# MEGAMAN
## NT WARRIOR

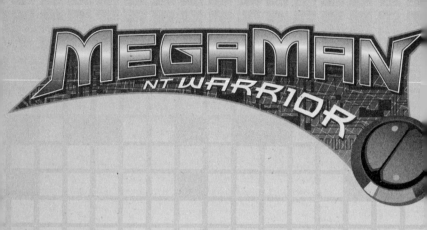

# MEGAMAN
## NT WARRIOR ™

Vol. 4
Action Edition

**Story and Art by Ryo Takamisaki**

English Adaptation/Gary Leach
Translation/Koji Goto
Touch-Up & Lettering/Gia Cam Luc
Cover Design/Mark Schumann
Graphic Design/Mark Schumann
Special Thanks/Hiromi Kadowaki & Jessica Villat
(ShoPro Entertainment)
Editor/Eric Searleman

Managing Editor/Annette Roman
Director of Production/Noboru Watanabe
Editorial Director/Alvin Lu
Sr. Director of Licensing & Acquisitions/Rika Inouye
Vice President of Sales & Marketing/Liza Coppola
Executive Vice President/Hyoe Narita
Publisher/Seiji Horibuchi

© 2001 Ryo Takamisaki/Shogakukan, Inc. © CAPCOM CO.,
LTD. ™ and ® are trademarks of CAPCOM CO., LTD. First
published by Shogakukan, Inc. in Japan as "Rokkuman
Eguze."

New and adapted artwork © 2004 VIZ, LLC. All rights
reserved.

*The stories, characters, and incidents mentioned in this
publication are entirely fictional. No portion of this book may
be reproduced or transmitted in any form or by any means
without written permission from the copyright holders.*

Printed in the U.S.A.

Published by VIZ, LLC
P.O. Box 77064
San Francisco, CA 94107

Action Edition
10 9 8 7 6 5 4 3 2 1
First printing, October 2004

For advertising rates or media kit,
e-mail advertising@viz.com

# CONTENTS

**PARENTAL ADVISORY**
MEGAMAN NT WARRIOR is rated A and is
recommended for readers of all ages. This
volume contains fantasy violence.

**store.viz.com**

www.animerica-mag.com

www.viz.com

Viz Graphic Novel

MEGAMAN
NT WARRIOR

TM

Vol. 4

Story and Art by
Ryo Takamisaki

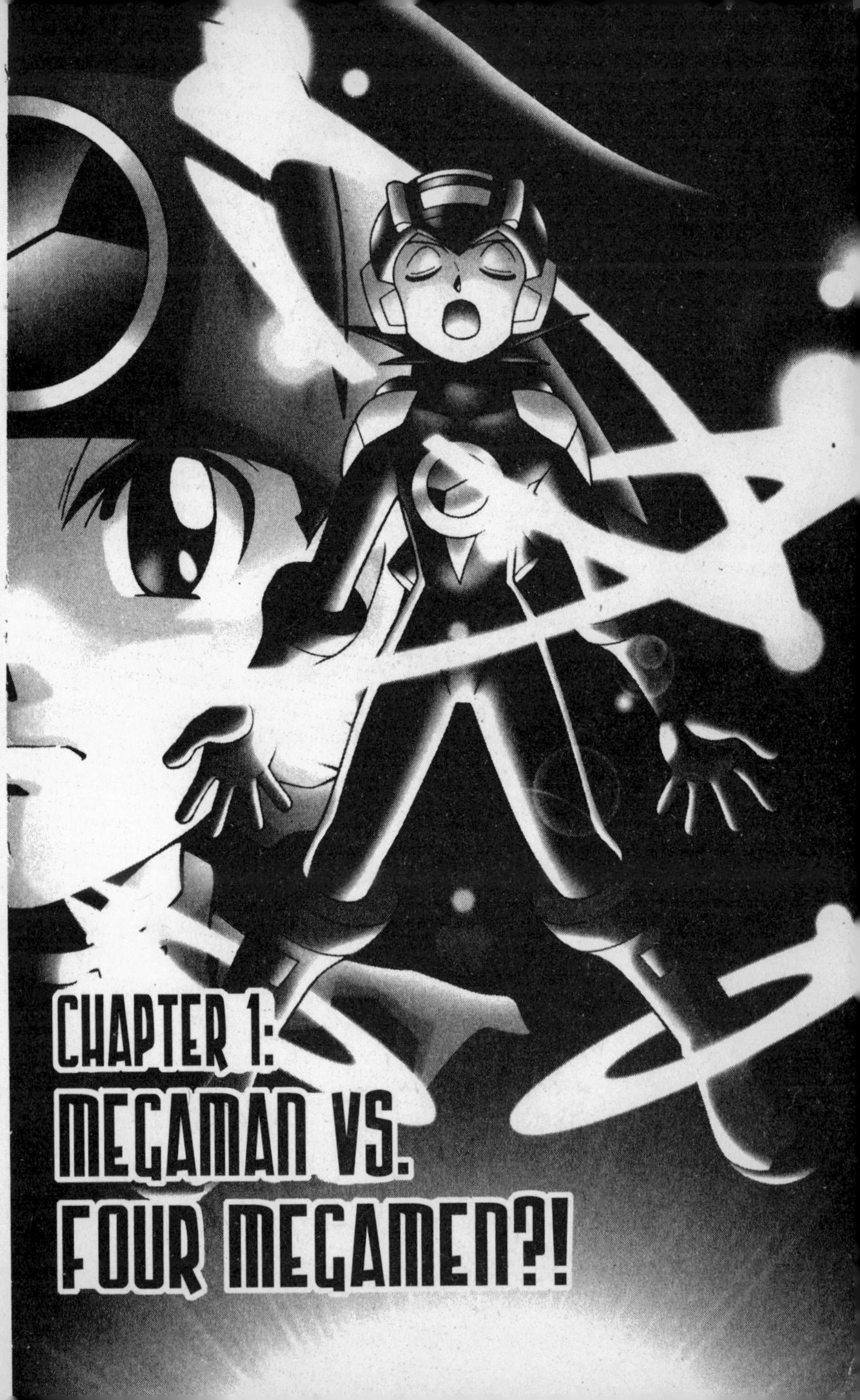
CHAPTER 1:
MEGAMAN VS.
FOUR MEGAMEN?!

WE EXIST TO DEFEAT ANY AND EVERY OPPONENT IMAGINABLE!!
OURS IS THE ABILITY TO REPLICATE OUR ADVERSARIES...
...AND ALSO-
THROUGH THE STYLE-CHANGE...
...ENHANCE OURSELVES INDIVIDUALLY!!
IN SHORT...
...YOU DON'T STAND A CHANCE IN A MILLION OF WINNIN'!!

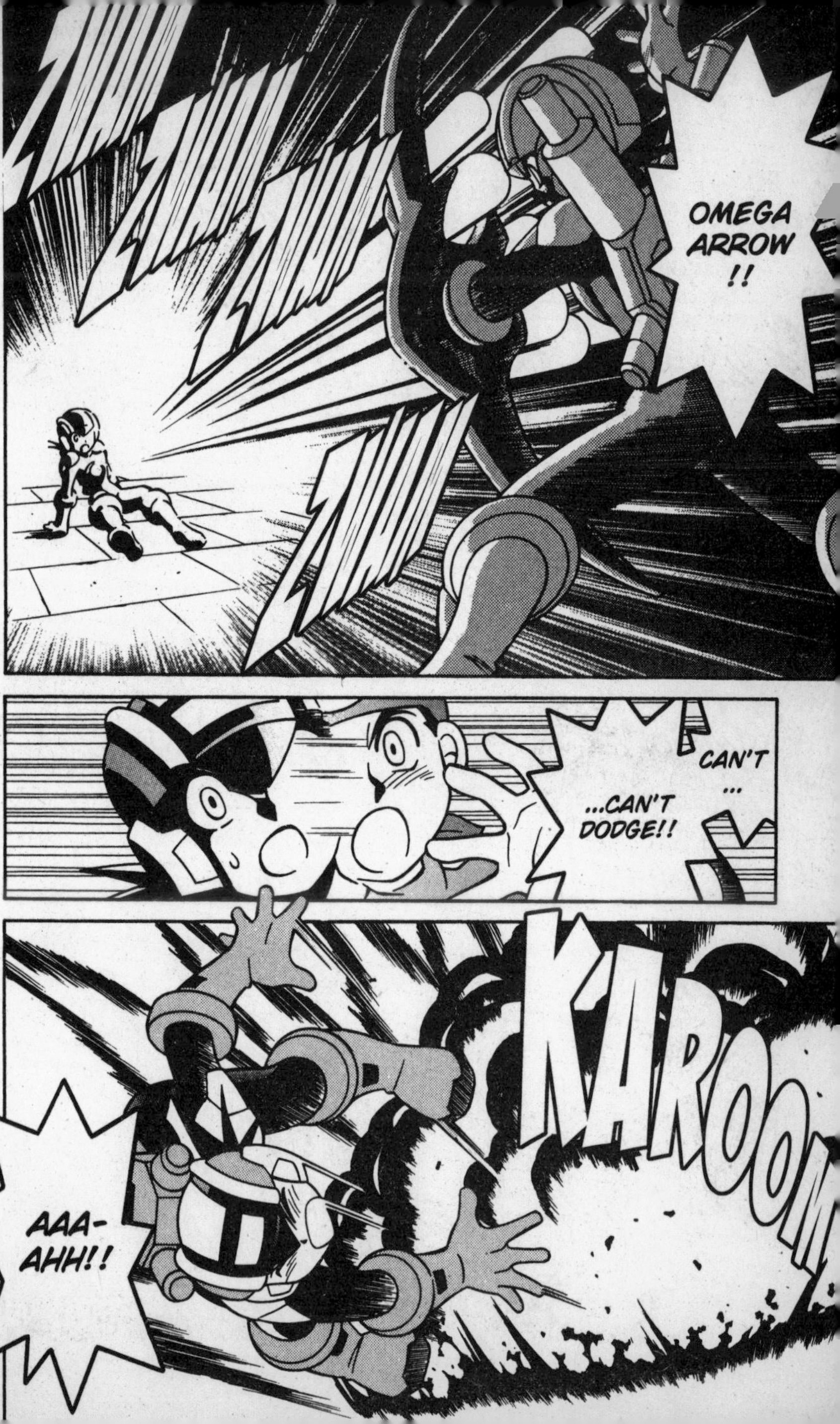
OMEGA ARROW !!
CAN'T ...
...CAN'T DODGE!!
KAROOM
AAA-AHH!!

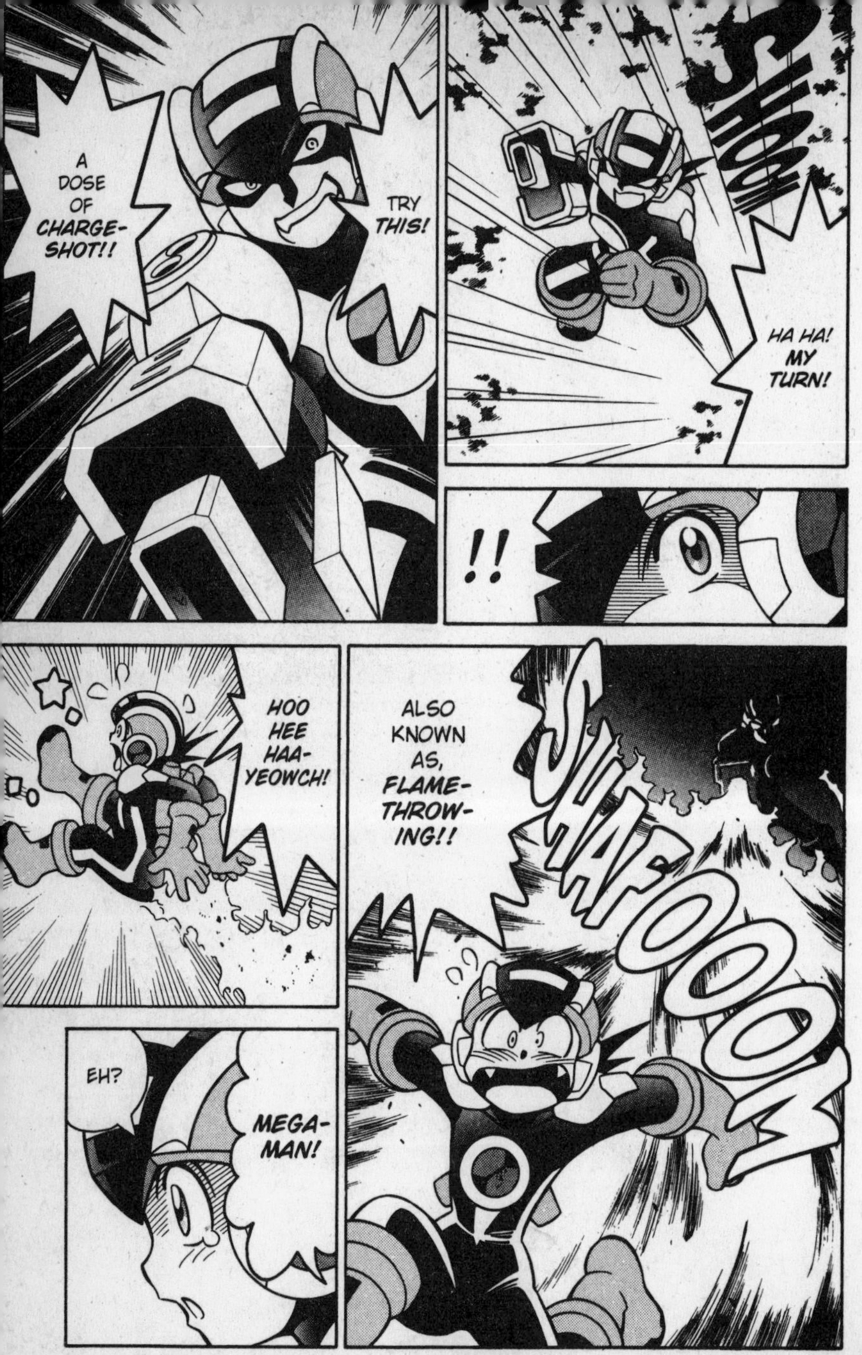
SHOOM
HA HA! MY TURN!
!!
TRY THIS!
A DOSE OF CHARGE-SHOT!!
ALSO KNOWN AS, FLAME-THROWING!!
SHAFOOOOM
HOO HEE HAA-YEOWCH!
EH?
MEGA-MAN!

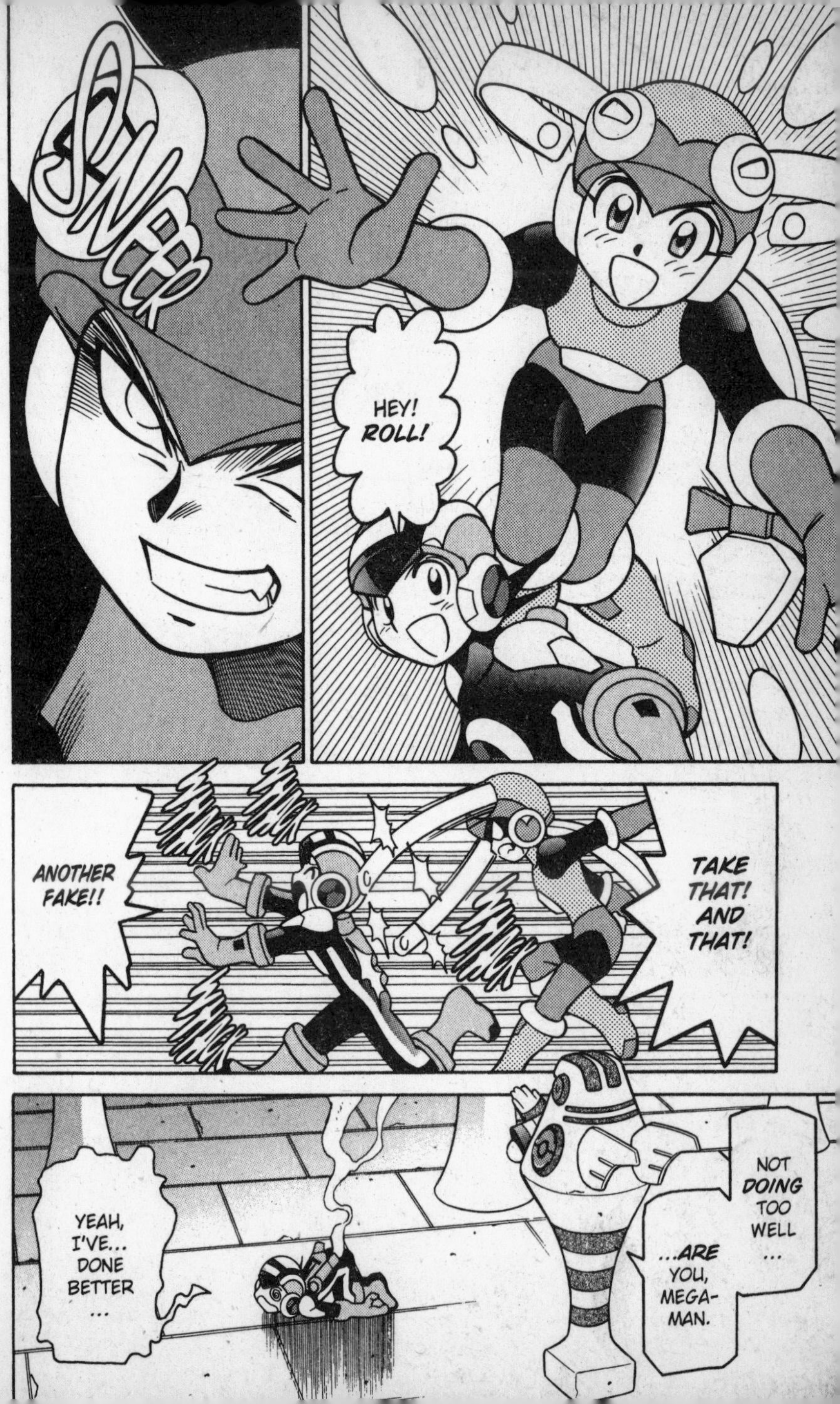
HEY! ROLL!
SNEER
TAKE THAT! AND THAT!
ANOTHER FAKE!!
NOT DOING TOO WELL ...
...ARE YOU, MEGA-MAN.
YEAH, I'VE... DONE BETTER ...

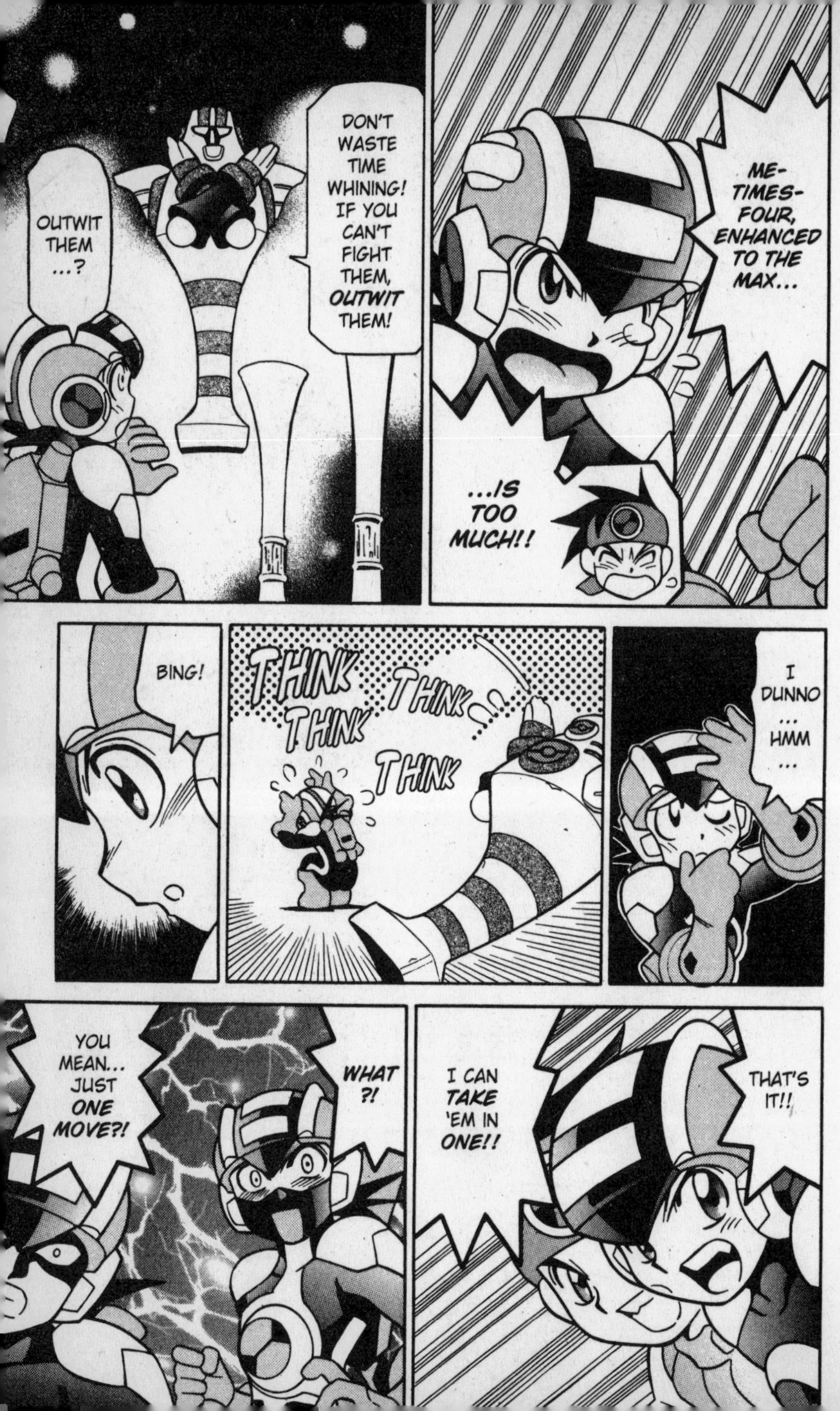
ME-TIMES-FOUR, ENHANCED TO THE MAX...
...IS TOO MUCH!!
DON'T WASTE TIME WHINING! IF YOU CAN'T FIGHT THEM, OUTWIT THEM!
OUTWIT THEM ...?
I DUNNO ... HMM ...
THINK
THINK
THINK
THINK
BING!
THAT'S IT!!
I CAN TAKE 'EM IN ONE!!
WHAT ?!
YOU MEAN... JUST ONE MOVE?!

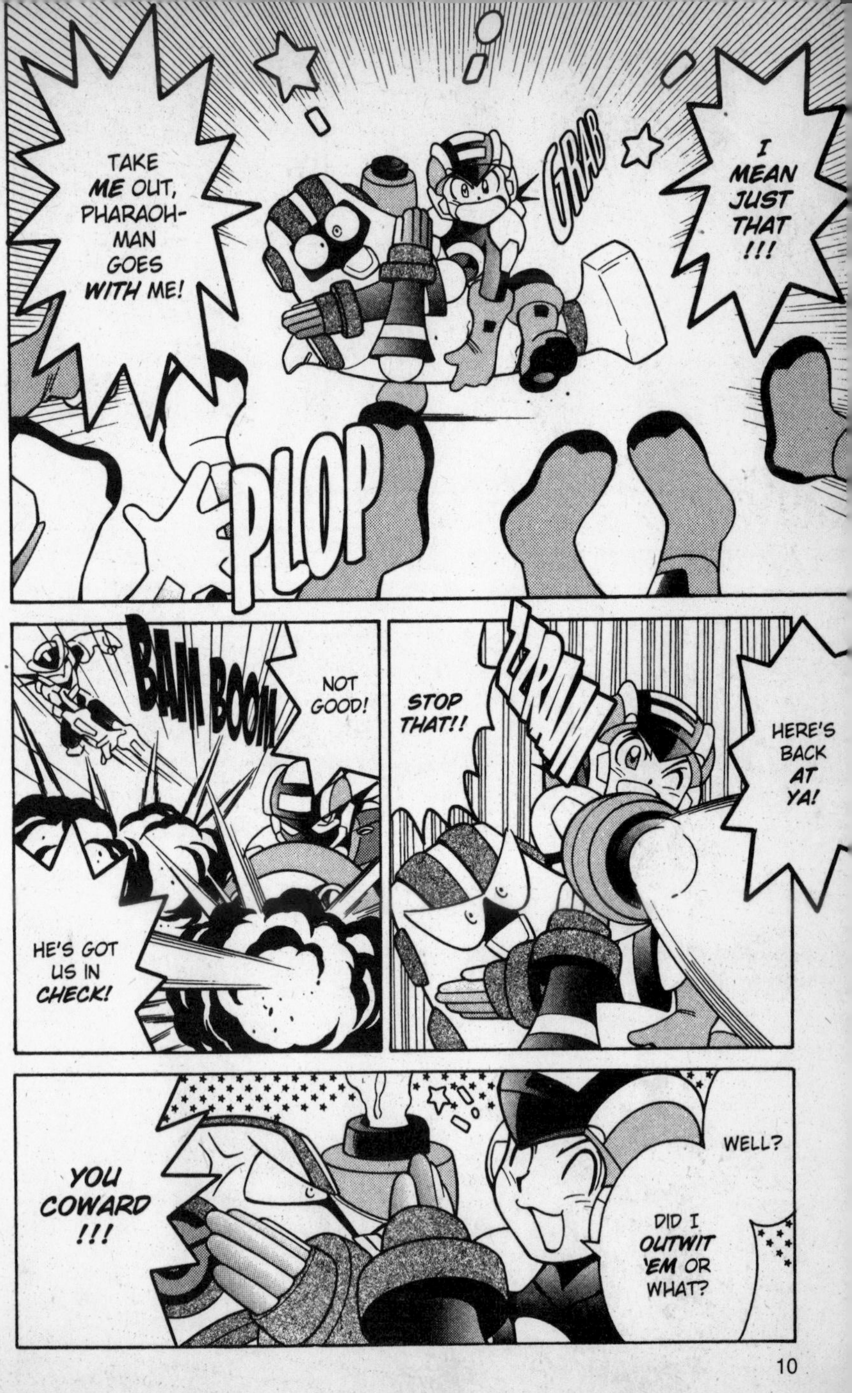
I MEAN JUST THAT!!!
GRAB
TAKE ME OUT, PHARAOH-MAN GOES WITH ME!
PLOP
HERE'S BACK AT YA!
ZZRAM
STOP THAT!!
NOT GOOD!
BAM BOOM
HE'S GOT US IN CHECK!
WELL?
DID I OUTWIT 'EM OR WHAT?
YOU COWARD!!!

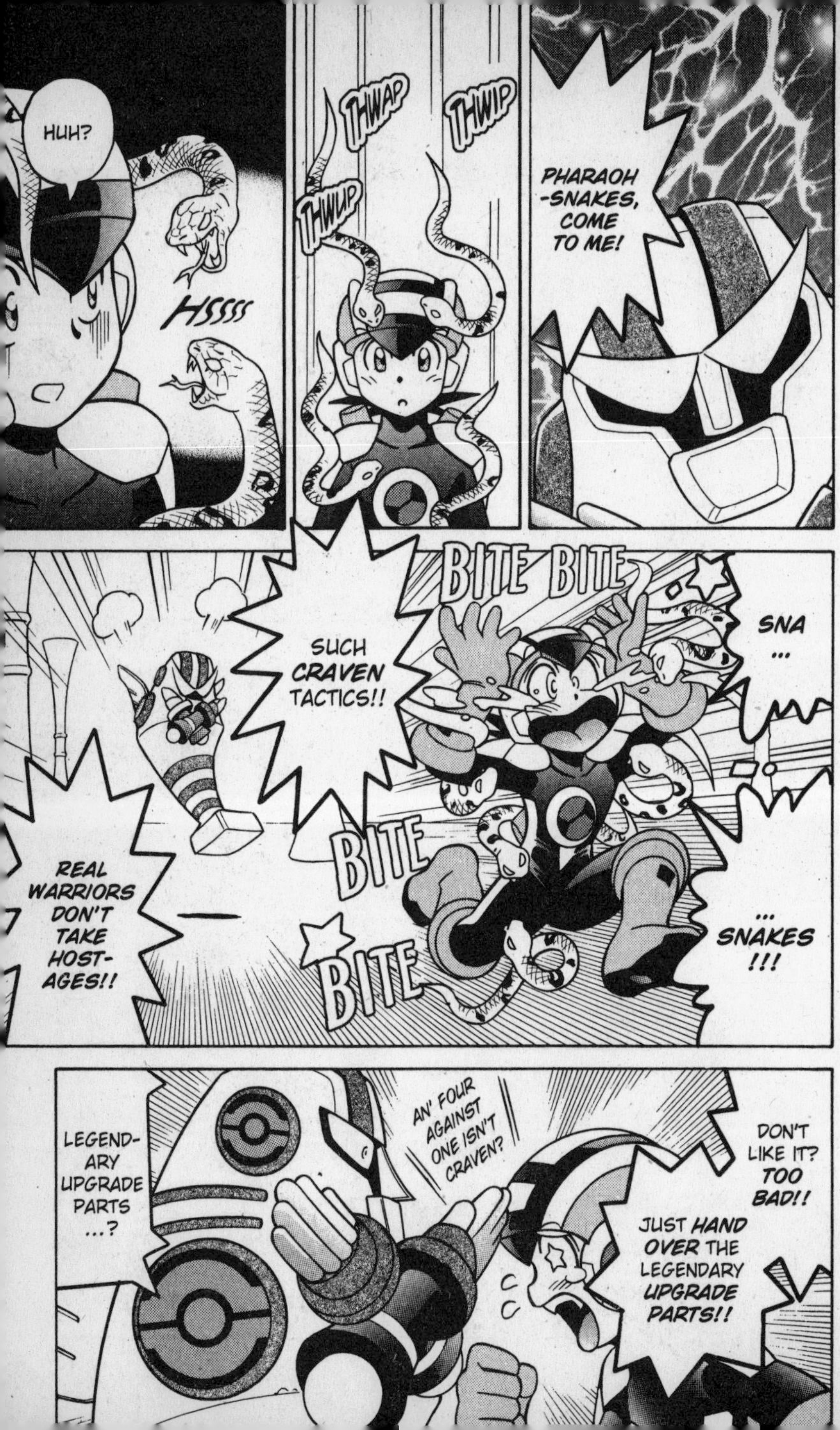
PHARAOH-SNAKES, COME TO ME!
THWIP
THWAP
THWUP
HUH?
HSSSS
SNA ...
BITE BITE
SUCH CRAVEN TACTICS!!
... SNAKES!!!
BITE
BITE
REAL WARRIORS DON'T TAKE HOST-AGES!!
DON'T LIKE IT? TOO BAD!!
JUST HAND OVER THE LEGENDARY UPGRADE PARTS!!
AN' FOUR AGAINST ONE ISN'T CRAVEN?
LEGEND-ARY UPGRADE PARTS ...?

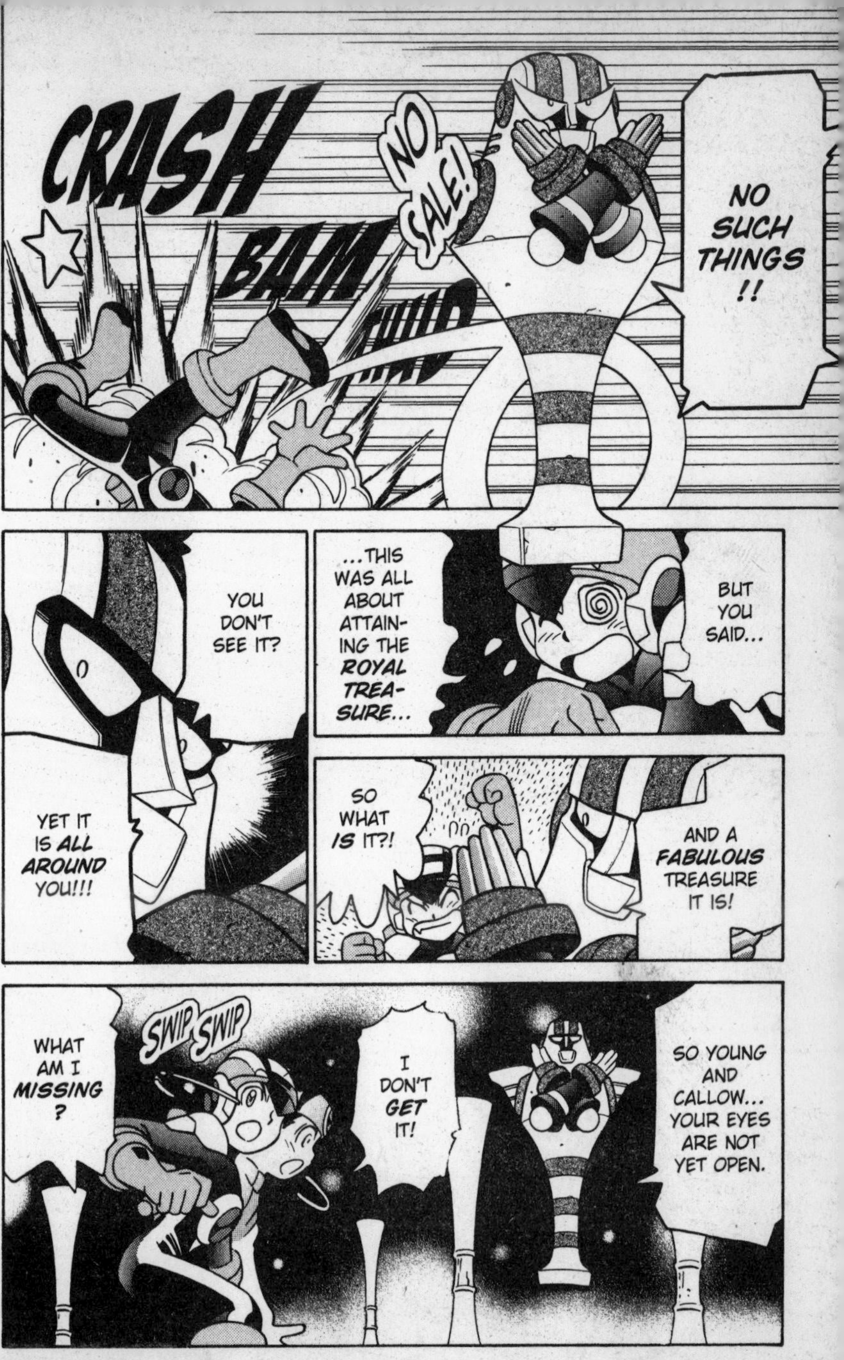
NO SUCH THINGS !!
NO SALE!
CRASH
BAM
THUD
BUT YOU SAID...
...THIS WAS ALL ABOUT ATTAINING THE ROYAL TREASURE...
AND A FABULOUS TREASURE IT IS!
SO WHAT IS IT?!
YOU DON'T SEE IT?
YET IT IS ALL AROUND YOU!!!
SO YOUNG AND CALLOW... YOUR EYES ARE NOT YET OPEN.
I DON'T GET IT!
SWIP SWIP
WHAT AM I MISSING ?

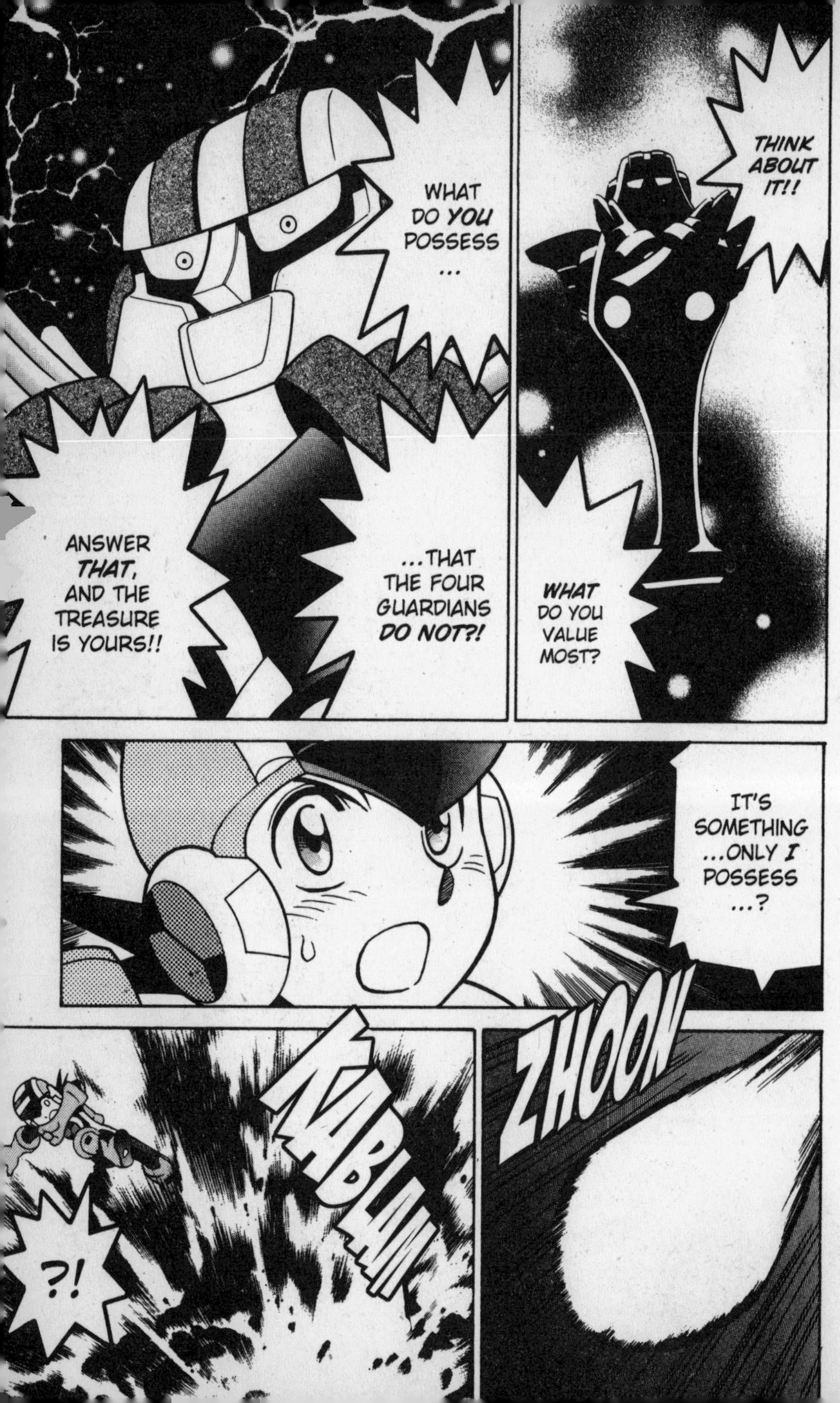
THINK ABOUT IT!!
WHAT DO YOU VALUE MOST?
WHAT DO YOU POSSESS ...
...THAT THE FOUR GUARDIANS DO NOT?!
ANSWER THAT, AND THE TREASURE IS YOURS!!
IT'S SOMETHING ...ONLY I POSSESS ...?
ZHOON
KABLAM
?!

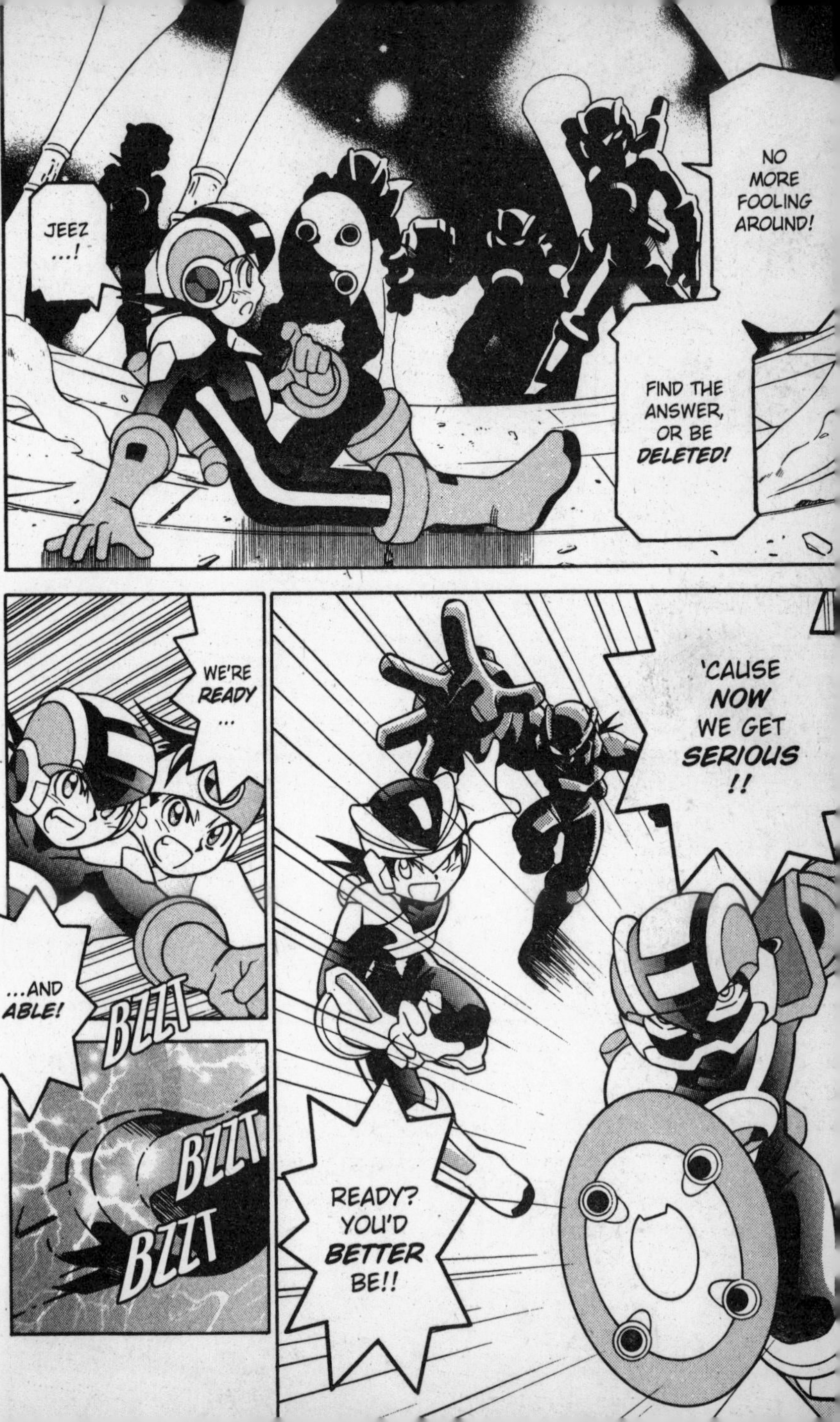
NO MORE FOOLING AROUND!
FIND THE ANSWER, OR BE DELETED!
JEEZ ...!
'CAUSE NOW WE GET SERIOUS !!
READY? YOU'D BETTER BE!!
WE'RE READY ...
...AND ABLE!
BZZT
BZZT
BZZT

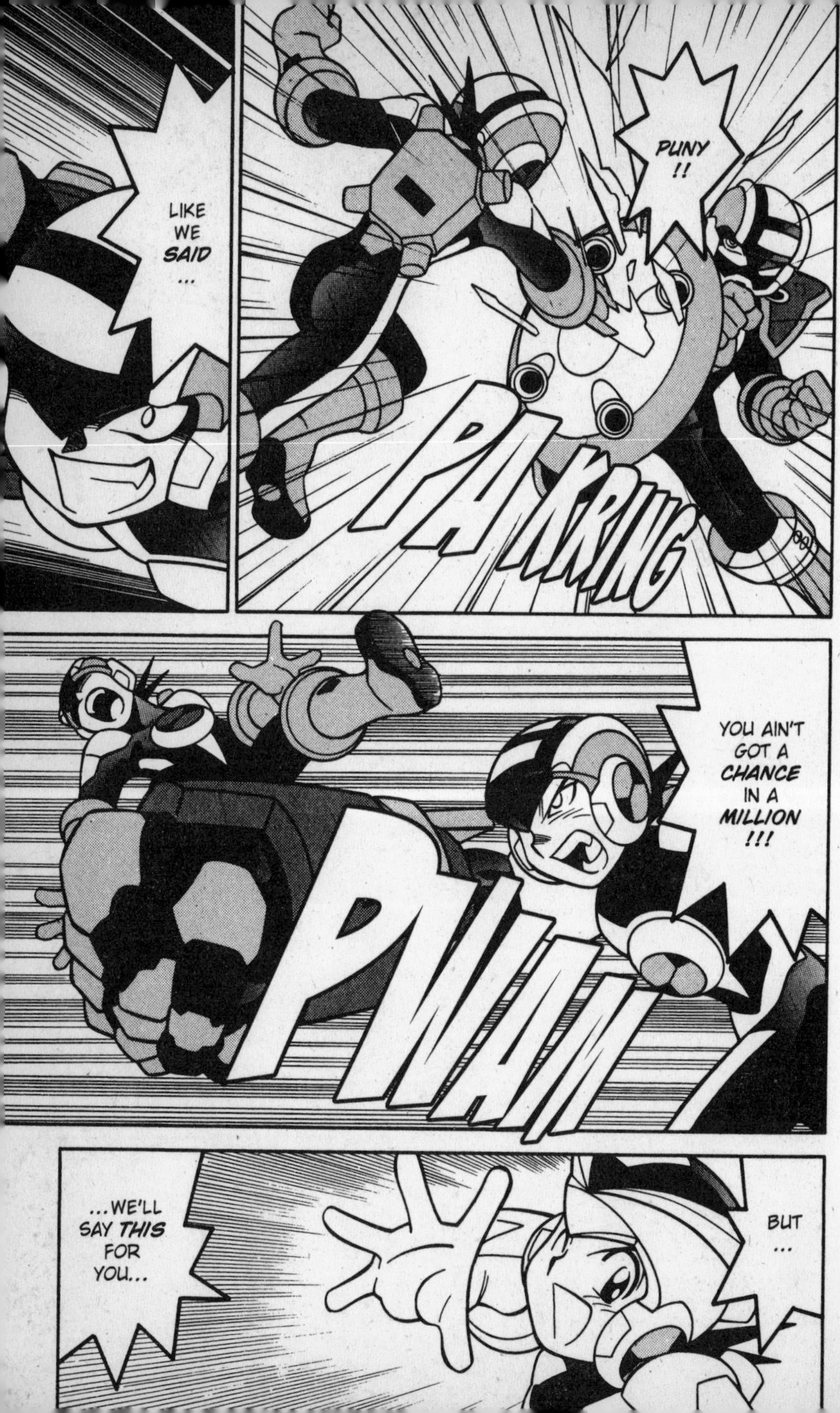
PUNY !!
PAKRING
LIKE WE SAID ...
YOU AIN'T GOT A CHANCE IN A MILLION !!!
PWAM
BUT ...
...WE'LL SAY THIS FOR YOU...

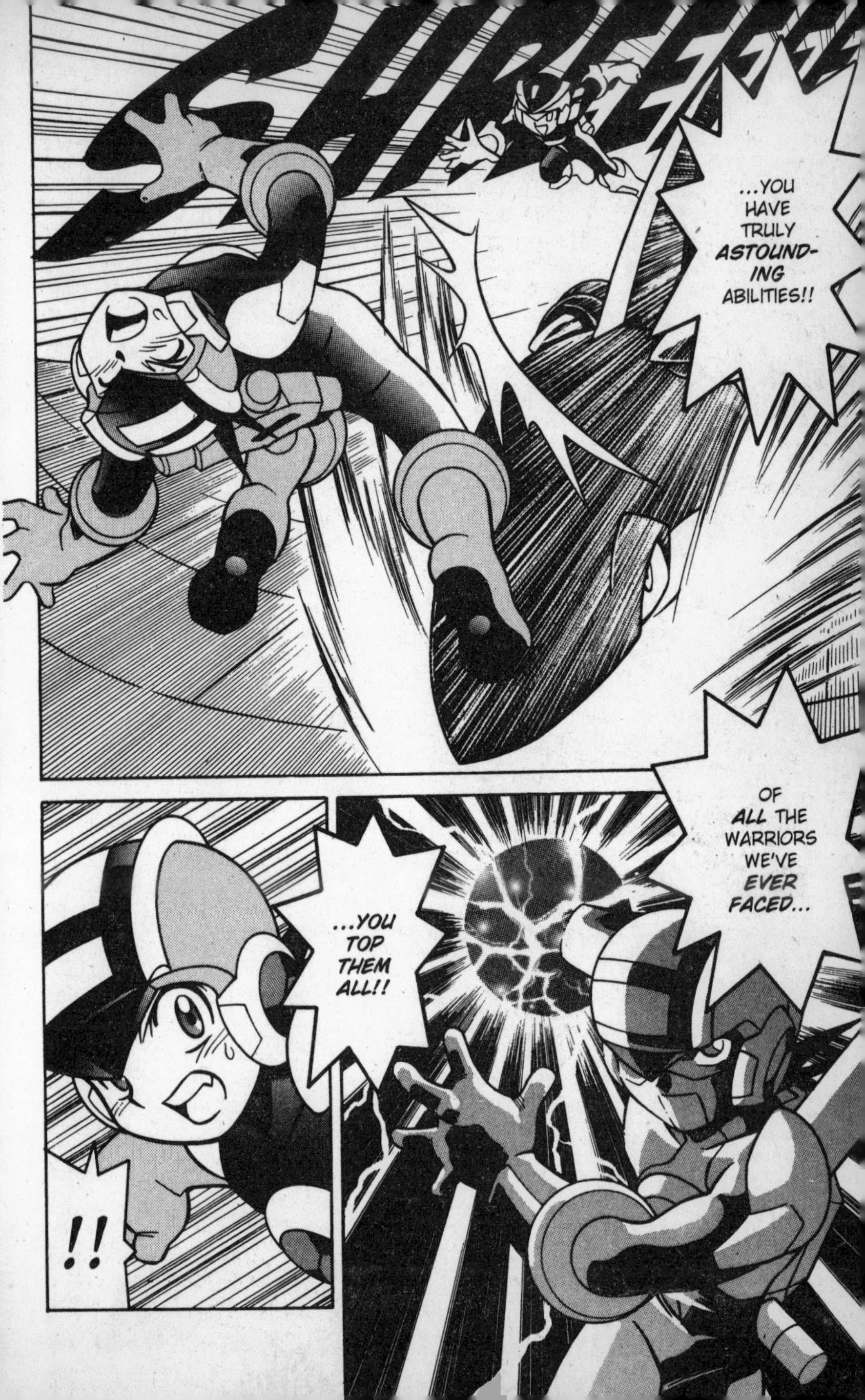
...YOU HAVE TRULY ASTOUNDING ABILITIES!!
OF ALL THE WARRIORS WE'VE EVER FACED...
...YOU TOP THEM ALL!!
!!

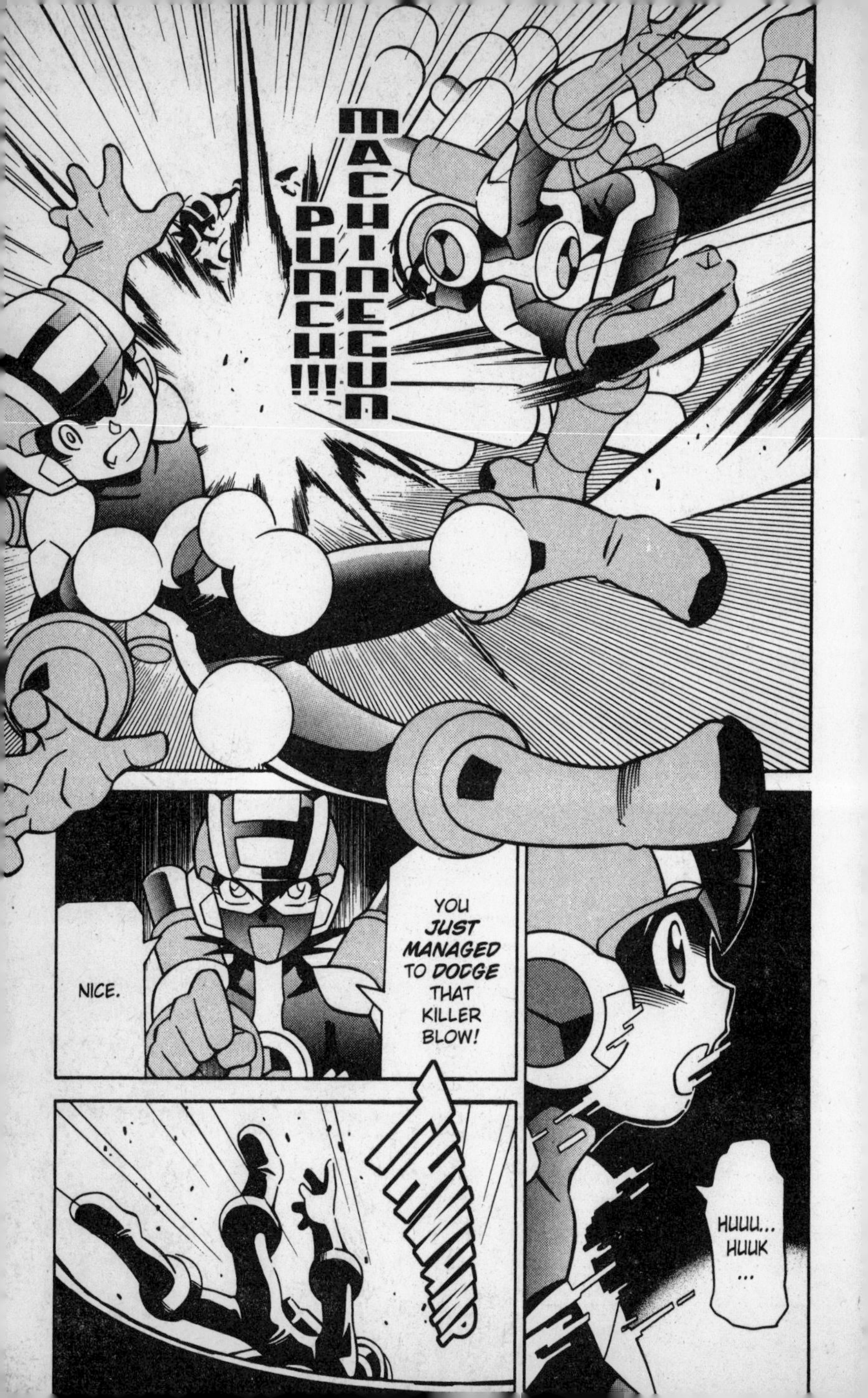
MACHINEGUN PUNCH!!!
HUUU... HUUK ...
YOU JUST MANAGED TO DODGE THAT KILLER BLOW!
NICE.
THWUMP

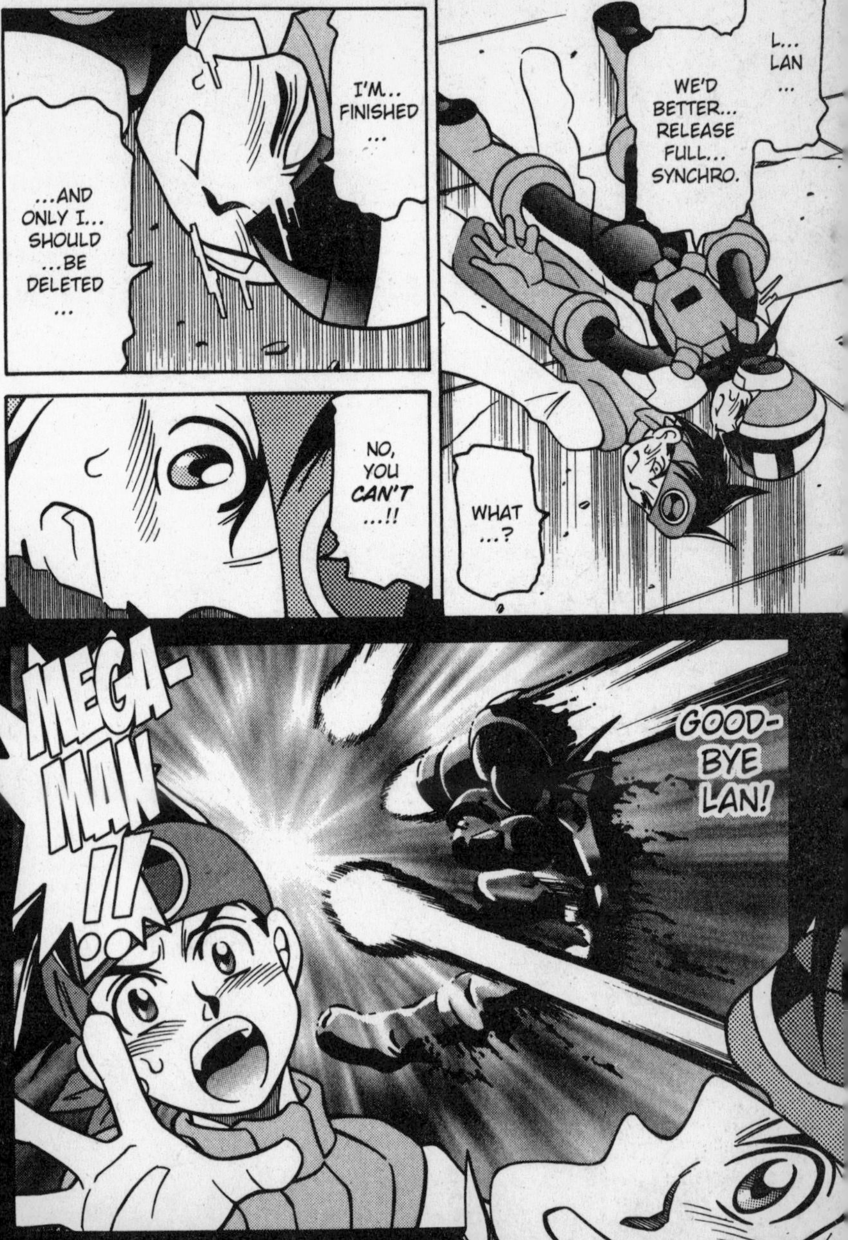
L... LAN ...
WE'D BETTER... RELEASE FULL... SYNCHRO.
WHAT ...?
I'M... FINISHED ...
...AND ONLY I... SHOULD ...BE DELETED ...
NO, YOU CAN'T ...!!
GOOD-BYE LAN!
MEGA-MAN !!

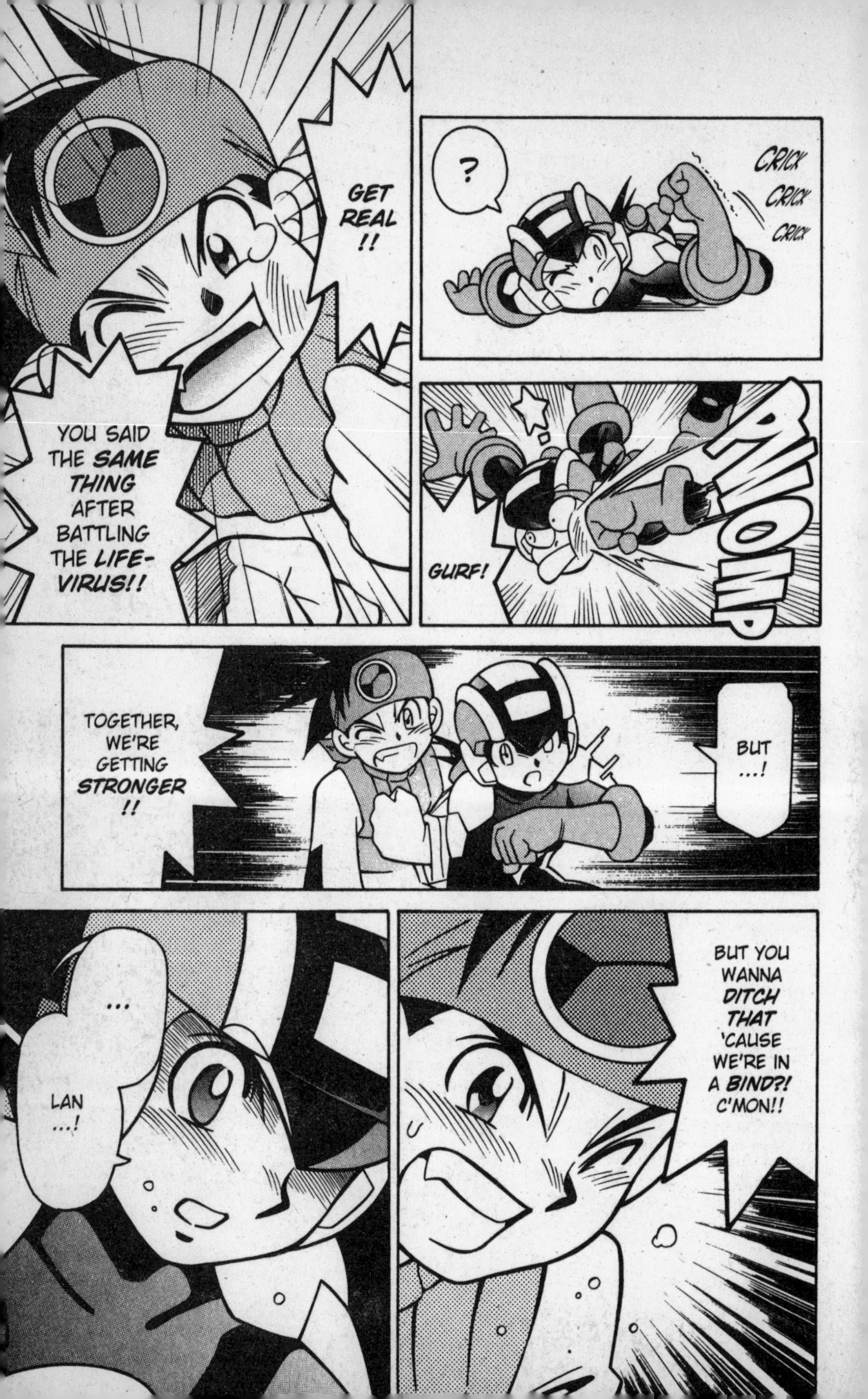
?
CRICK
CRICK
CRICK
PWOMP
GURF!
GET REAL!!
YOU SAID THE SAME THING AFTER BATTLING THE LIFE-VIRUS!!
BUT ...!
TOGETHER, WE'RE GETTING STRONGER!!
BUT YOU WANNA DITCH THAT 'CAUSE WE'RE IN A BIND?! C'MON!!
...
LAN ...!

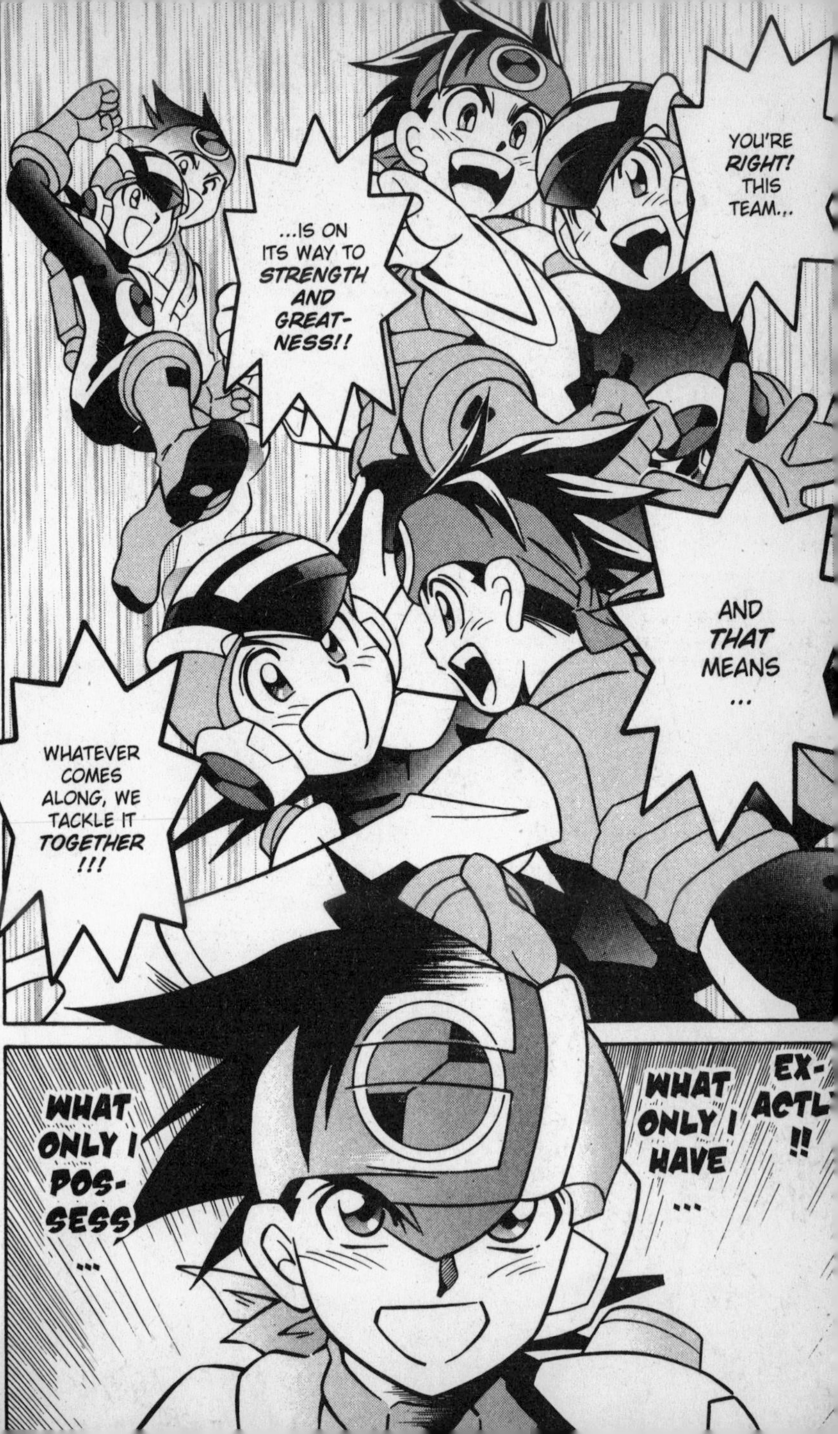
YOU'RE RIGHT! THIS TEAM...
...IS ON ITS WAY TO STRENGTH AND GREAT-NESS!!
AND THAT MEANS ...
WHATEVER COMES ALONG, WE TACKLE IT TOGETHER !!!
EX-ACTL !!
WHAT ONLY I HAVE ...
WHAT ONLY I POS-SESS ...

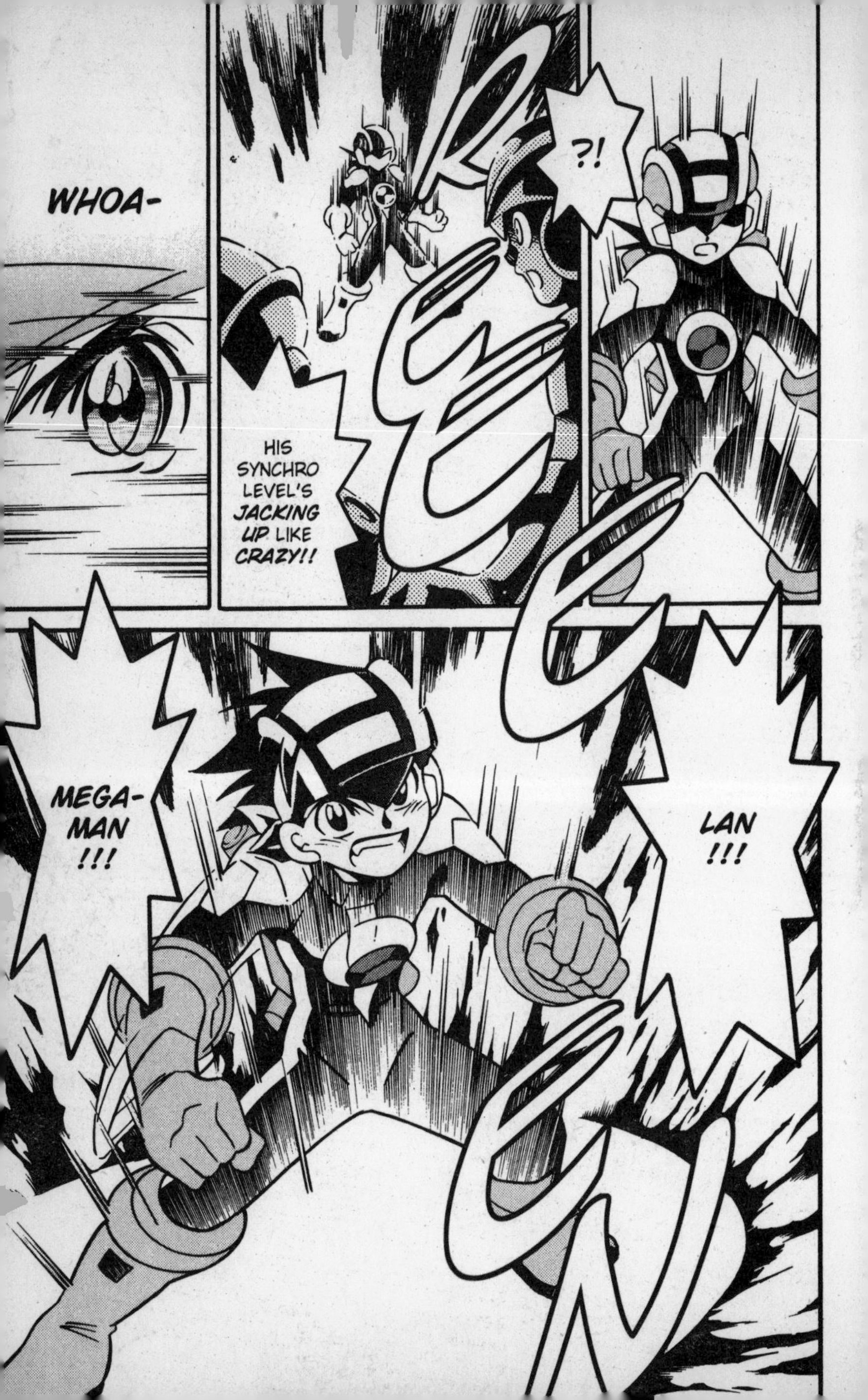
?!
HIS SYNCHRO LEVEL'S JACKING UP LIKE CRAZY!!
WHOA-
LAN!!!
MEGA-MAN!!!

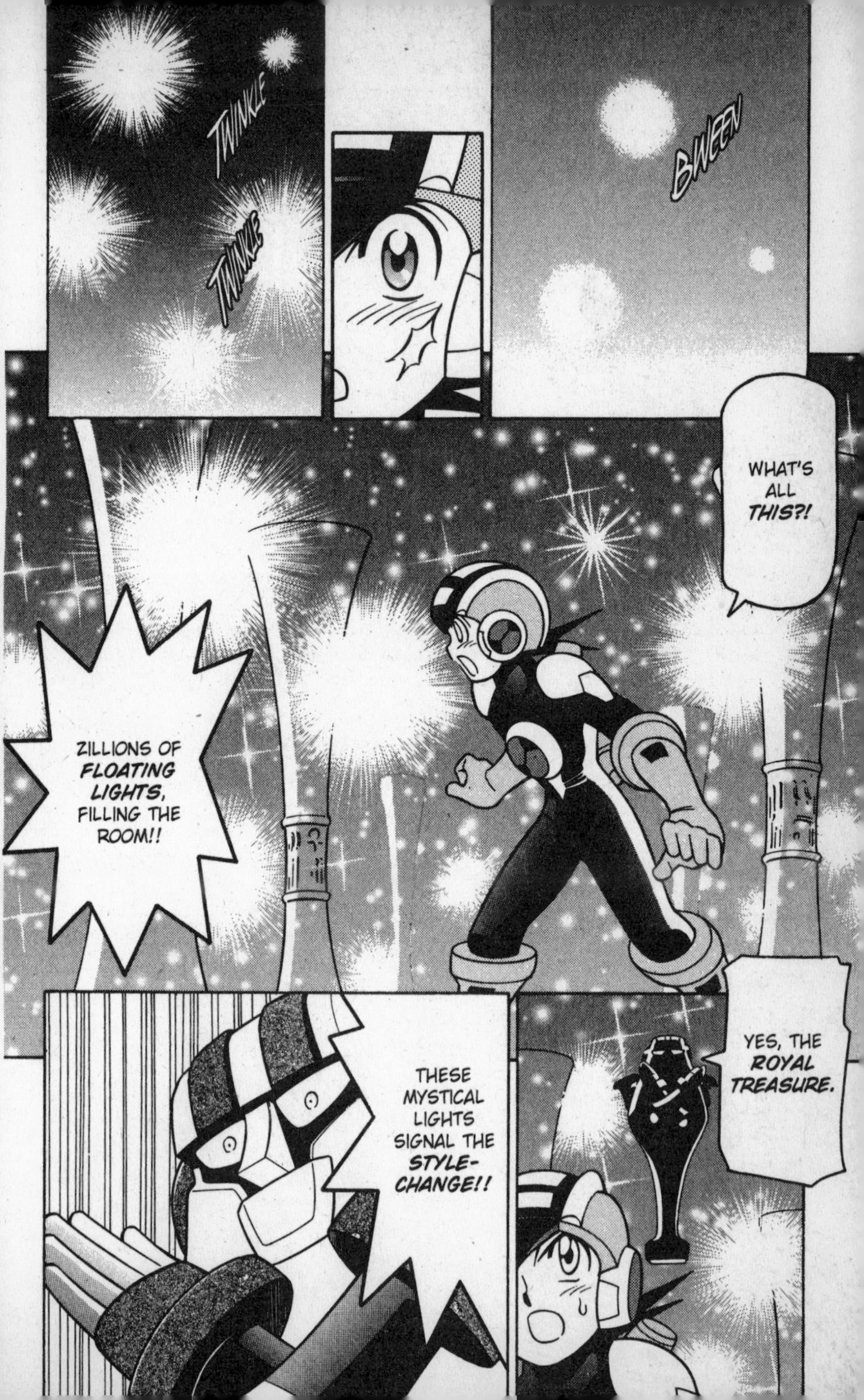
BWEEN
TWINKLE
TWINKLE
WHAT'S ALL *THIS?!*
ZILLIONS OF *FLOATING LIGHTS,* FILLING THE ROOM!!
YES, THE *ROYAL TREASURE.*
THESE MYSTICAL LIGHTS SIGNAL THE *STYLE-CHANGE!!*

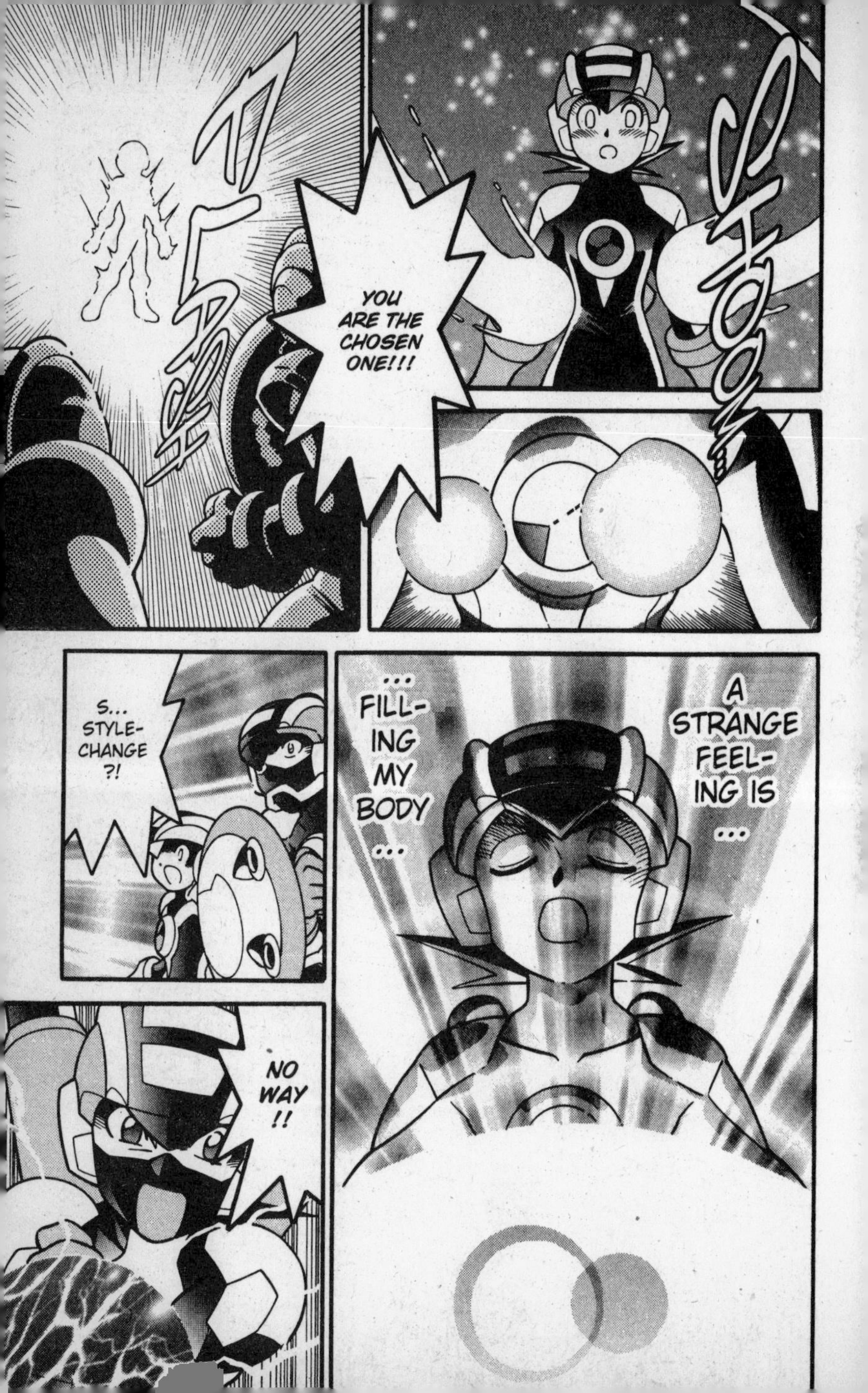
CHOOOM
YOU ARE THE CHOSEN ONE!!!
FLASH
A STRANGE FEELING IS ...
... FILLING MY BODY ...
S... STYLE-CHANGE ?!
NO WAY !!

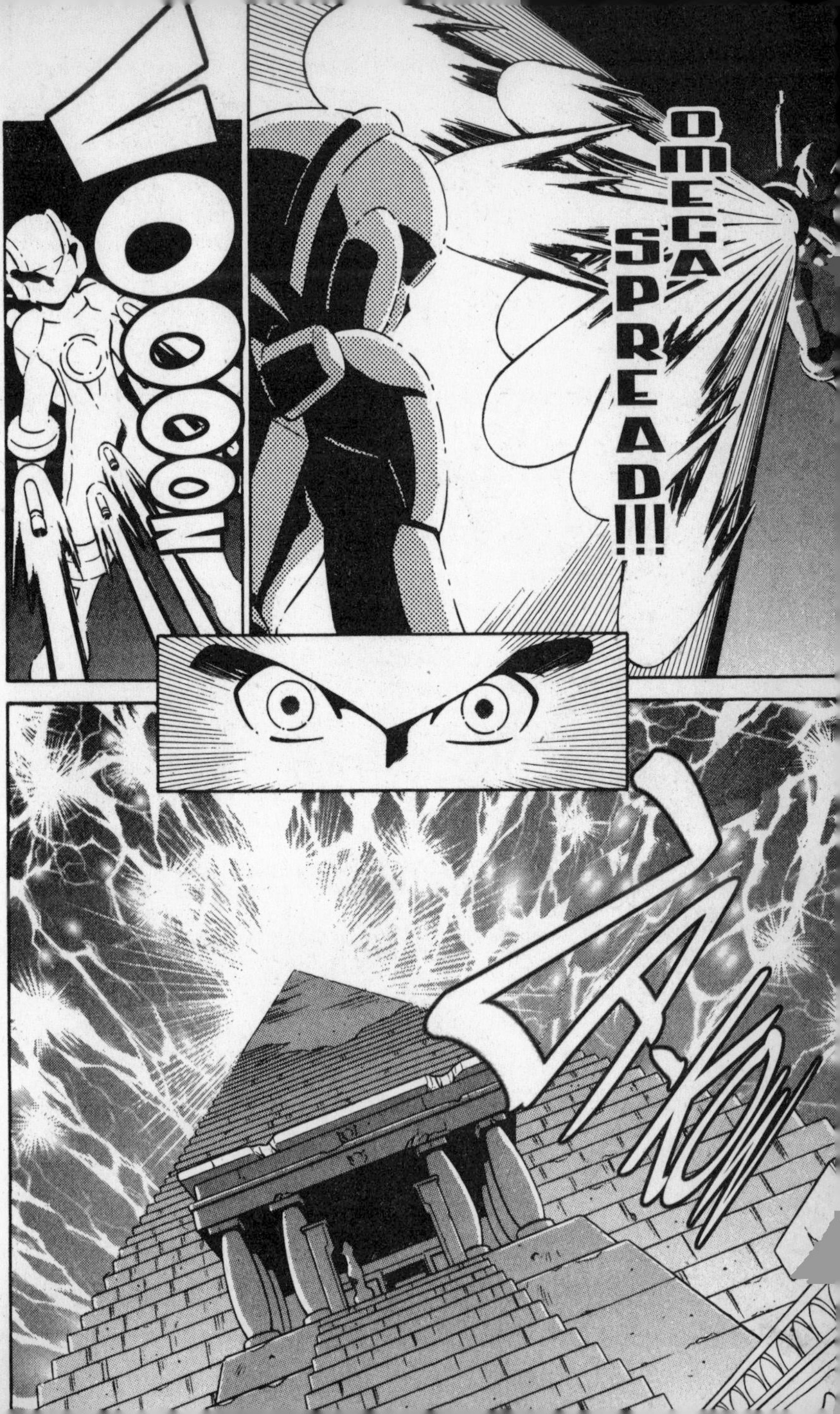
OMEGA SPREAD!!!
VOOOON

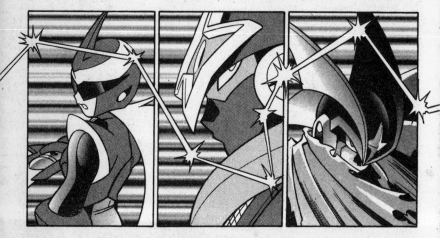

RUMM RUMM RUMM

...DID YOU *GET* HIM?!

DID...

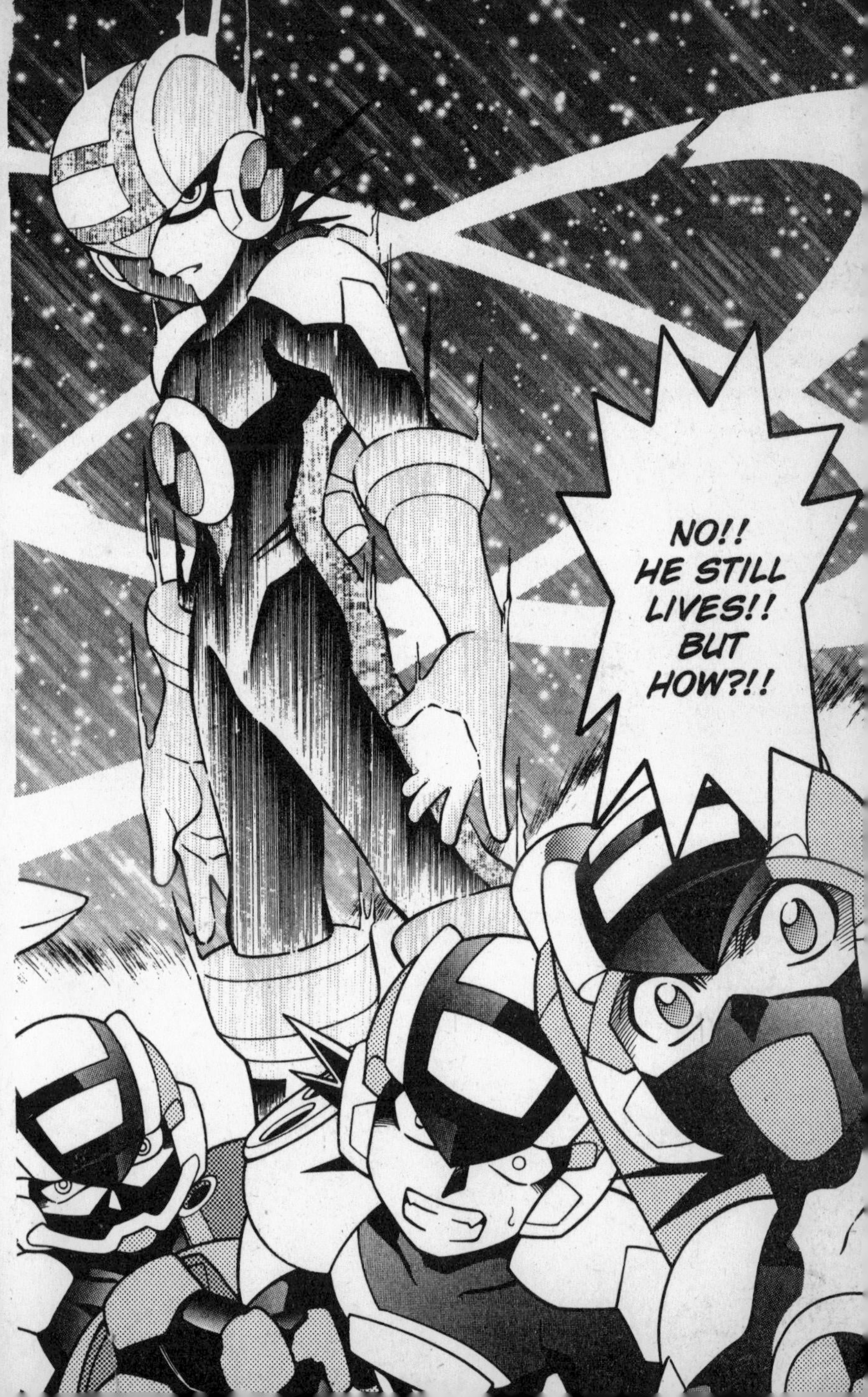
NO!! HE STILL LIVES!! BUT HOW?!!

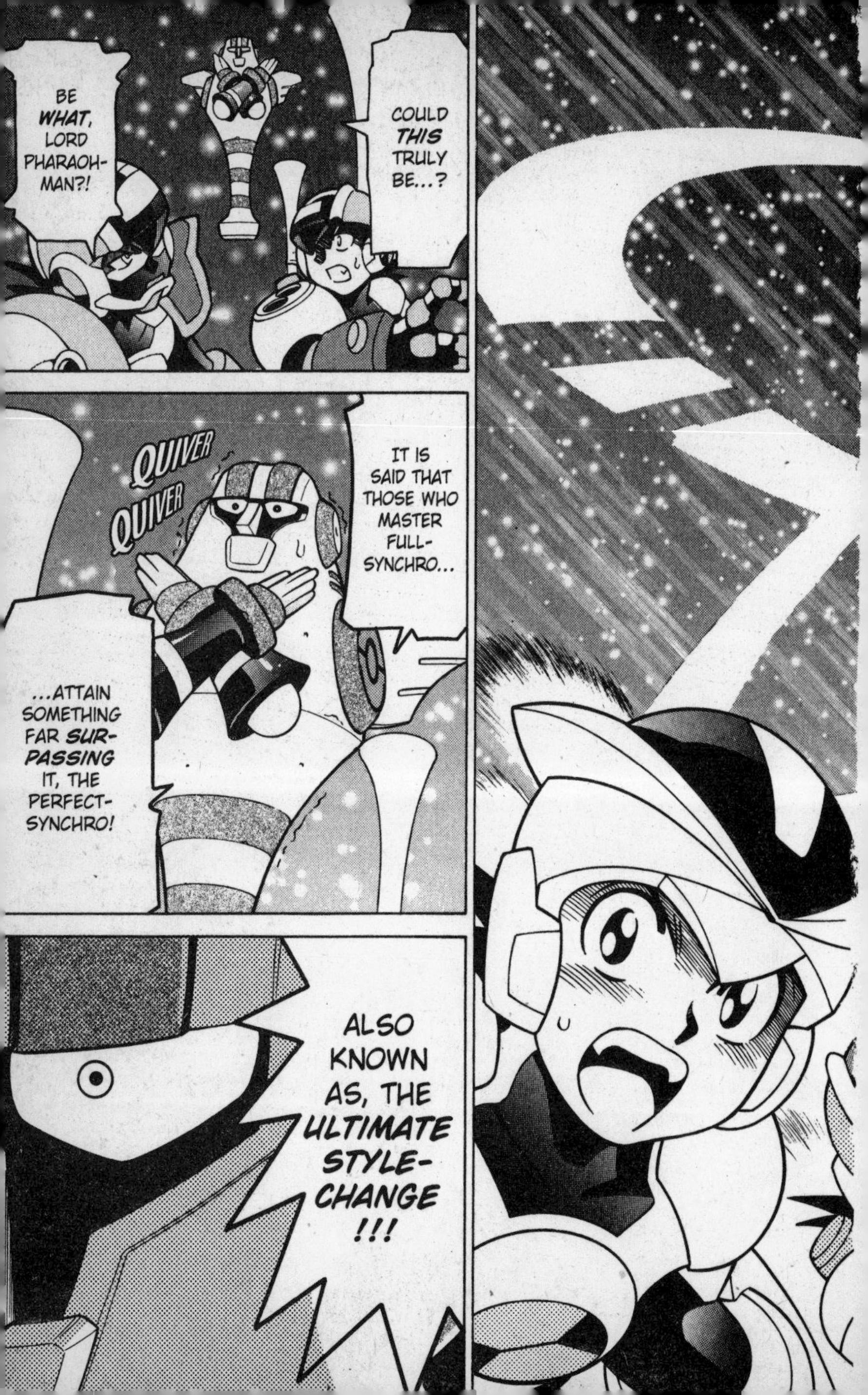
COULD THIS TRULY BE...?
BE WHAT, LORD PHARAOH-MAN?!
IT IS SAID THAT THOSE WHO MASTER FULL-SYNCHRO...
QUIVER QUIVER
...ATTAIN SOMETHING FAR SURPASSING IT, THE PERFECT-SYNCHRO!
ALSO KNOWN AS, THE ULTIMATE STYLE-CHANGE!!!

HUFF
...

HUFF
...

HUFF
...

HUFF
...

HUFF
...

HUFF
...

TINK↓
TINK↓

HE... CAUGHT IT!!

THE. OMEGA-SPREAD...

WELL, THEN...

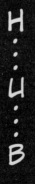

H...U...B

U... B...

HUFF
...

HUFF
...

HU... B...

SOMEONE'S VOICE... INSIDE MY HEAD...

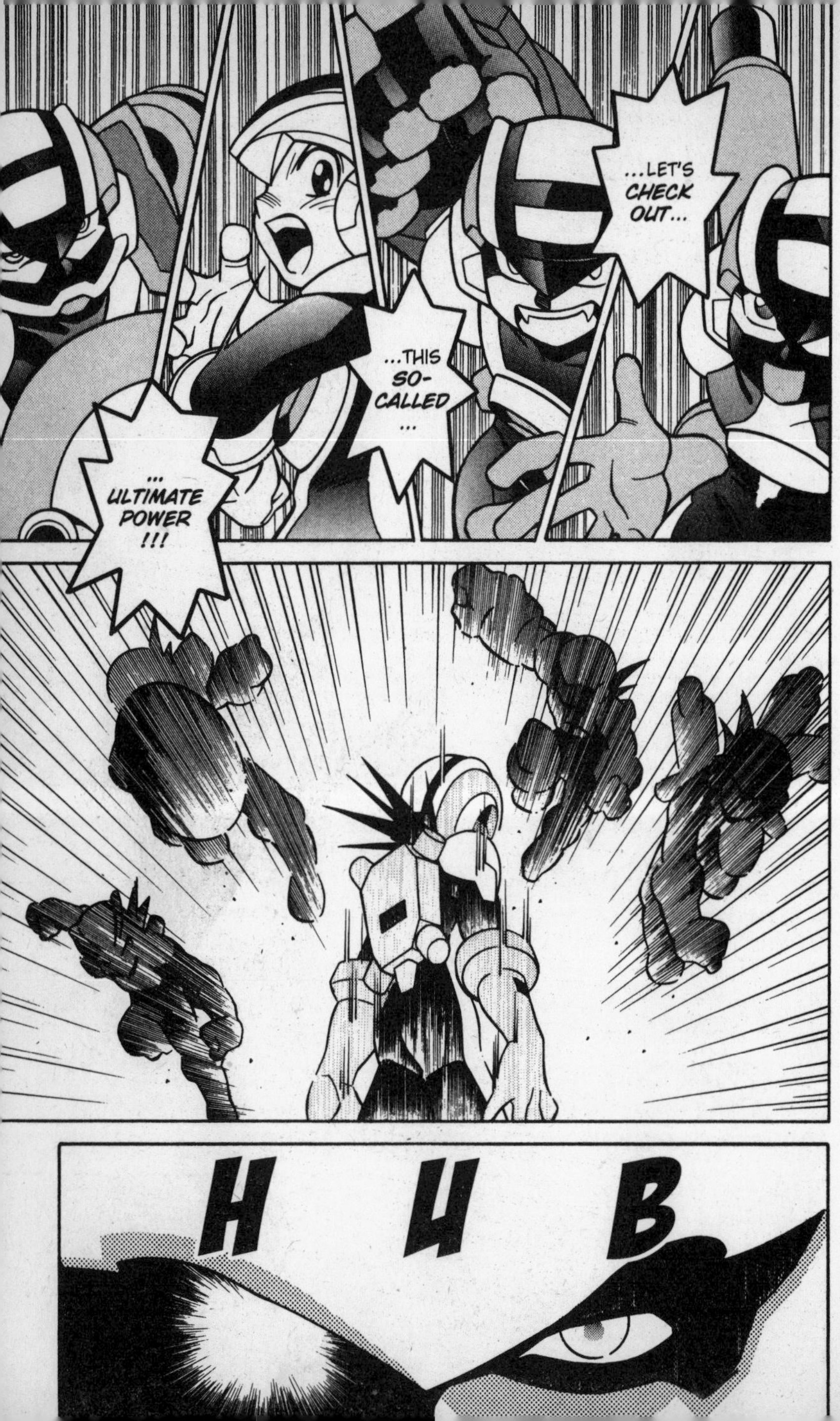
...LET'S CHECK OUT...
...THIS SO-CALLED...
...ULTIMATE POWER!!!
H U B

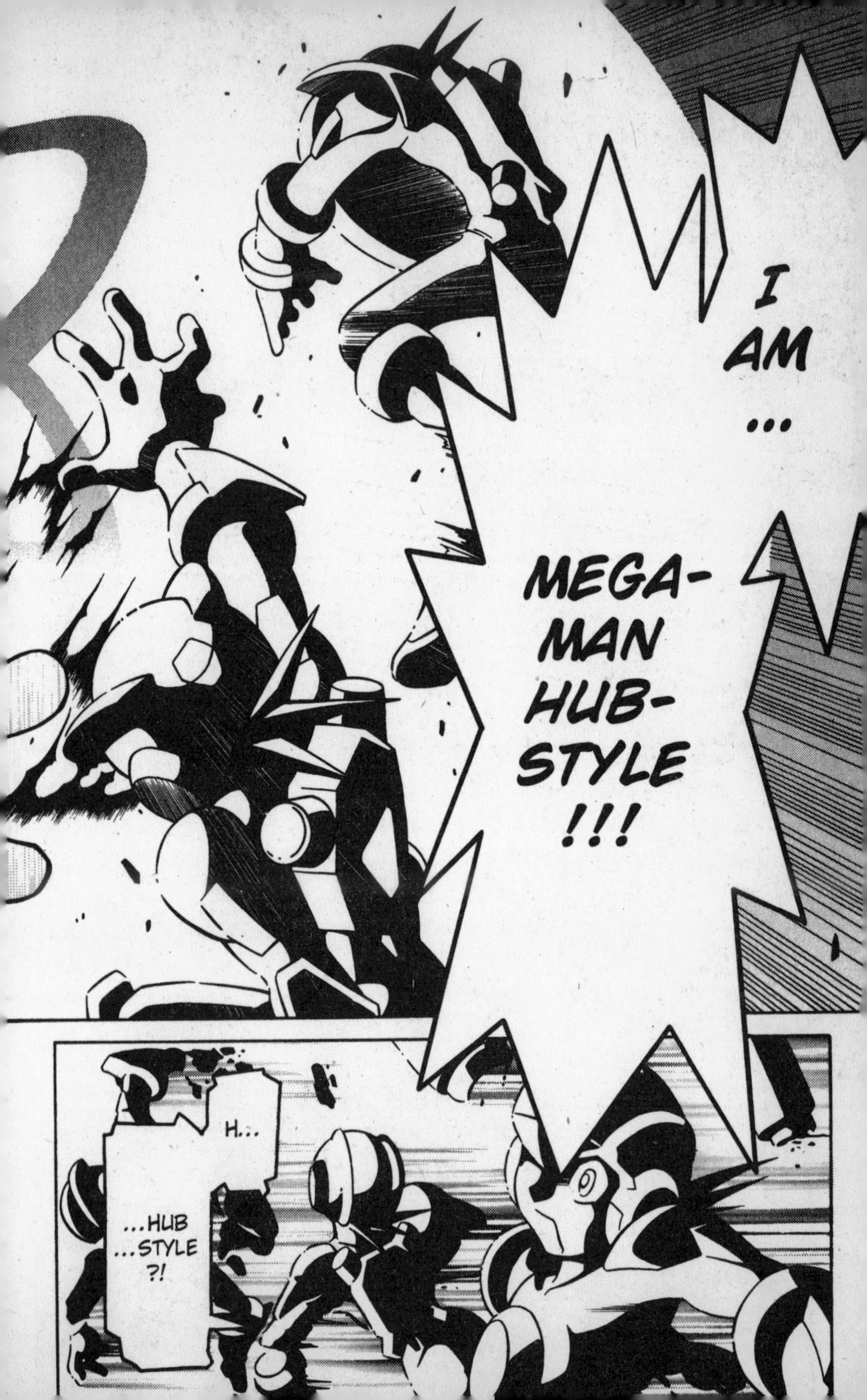
I AM ...
MEGA-MAN HUB-STYLE !!!
H...
...HUB ...STYLE ?!

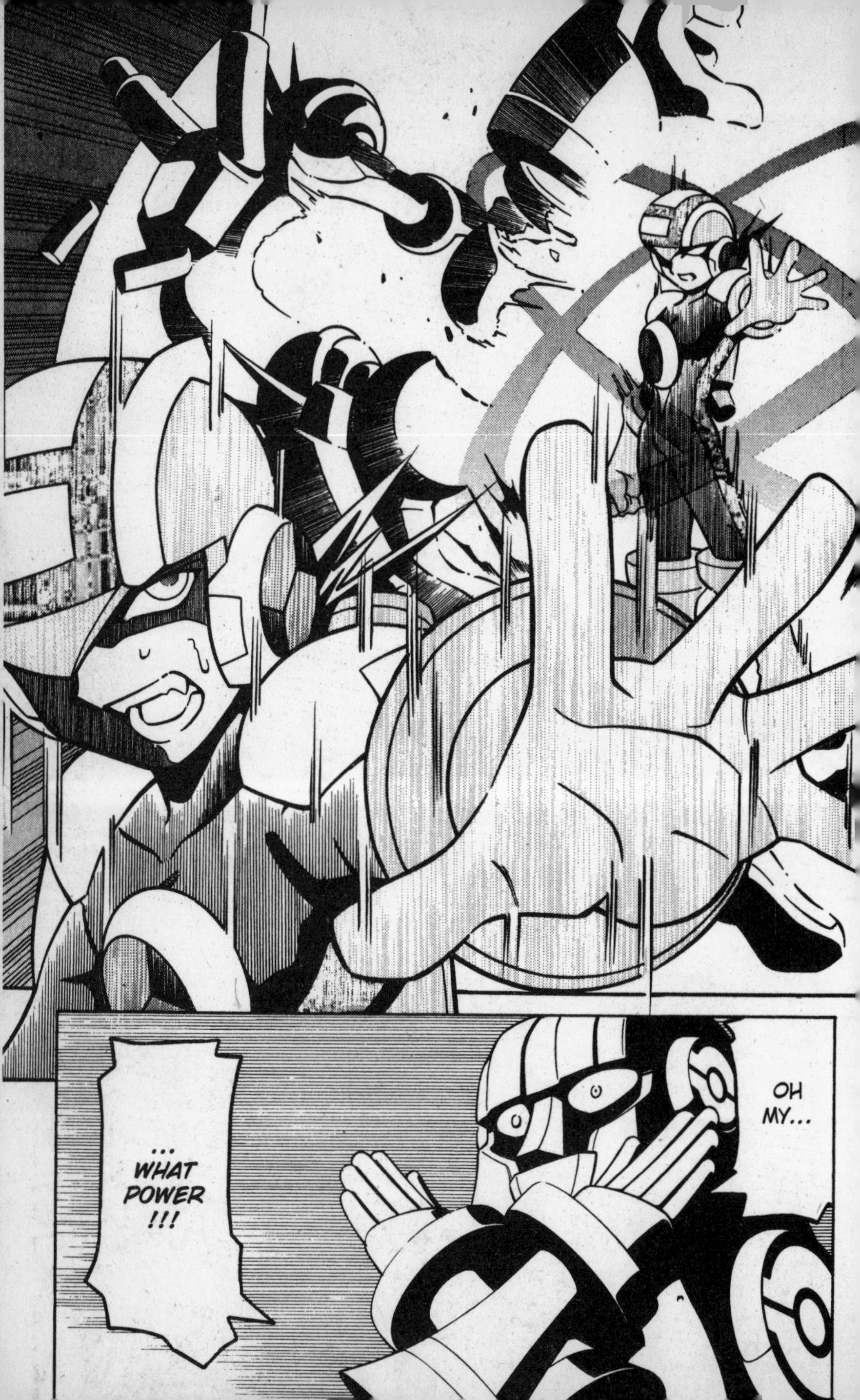
OH MY...
... WHAT POWER !!!

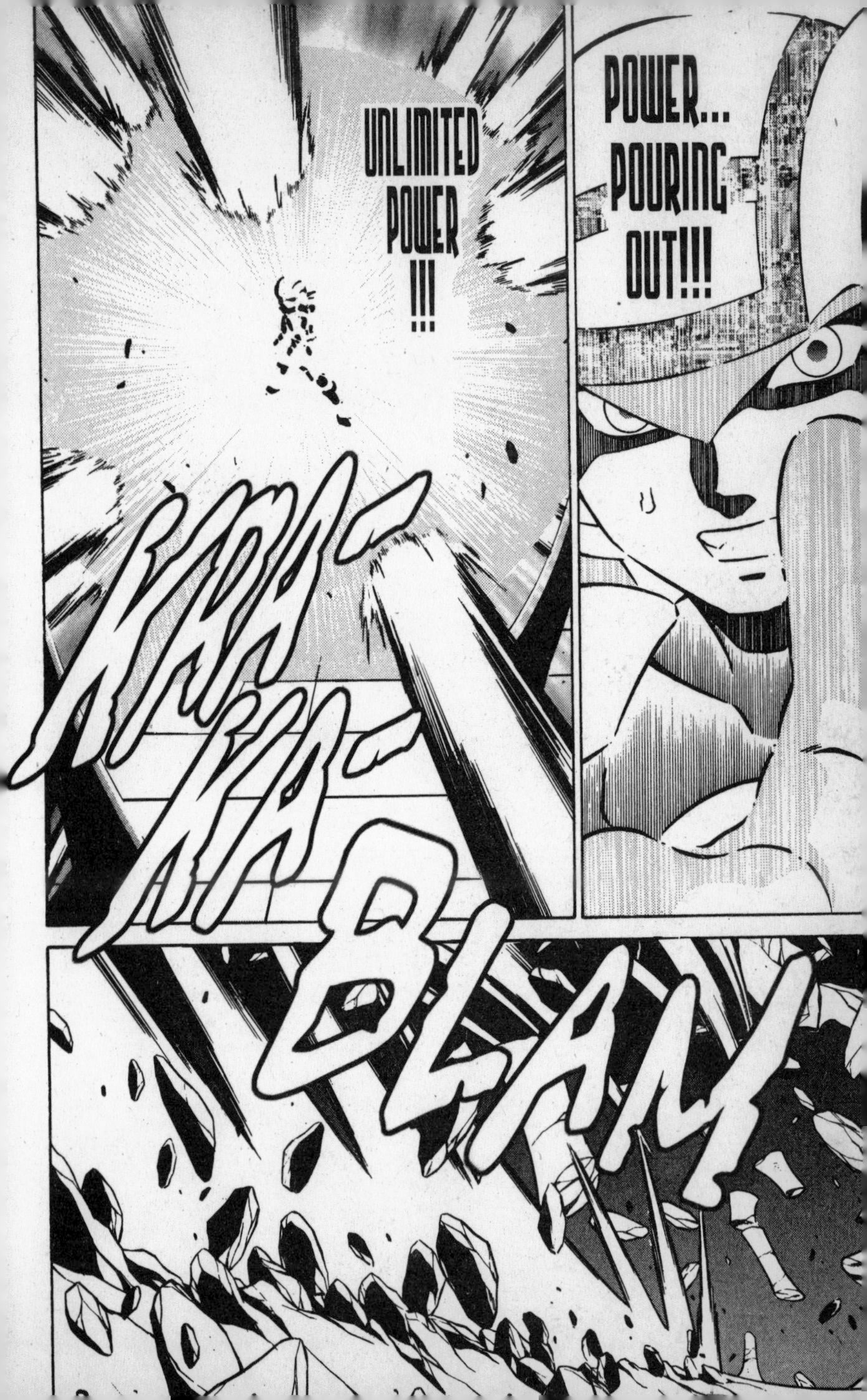
POWER... POURING OUT!!!
UNLIMITED POWER!!!
BLAM

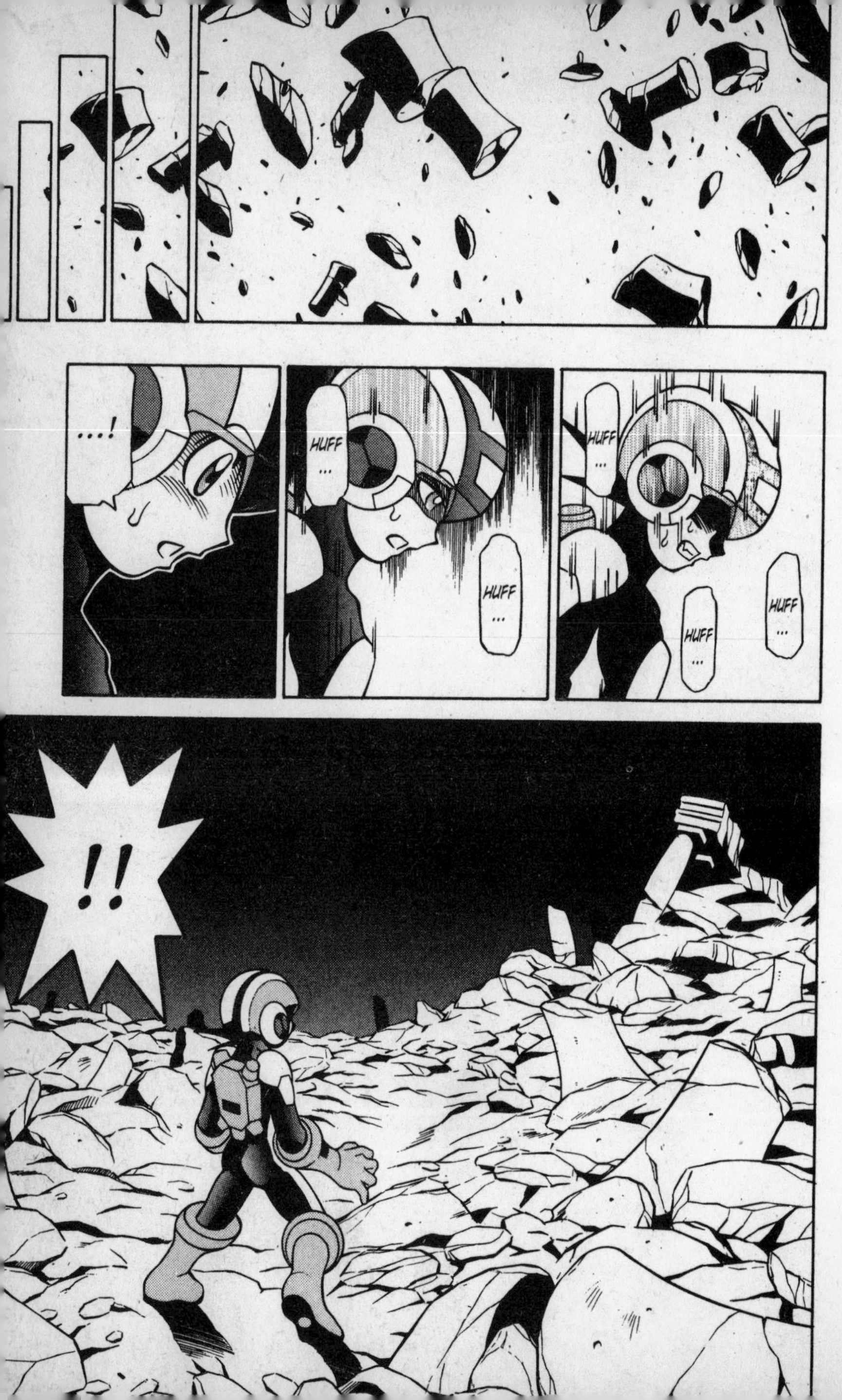

HUFF ...
HUFF ...
HUFF ...
HUFF ...
HUFF ...
...!
!!

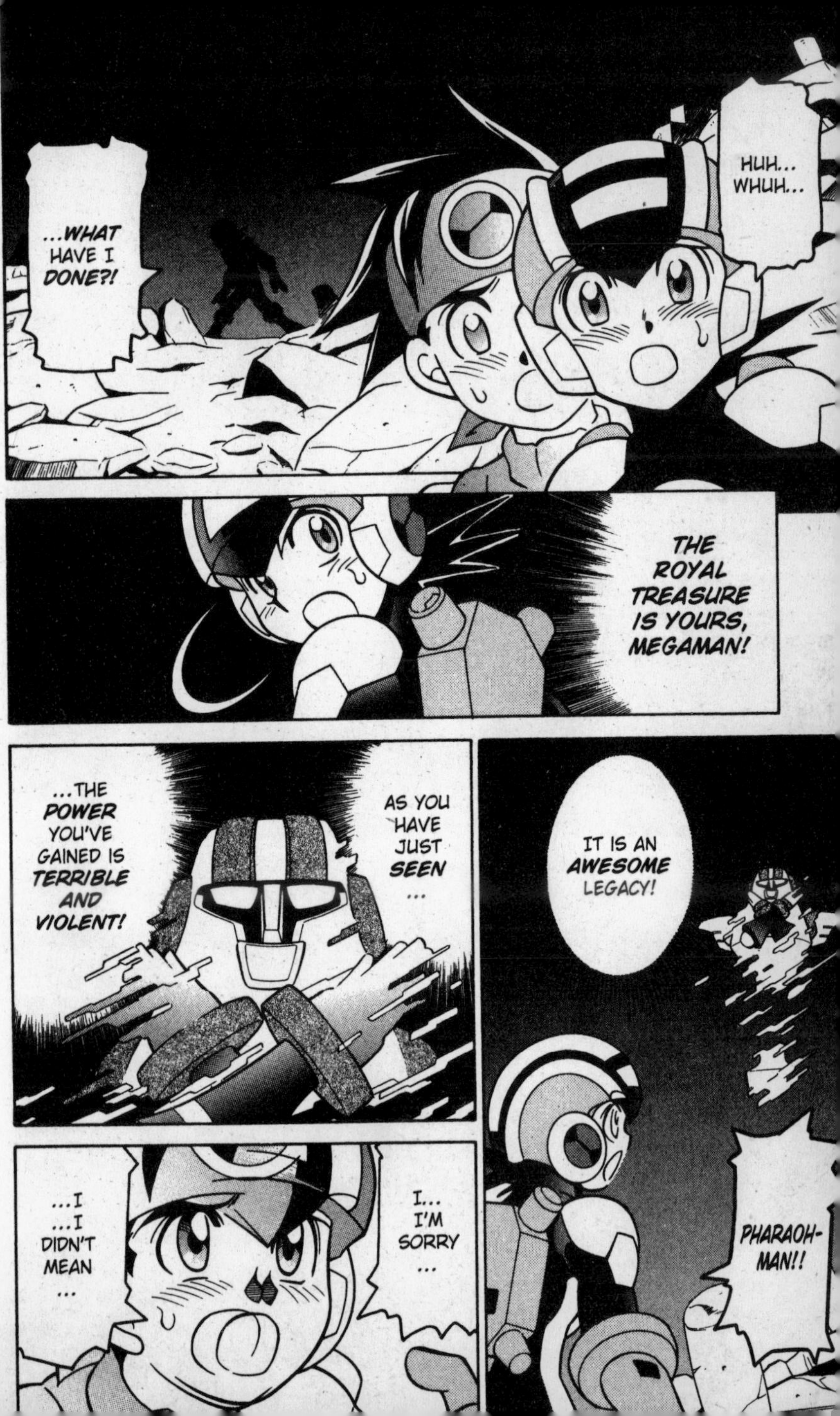
HUH... WHUH...
...WHAT HAVE I DONE?!
THE ROYAL TREASURE IS YOURS, MEGAMAN!
IT IS AN AWESOME LEGACY!
PHARAOH-MAN!!
AS YOU HAVE JUST SEEN...
...THE POWER YOU'VE GAINED IS TERRIBLE AND VIOLENT!
I... I'M SORRY...
...I ...I DIDN'T MEAN...

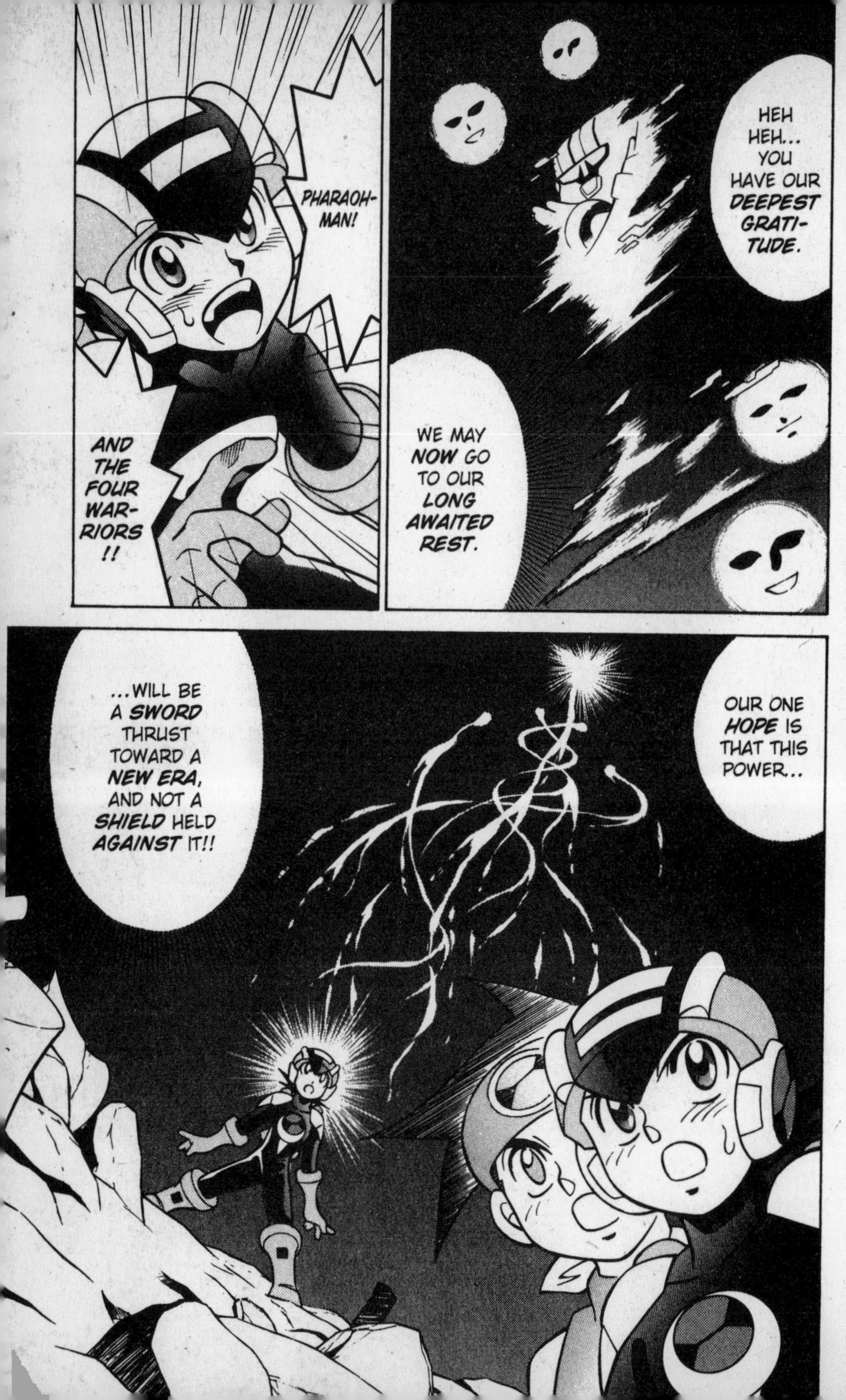
HEH HEH... YOU HAVE OUR DEEPEST GRATITUDE.
WE MAY NOW GO TO OUR LONG AWAITED REST.
PHARAOH-MAN!
AND THE FOUR WARRIORS!!
OUR ONE HOPE IS THAT THIS POWER...
...WILL BE A SWORD THRUST TOWARD A NEW ERA, AND NOT A SHIELD HELD AGAINST IT!!

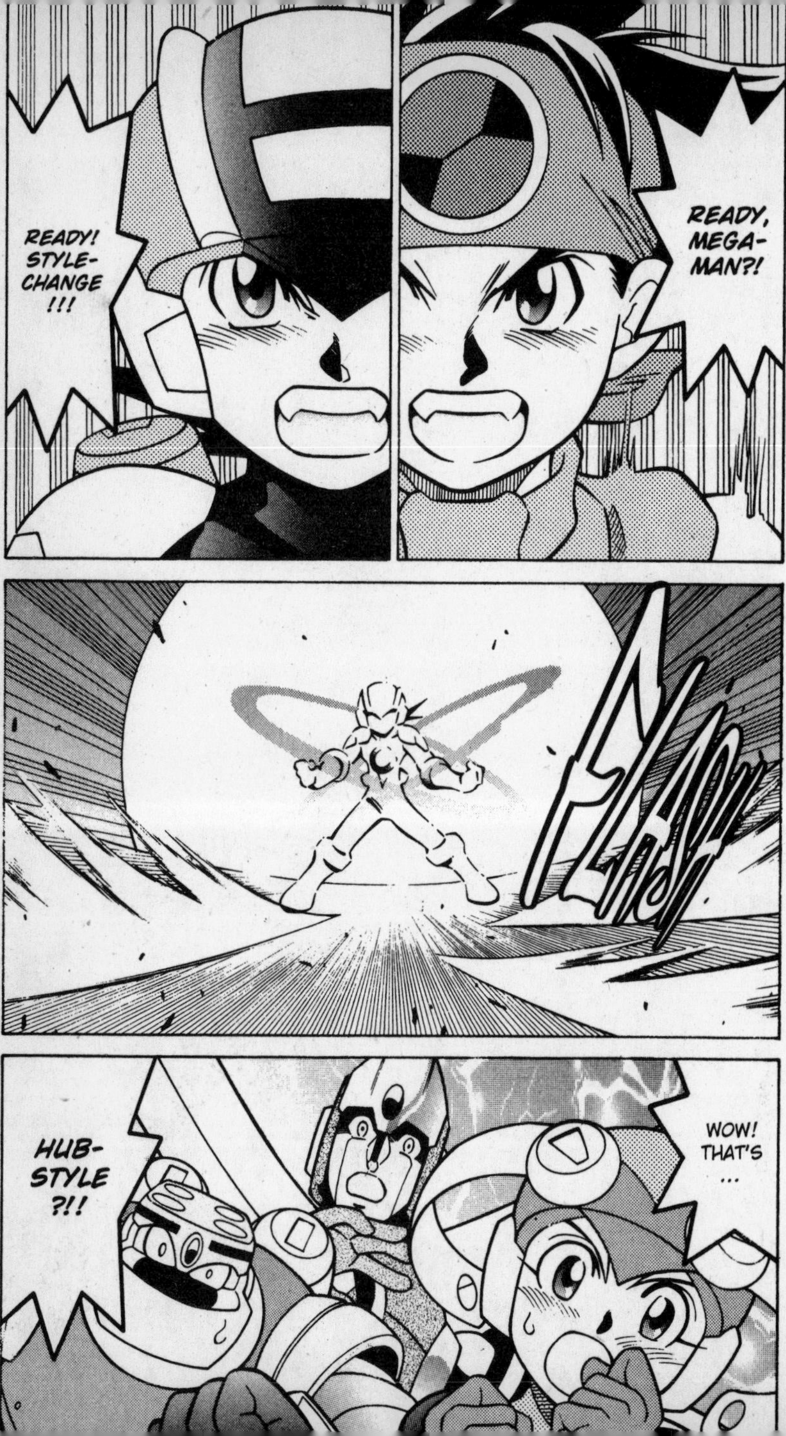
READY, MEGA-MAN?!
READY! STYLE-CHANGE !!!
WOW! THAT'S ...
HUB-STYLE ?!!

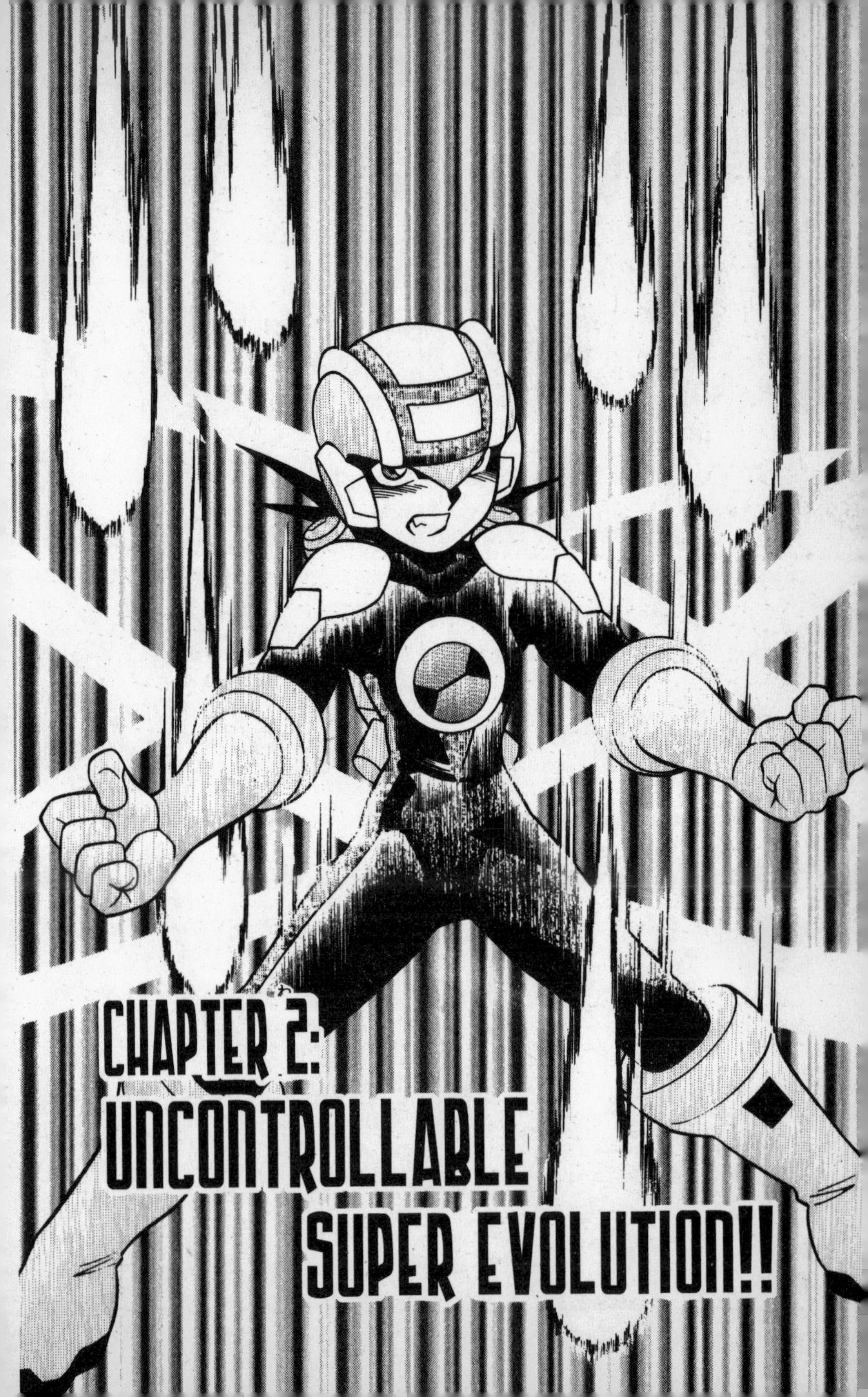
CHAPTER 2:
UNCONTROLLABLE
SUPER EVOLUTION!!

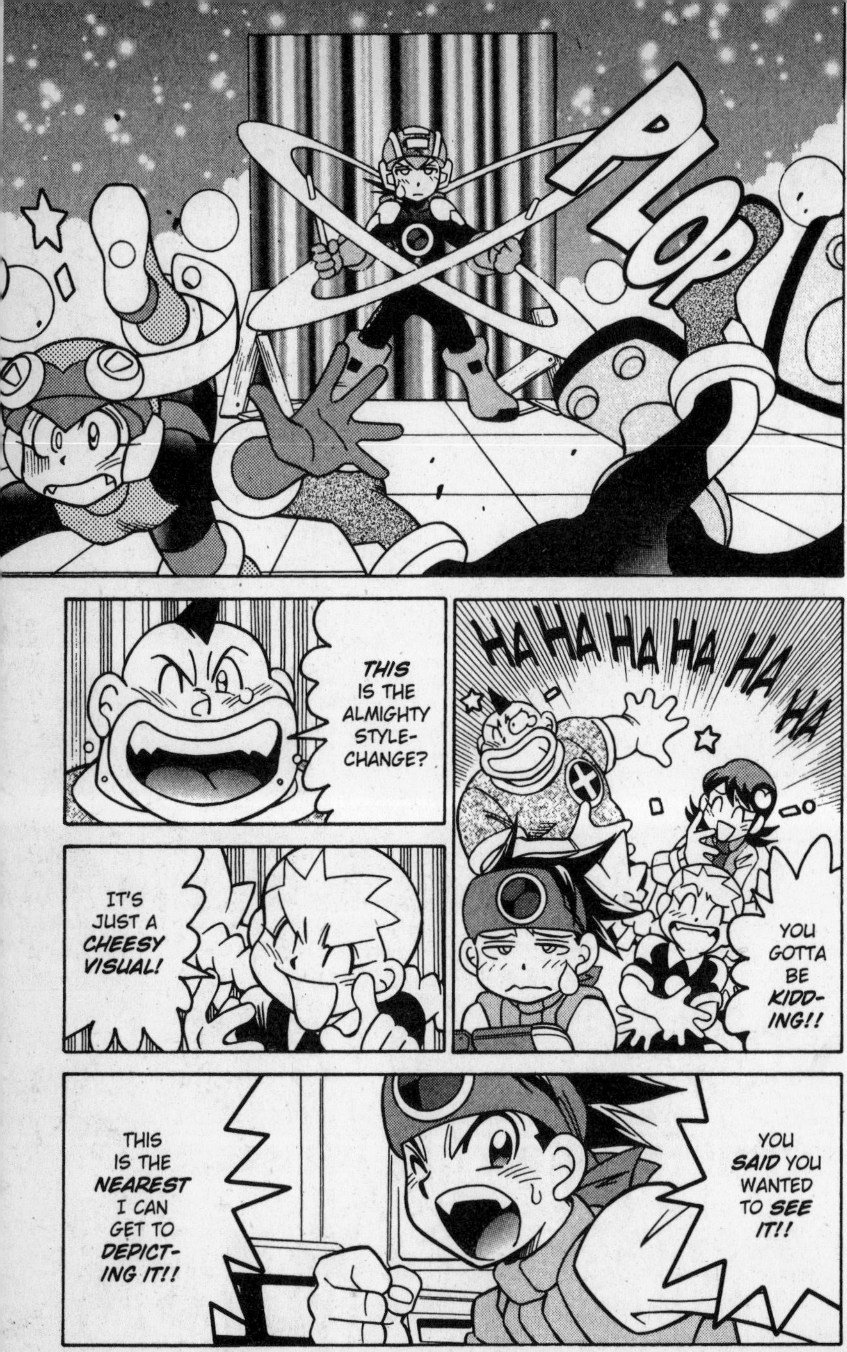
PLOP
HA HA HA HA HA HA HA HA
YOU GOTTA BE KIDDING!!
THIS IS THE ALMIGHTY STYLE-CHANGE?
IT'S JUST A CHEESY VISUAL!
YOU SAID YOU WANTED TO SEE IT!!
THIS IS THE NEAREST I CAN GET TO DEPICTING IT!!

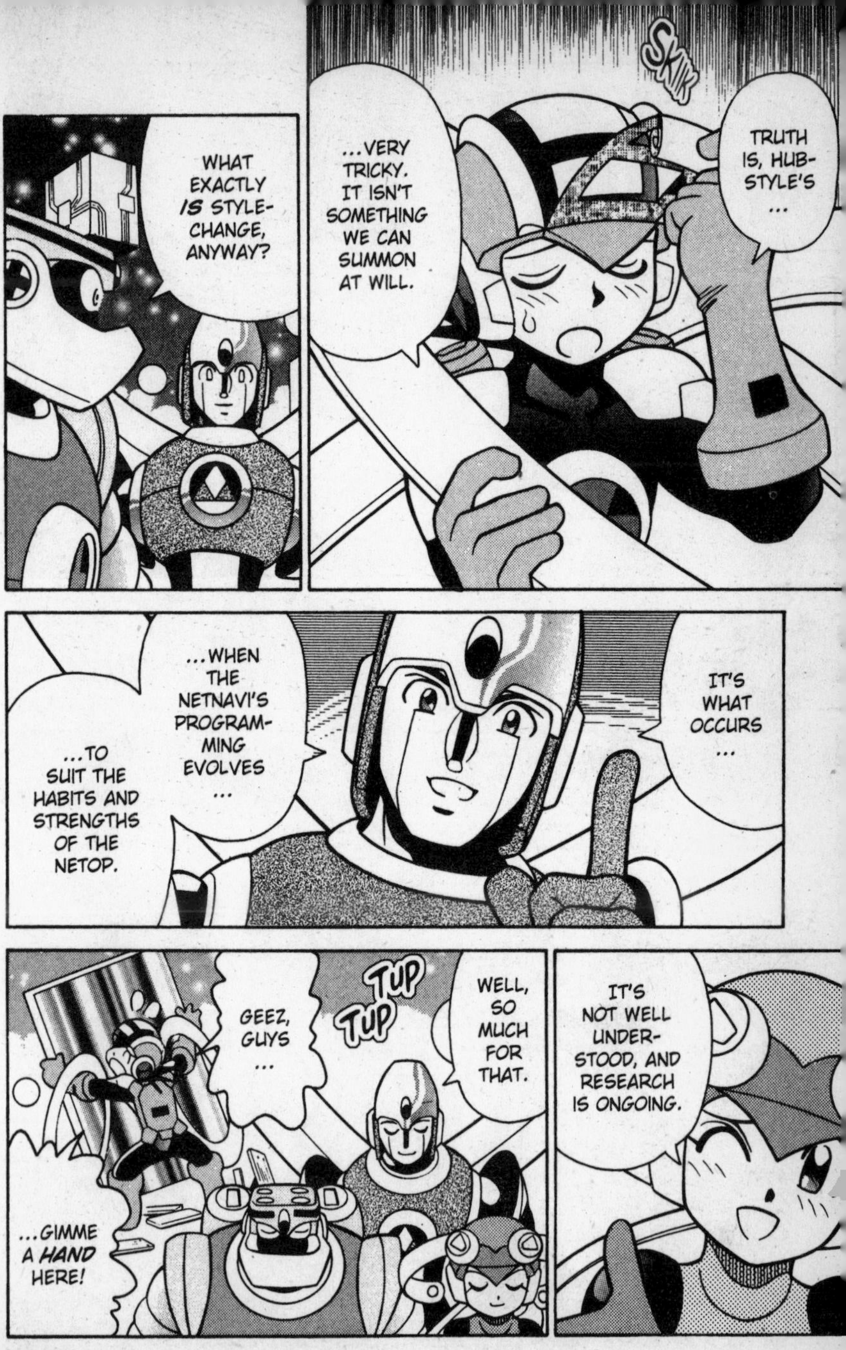
SKIIK
TRUTH IS, HUB-STYLE'S ...
...VERY TRICKY. IT ISN'T SOMETHING WE CAN SUMMON AT WILL.
WHAT EXACTLY *IS* STYLE-CHANGE, ANYWAY?
IT'S WHAT OCCURS ...
...WHEN THE NETNAVI'S PROGRAMMING EVOLVES ...
...TO SUIT THE HABITS AND STRENGTHS OF THE NETOP.
IT'S NOT WELL UNDERSTOOD, AND RESEARCH IS ONGOING.
WELL, SO MUCH FOR THAT.
TUP TUP
GEEZ, GUYS ...
...GIMME A **HAND** HERE!

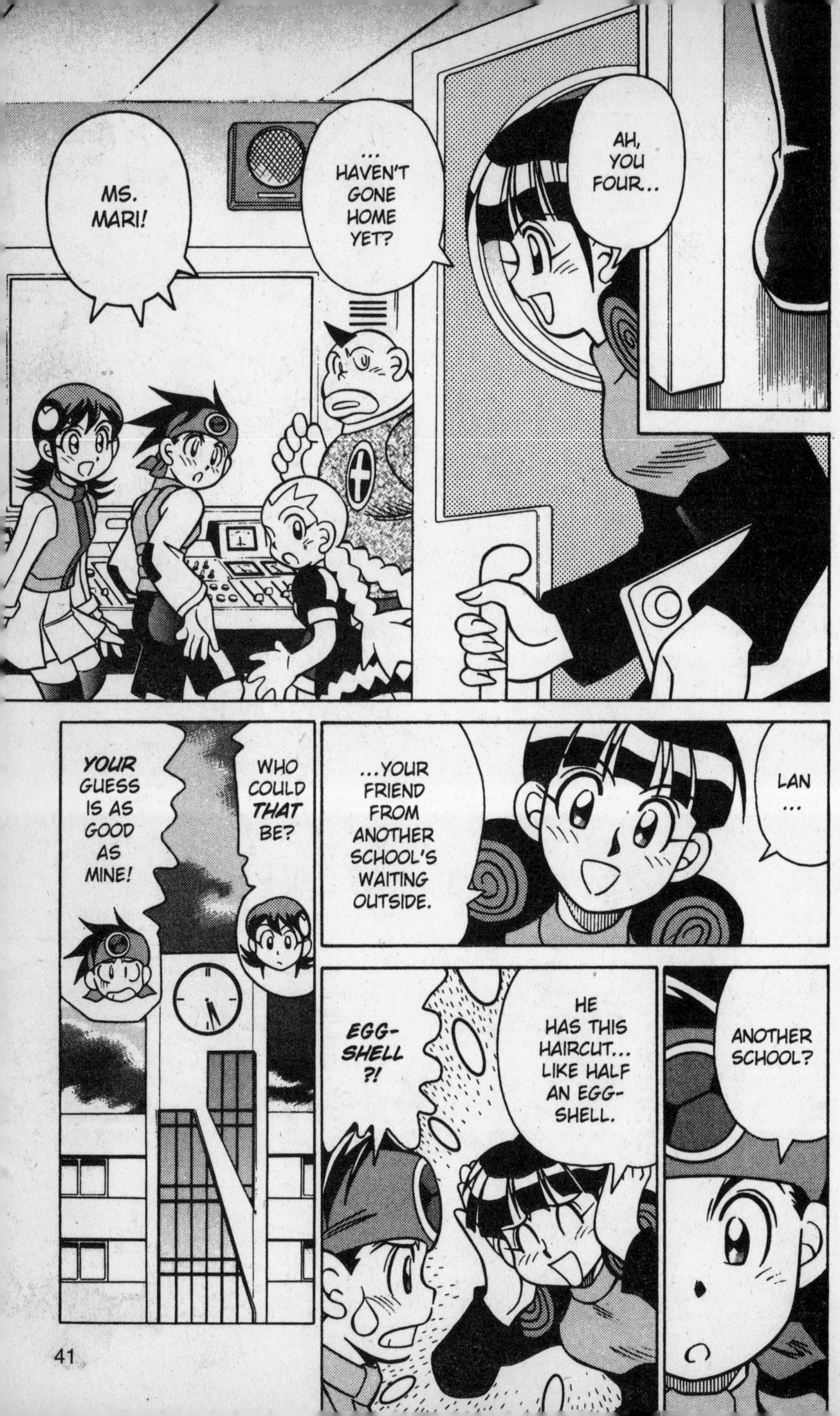
AH, YOU FOUR...
... HAVEN'T GONE HOME YET?
MS. MARI!
LAN ...
...YOUR FRIEND FROM ANOTHER SCHOOL'S WAITING OUTSIDE.
ANOTHER SCHOOL?
HE HAS THIS HAIRCUT... LIKE HALF AN EGG-SHELL.
EGG-SHELL ?!
WHO COULD *THAT* BE?
*YOUR* GUESS IS AS GOOD AS MINE!

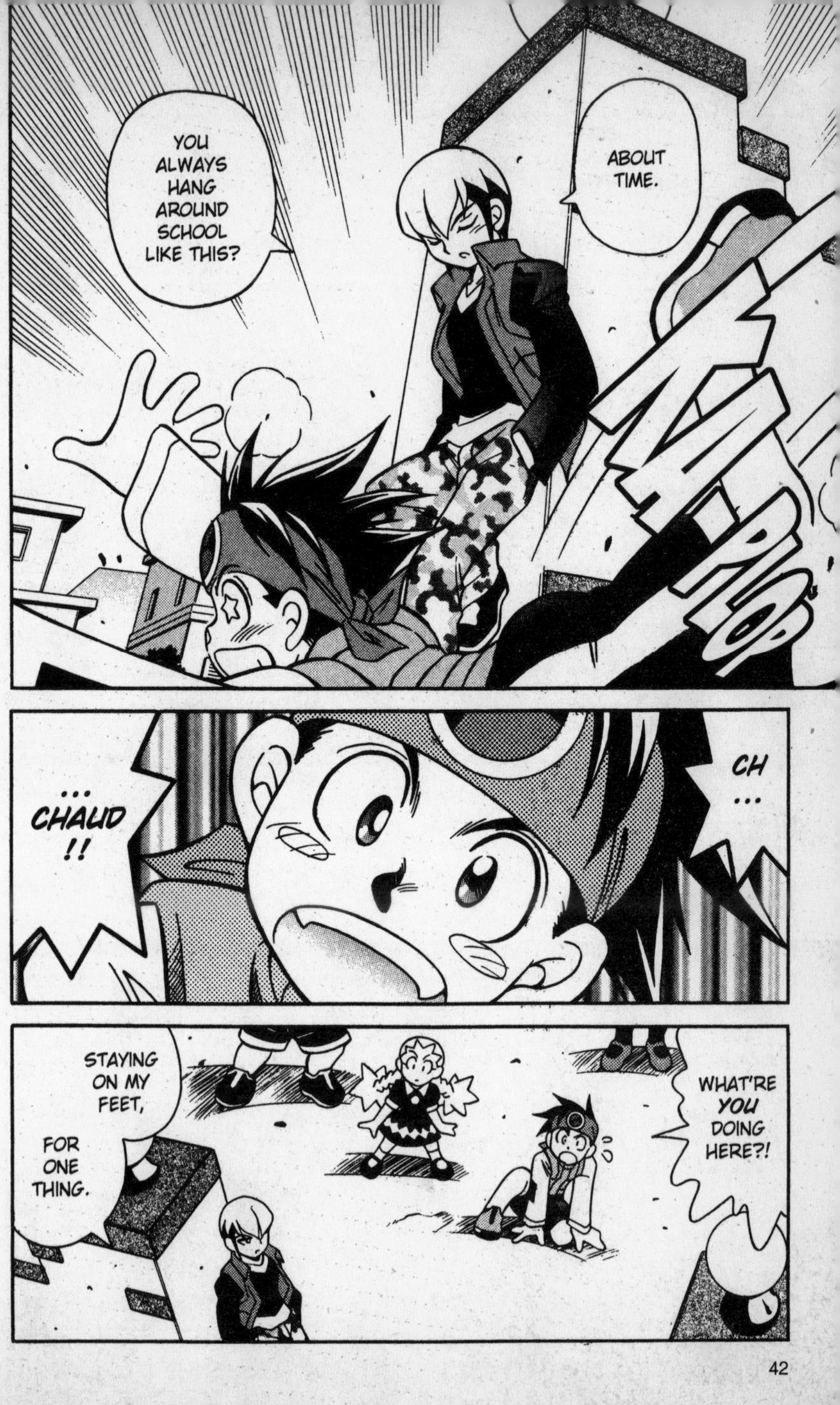
ABOUT TIME.
YOU ALWAYS HANG AROUND SCHOOL LIKE THIS?
CH ...
... CHAUD !!
WHAT'RE *YOU* DOING HERE?!
STAYING ON MY FEET,
FOR ONE THING.

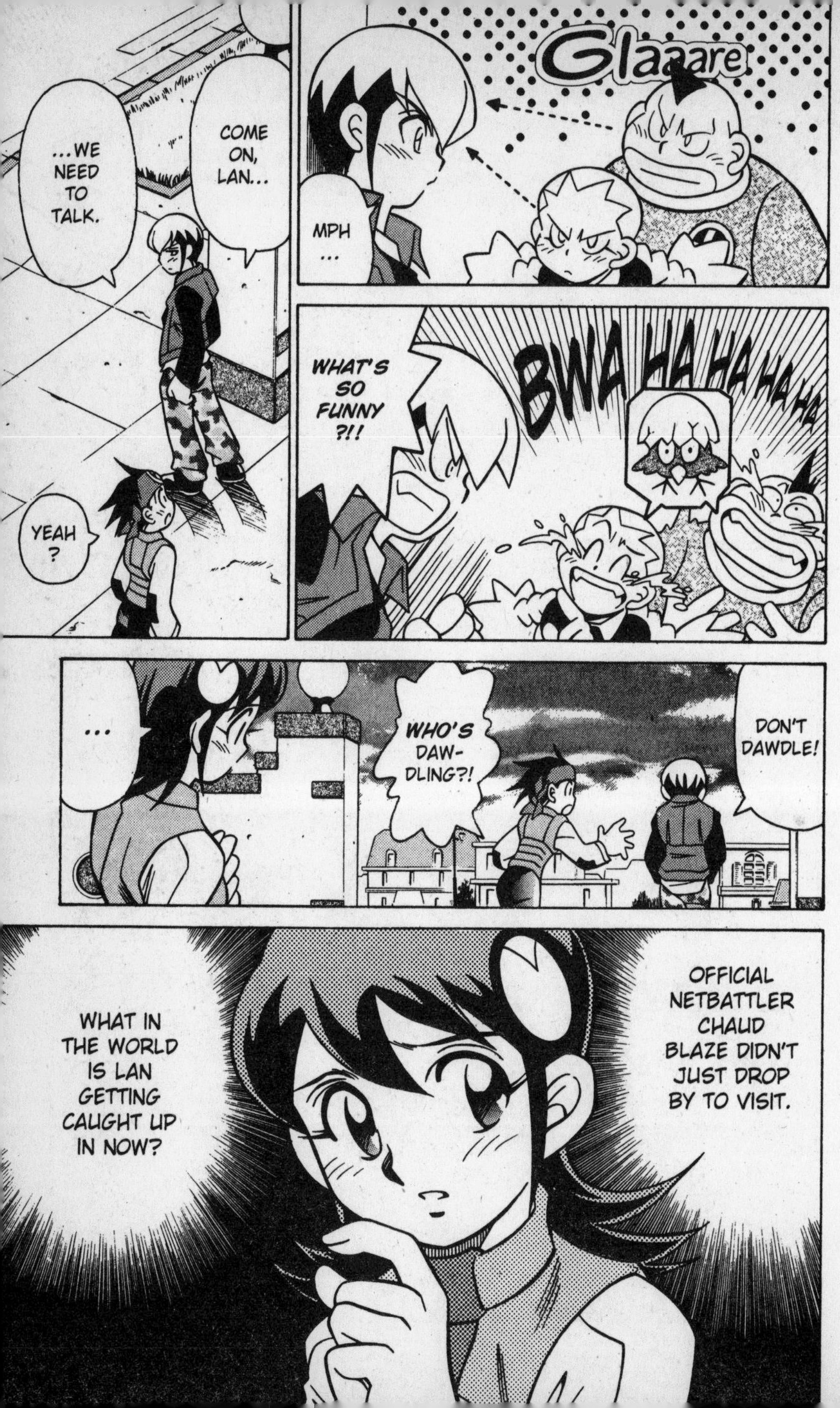
Glaaare
MPH ...
BWA HA HA HA HA HA
WHAT'S SO FUNNY ?!!
COME ON, LAN...
...WE NEED TO TALK.
YEAH ?
DON'T DAWDLE!
WHO'S DAW-DLING?!
...
OFFICIAL NETBATTLER CHAUD BLAZE DIDN'T JUST DROP BY TO VISIT.
WHAT IN THE WORLD IS LAN GETTING CAUGHT UP IN NOW?

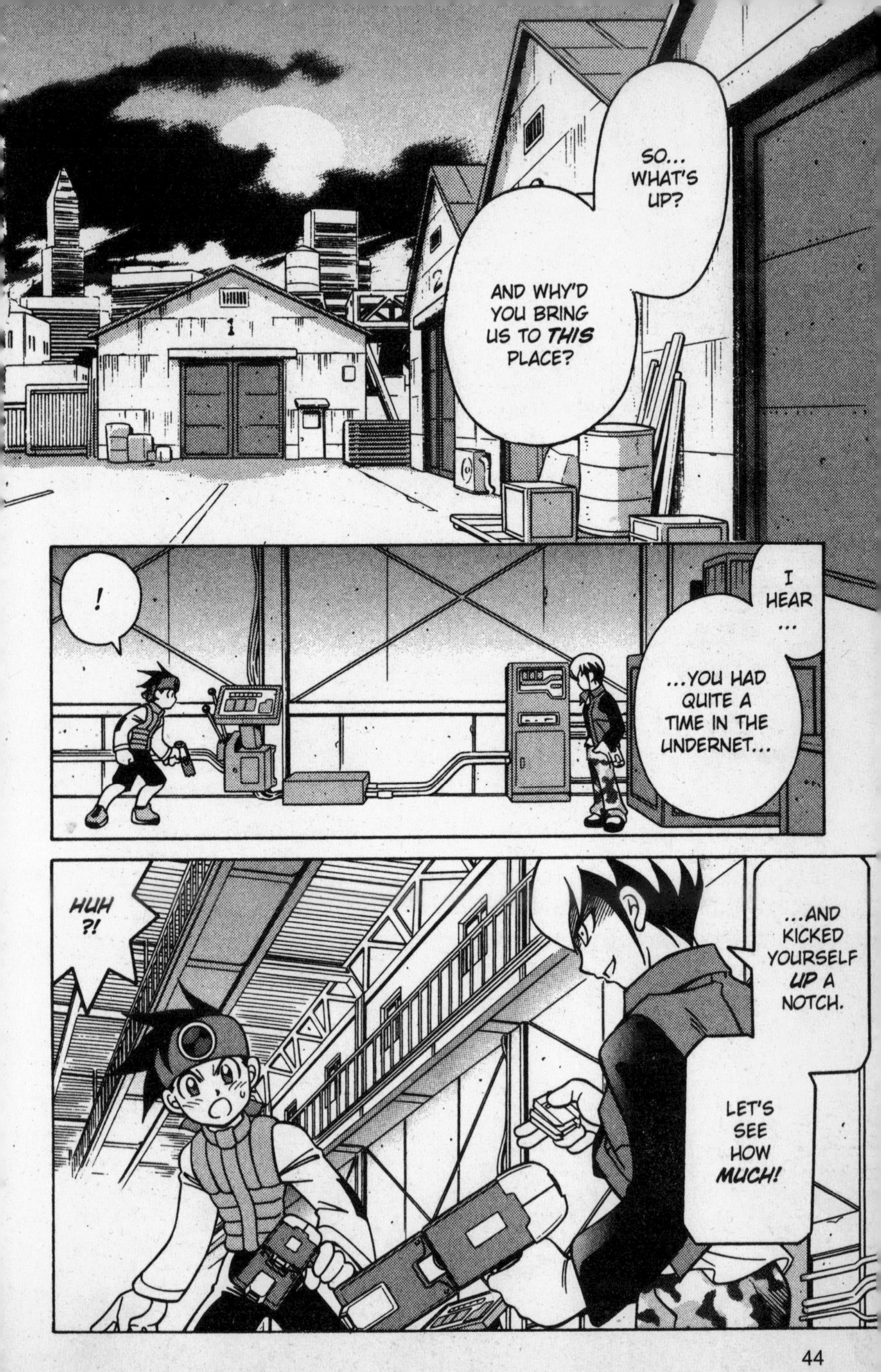
SO... WHAT'S UP?
AND WHY'D YOU BRING US TO *THIS* PLACE?
I HEAR...
...YOU HAD QUITE A TIME IN THE UNDERNET...
!
...AND KICKED YOURSELF *UP* A NOTCH.
LET'S SEE HOW *MUCH!*
HUH ?!

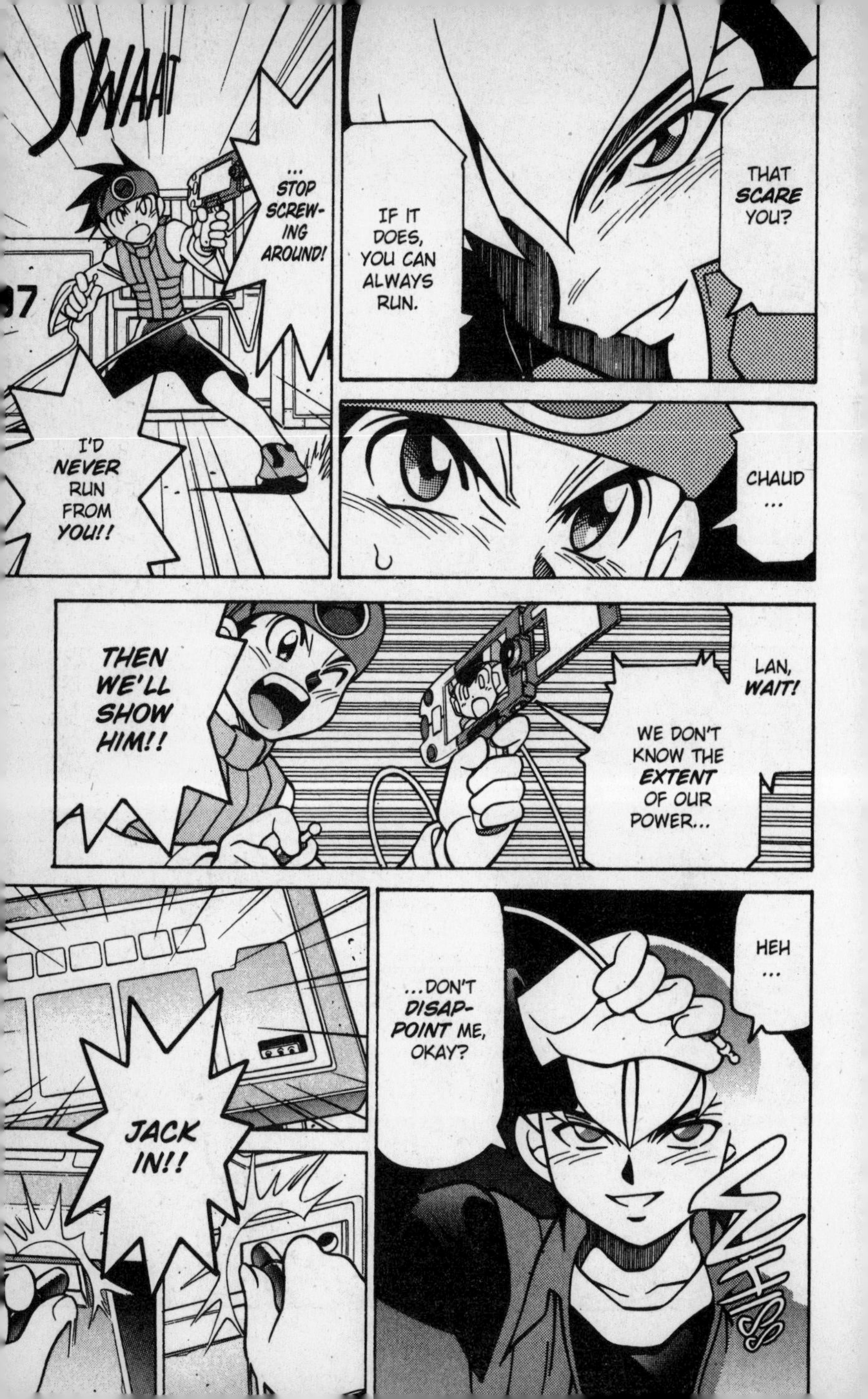
THAT SCARE YOU?
IF IT DOES, YOU CAN ALWAYS RUN.
CHAUD ...
SWAAT
... STOP SCREWING AROUND!
I'D NEVER RUN FROM YOU!!
LAN, WAIT!
WE DON'T KNOW THE EXTENT OF OUR POWER...
THEN WE'LL SHOW HIM!!
HEH ...
...DON'T DISAPPOINT ME, OKAY?
JACK IN!!

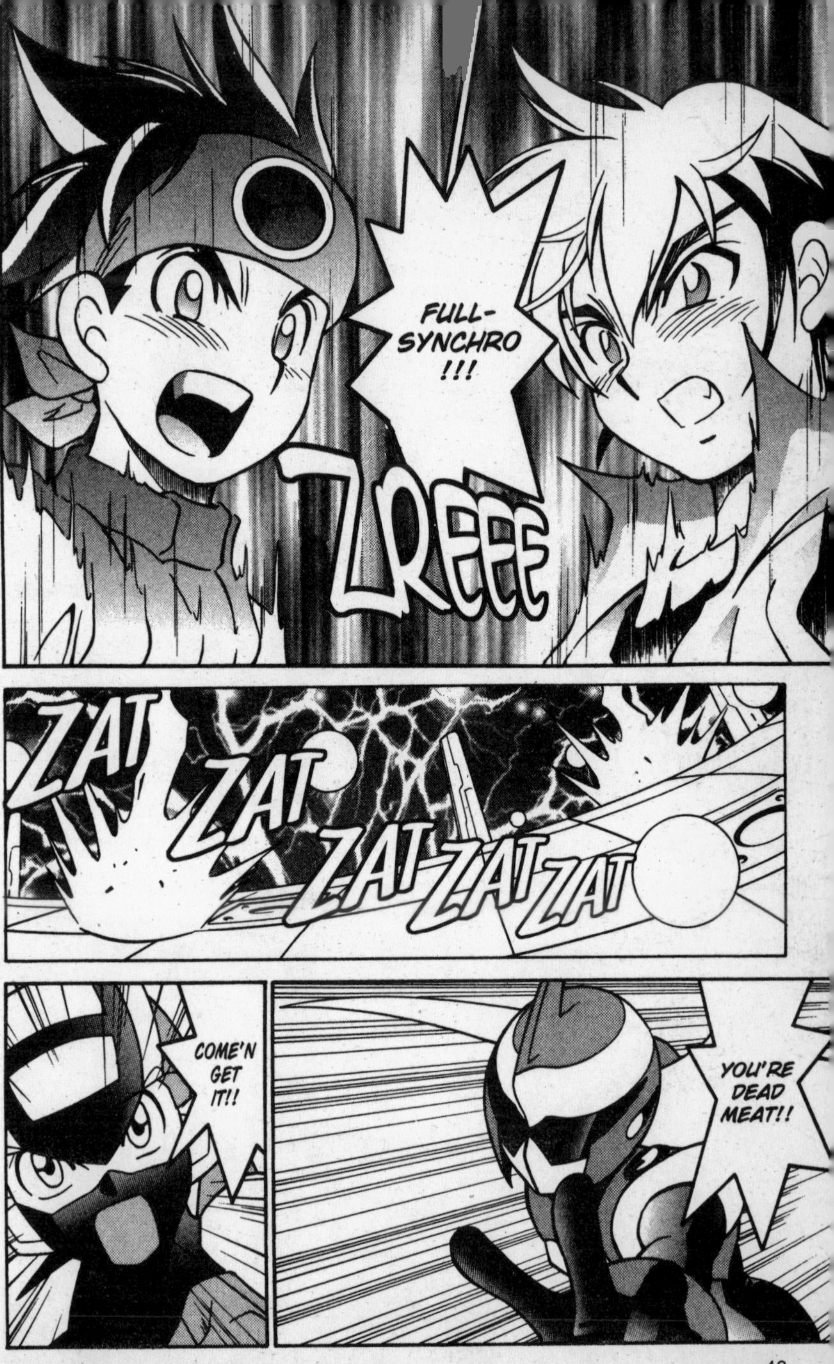
FULL-SYNCHRO !!!
ZREEE
ZAT ZAT ZAT ZAT ZAT
YOU'RE DEAD MEAT!!
COME'N GET IT!!

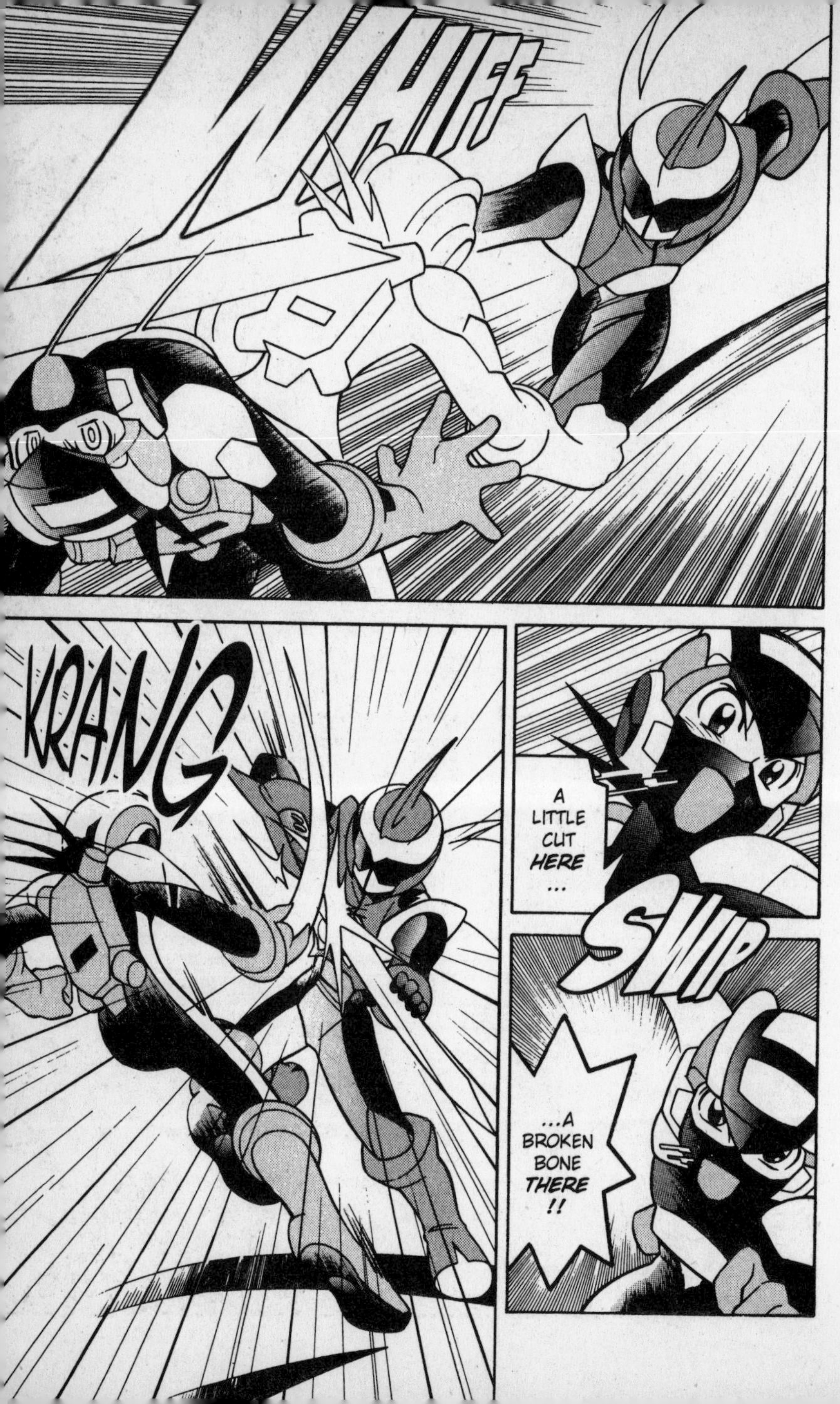
WHIFF
A LITTLE CUT *HERE* ...
SWIP
...A BROKEN BONE *THERE* !!
KRANG

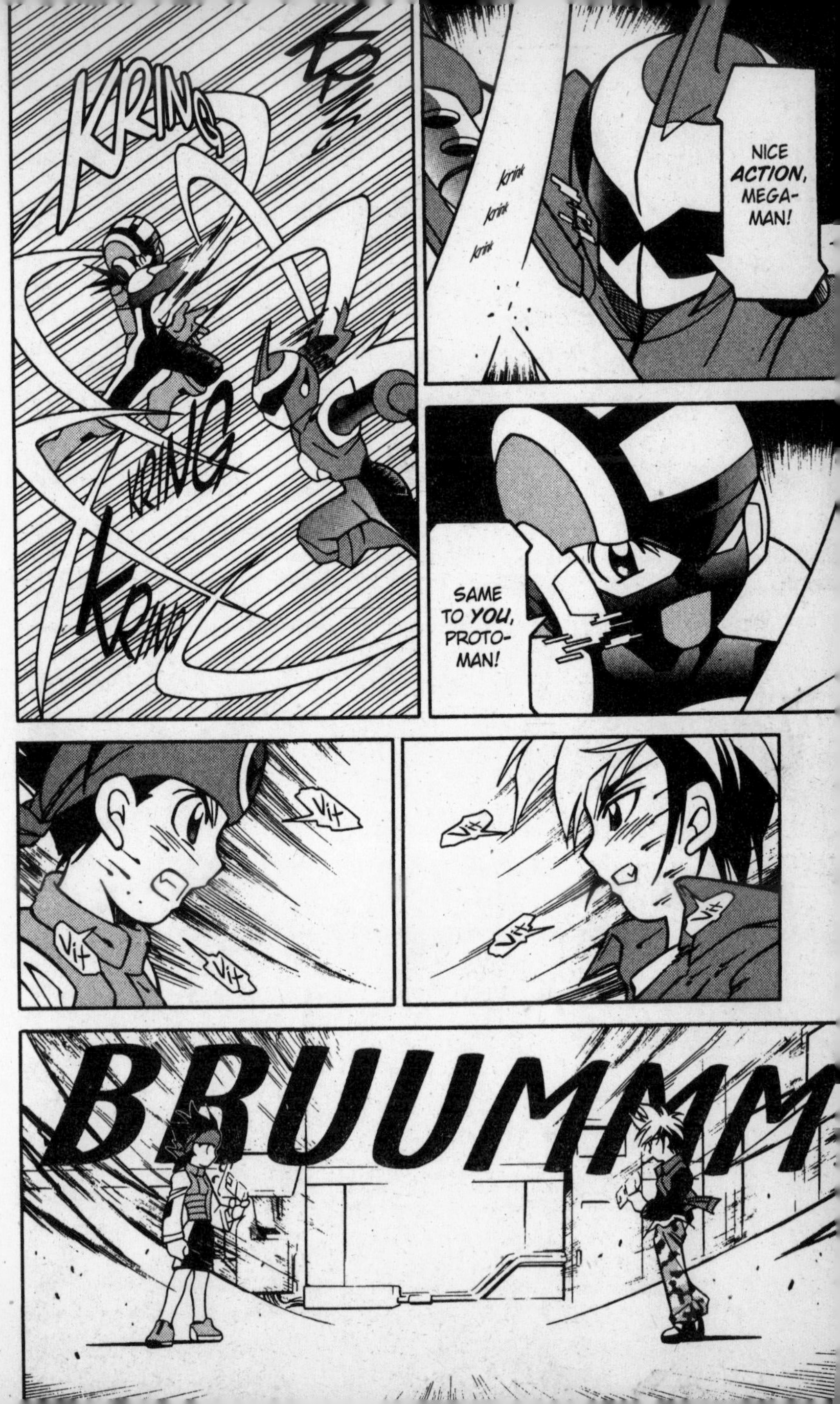
krink
krink
krink
NICE ACTION, MEGA-MAN!
SAME TO YOU, PROTO-MAN!
KRING
KRING
KRING
KRING
Vit
Vit
Vit
Vit
Vit
Vit
BRUUMMM

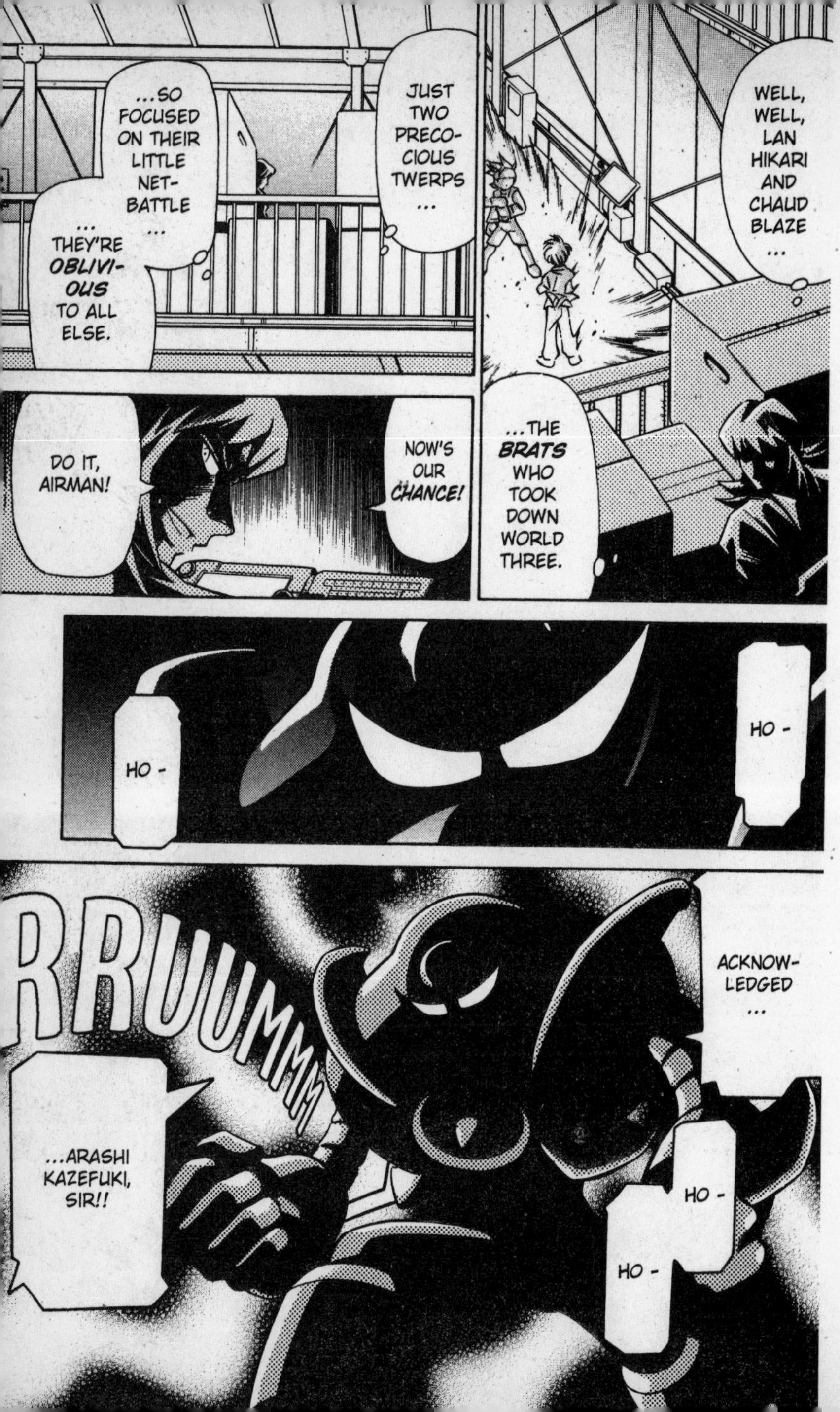
WELL, WELL, LAN HIKARI AND CHAUD BLAZE ...
...THE BRATS WHO TOOK DOWN WORLD THREE.
JUST TWO PRECOCIOUS TWERPS ...
...SO FOCUSED ON THEIR LITTLE NET-BATTLE ...
... THEY'RE OBLIVIOUS TO ALL ELSE.
NOW'S OUR CHANCE!
DO IT, AIRMAN!
HO -
HO -
ACKNOWLEDGED ...
HO -
HO -
RRUUMMM
...ARASHI KAZEFUKI, SIR!!

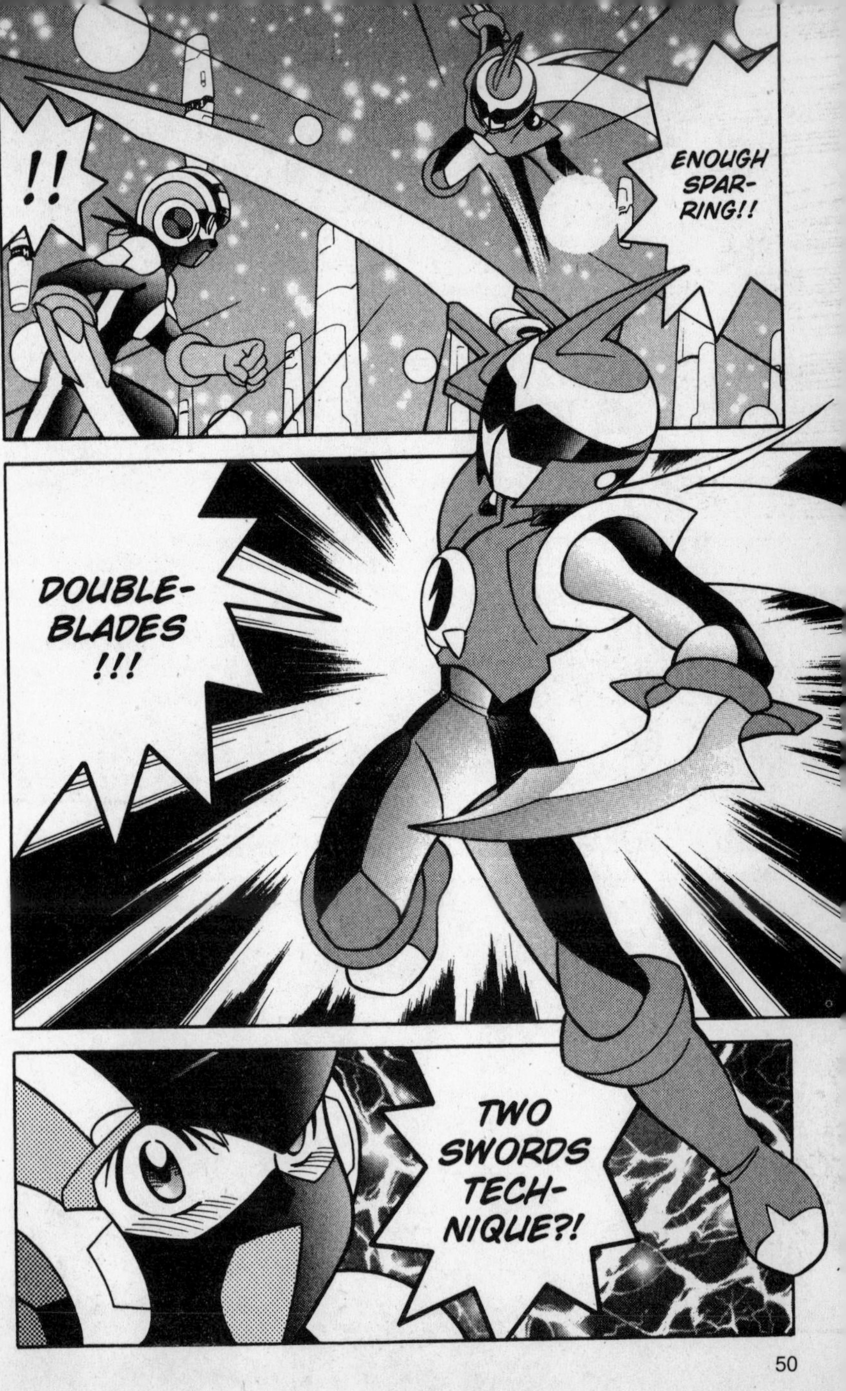
ENOUGH SPAR-RING!!
!!
DOUBLE-BLADES!!!
TWO SWORDS TECH-NIQUE?!

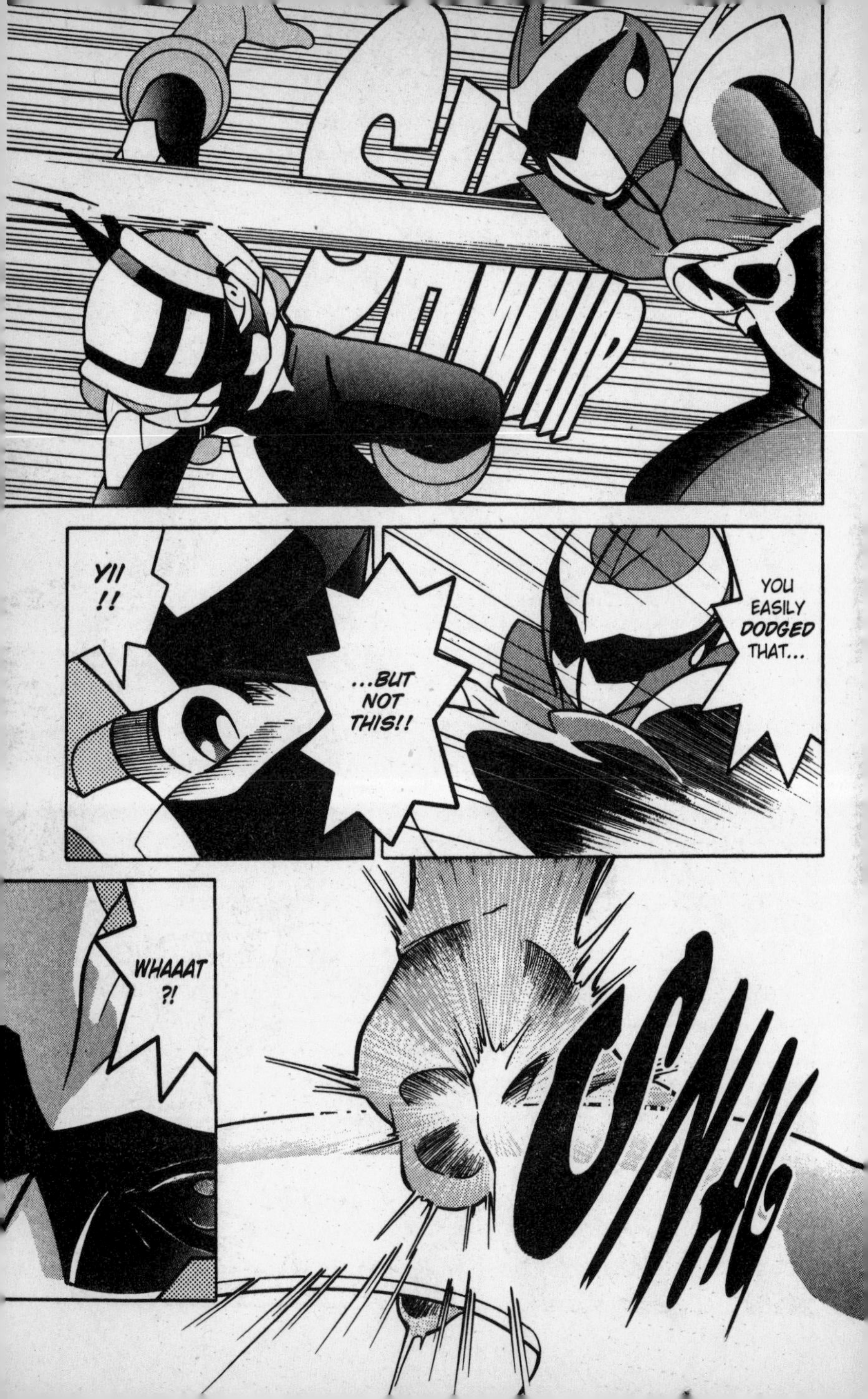
YOU EASILY DODGED THAT...
...BUT NOT THIS!!
YII !!
WHAAAT ?!

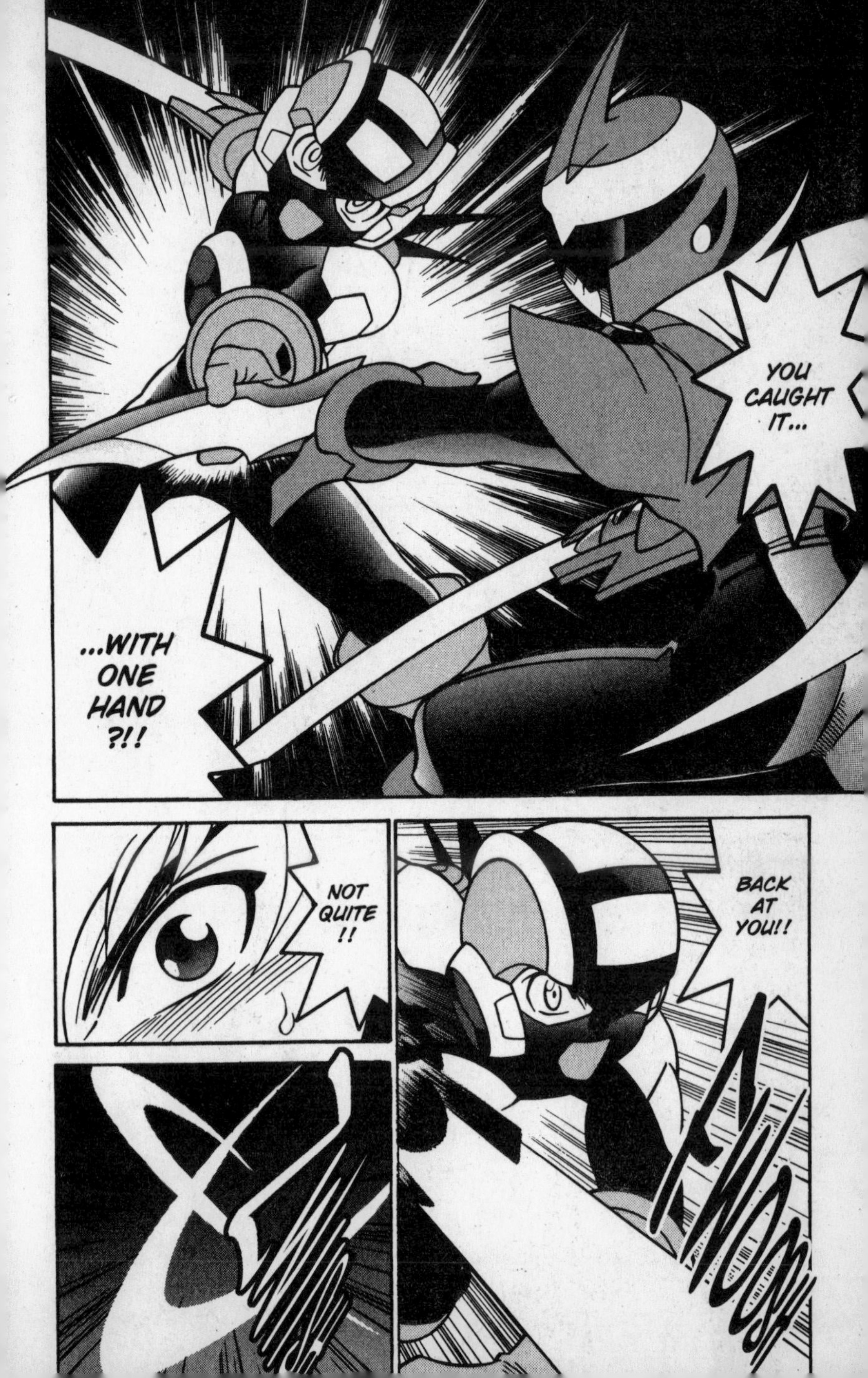
YOU CAUGHT IT...
...WITH ONE HAND ?!!
BACK AT YOU!!
NOT QUITE !!

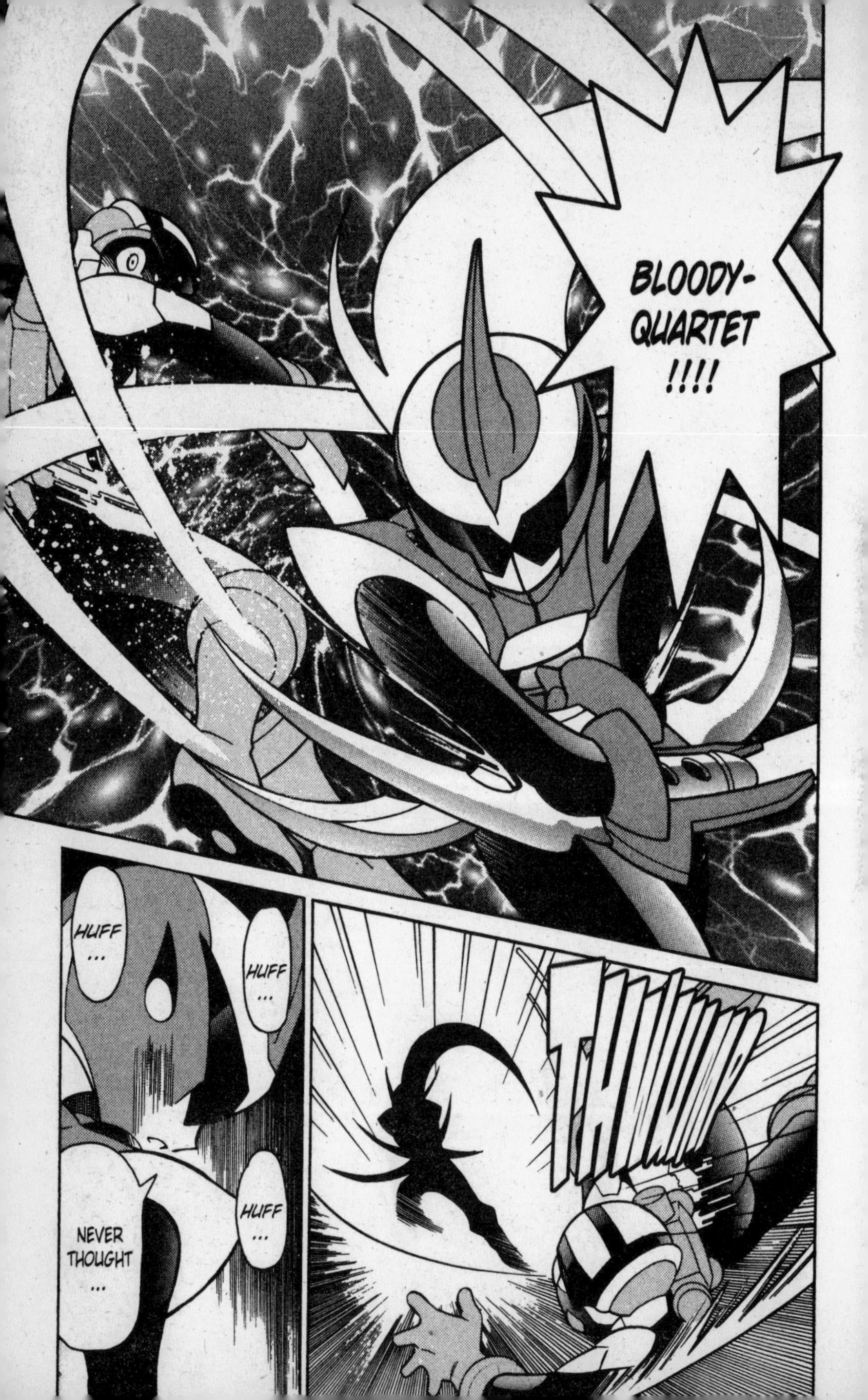
BLOODY-QUARTET!!!!
HUFF...
HUFF...
HUFF...
NEVER THOUGHT...

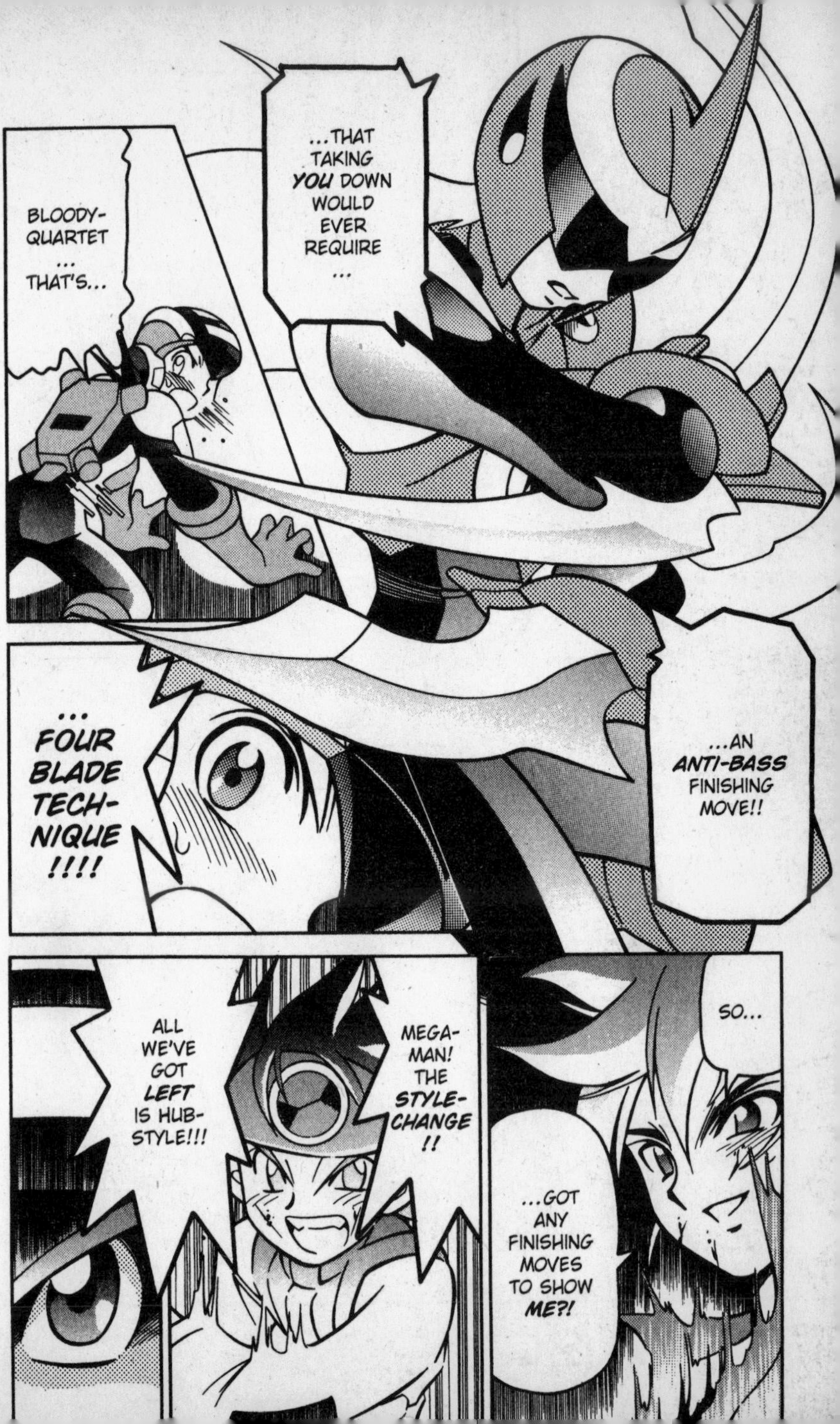
...THAT TAKING *YOU* DOWN WOULD EVER REQUIRE...
BLOODY-QUARTET... THAT'S...
...AN *ANTI-BASS* FINISHING MOVE!!
...*FOUR BLADE TECHNIQUE!!!!*
SO...
...GOT ANY FINISHING MOVES TO SHOW *ME?!*
MEGA-MAN! THE *STYLE-CHANGE!!*
ALL WE'VE GOT *LEFT* IS HUB-STYLE!!!

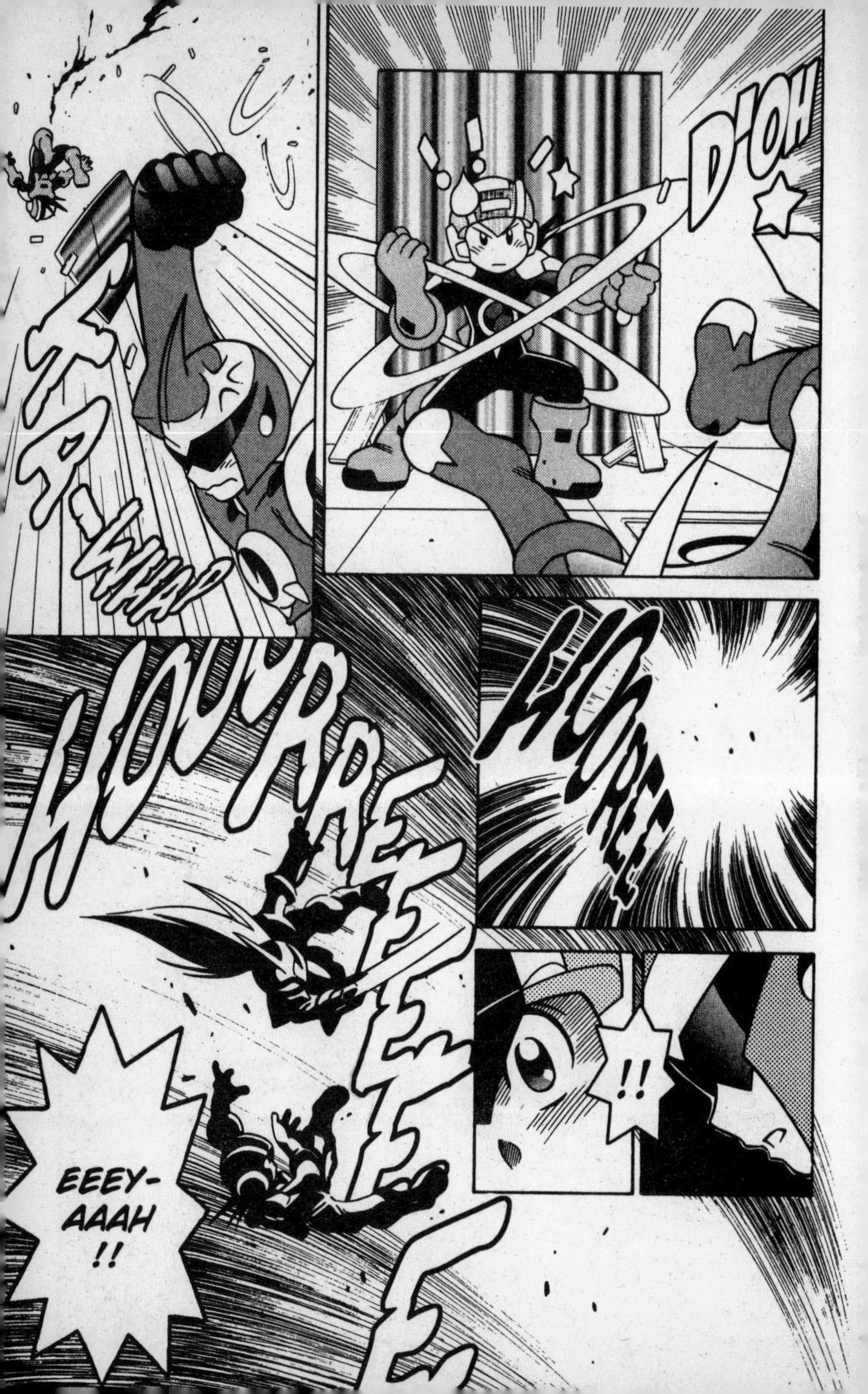
D'OH
HA
WHA?
YOU'RE!
!!
YOU'RE FREE
EEEY-AAAH !!

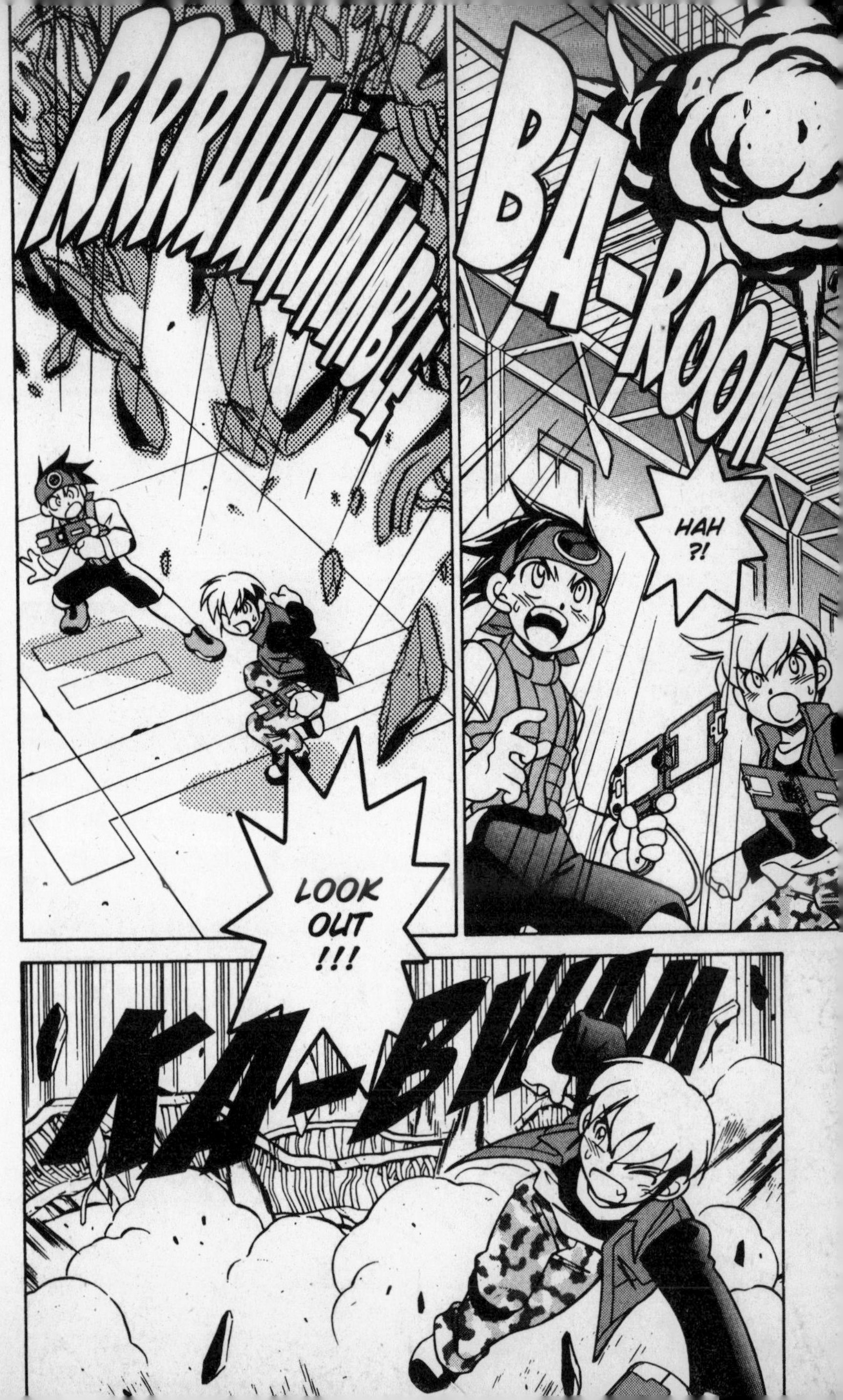
BA-ROOM
HAH ?!
RRRUMMMBLE
LOOK OUT !!!
KA-BWAM

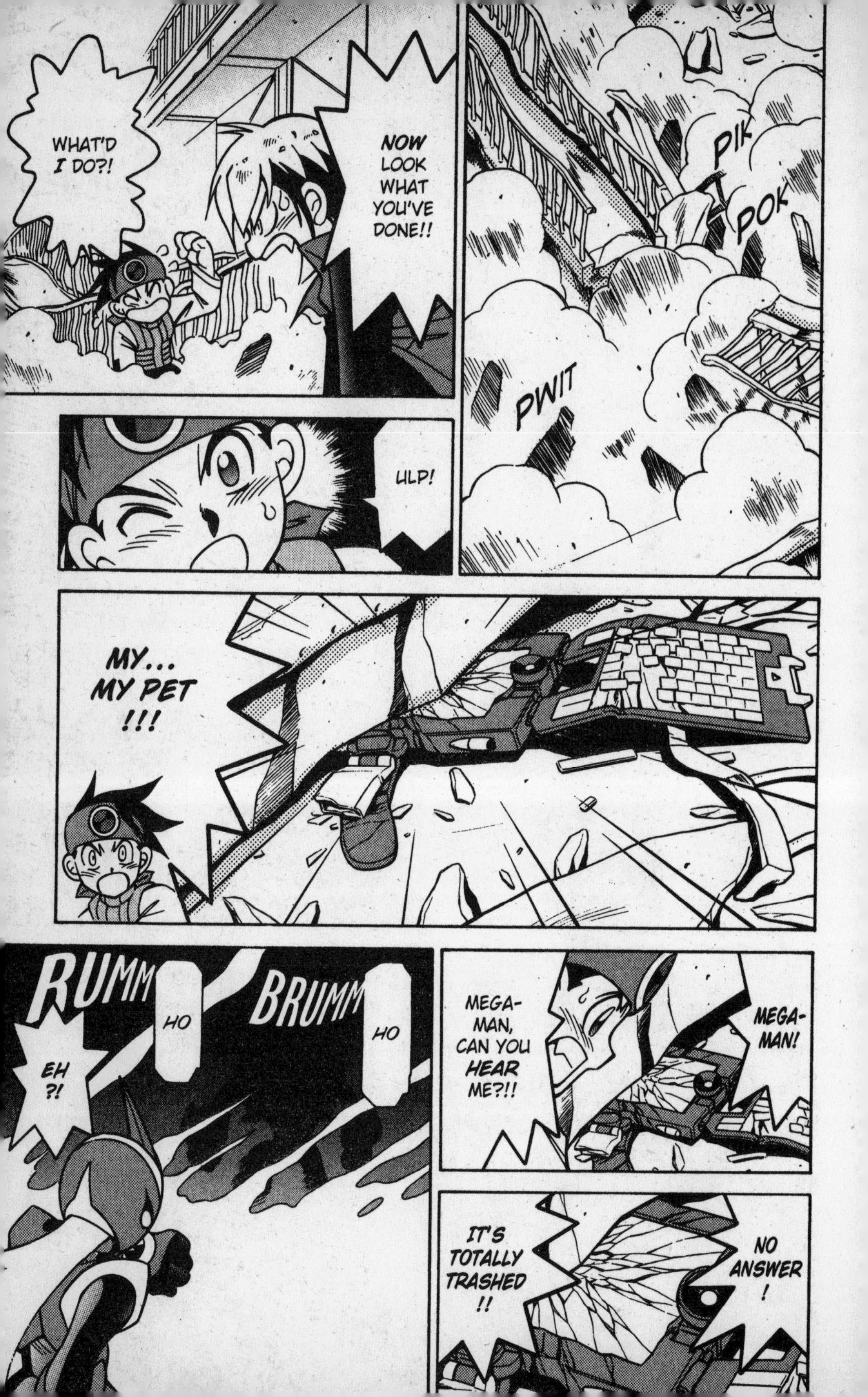
PIK
POK
PWIT
NOW LOOK WHAT YOU'VE DONE!!
WHAT'D I DO?!
ULP!
MY... MY PET !!!
MEGA-MAN!
MEGA-MAN, CAN YOU HEAR ME?!!
NO ANSWER !
IT'S TOTALLY TRASHED !!
BRUMM
HO
RUMM
HO
EH ?!

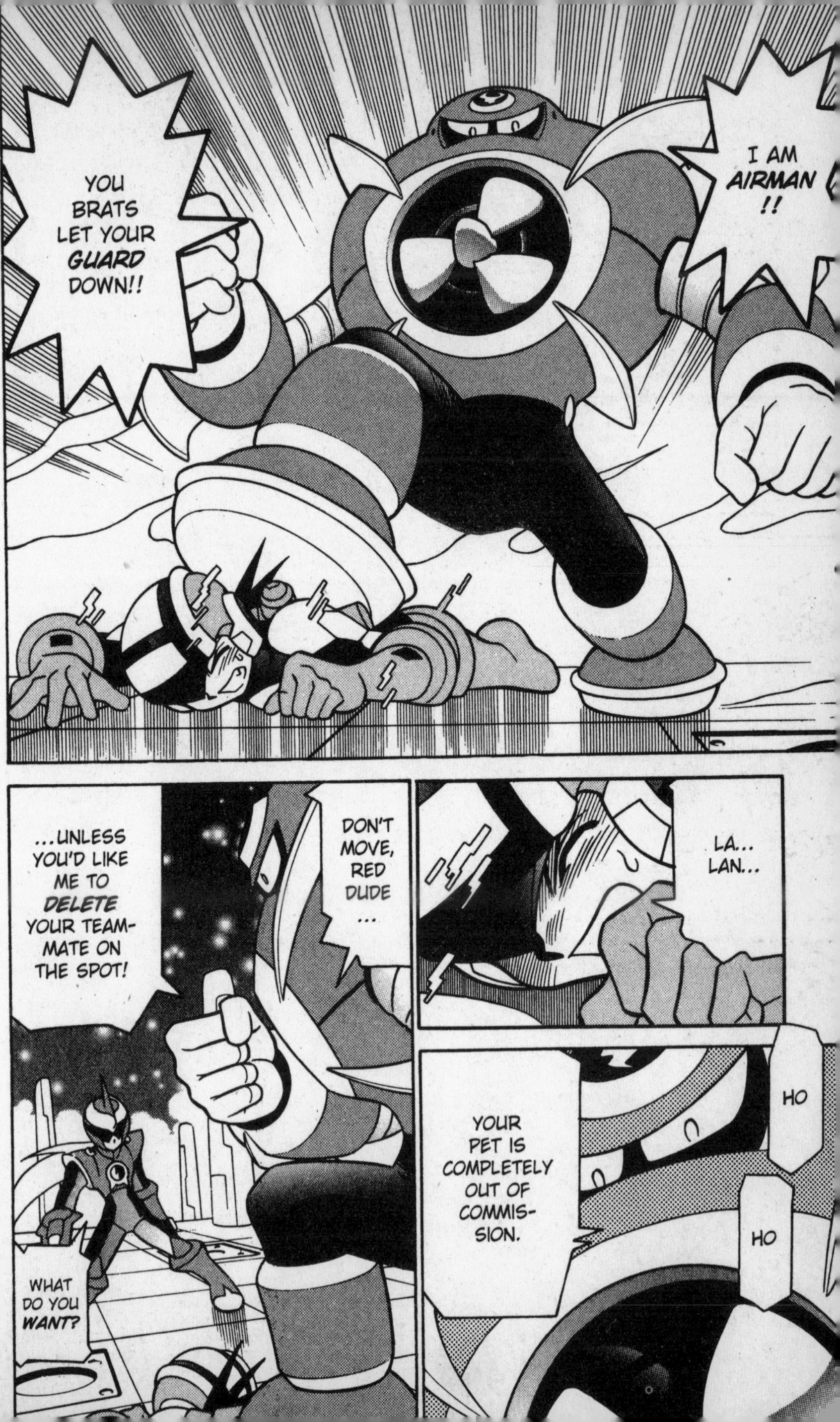

I AM AIRMAN !!
YOU BRATS LET YOUR GUARD DOWN!!
LA... LAN...
HO
YOUR PET IS COMPLETELY OUT OF COMMISSION.
HO
DON'T MOVE, RED DUDE ...
...UNLESS YOU'D LIKE ME TO DELETE YOUR TEAMMATE ON THE SPOT!
WHAT DO YOU WANT?

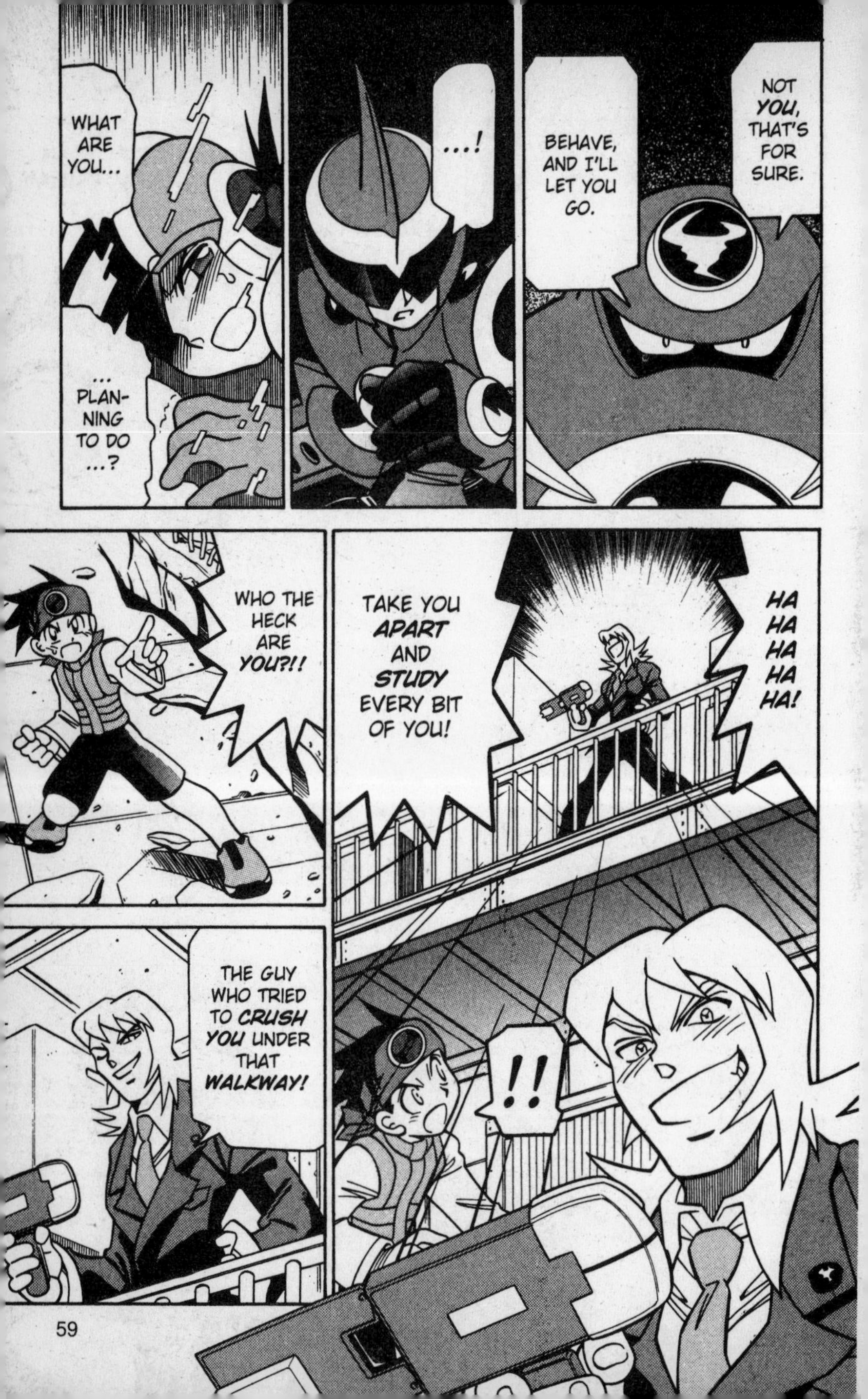

NOT *YOU*, THAT'S FOR SURE.
BEHAVE, AND I'LL LET YOU GO.
...!
WHAT ARE YOU...
...PLAN-NING TO DO ...?
*HA HA HA HA HA!*
TAKE YOU *APART* AND *STUDY* EVERY BIT OF YOU!
!!
WHO THE HECK ARE *YOU?!!*
THE GUY WHO TRIED TO *CRUSH YOU* UNDER THAT *WALKWAY!*

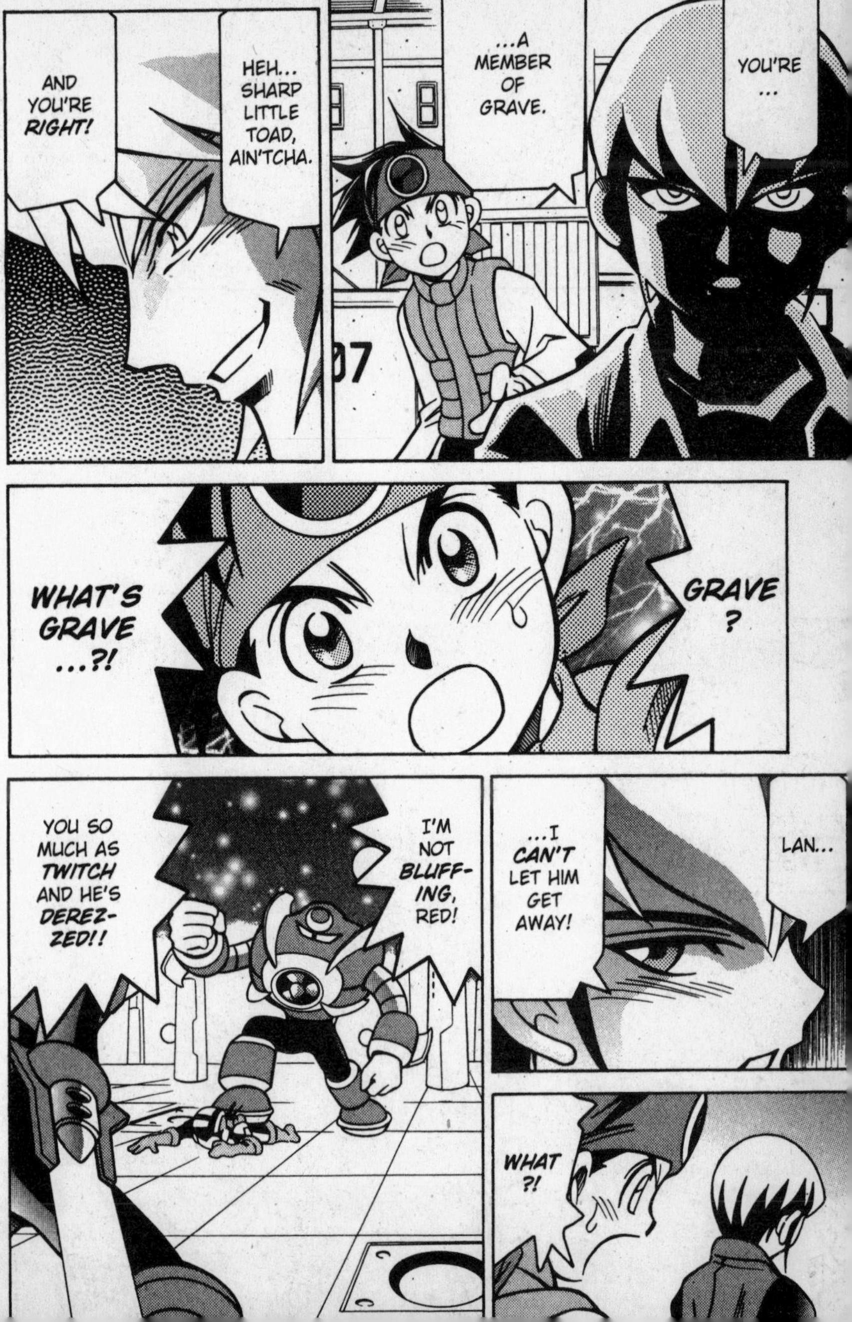
YOU'RE ...
...A MEMBER OF GRAVE.
07
HEH... SHARP LITTLE TOAD, AIN'TCHA.
AND YOU'RE *RIGHT!*
*GRAVE ?*
*WHAT'S GRAVE ...?!*
LAN...
...I *CAN'T* LET HIM GET AWAY!
*WHAT ?!*
I'M NOT *BLUFF-ING*, RED!
YOU SO MUCH AS *TWITCH* AND HE'S *DEREZ-ZED!!*

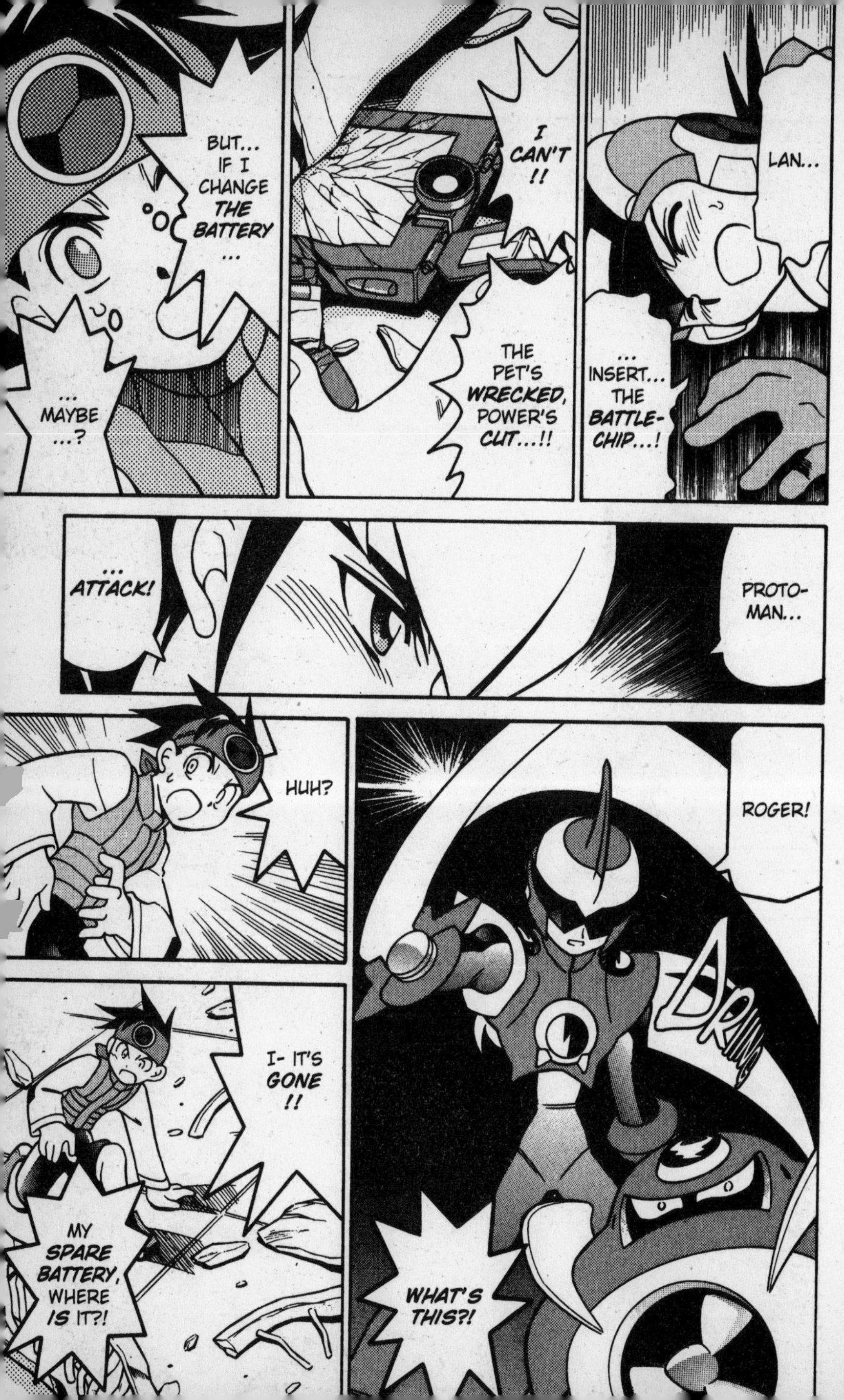
LAN...
...INSERT... THE BATTLE-CHIP...!
I CAN'T !!
THE PET'S WRECKED, POWER'S CUT...!!
BUT... IF I CHANGE THE BATTERY ...
... MAYBE ...?
PROTO-MAN...
... ATTACK!
ROGER!
WHAT'S THIS?!
HUH?
I- IT'S GONE !!
MY SPARE BATTERY, WHERE IS IT?!

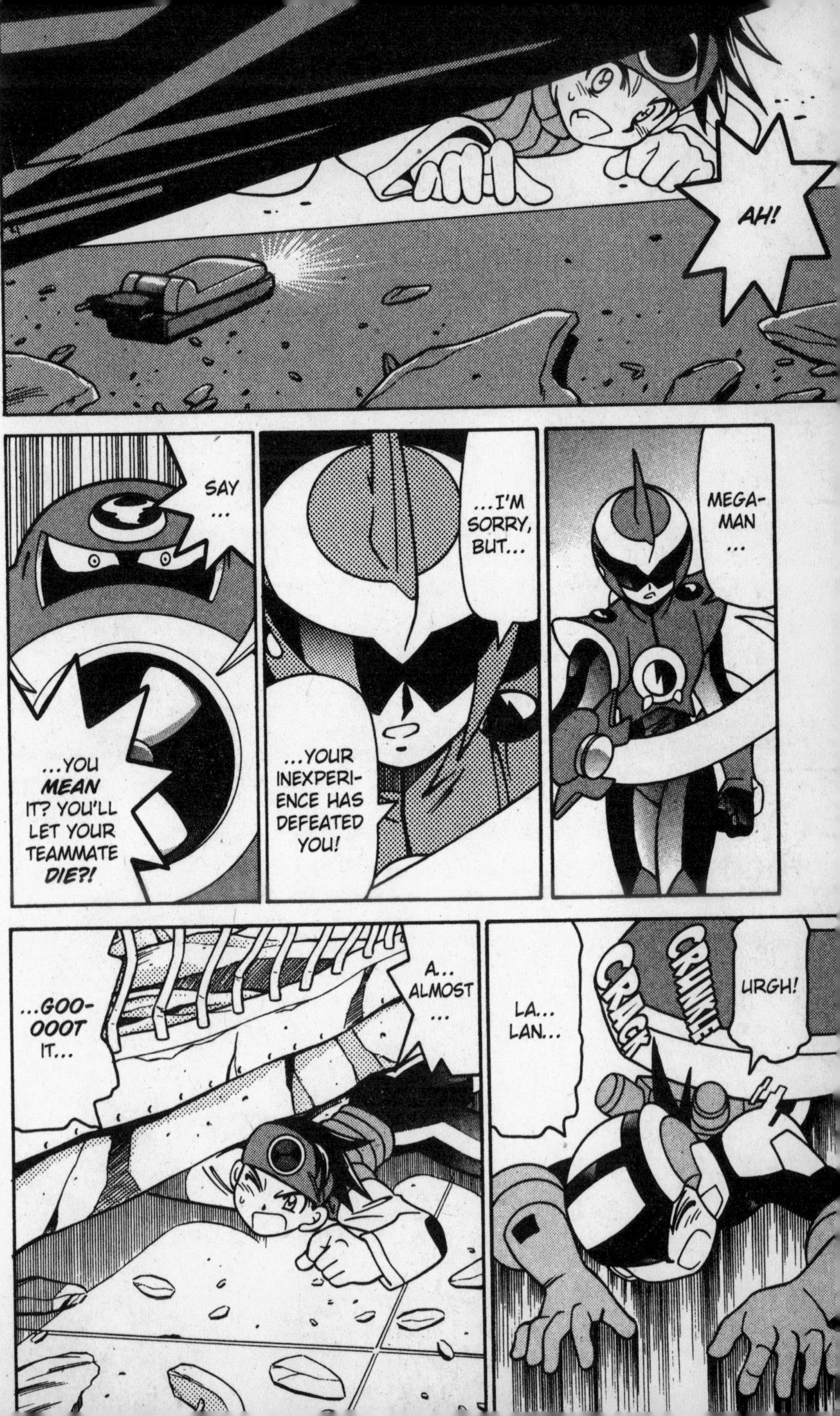
AH!
MEGA-MAN ...
...I'M SORRY, BUT...
...YOUR INEXPERIENCE HAS DEFEATED YOU!
SAY ...
...YOU MEAN IT? YOU'LL LET YOUR TEAMMATE DIE?!
URGH!
CRUNKLE
CRACK
LA... LAN...
A... ALMOST ...
...GOO-OOOT IT...

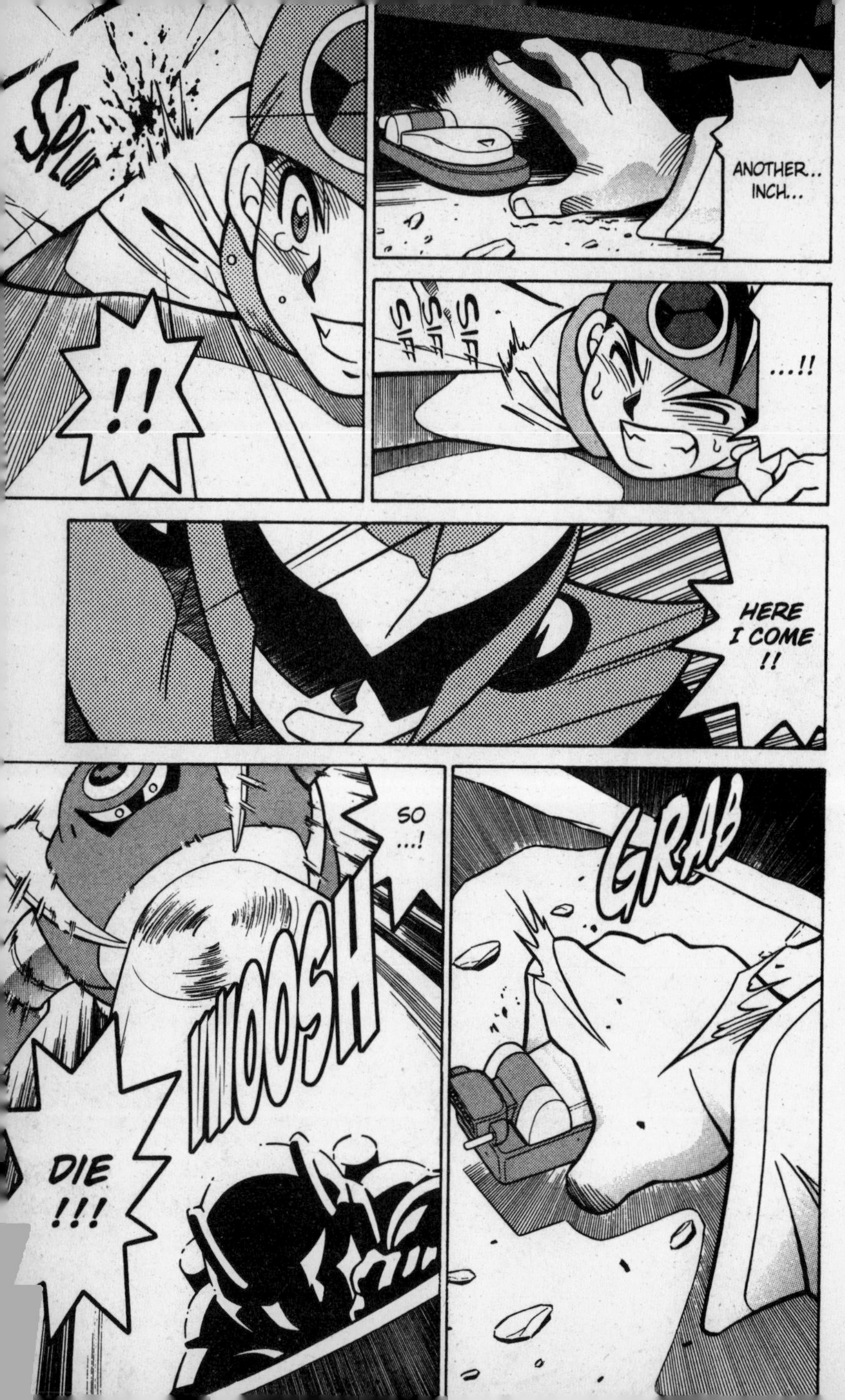

ANOTHER... INCH...
SIFF SIFF SIFF
...!!
SPLU
!!
HERE I COME !!
GRAB
SO ...!
WOOSH
DIE !!!

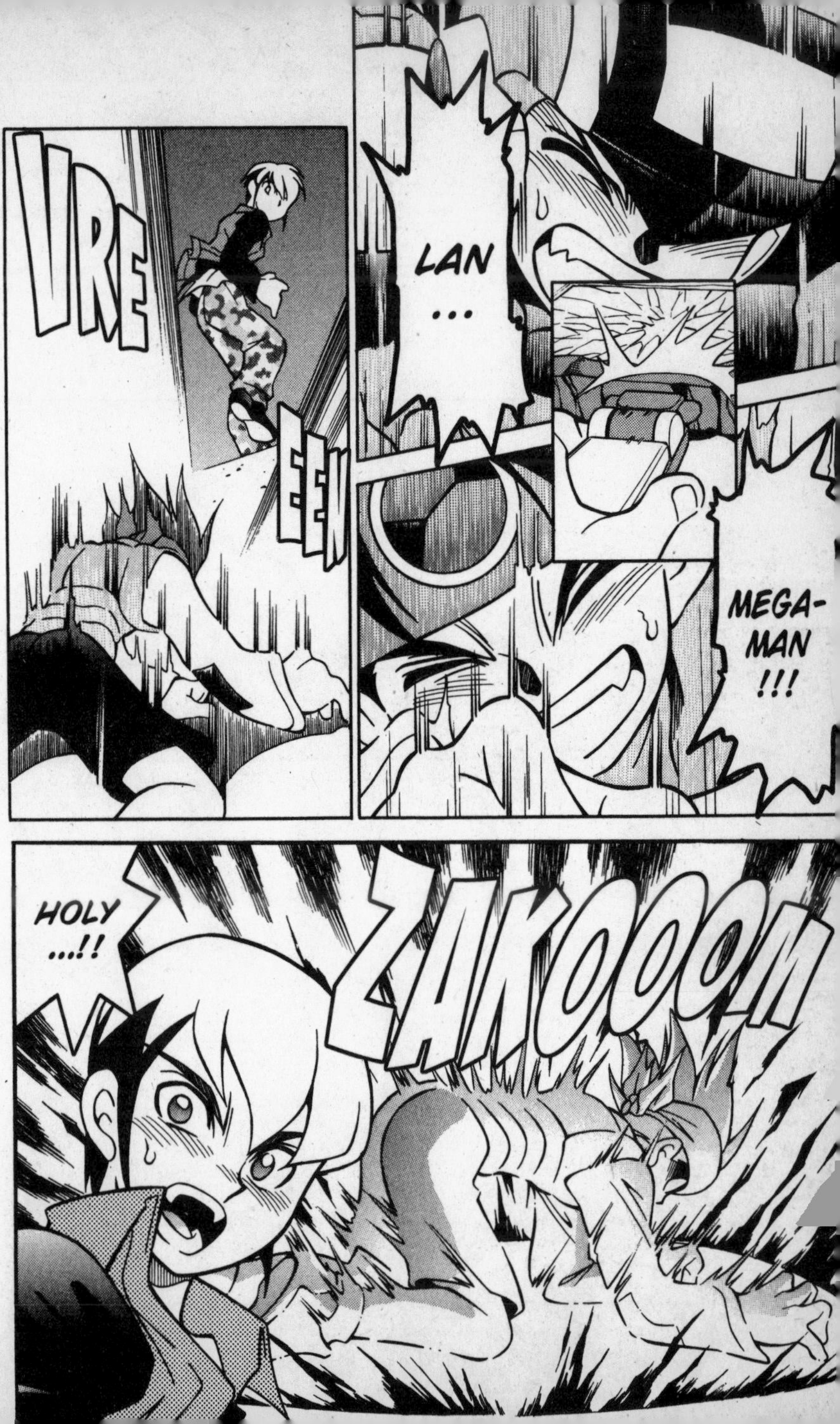
LAN ...
MEGA-MAN !!!
VRE
EEN
ZAKOOOM
HOLY ...!!

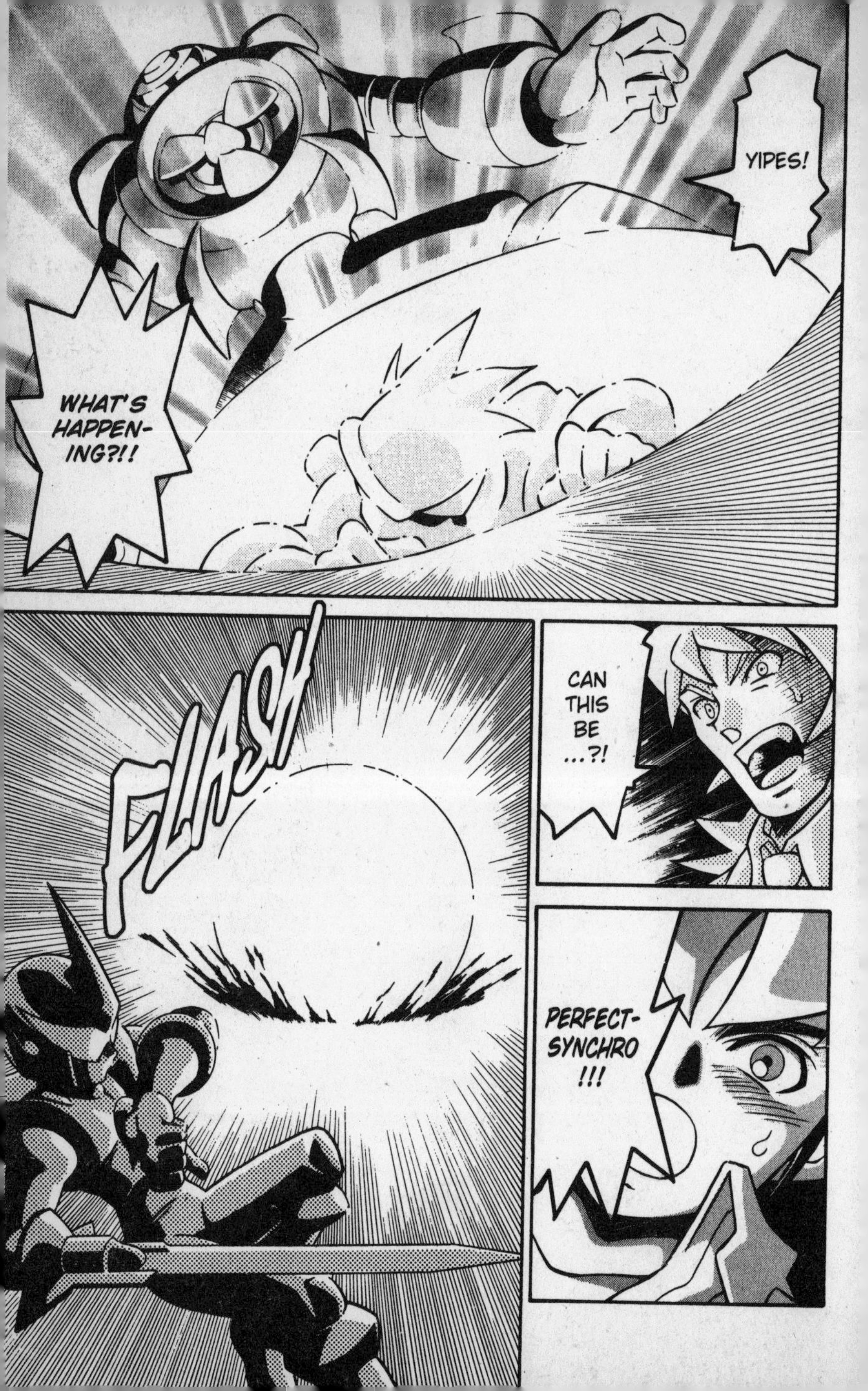
YIPES!
WHAT'S HAPPENING?!!
CAN THIS BE ...?!
PERFECT-SYNCHRO!!!
FLASH

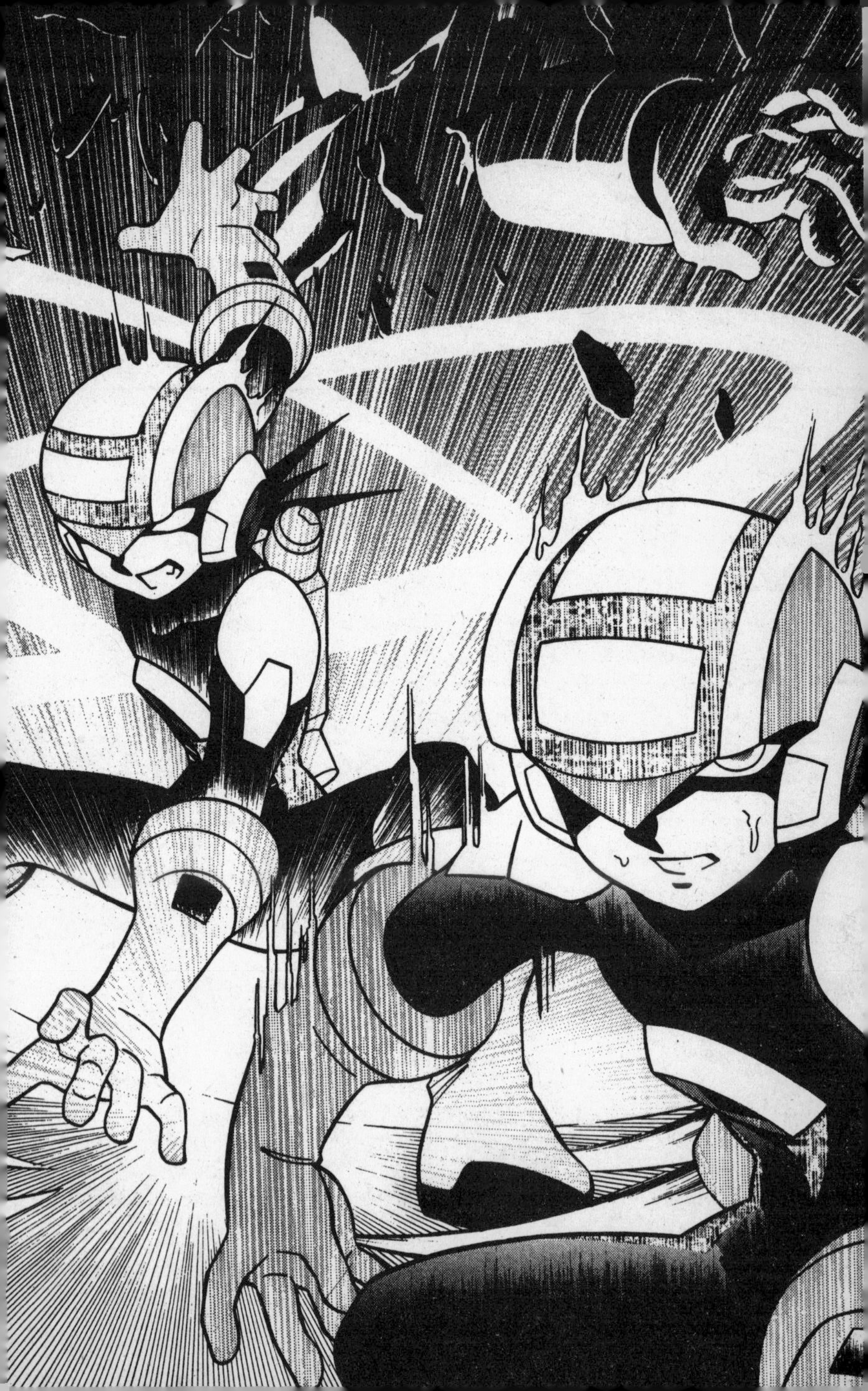

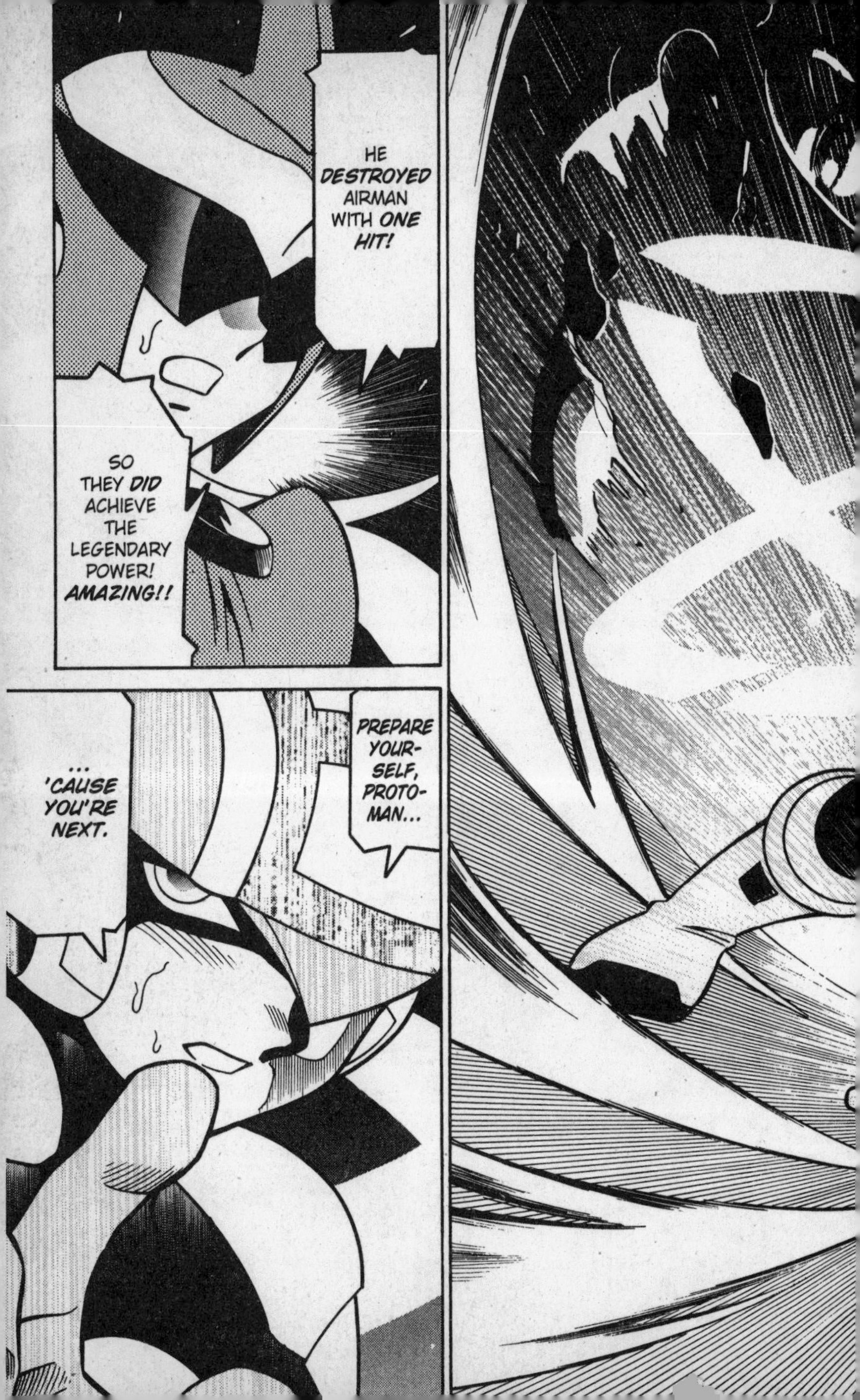
HE DESTROYED AIRMAN WITH ONE HIT!
SO THEY DID ACHIEVE THE LEGENDARY POWER! AMAZING!!
PREPARE YOURSELF, PROTOMAN...
...'CAUSE YOU'RE NEXT.

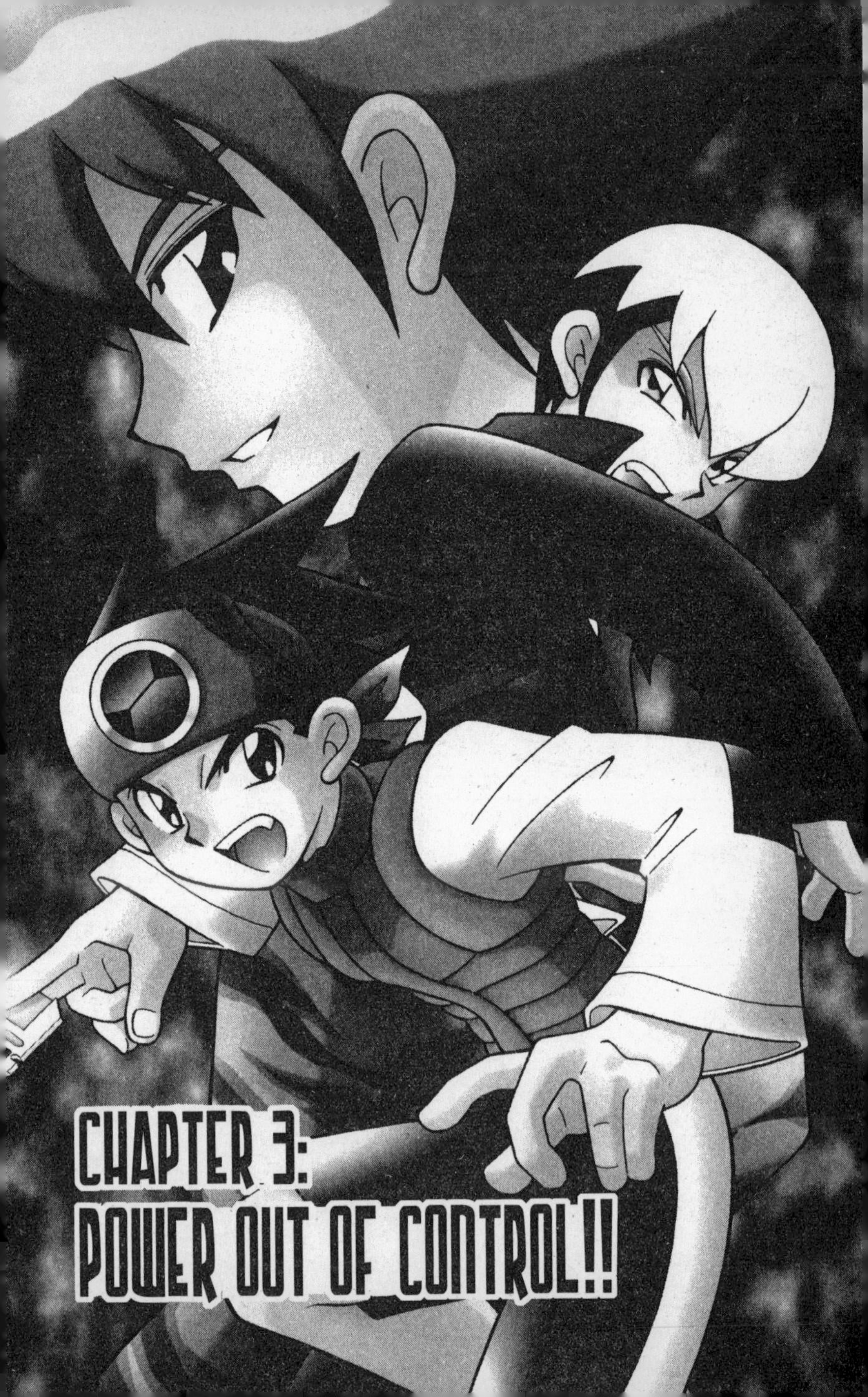
CHAPTER 3:
POWER OUT OF CONTROL!!

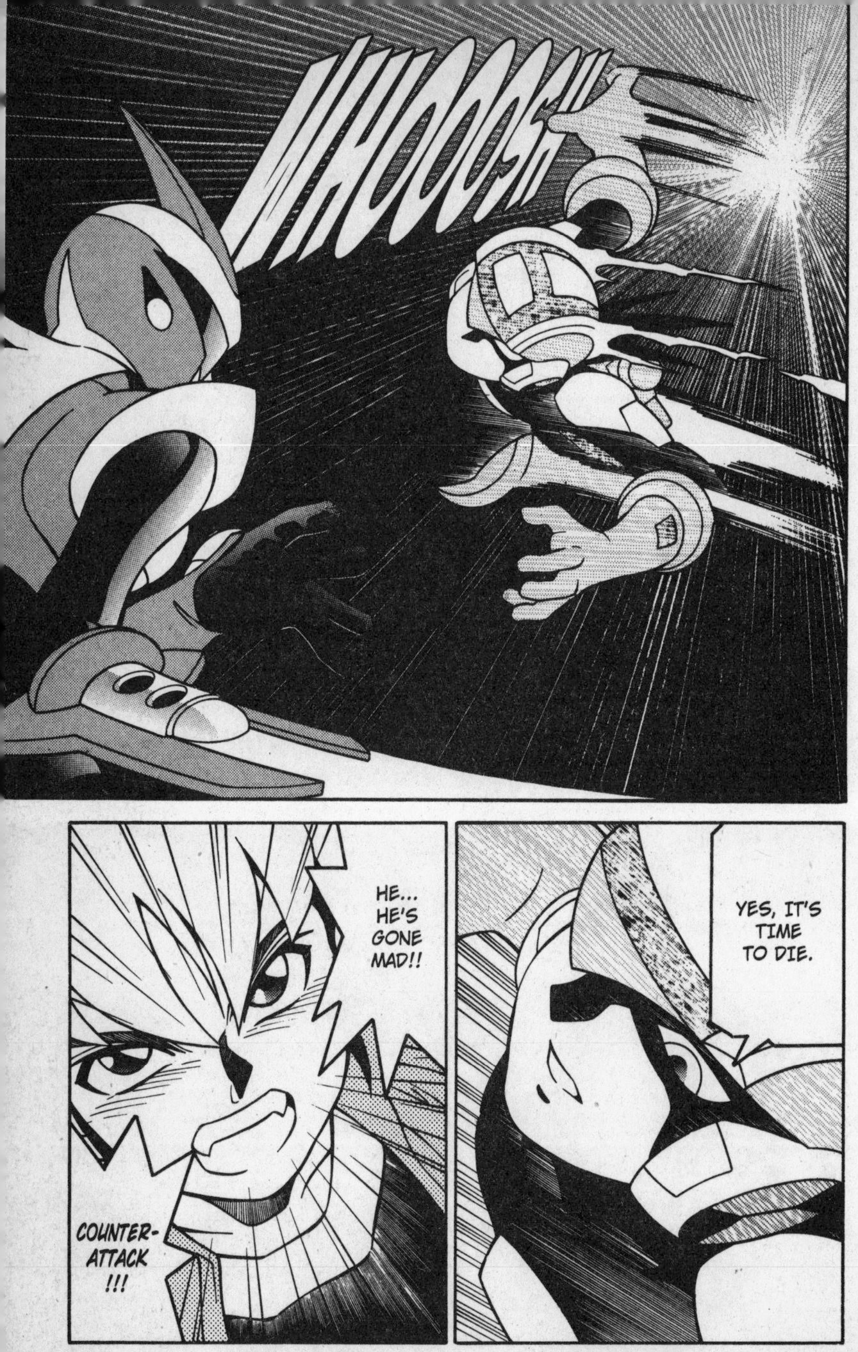
WHOOOSH!!
YES, IT'S TIME TO DIE.
HE... HE'S GONE MAD!!
COUNTER-ATTACK!!!

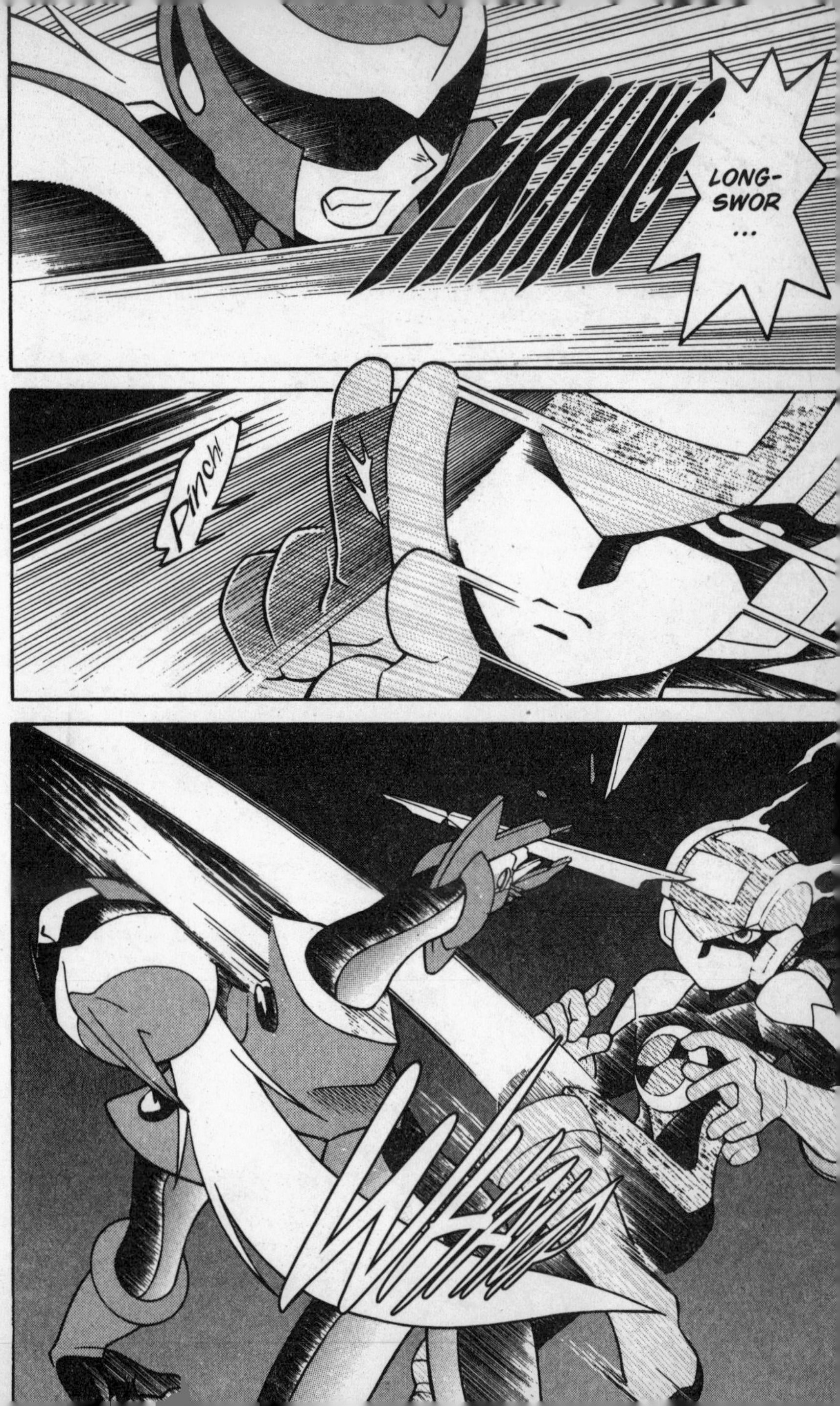
LONG-SWOR...
FZING
Pinch!
WHAP

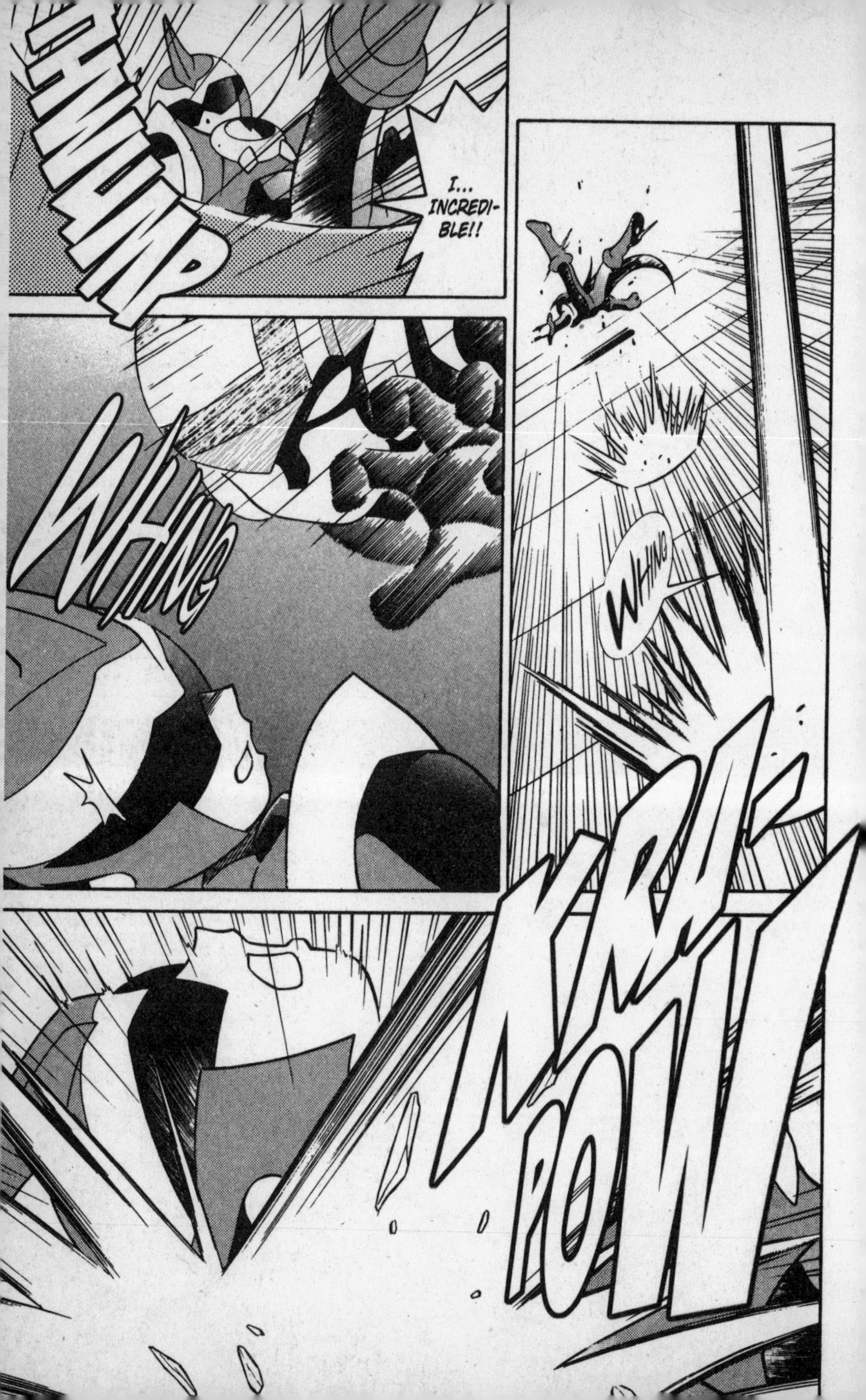
WHING
KRAK-POW!!
I... INCREDIBLE!!
WHING

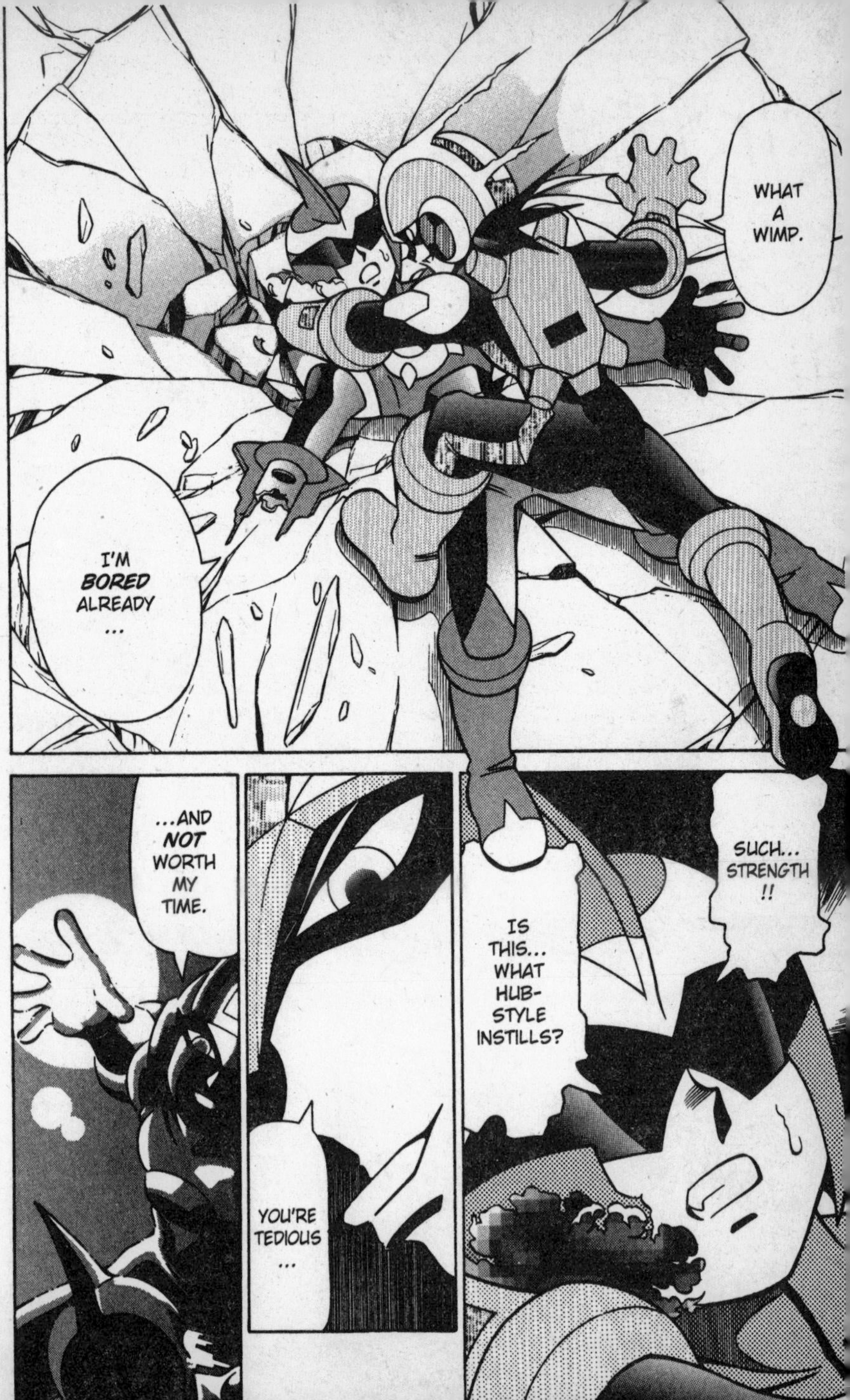
WHAT A WIMP.
I'M **BORED** ALREADY ...
SUCH... STRENGTH !!
IS THIS... WHAT HUB-STYLE INSTILLS?
YOU'RE TEDIOUS ...
...AND **NOT** WORTH MY TIME.

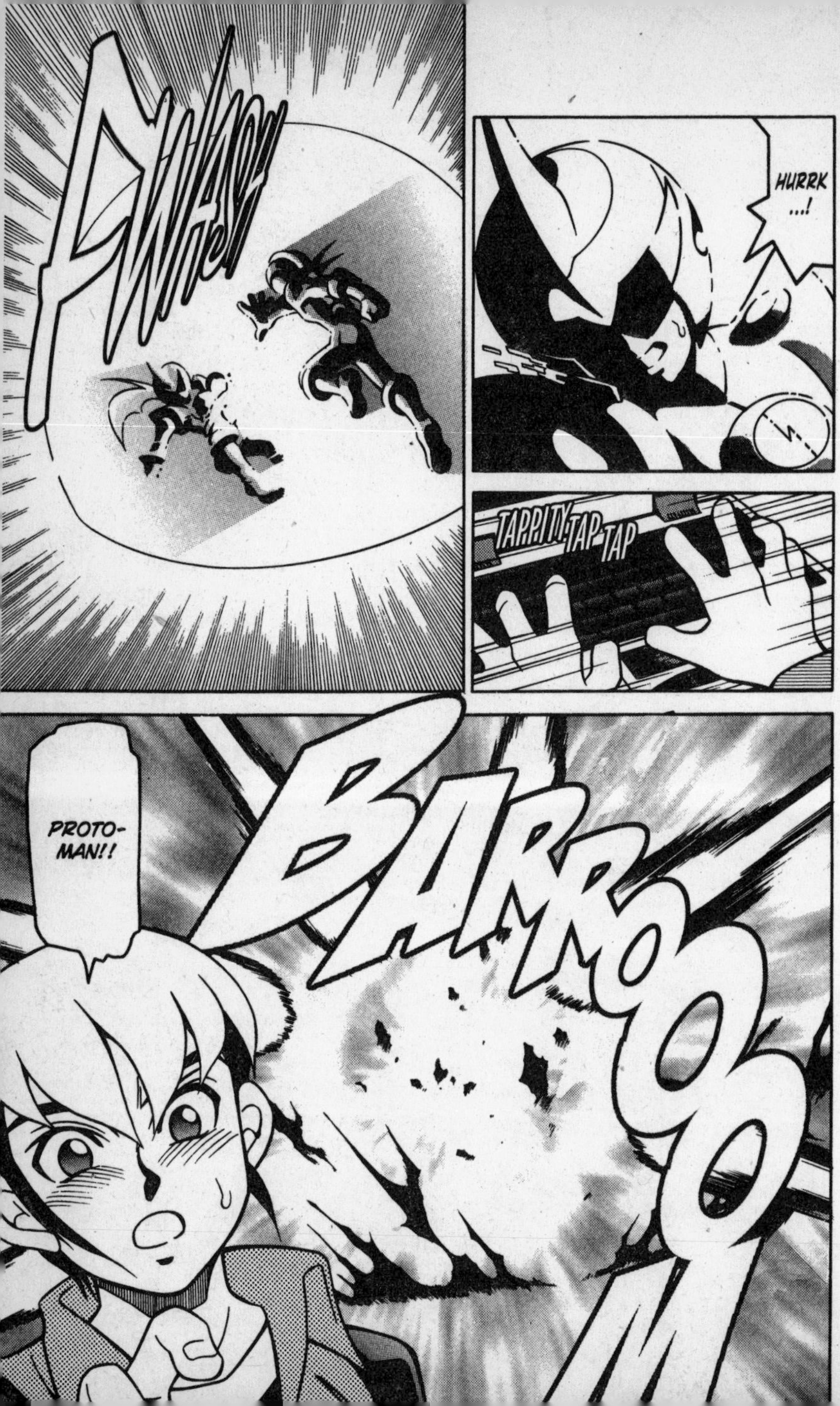
HURRK ...!
TAPPITY TAP TAP
BARROOOM
PROTO-MAN!!

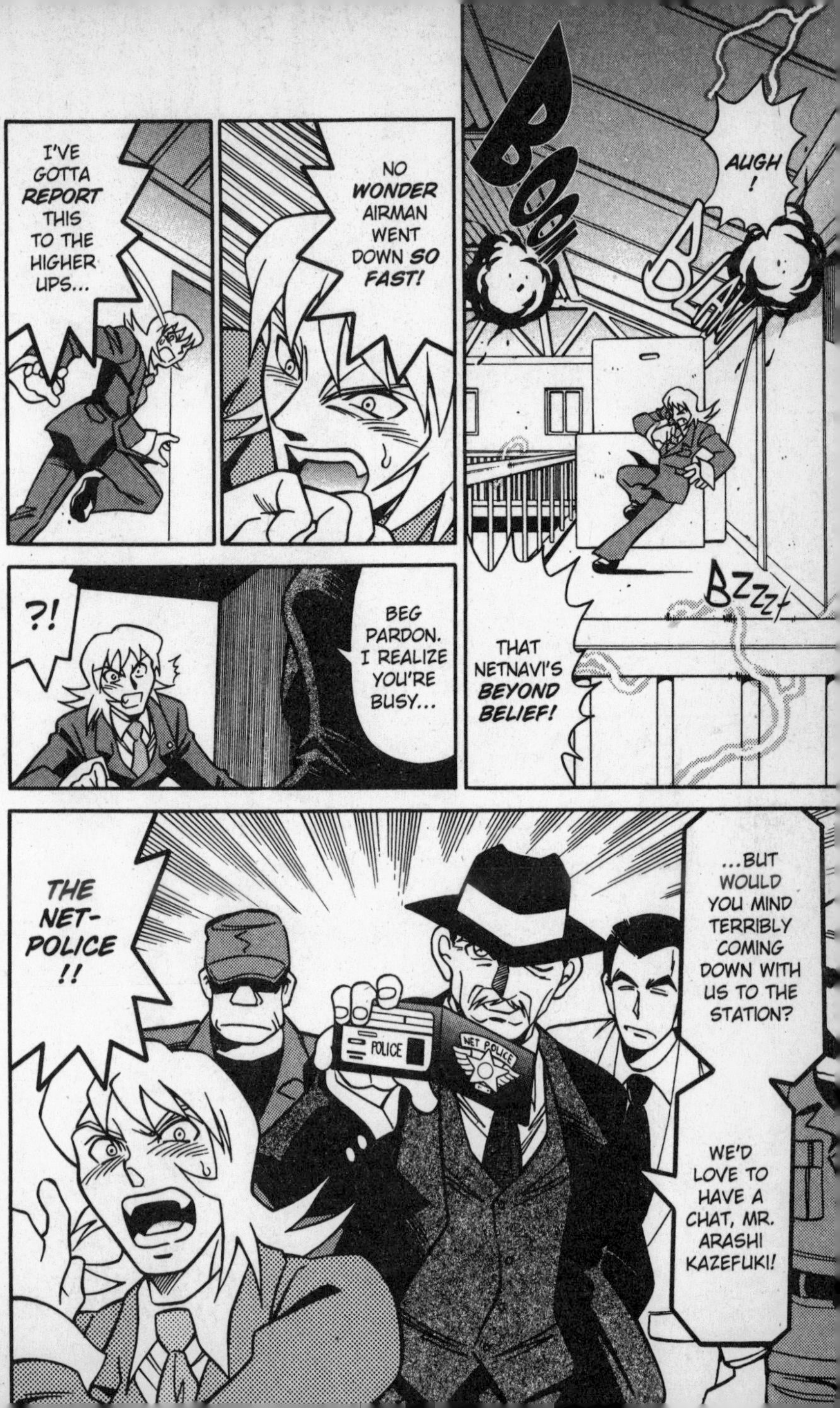
AUGH!
BOOM
BLAM
BZZZT
THAT NETNAVI'S BEYOND BELIEF!
NO WONDER AIRMAN WENT DOWN SO FAST!
I'VE GOTTA REPORT THIS TO THE HIGHER UPS...
BEG PARDON. I REALIZE YOU'RE BUSY...
?!
...BUT WOULD YOU MIND TERRIBLY COMING DOWN WITH US TO THE STATION?
WE'D LOVE TO HAVE A CHAT, MR. ARASHI KAZEFUKI!
THE NET-POLICE!!
POLICE
NET POLICE

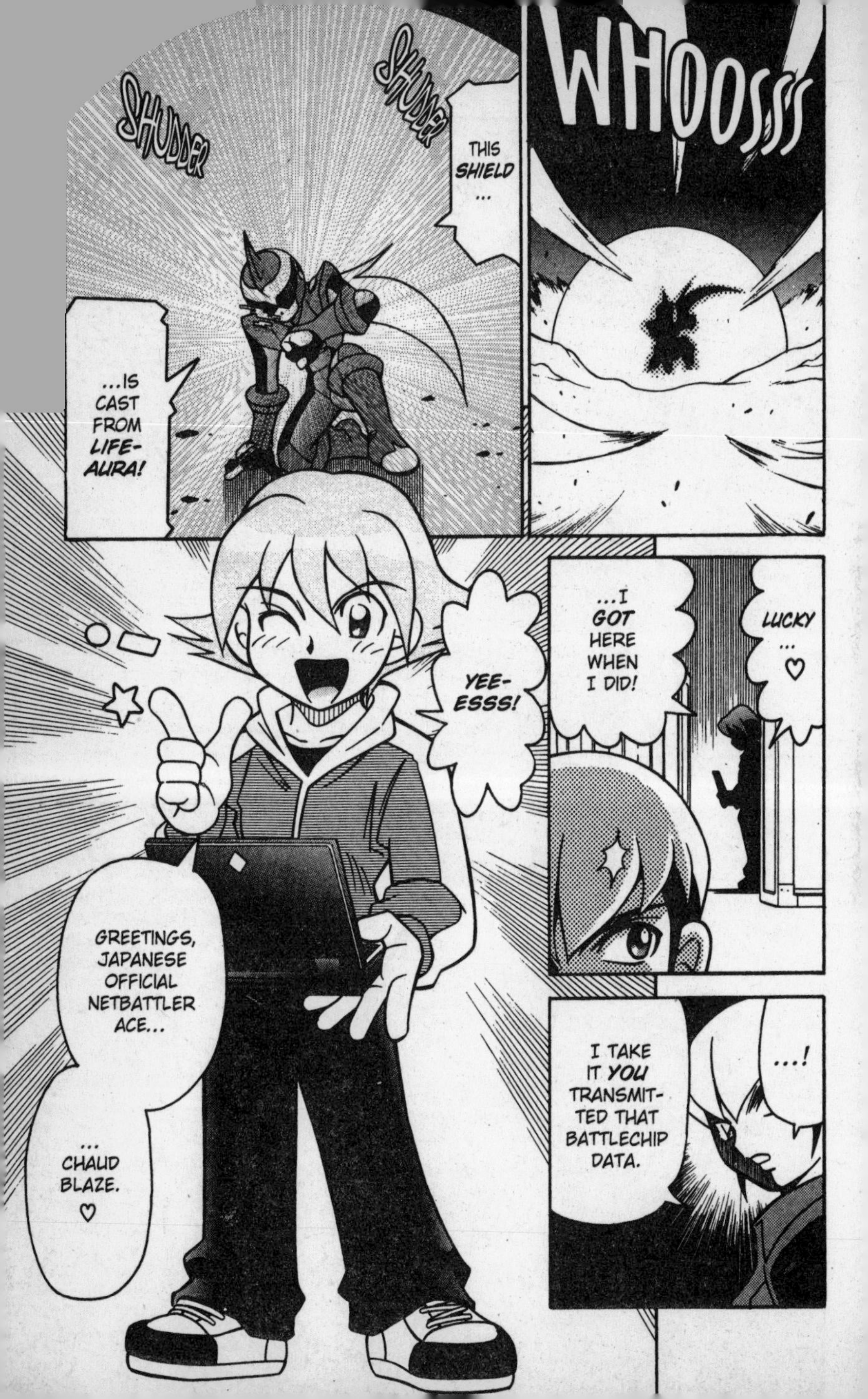
WHOOSSS
SHUDDER
SHUDDER
THIS SHIELD ...
...IS CAST FROM LIFE-AURA!
LUCKY ... ♡
...I GOT HERE WHEN I DID!
...!
I TAKE IT YOU TRANSMITTED THAT BATTLECHIP DATA.
YEE-ESSS!
GREETINGS, JAPANESE OFFICIAL NETBATTLER ACE...
... CHAUD BLAZE. ♡

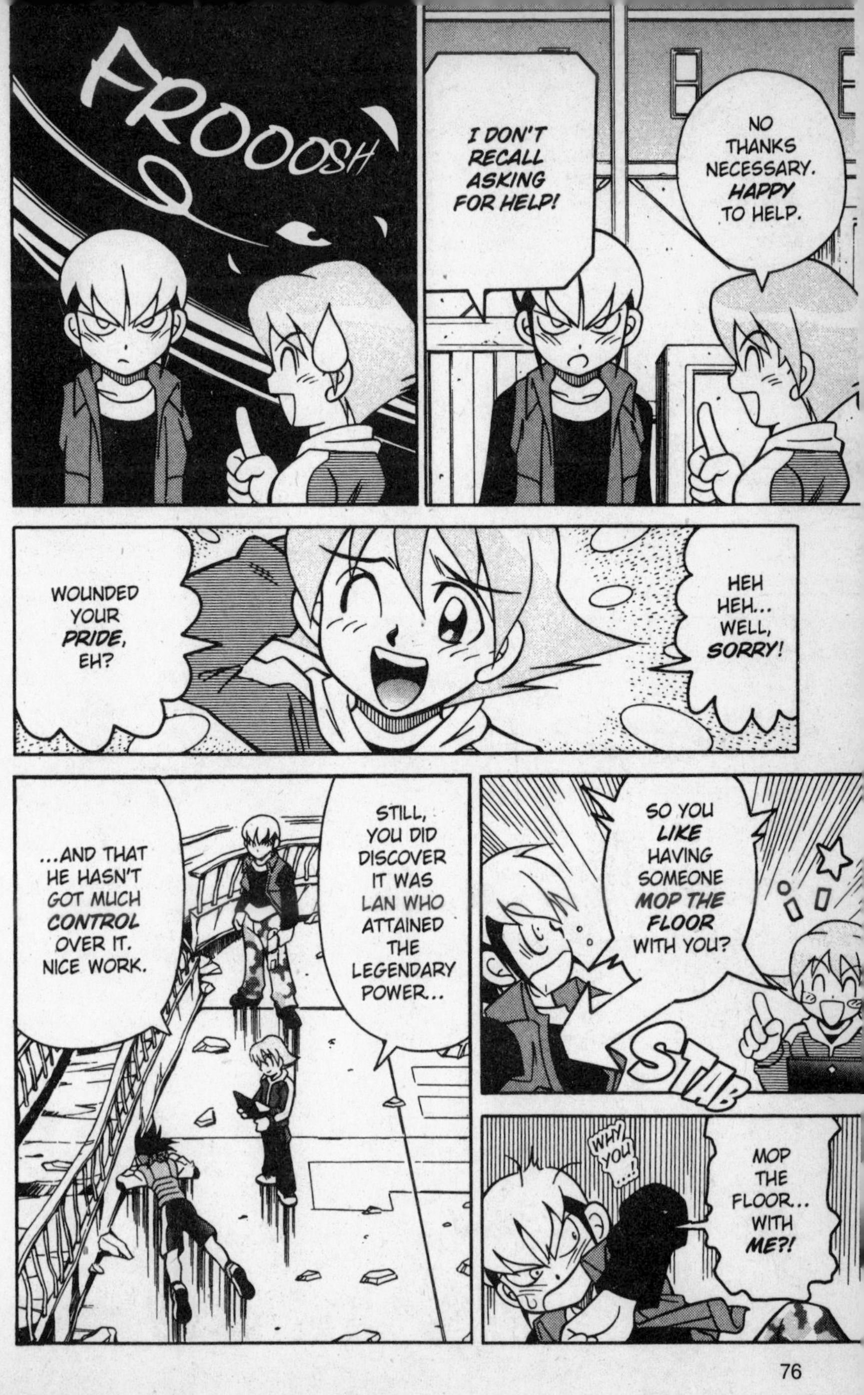
I DON'T RECALL ASKING FOR HELP!
NO THANKS NECESSARY. HAPPY TO HELP.
FROOOSH
HEH HEH... WELL, SORRY!
WOUNDED YOUR PRIDE, EH?
SO YOU LIKE HAVING SOMEONE MOP THE FLOOR WITH YOU?
STAB
MOP THE FLOOR... WITH ME?!
WHY YOU...!
STILL, YOU DID DISCOVER IT WAS LAN WHO ATTAINED THE LEGENDARY POWER...
...AND THAT HE HASN'T GOT MUCH CONTROL OVER IT. NICE WORK.

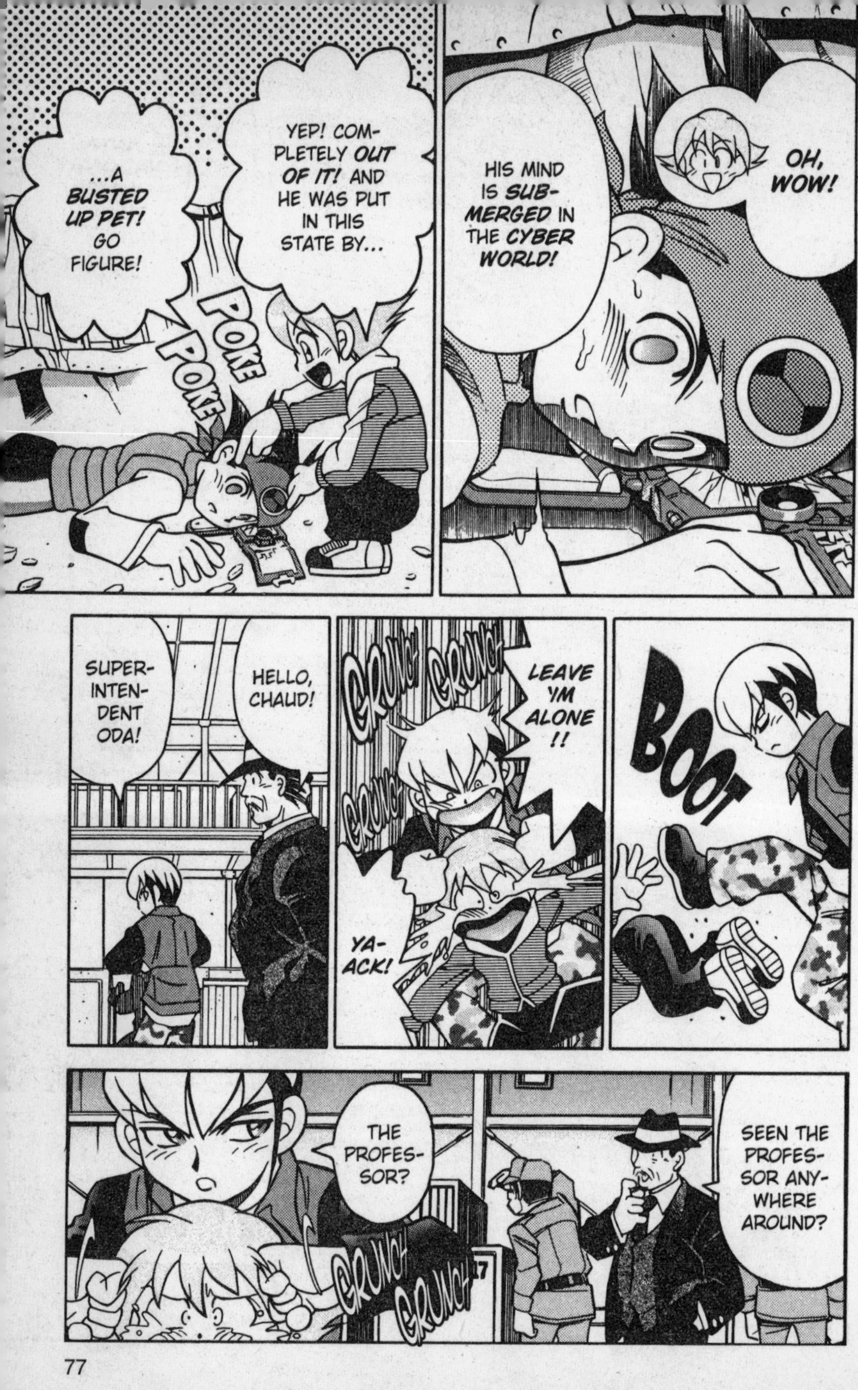
OH, WOW!
HIS MIND IS SUBMERGED IN THE CYBER WORLD!
YEP! COMPLETELY OUT OF IT! AND HE WAS PUT IN THIS STATE BY...
...A BUSTED UP PET! GO FIGURE!
POKE POKE
BOOT
LEAVE 'YM ALONE !!
GRUNCH GRUNCH GRUNCH
YA-ACK!
HELLO, CHAUD!
SUPERINTENDENT ODA!
SEEN THE PROFESSOR ANYWHERE AROUND?
THE PROFESSOR?
GRUNCH GRUNCH

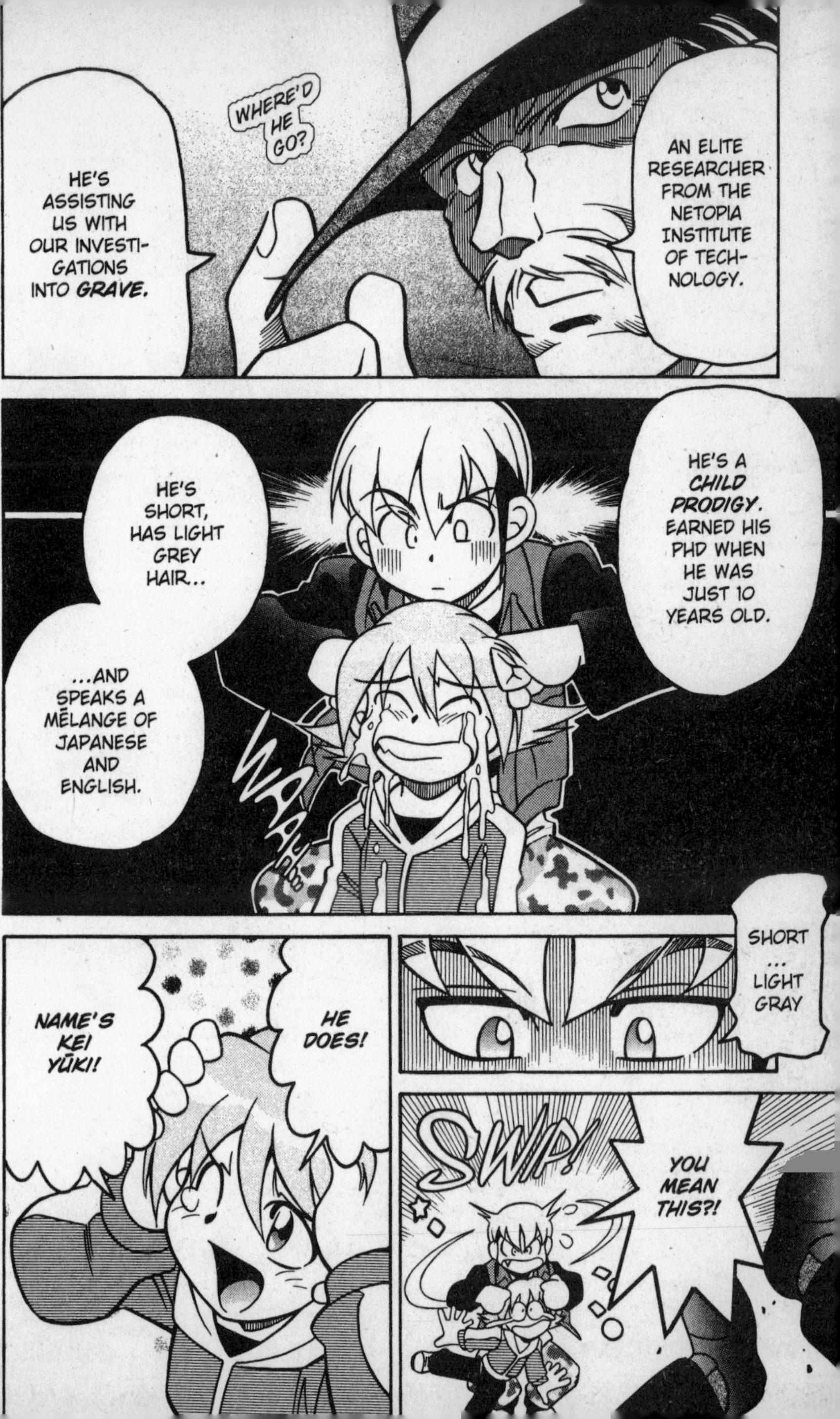
AN ELITE RESEARCHER FROM THE NETOPIA INSTITUTE OF TECH-NOLOGY.
WHERE'D HE GO?
HE'S ASSISTING US WITH OUR INVESTI-GATIONS INTO GRAVE.
HE'S A CHILD PRODIGY. EARNED HIS PHD WHEN HE WAS JUST 10 YEARS OLD.
HE'S SHORT, HAS LIGHT GREY HAIR...
...AND SPEAKS A MÉLANGE OF JAPANESE AND ENGLISH.
SHORT ... LIGHT GRAY
SWIP!
YOU MEAN THIS?!
HE DOES!
NAME'S KEI YŪKI!

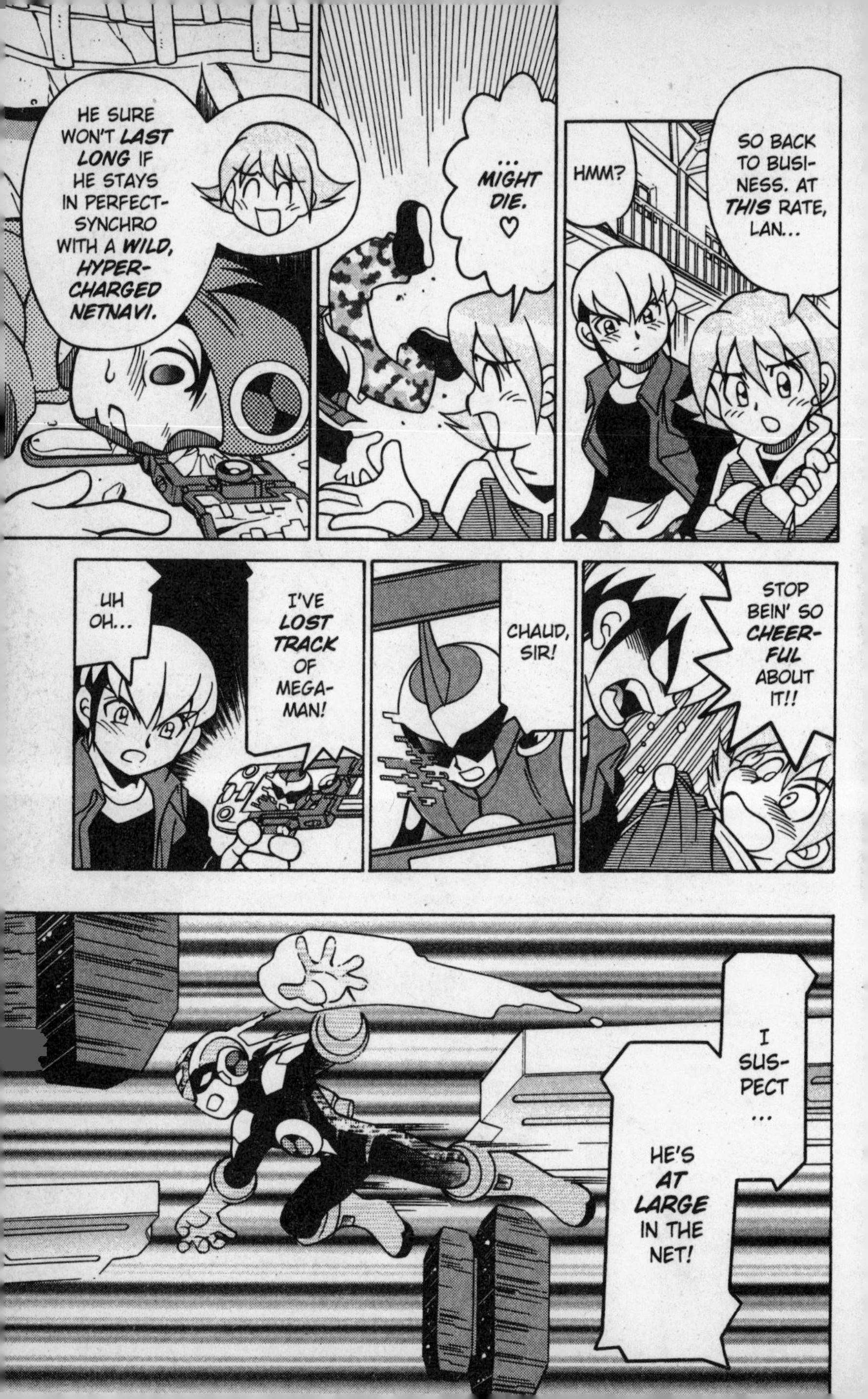
SO BACK TO BUSINESS. AT THIS RATE, LAN...
HMM?
...MIGHT DIE. ♡
HE SURE WON'T LAST LONG IF HE STAYS IN PERFECT-SYNCHRO WITH A WILD, HYPER-CHARGED NETNAVI.
STOP BEIN' SO CHEERFUL ABOUT IT!!
CHAUD, SIR!
I'VE LOST TRACK OF MEGAMAN!
UH OH...
I SUSPECT...
HE'S AT LARGE IN THE NET!

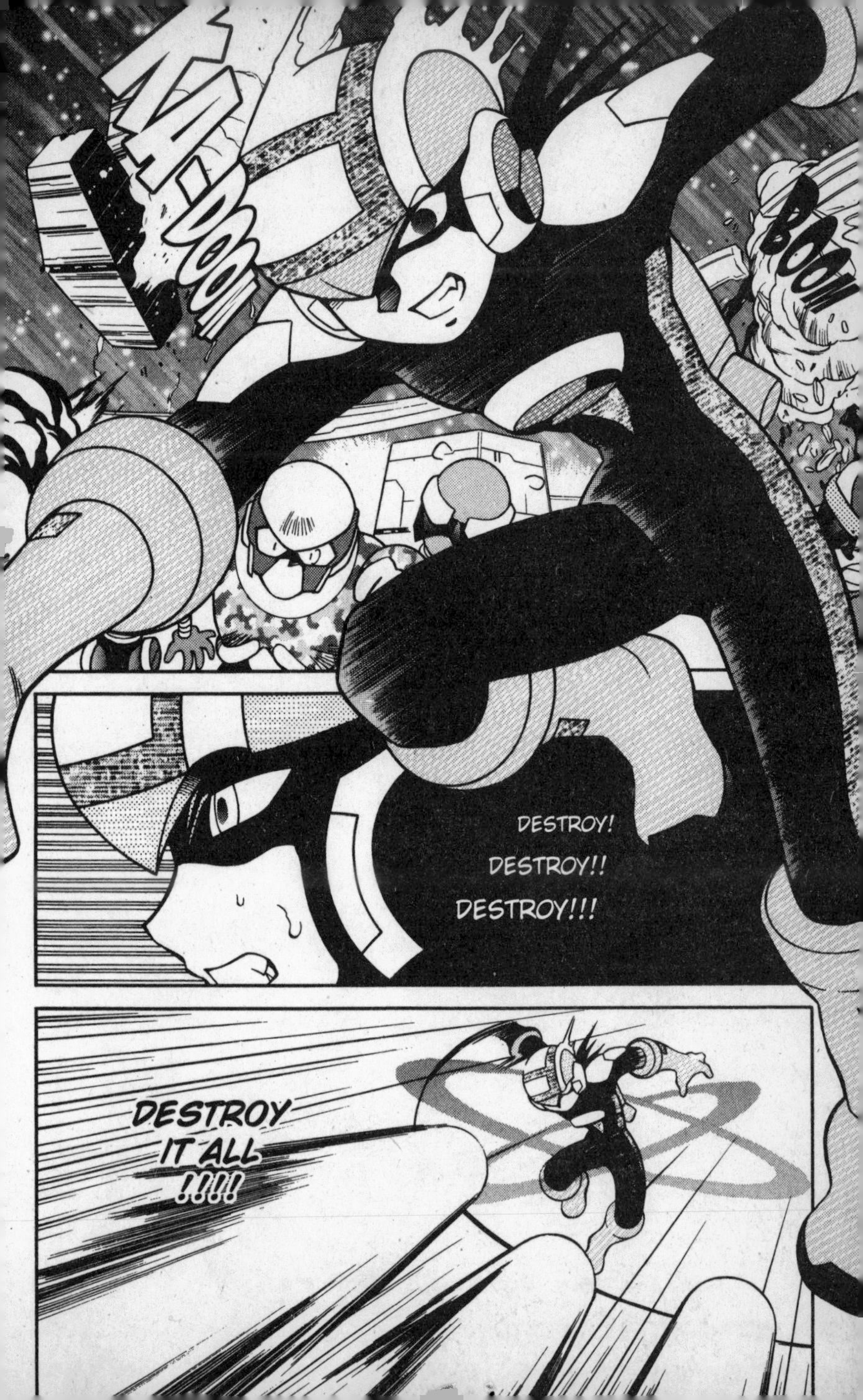
BOOM
KA-DOOOM
DESTROY!
DESTROY!!
DESTROY!!!
DESTROY IT ALL !!!!

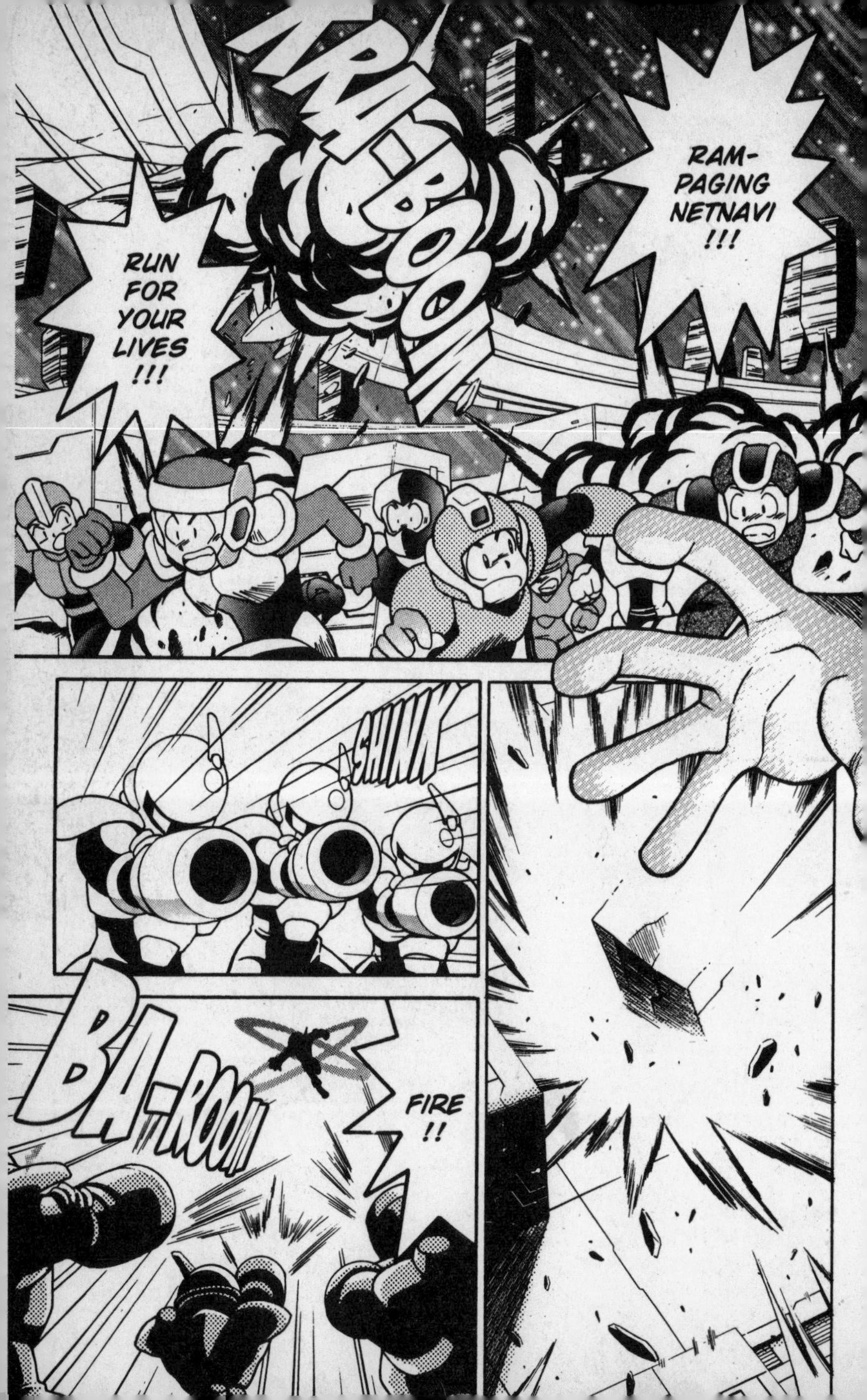
RAM-PAGING NETNAVI !!!
RUN FOR YOUR LIVES !!!
SHINK
FIRE !!
BA-ROOM

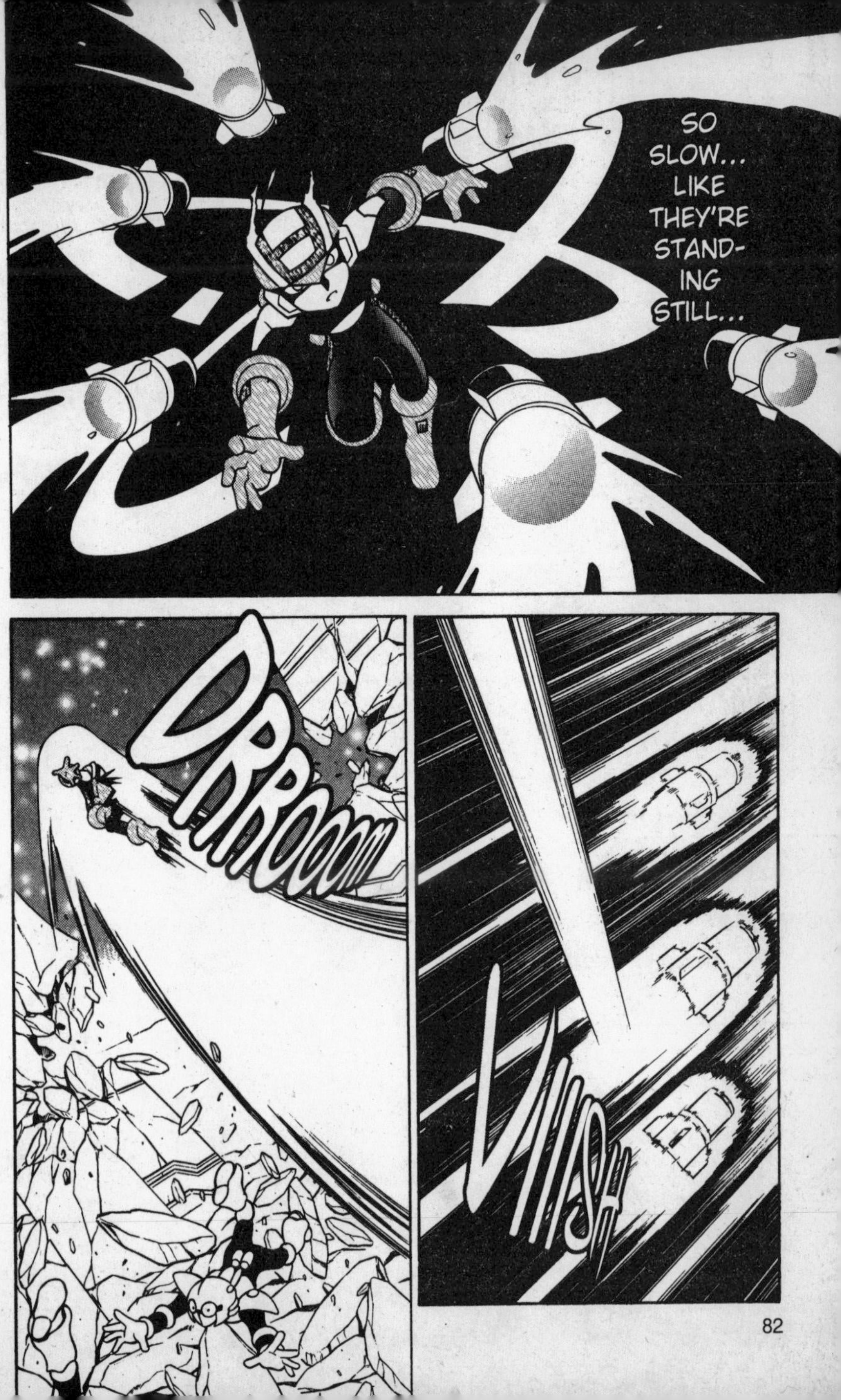
SO SLOW... LIKE THEY'RE STAND-ING STILL...
VWISH
DRROOOM

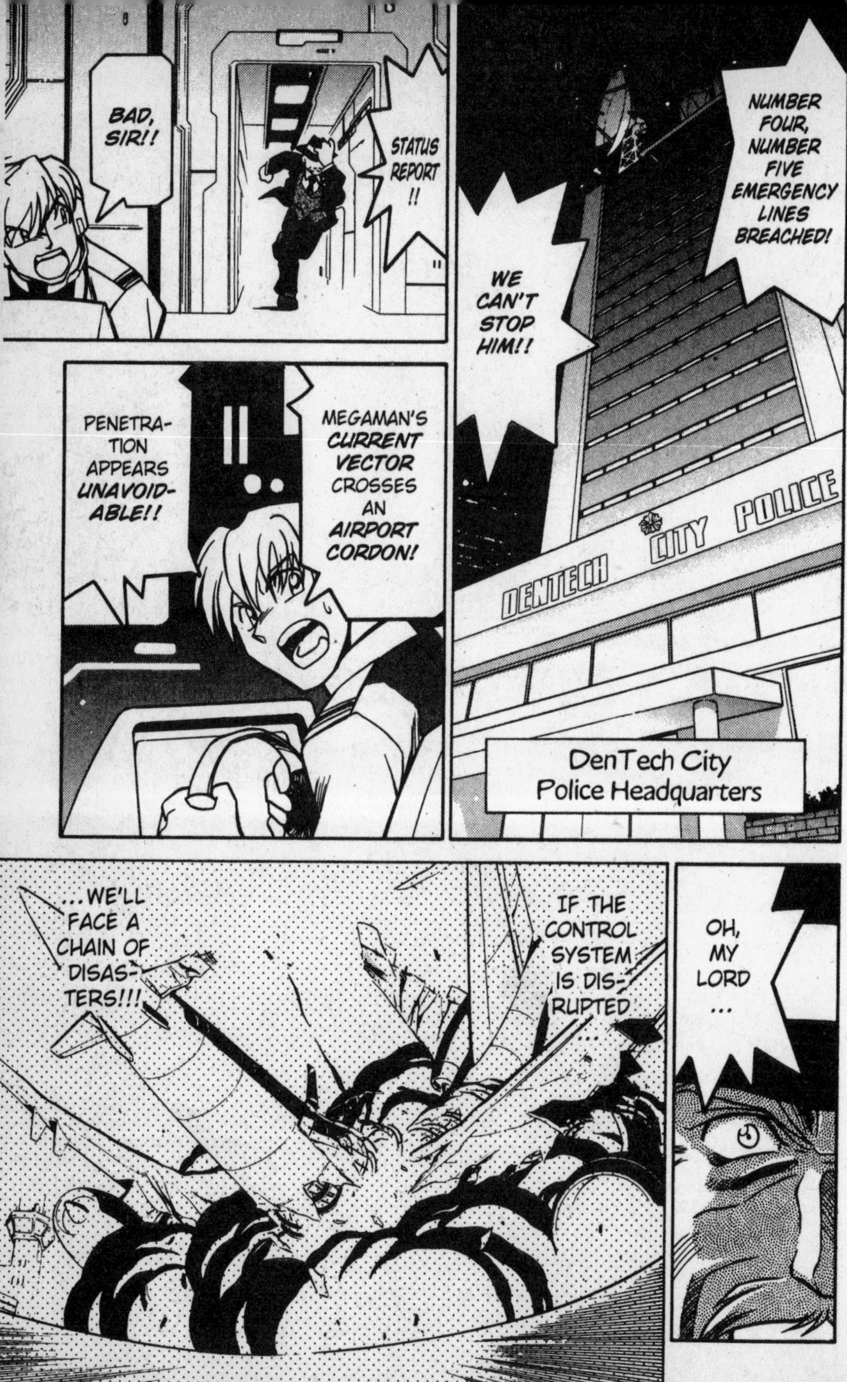
NUMBER FOUR, NUMBER FIVE EMERGENCY LINES BREACHED!
WE CAN'T STOP HIM!!
DENTECH CITY POLICE
DenTech City Police Headquarters
STATUS REPORT!!
BAD, SIR!!
MEGAMAN'S CURRENT VECTOR CROSSES AN AIRPORT CORDON!
PENETRATION APPEARS UNAVOIDABLE!!
OH, MY LORD...
IF THE CONTROL SYSTEM IS DISRUPTED...
...WE'LL FACE A CHAIN OF DISASTERS!!!

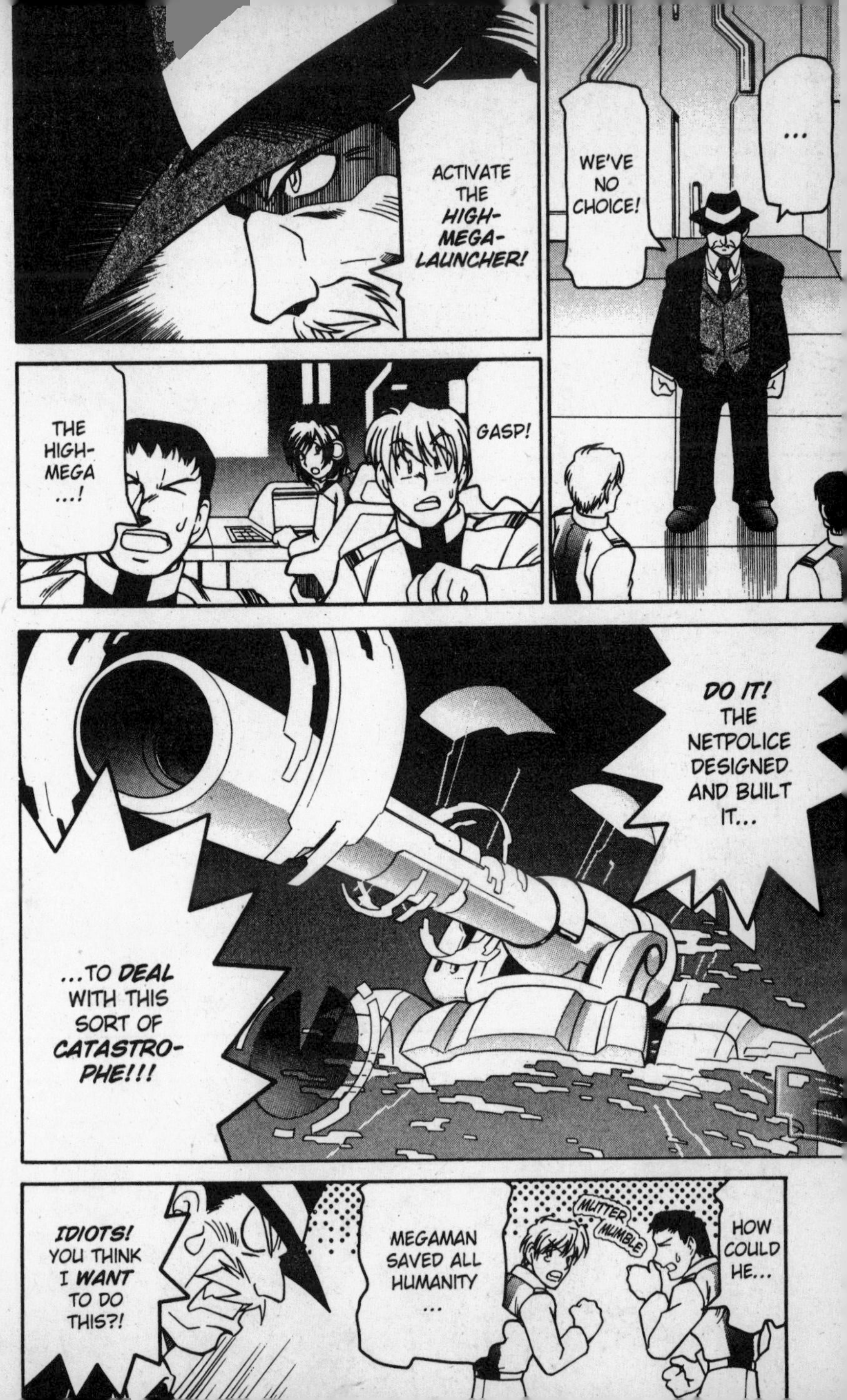
...
WE'VE NO CHOICE!
ACTIVATE THE HIGH-MEGA-LAUNCHER!
GASP!
THE HIGH-MEGA ...!
DO IT! THE NETPOLICE DESIGNED AND BUILT IT...
...TO DEAL WITH THIS SORT OF CATASTROPHE!!!
HOW COULD HE...
MUTTER
MUMBLE
MEGAMAN SAVED ALL HUMANITY ...
IDIOTS! YOU THINK I WANT TO DO THIS?!

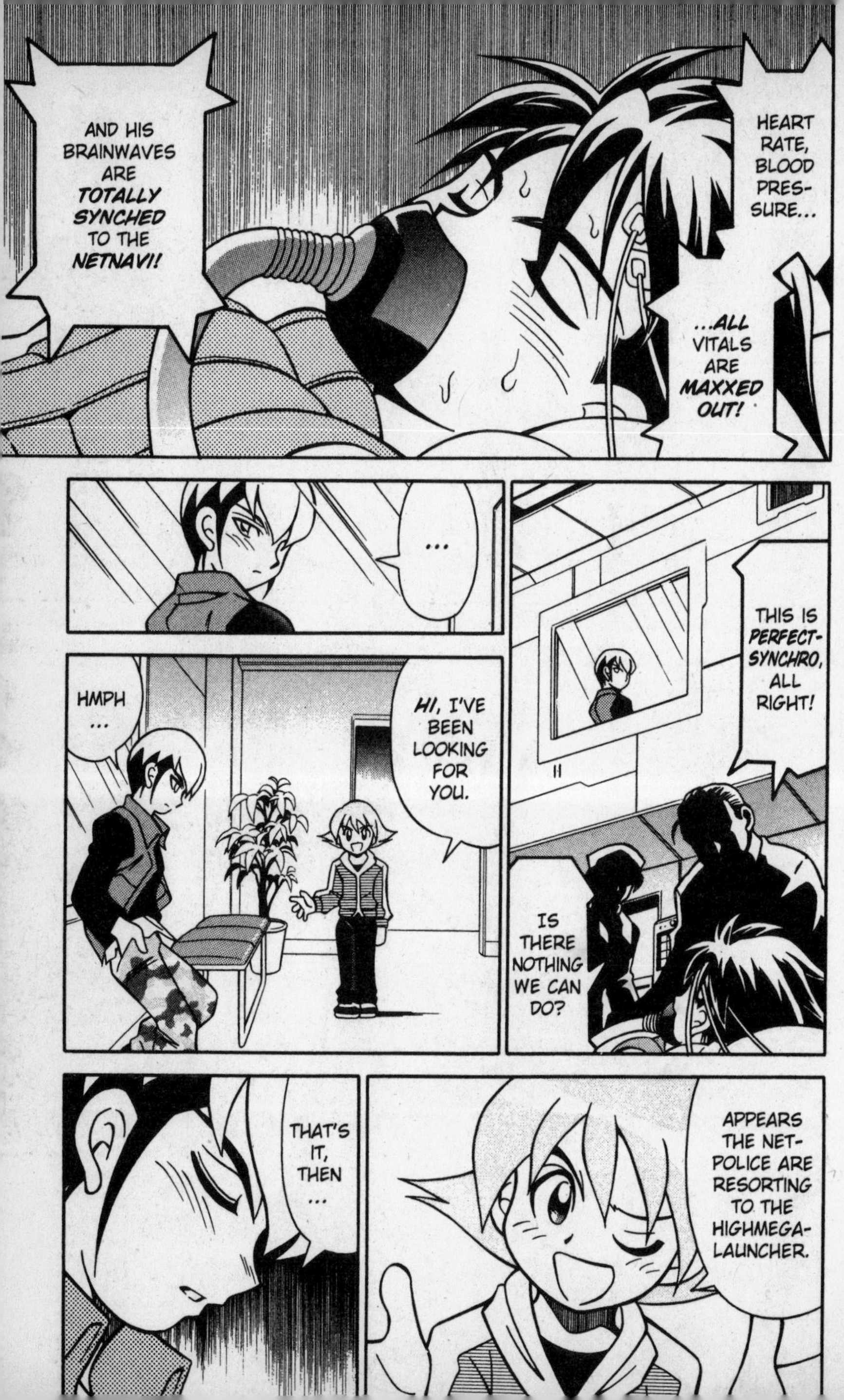
HEART RATE, BLOOD PRESSURE...
...ALL VITALS ARE MAXXED OUT!
AND HIS BRAINWAVES ARE TOTALLY SYNCHED TO THE NETNAVI!
THIS IS PERFECT-SYNCHRO, ALL RIGHT!
IS THERE NOTHING WE CAN DO?
...
HI, I'VE BEEN LOOKING FOR YOU.
HMPH ...
APPEARS THE NET-POLICE ARE RESORTING TO THE HIGHMEGA-LAUNCHER.
THAT'S IT, THEN ...

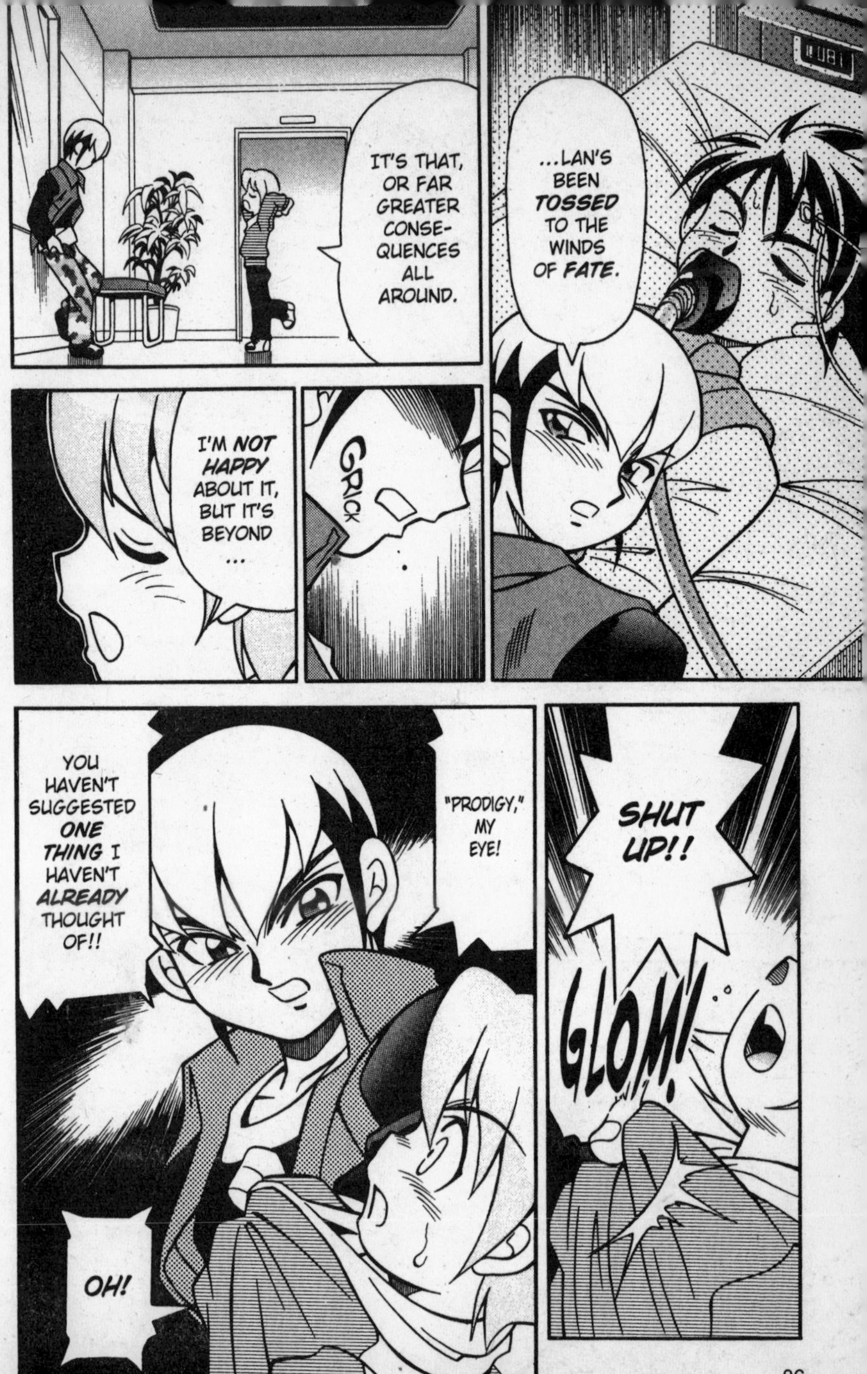
...LAN'S BEEN TOSSED TO THE WINDS OF FATE.
IT'S THAT, OR FAR GREATER CONSE-QUENCES ALL AROUND.
GRICK
I'M NOT HAPPY ABOUT IT, BUT IT'S BEYOND ...
SHUT UP!!
GLOM!
YOU HAVEN'T SUGGESTED ONE THING I HAVEN'T ALREADY THOUGHT OF!!
"PRODIGY," MY EYE!
OH!

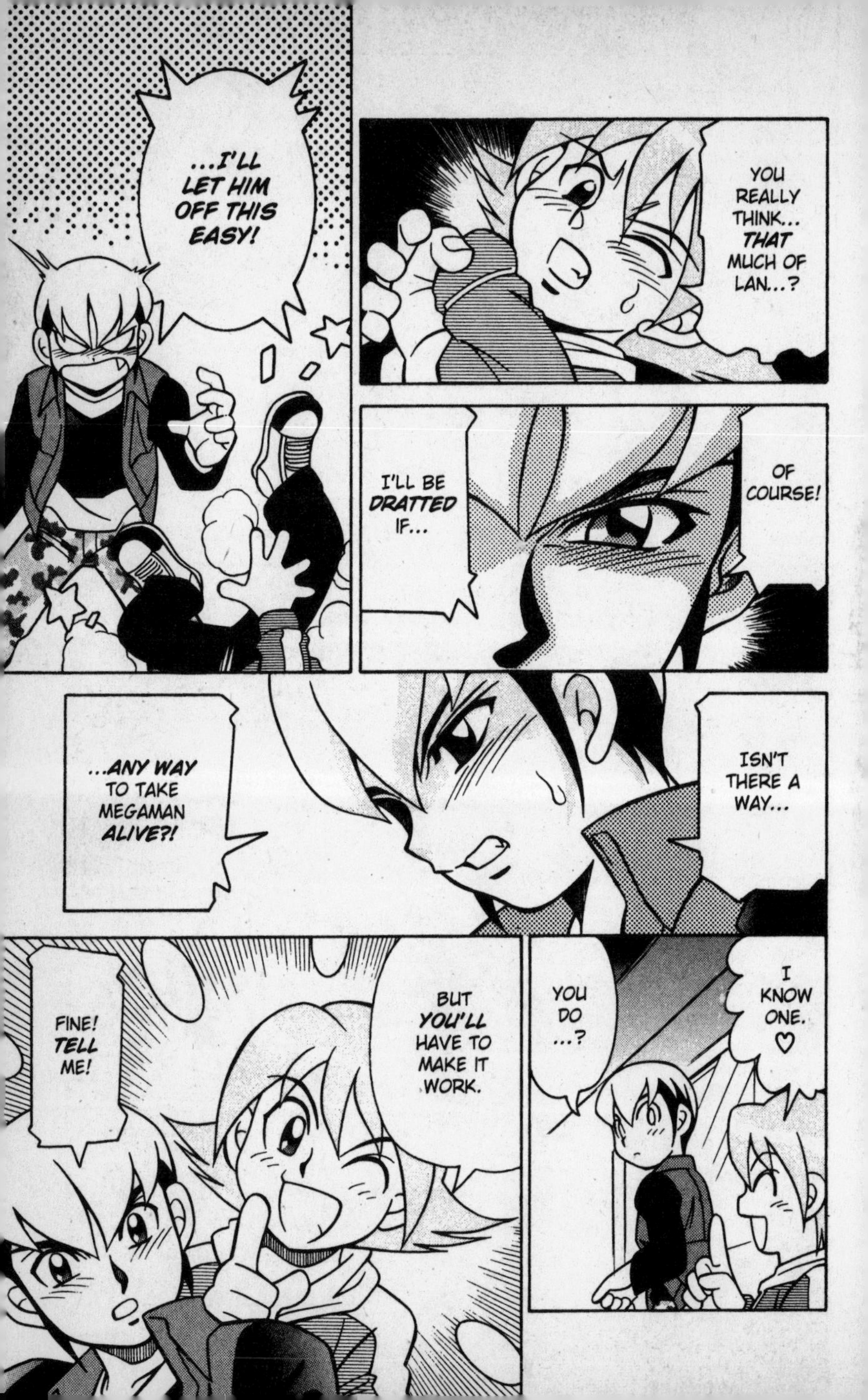
YOU REALLY THINK... THAT MUCH OF LAN...?
OF COURSE!
I'LL BE DRATTED IF...
...I'LL LET HIM OFF THIS EASY!
ISN'T THERE A WAY...
...ANY WAY TO TAKE MEGAMAN ALIVE?!
I KNOW ONE. ♡
YOU DO ...?
BUT YOU'LL HAVE TO MAKE IT WORK.
FINE! TELL ME!

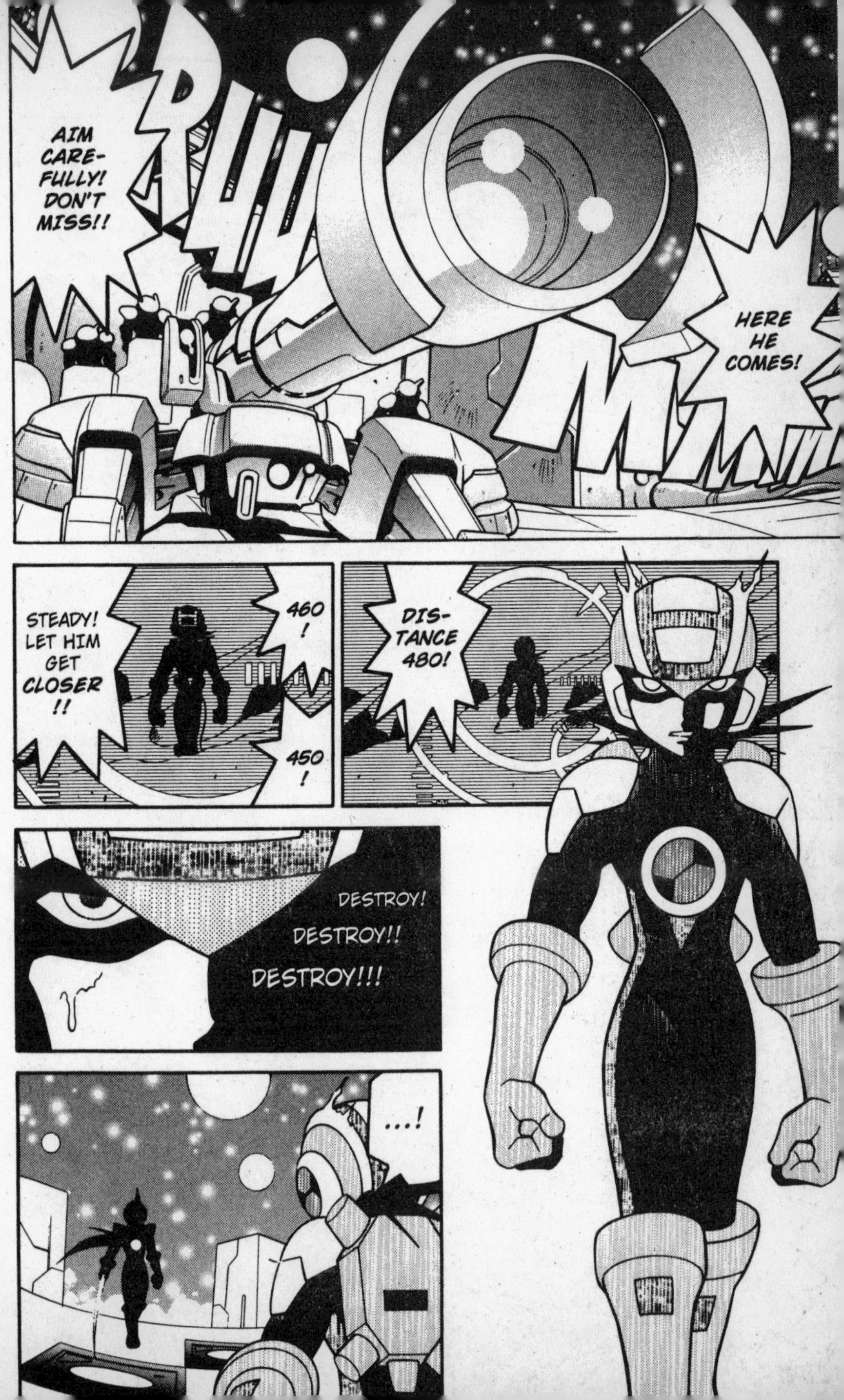
HERE HE COMES!
AIM CARE-FULLY! DON'T MISS!!
DIS-TANCE 480!
460!
STEADY! LET HIM GET CLOSER!!
450!
DESTROY!
DESTROY!!
DESTROY!!!
...!

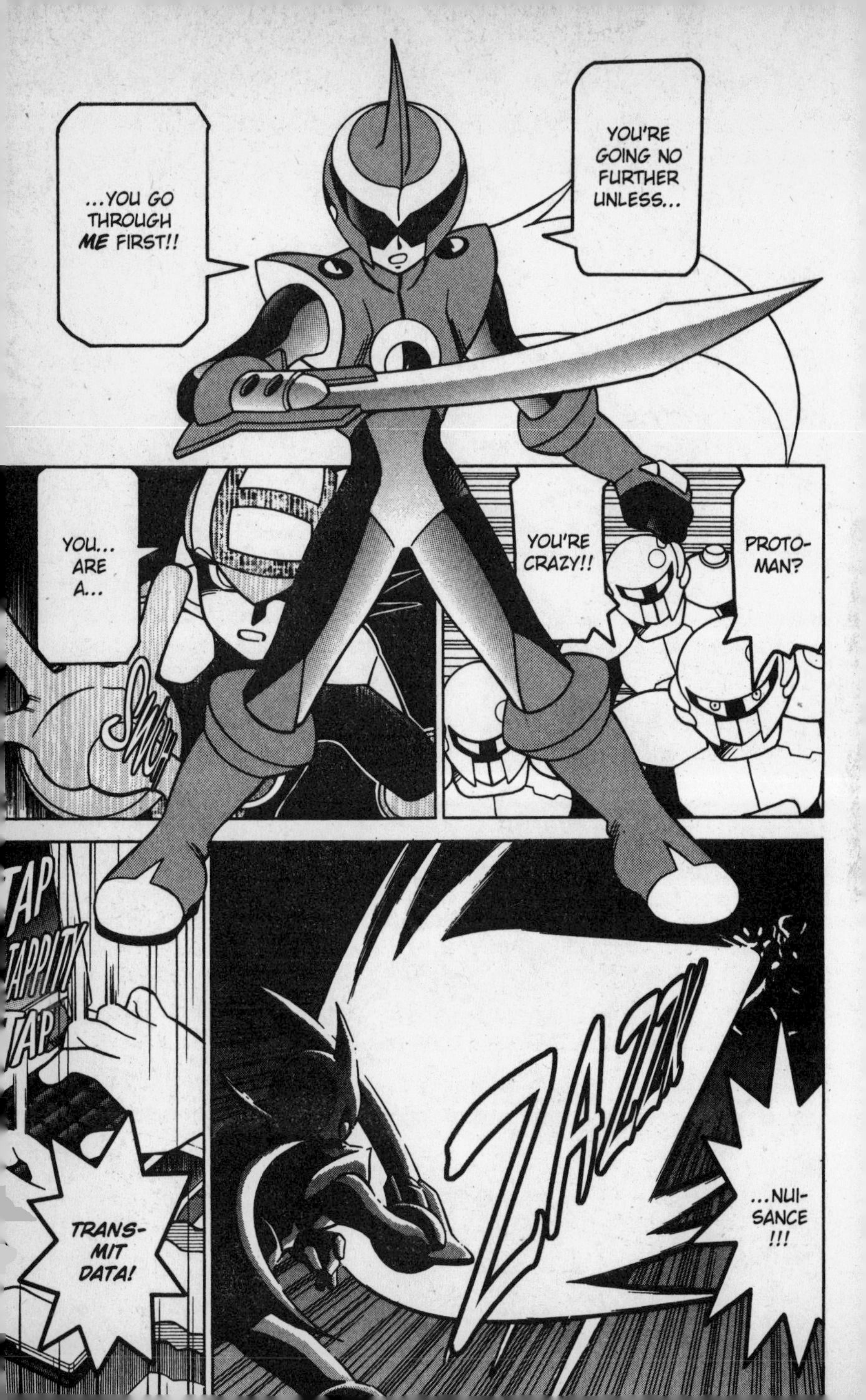
YOU'RE GOING NO FURTHER UNLESS...
...YOU GO THROUGH **ME** FIRST!!
PROTO-MAN?
YOU'RE CRAZY!!
YOU... ARE A...
...NUI-SANCE!!!
TAP TAPPITY TAP
TRANS-MIT DATA!

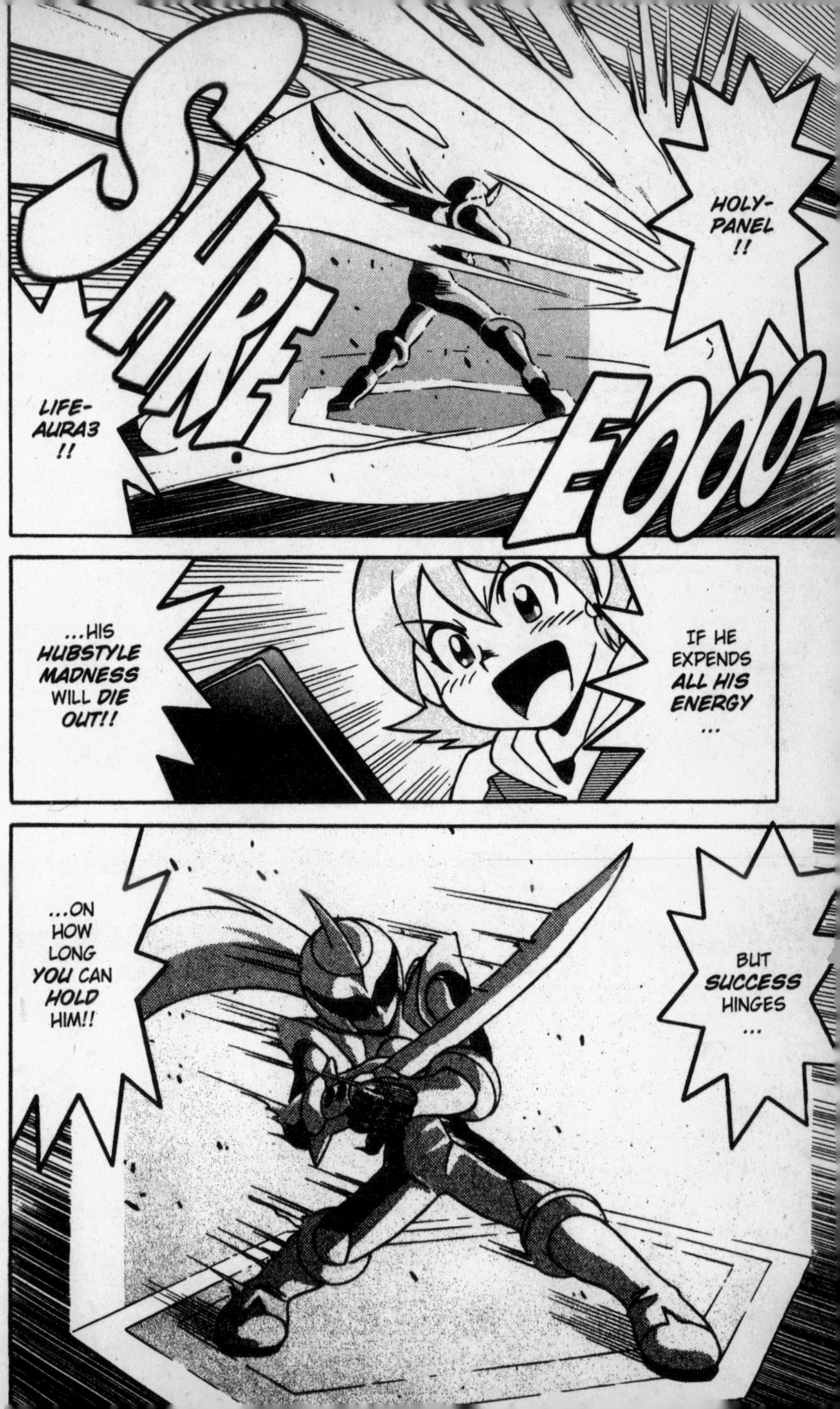
HOLY-PANEL !!
SHRE
EOOO
LIFE-AURA3 !!
IF HE EXPENDS ALL HIS ENERGY ...
...HIS HUBSTYLE MADNESS WILL DIE OUT!!
BUT SUCCESS HINGES ...
...ON HOW LONG YOU CAN HOLD HIM!!

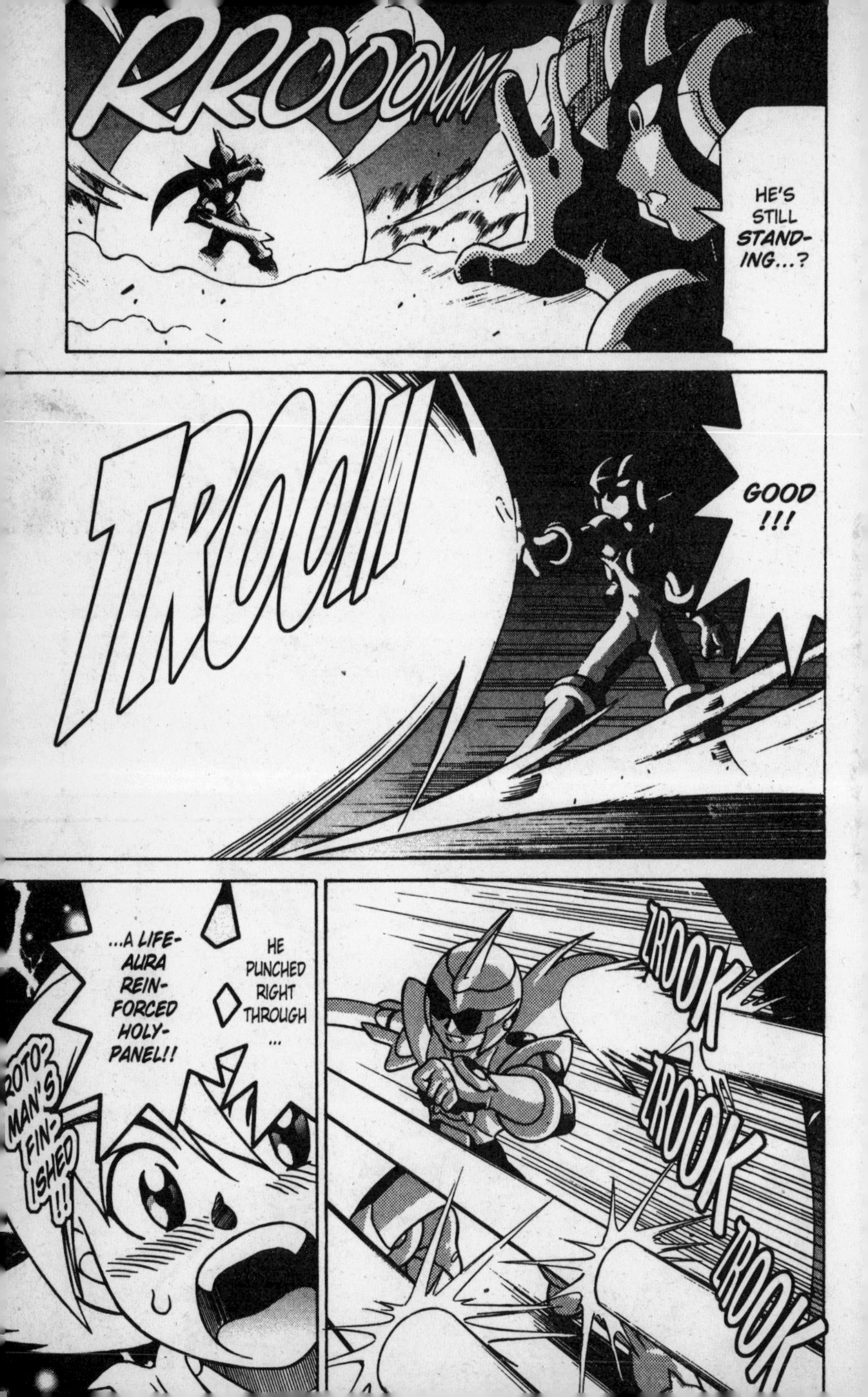
RRROOOM
HE'S STILL STANDING...?
GOOD!!!
TROOM
TROOK
TROOK
TROOK
HE PUNCHED RIGHT THROUGH...
...A LIFE-AURA REINFORCED HOLY-PANEL!!
ROTO-MAN'S FINISHED!!

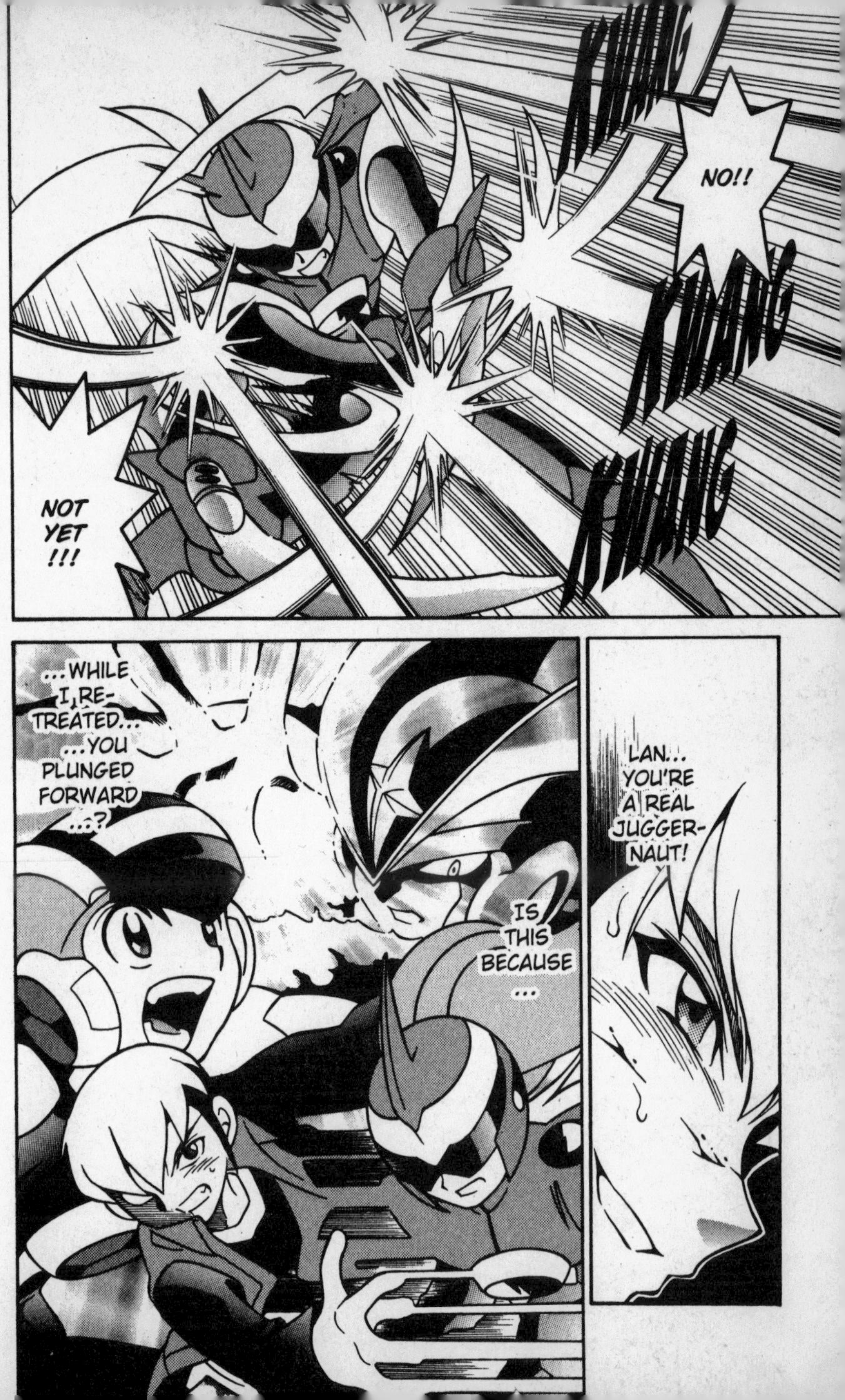
KWANG
NO!!
KWANG
KWANG
NOT YET!!!
LAN... YOU'RE A REAL JUGGER-NAUT!
...WHILE I RE-TREATED... ...YOU PLUNGED FORWARD ...?
IS THIS BECAUSE ...

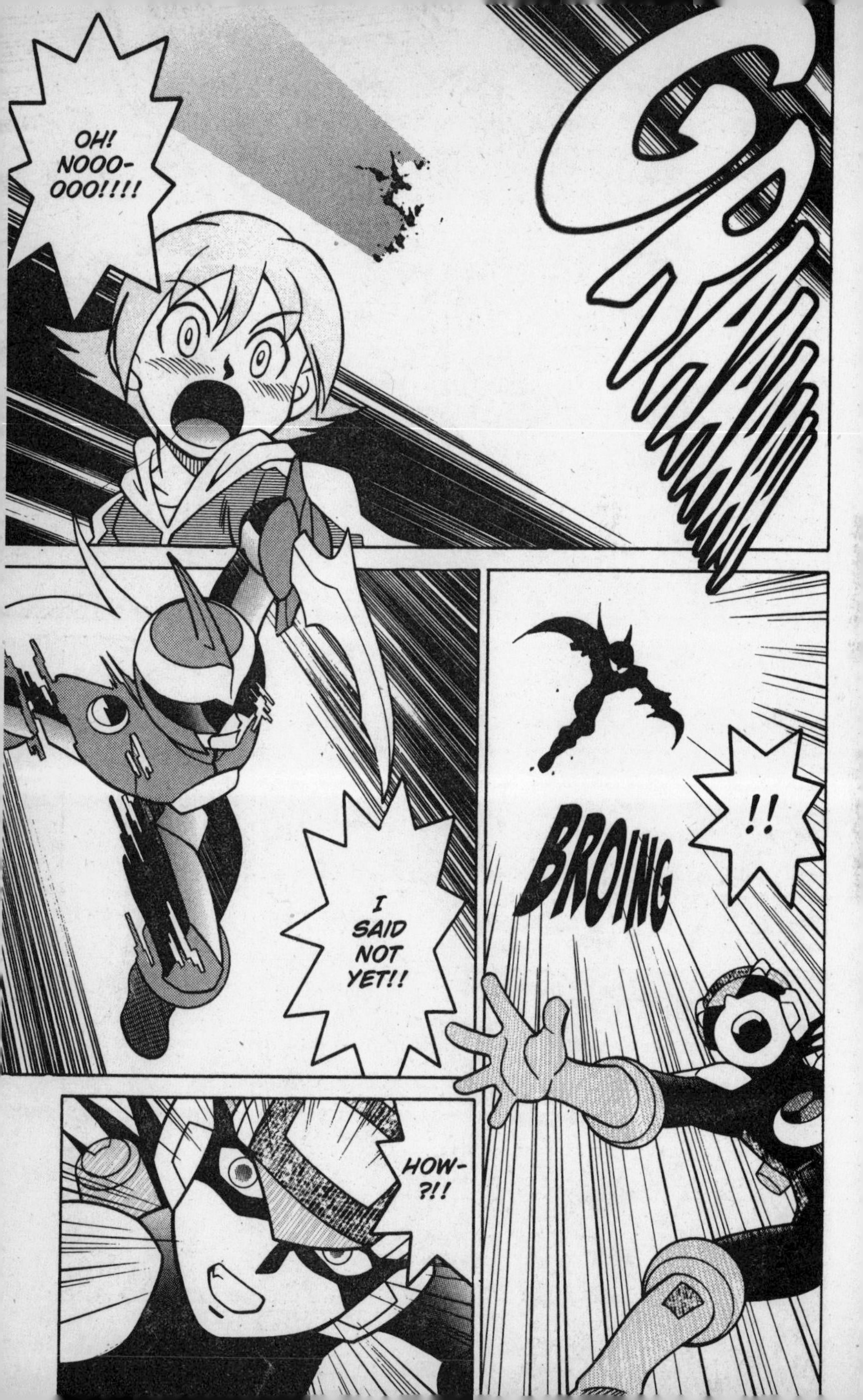
OH! NOOO-OOO!!!!
BROING
!!
I SAID NOT YET!!
HOW-?!!

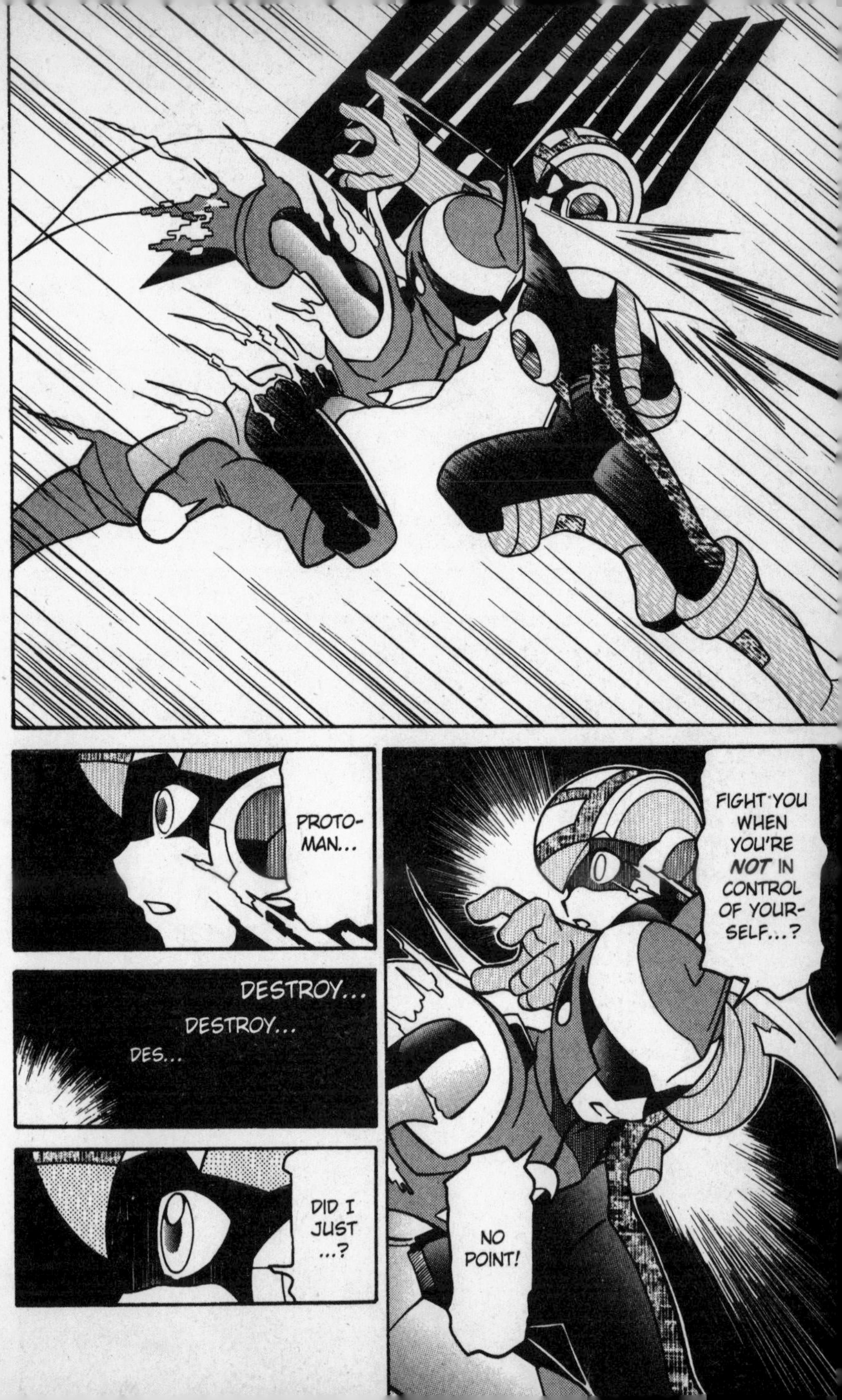
FIGHT YOU WHEN YOU'RE *NOT* IN CONTROL OF YOUR-SELF...?
NO POINT!
PROTO-MAN...
DESTROY...
DESTROY...
DES...
DID I JUST ...?

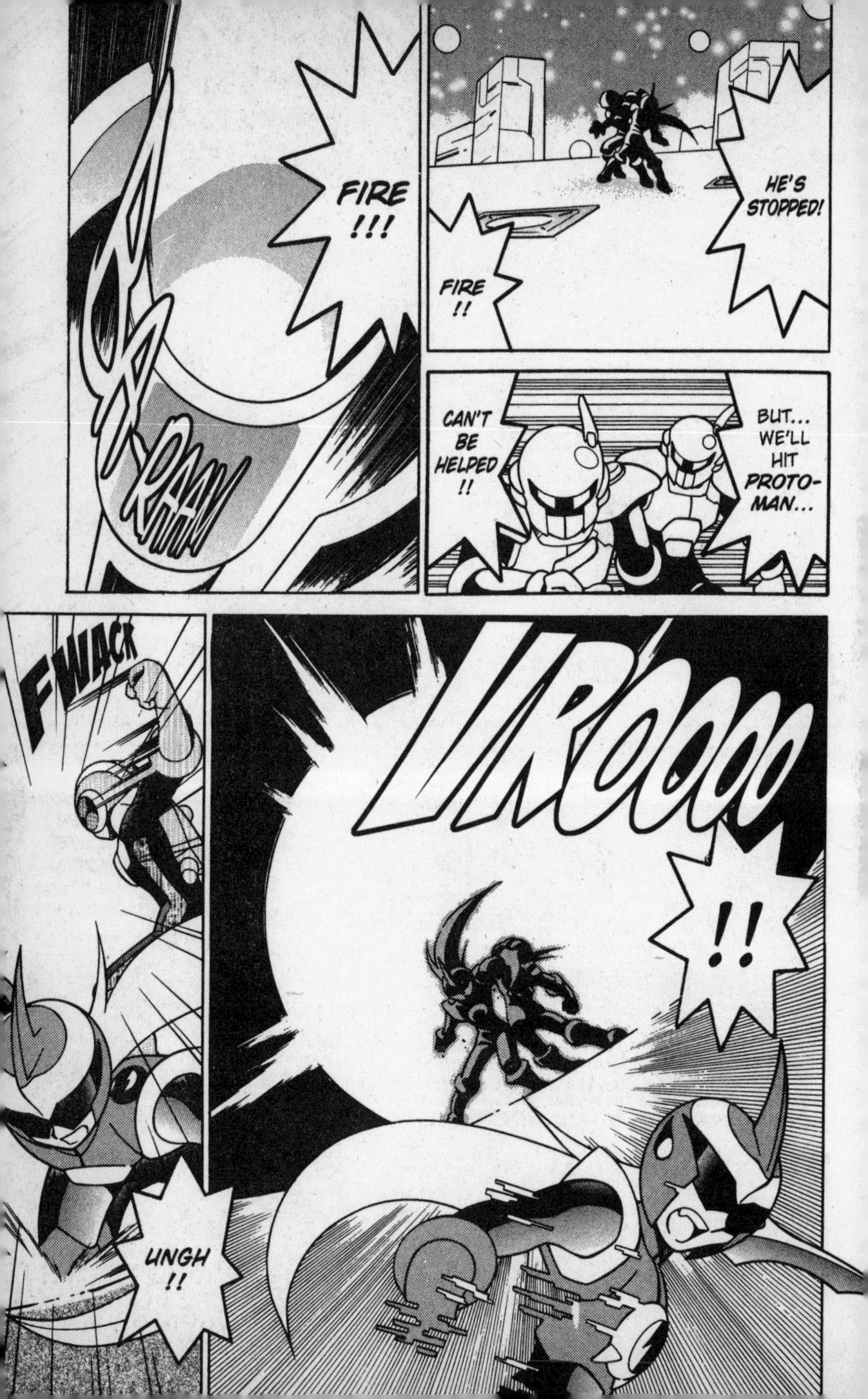
HE'S STOPPED!
FIRE !!
BUT... WE'LL HIT PROTO-MAN...
CAN'T BE HELPED !!
FIRE !!!
!!
FWACK
UNGH !!

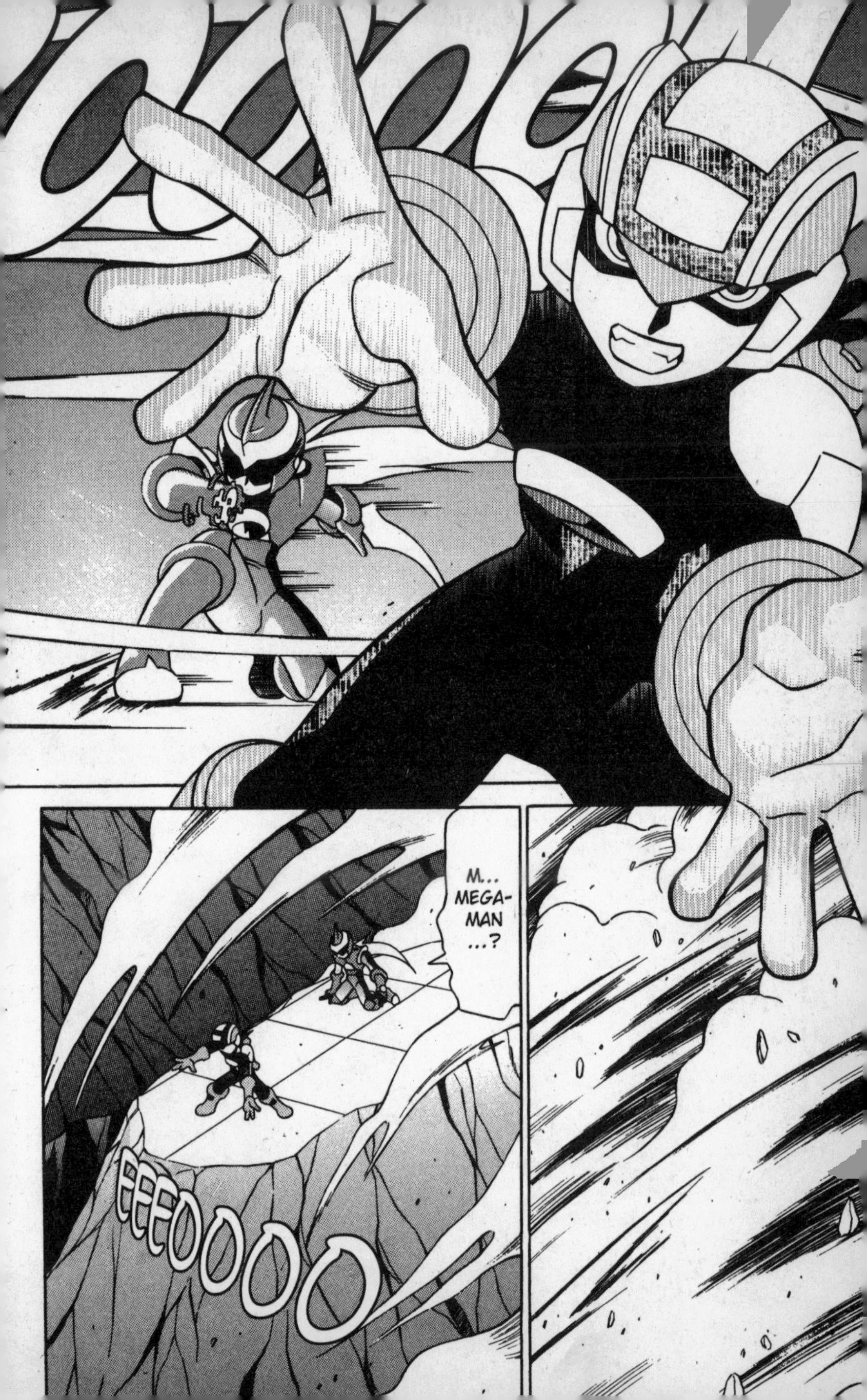
M... MEGA-MAN ...?
EEEOOOOO

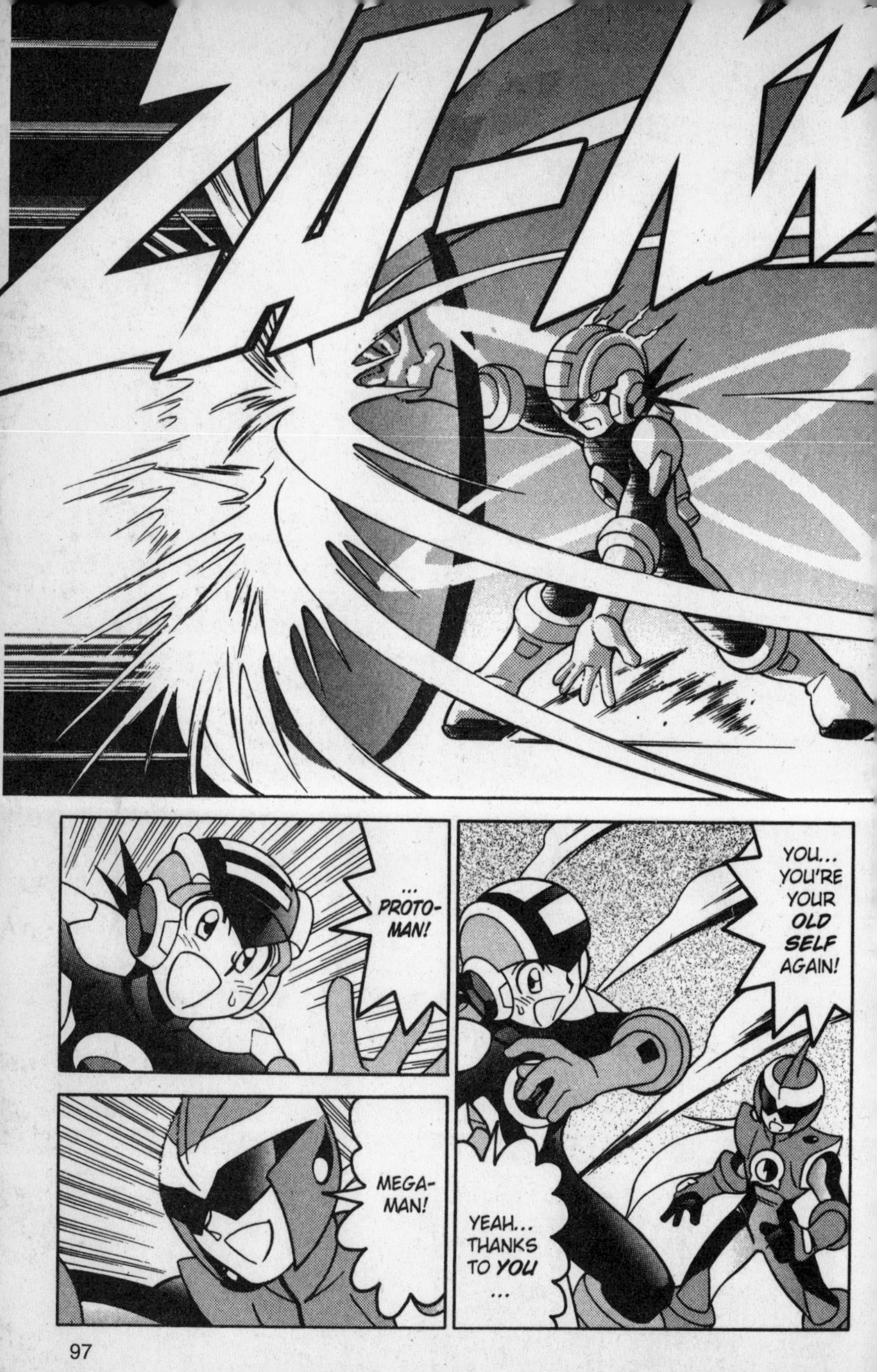
YOU... YOU'RE YOUR OLD SELF AGAIN!
YEAH... THANKS TO YOU ...
... PROTO-MAN!
MEGA-MAN!

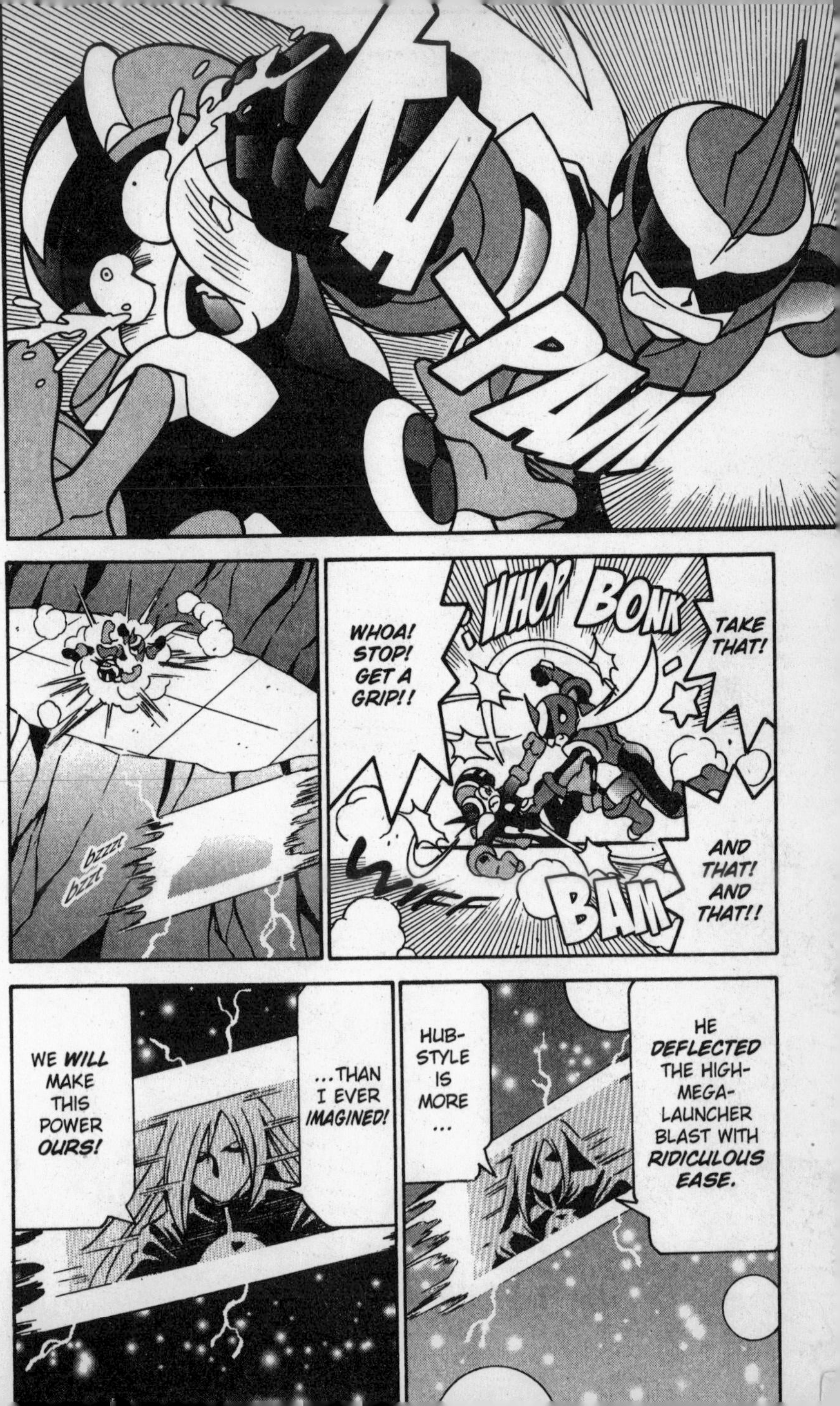
KA-PAM
TAKE THAT!
WHOP BONK
WHOA! STOP! GET A GRIP!!
AND THAT! AND THAT!!
BAM
WIFF
bzzzt bzzzt
HE *DEFLECTED* THE HIGH-MEGA-LAUNCHER BLAST WITH *RIDICULOUS EASE.*
HUB-STYLE IS MORE ...
...THAN I EVER *IMAGINED!*
WE *WILL* MAKE THIS POWER *OURS!*

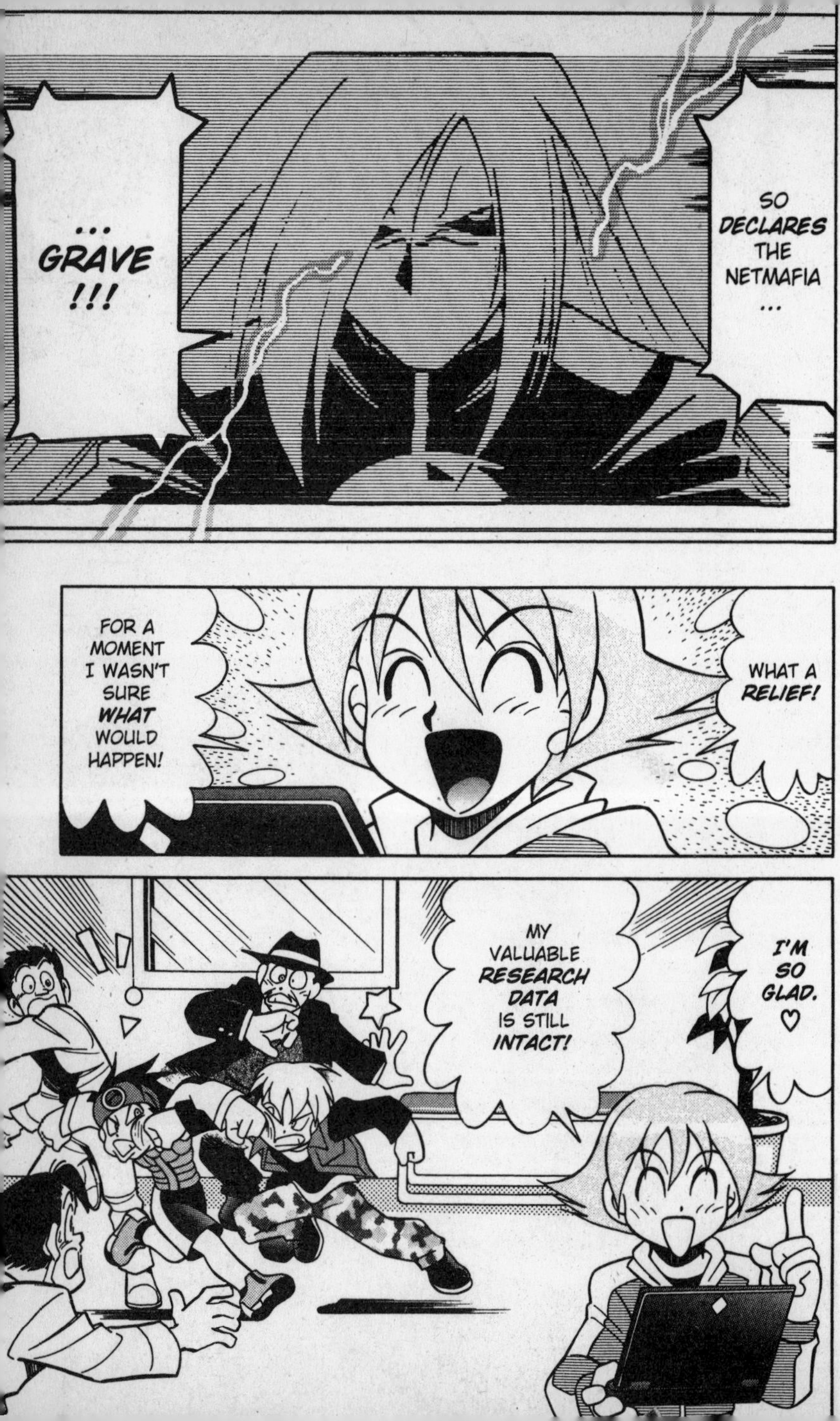
SO DECLARES THE NETMAFIA ...
... GRAVE !!!
WHAT A RELIEF!
FOR A MOMENT I WASN'T SURE WHAT WOULD HAPPEN!
I'M SO GLAD. ♡
MY VALUABLE RESEARCH DATA IS STILL INTACT!

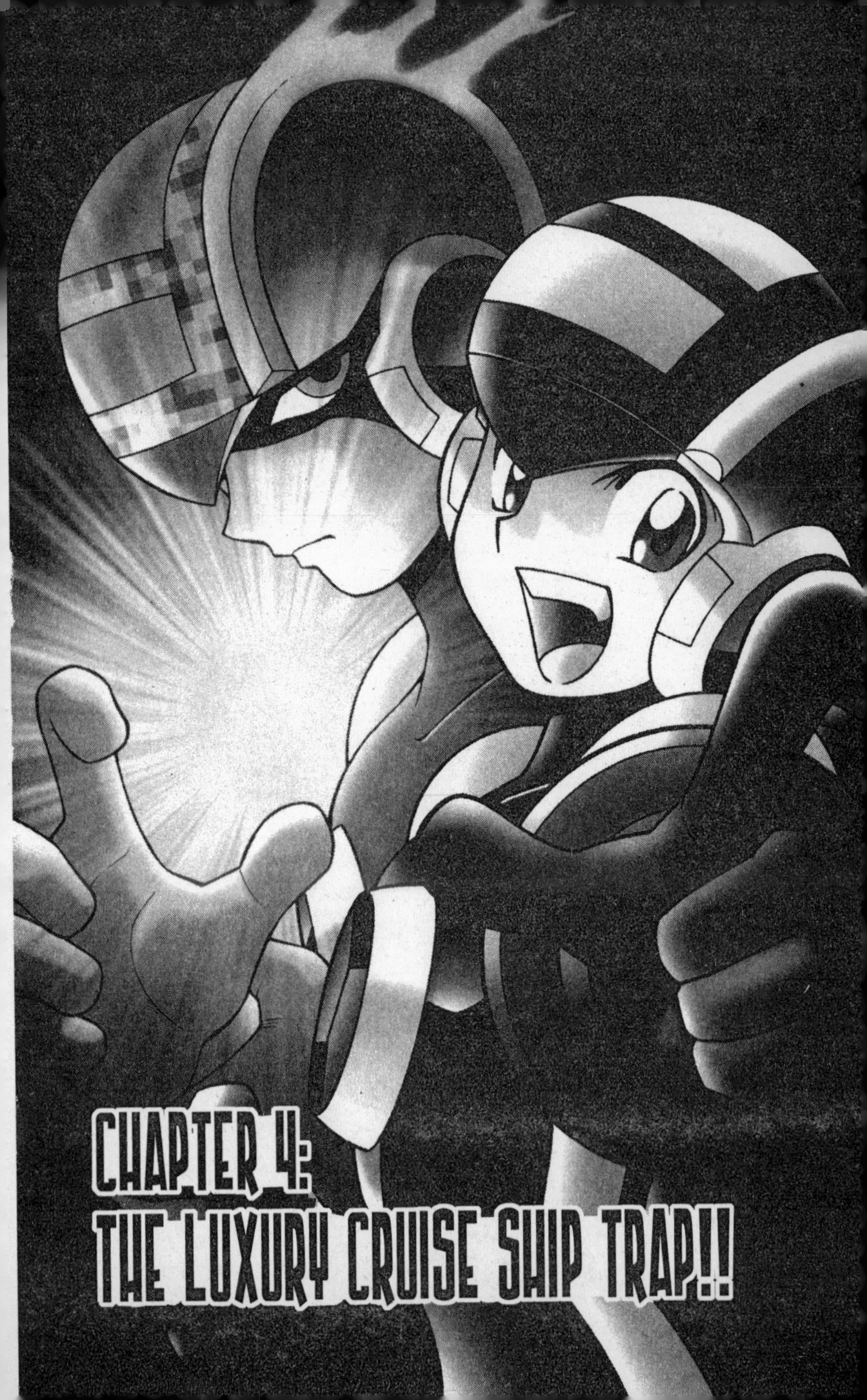
CHAPTER 4:
THE LUXURY CRUISE SHIP TRAP!!

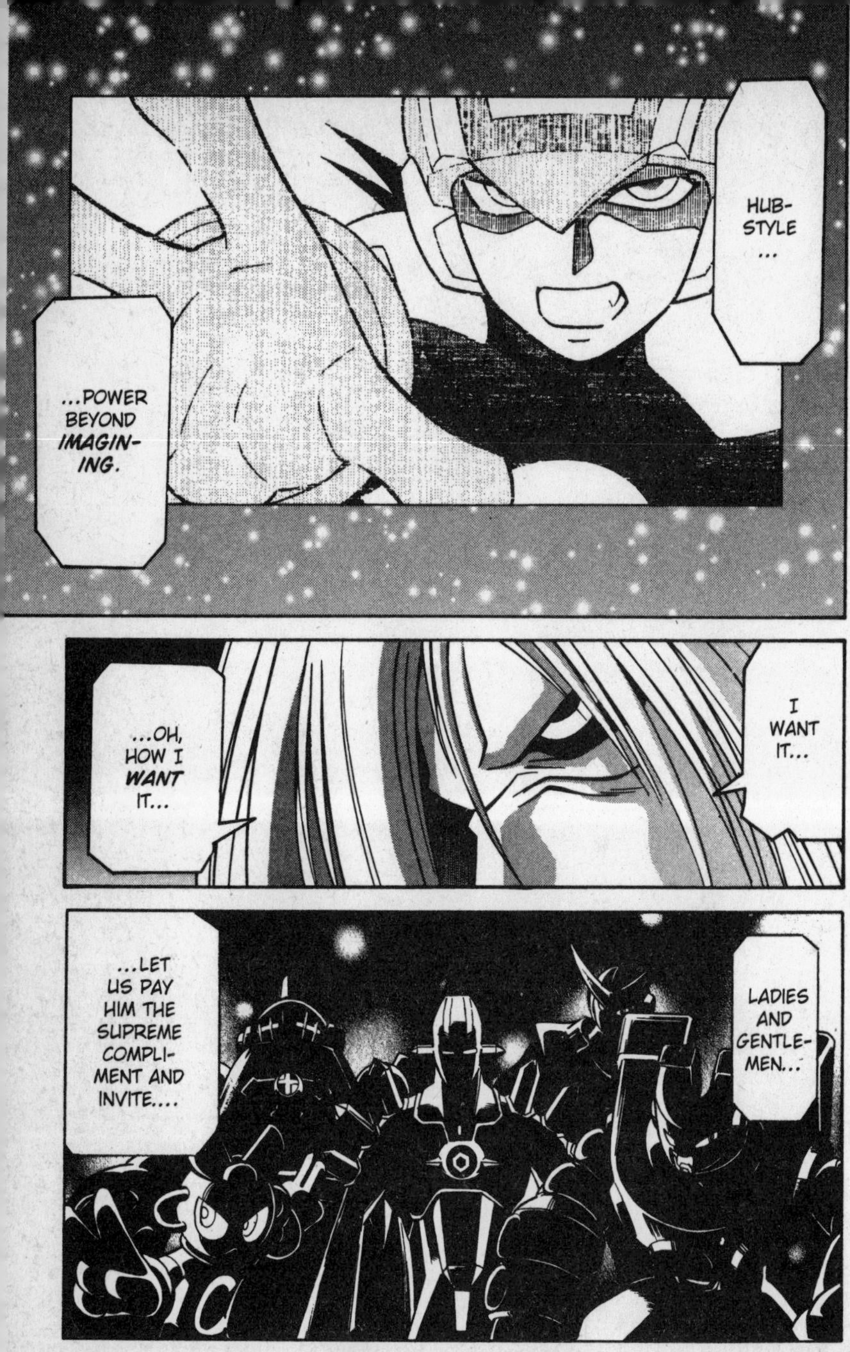
HUB-STYLE ...
...POWER BEYOND *IMAGIN-ING*.
I WANT IT...
...OH, HOW I *WANT* IT...
LADIES AND GENTLE-MEN...
...LET US PAY HIM THE SUPREME COMPLI-MENT AND INVITE....

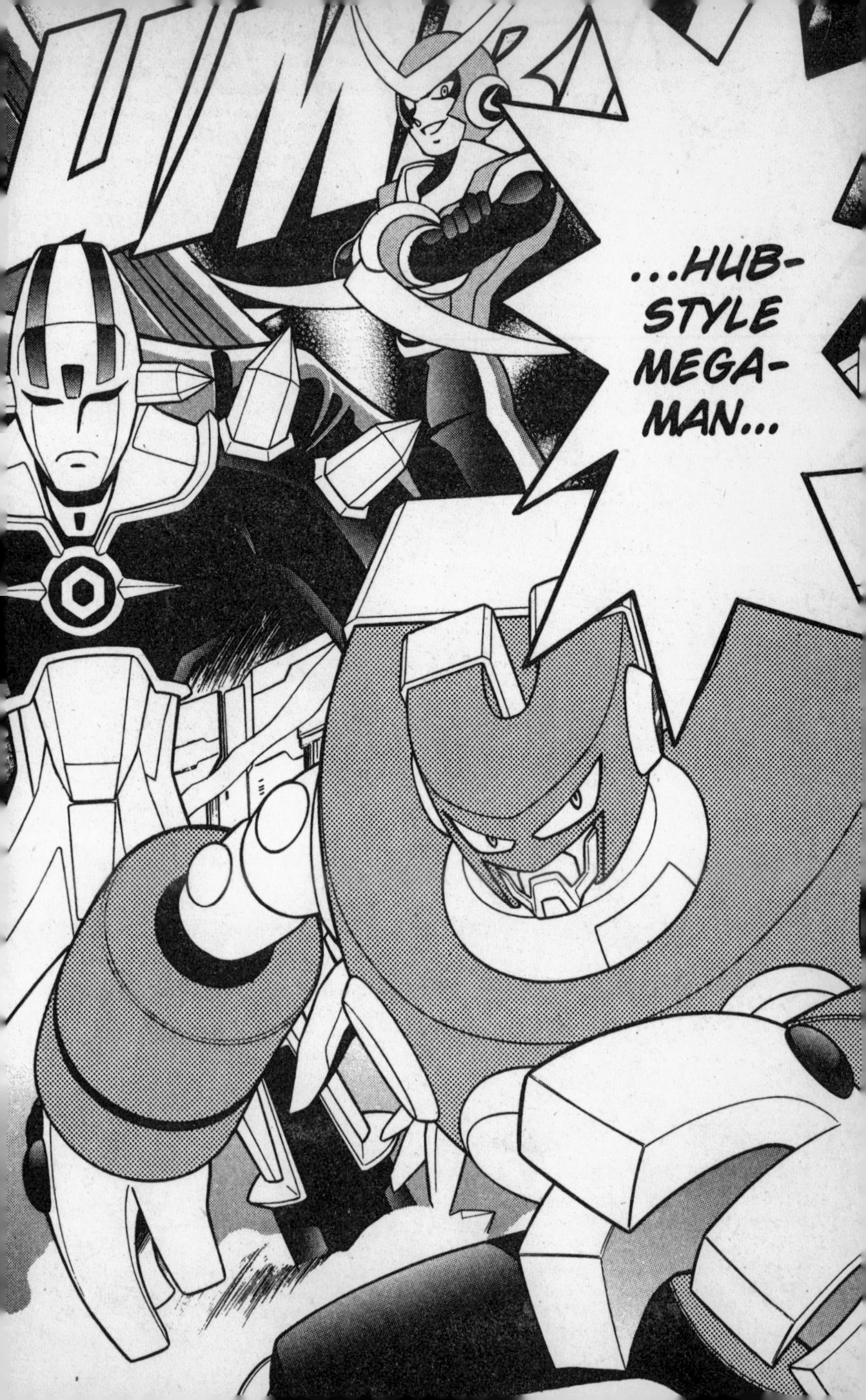
...HUB-STYLE MEGA-MAN...

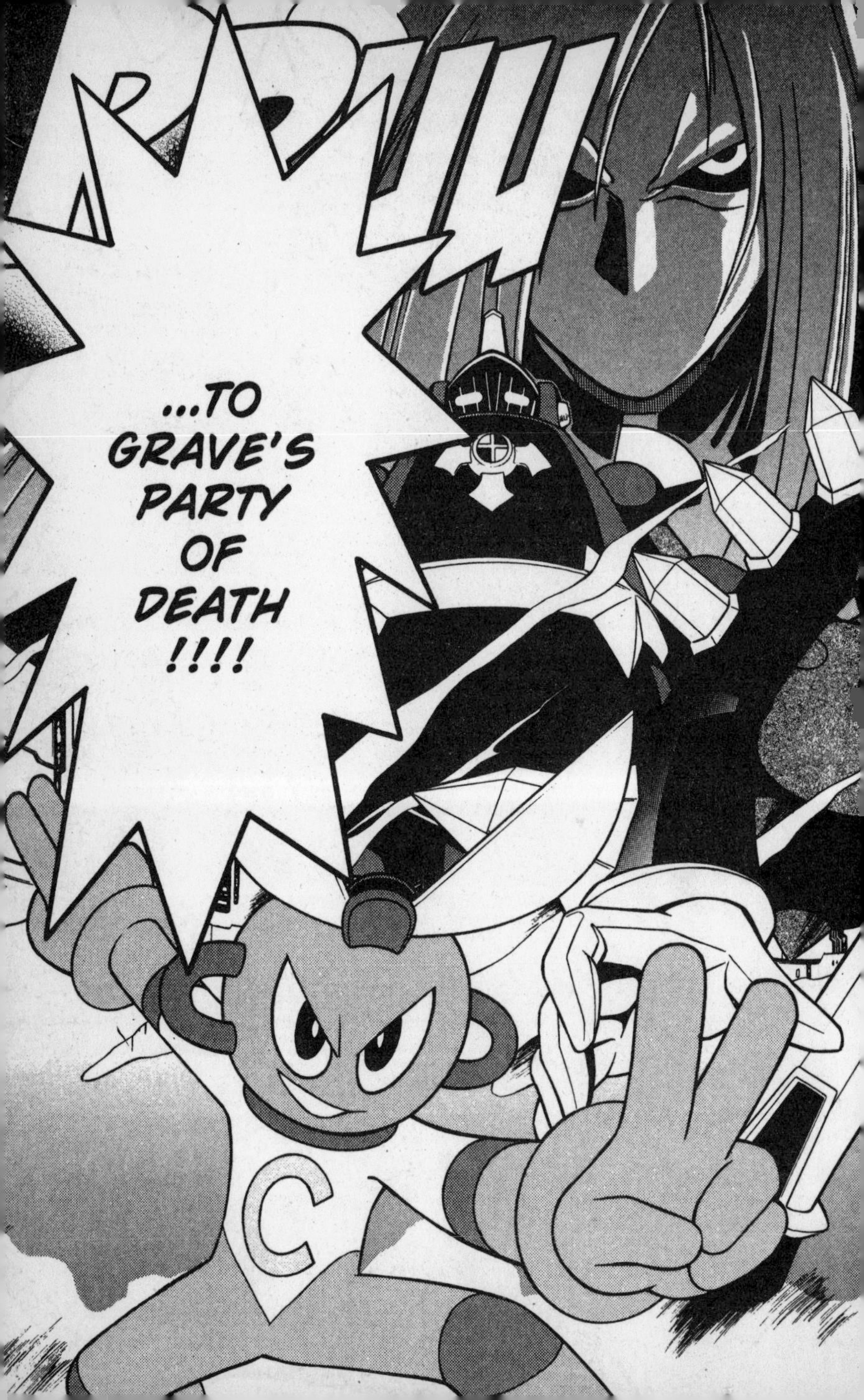
...TO GRAVE'S PARTY OF DEATH !!!!

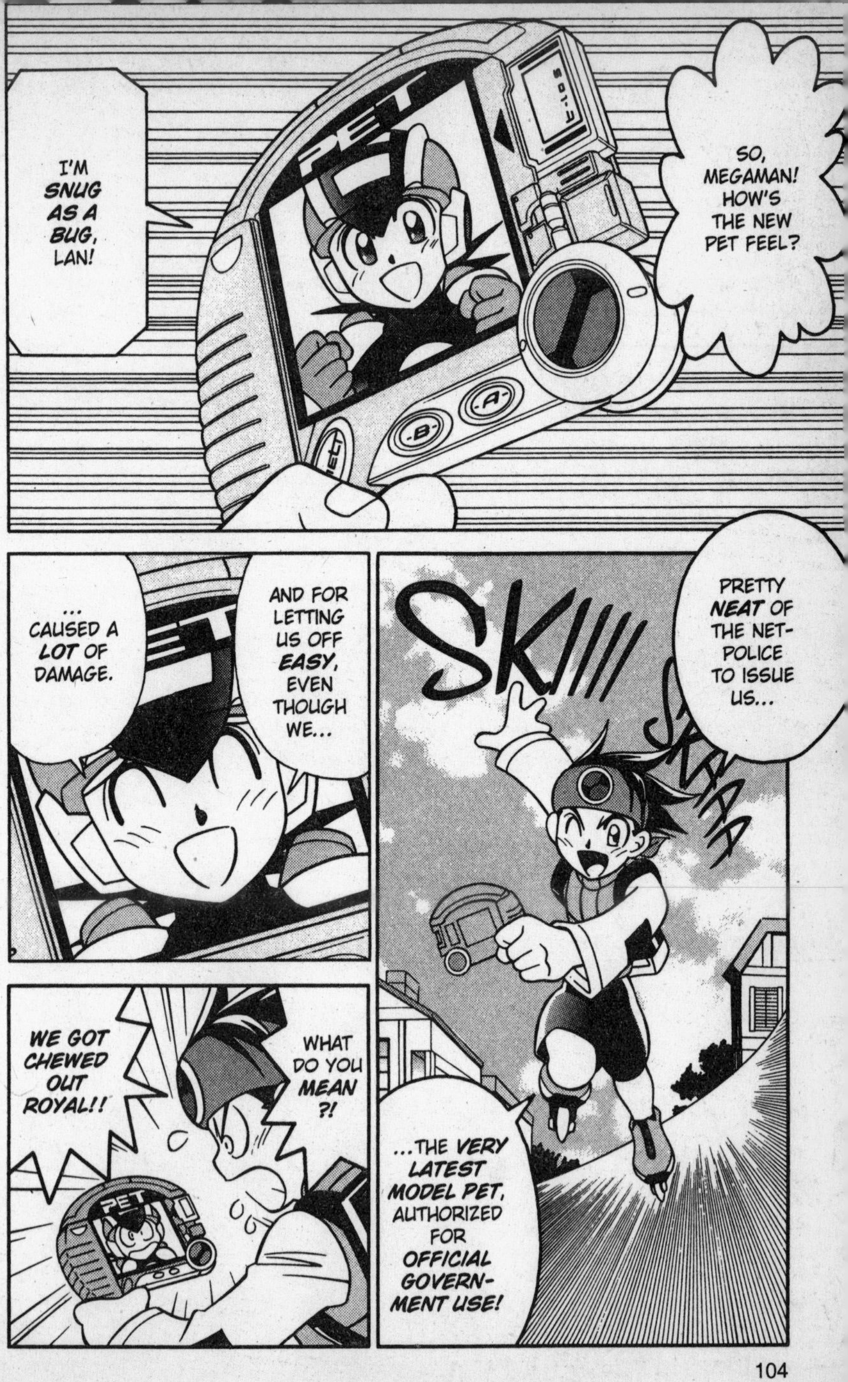
SO, MEGAMAN! HOW'S THE NEW PET FEEL?
I'M SNUG AS A BUG, LAN!
PRETTY NEAT OF THE NET-POLICE TO ISSUE US...
...THE VERY LATEST MODEL PET, AUTHORIZED FOR OFFICIAL GOVERNMENT USE!
AND FOR LETTING US OFF EASY, EVEN THOUGH WE...
...CAUSED A LOT OF DAMAGE.
WHAT DO YOU MEAN?!
WE GOT CHEWED OUT ROYAL!!

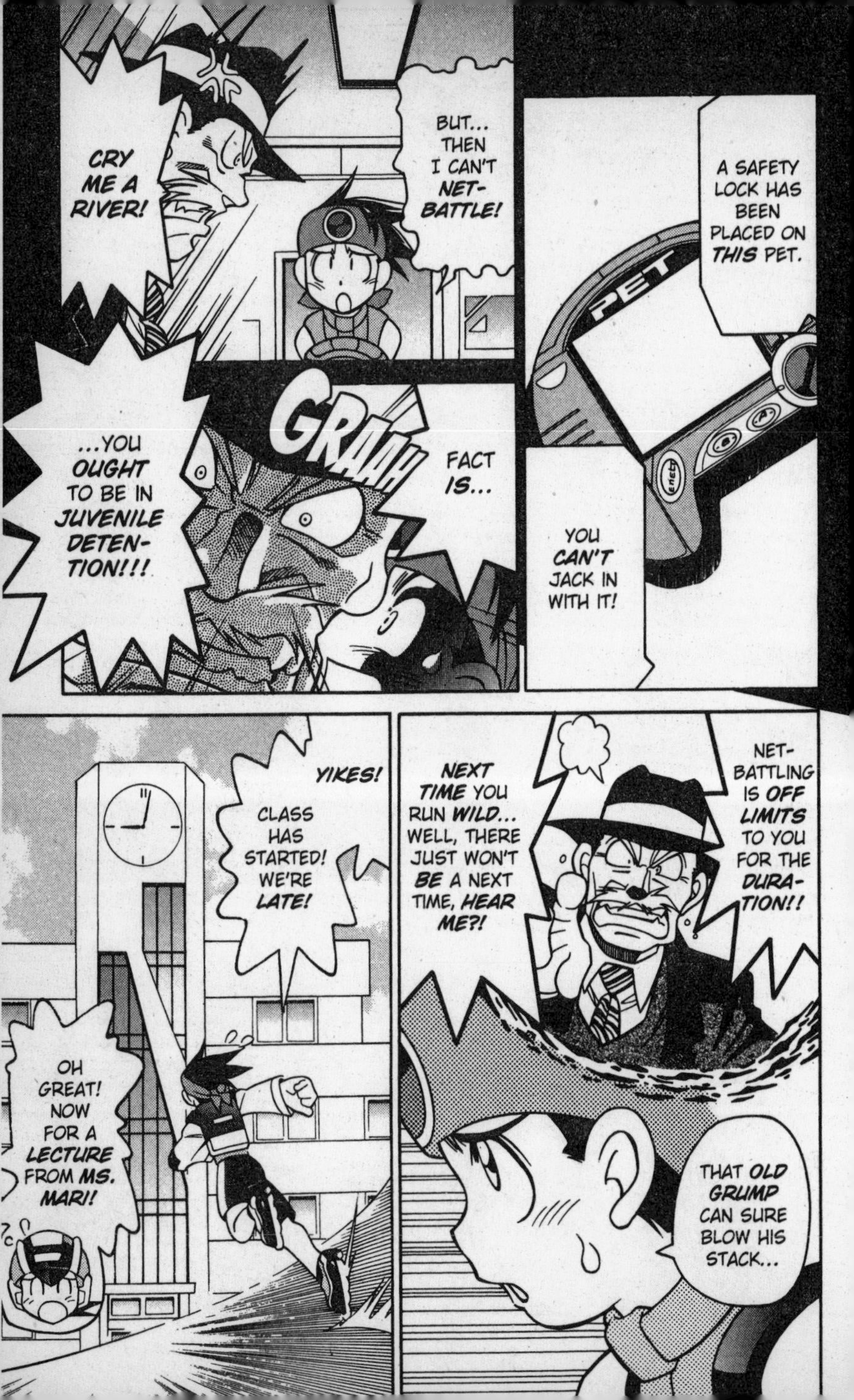

A SAFETY LOCK HAS BEEN PLACED ON THIS PET.
PET
YOU CAN'T JACK IN WITH IT!
BUT... THEN I CAN'T NET-BATTLE!
CRY ME A RIVER!
FACT IS...
GRAAAH
...YOU OUGHT TO BE IN JUVENILE DETENTION!!!
NET-BATTLING IS OFF LIMITS TO YOU FOR THE DURATION!!
NEXT TIME YOU RUN WILD... WELL, THERE JUST WON'T BE A NEXT TIME, HEAR ME?!
THAT OLD GRUMP CAN SURE BLOW HIS STACK...
YIKES!
CLASS HAS STARTED! WE'RE LATE!
OH GREAT! NOW FOR A LECTURE FROM MS. MARI!

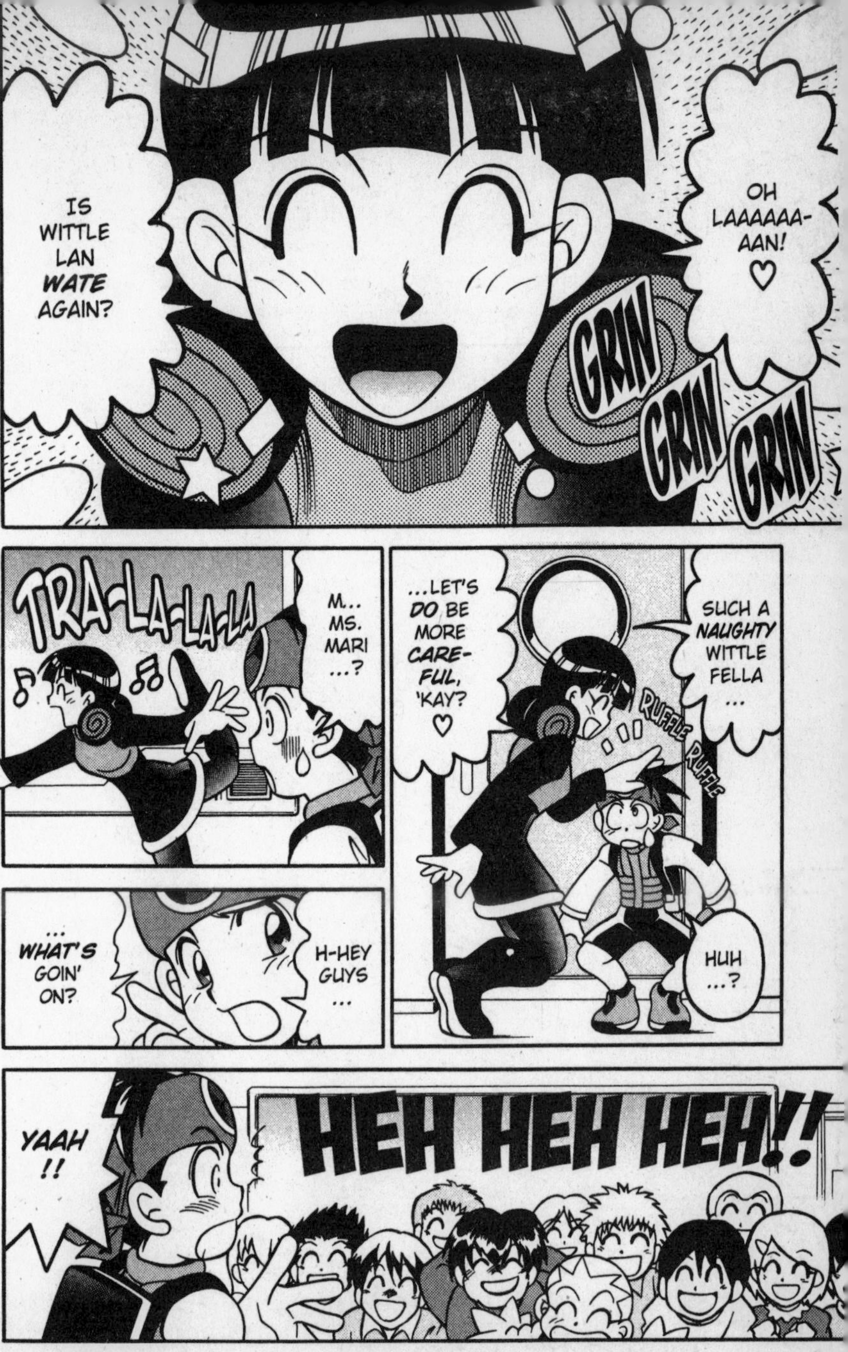
OH LAAAAAAA-AAN! ♡
GRIN GRIN GRIN
IS WITTLE LAN WATE AGAIN?
SUCH A NAUGHTY WITTLE FELLA ...
RUFFLE RUFFLE
...LET'S DO BE MORE CAREFUL, 'KAY? ♡
HUH ...?
M... MS. MARI ...?
TRA-LA-LA-LA
H-HEY GUYS ...
... WHAT'S GOIN' ON?
HEH HEH HEH!!
YAAH !!

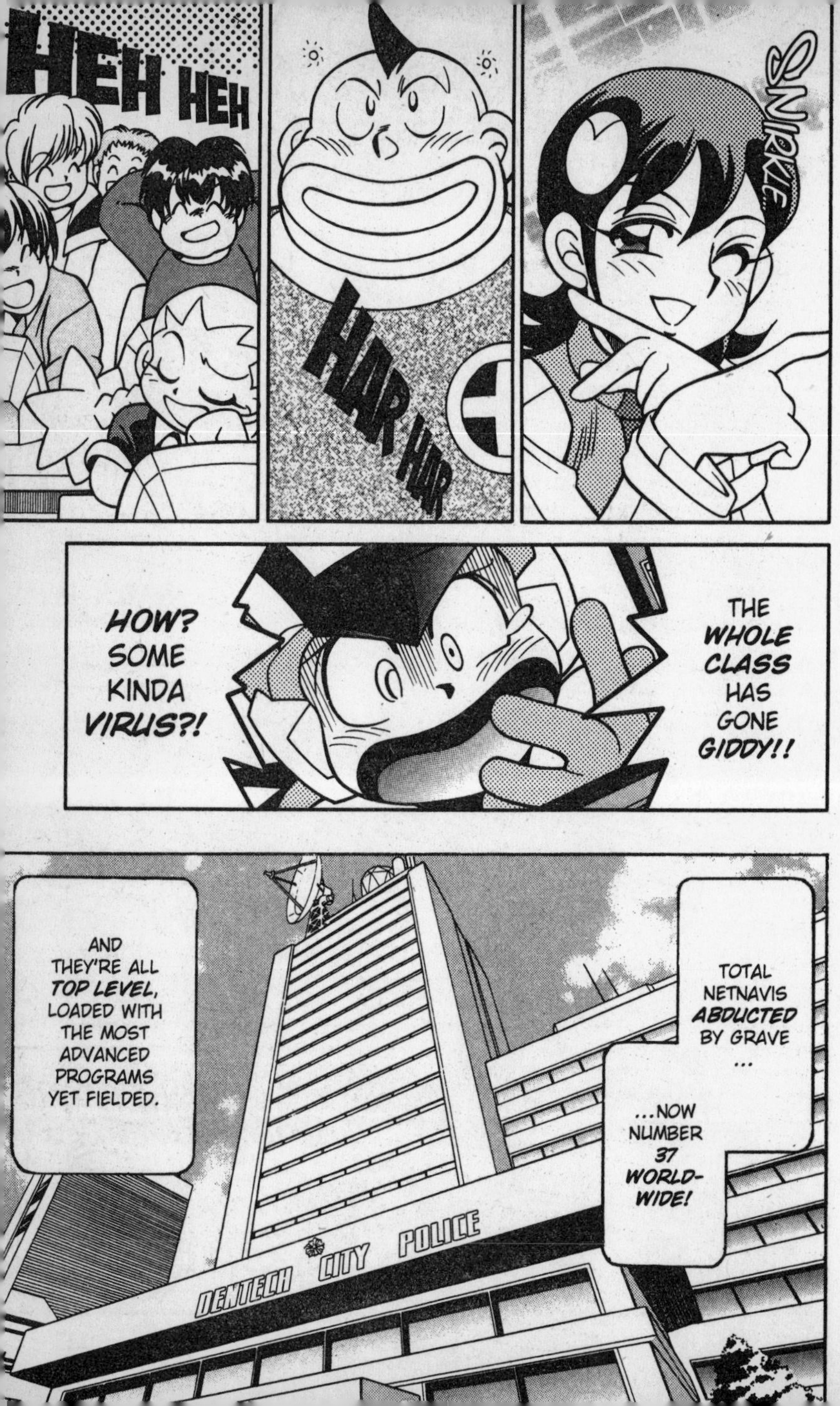
SNIRKLE
HAR HAR
HEH HEH
THE WHOLE CLASS HAS GONE GIDDY!!
HOW? SOME KINDA VIRUS?!
TOTAL NETNAVIS ABDUCTED BY GRAVE...
...NOW NUMBER 37 WORLD-WIDE!
AND THEY'RE ALL TOP LEVEL, LOADED WITH THE MOST ADVANCED PROGRAMS YET FIELDED.
DENTECH CITY POLICE

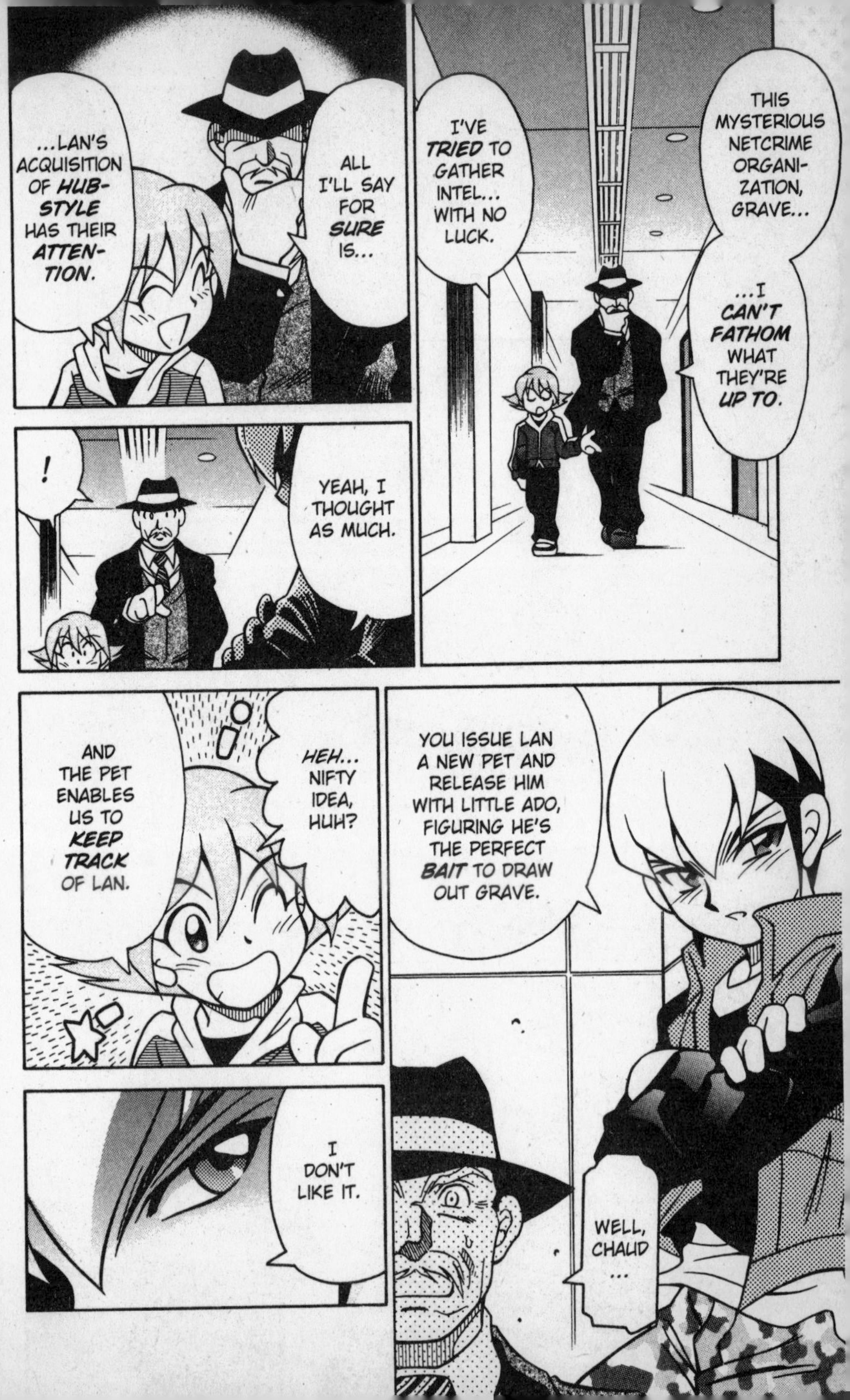
THIS MYSTERIOUS NETCRIME ORGANI-ZATION, GRAVE...
...I CAN'T FATHOM WHAT THEY'RE UP TO.
I'VE TRIED TO GATHER INTEL... WITH NO LUCK.
ALL I'LL SAY FOR SURE IS...
...LAN'S ACQUISITION OF HUB-STYLE HAS THEIR ATTEN-TION.
YEAH, I THOUGHT AS MUCH.
!
YOU ISSUE LAN A NEW PET AND RELEASE HIM WITH LITTLE ADO, FIGURING HE'S THE PERFECT BAIT TO DRAW OUT GRAVE.
WELL, CHAUD...
HEH... NIFTY IDEA, HUH?
AND THE PET ENABLES US TO KEEP TRACK OF LAN.
I DON'T LIKE IT.

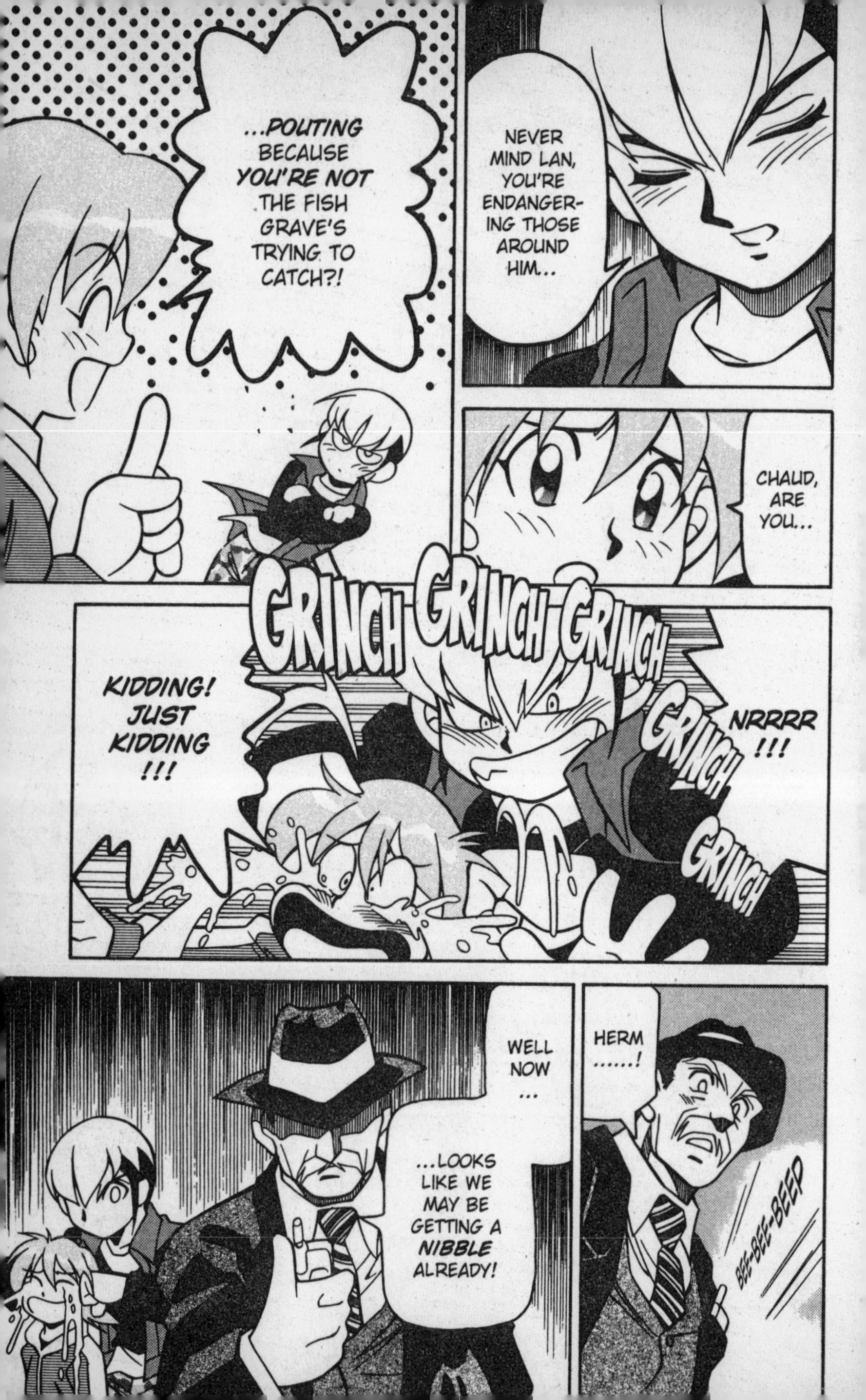
NEVER MIND LAN, YOU'RE ENDANGER-ING THOSE AROUND HIM...
CHAUD, ARE YOU...
...POUTING BECAUSE YOU'RE NOT THE FISH GRAVE'S TRYING TO CATCH?!
NRRRR !!!
GRINCH GRINCH GRINCH GRINCH GRINCH
KIDDING! JUST KIDDING !!!
HERM ......!
BEE-BEE-BEEP
WELL NOW ...
...LOOKS LIKE WE MAY BE GETTING A NIBBLE ALREADY!

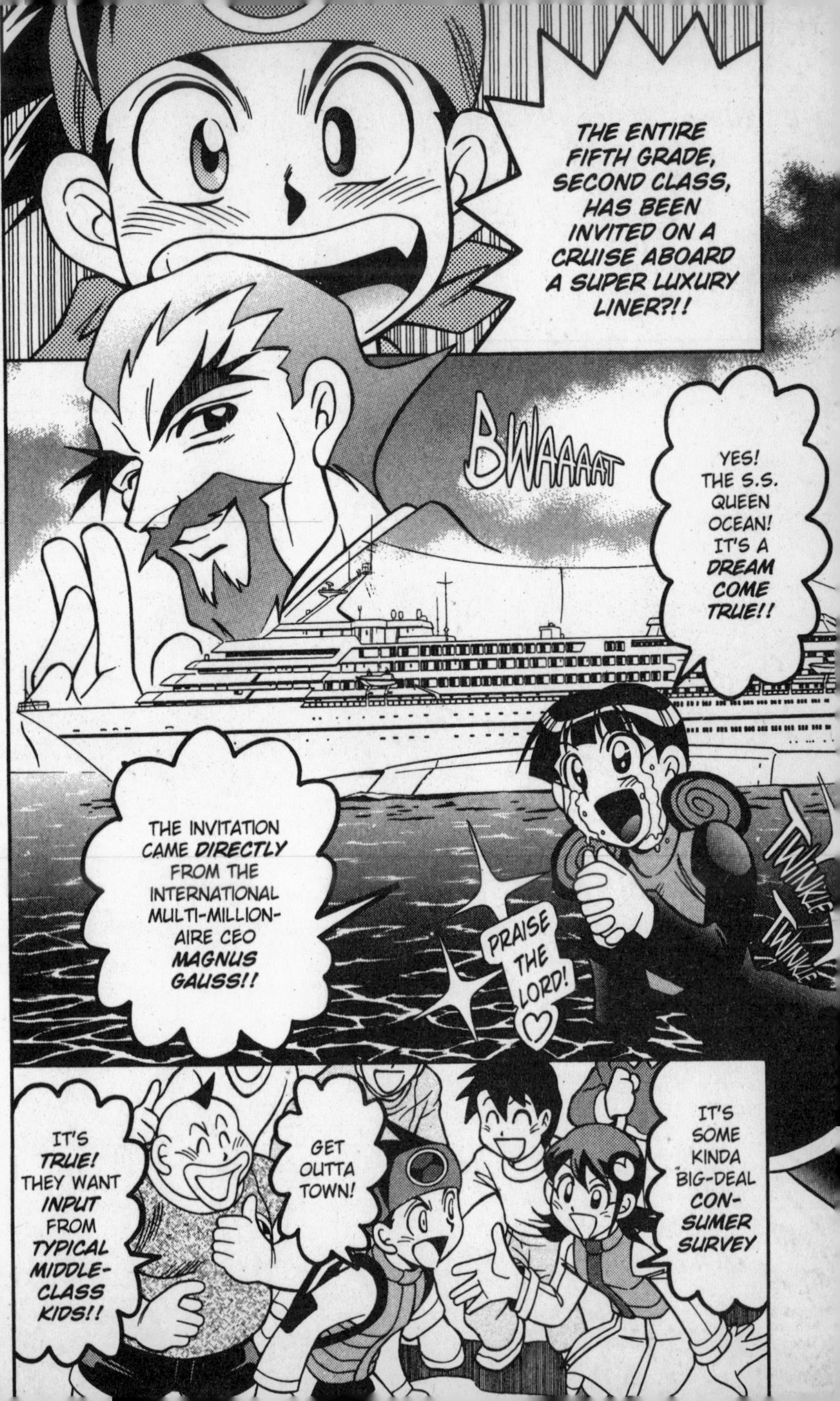
THE ENTIRE FIFTH GRADE, SECOND CLASS, HAS BEEN INVITED ON A CRUISE ABOARD A SUPER LUXURY LINER?!!
YES! THE S.S. QUEEN OCEAN! IT'S A DREAM COME TRUE!!
BWAAAAT
TWINKLE TWINKLE
PRAISE THE LORD! ♡
THE INVITATION CAME DIRECTLY FROM THE INTERNATIONAL MULTI-MILLION-AIRE CEO MAGNUS GAUSS!!
IT'S SOME KINDA BIG-DEAL CON-SUMER SURVEY
GET OUTTA TOWN!
IT'S TRUE! THEY WANT INPUT FROM TYPICAL MIDDLE-CLASS KIDS!!

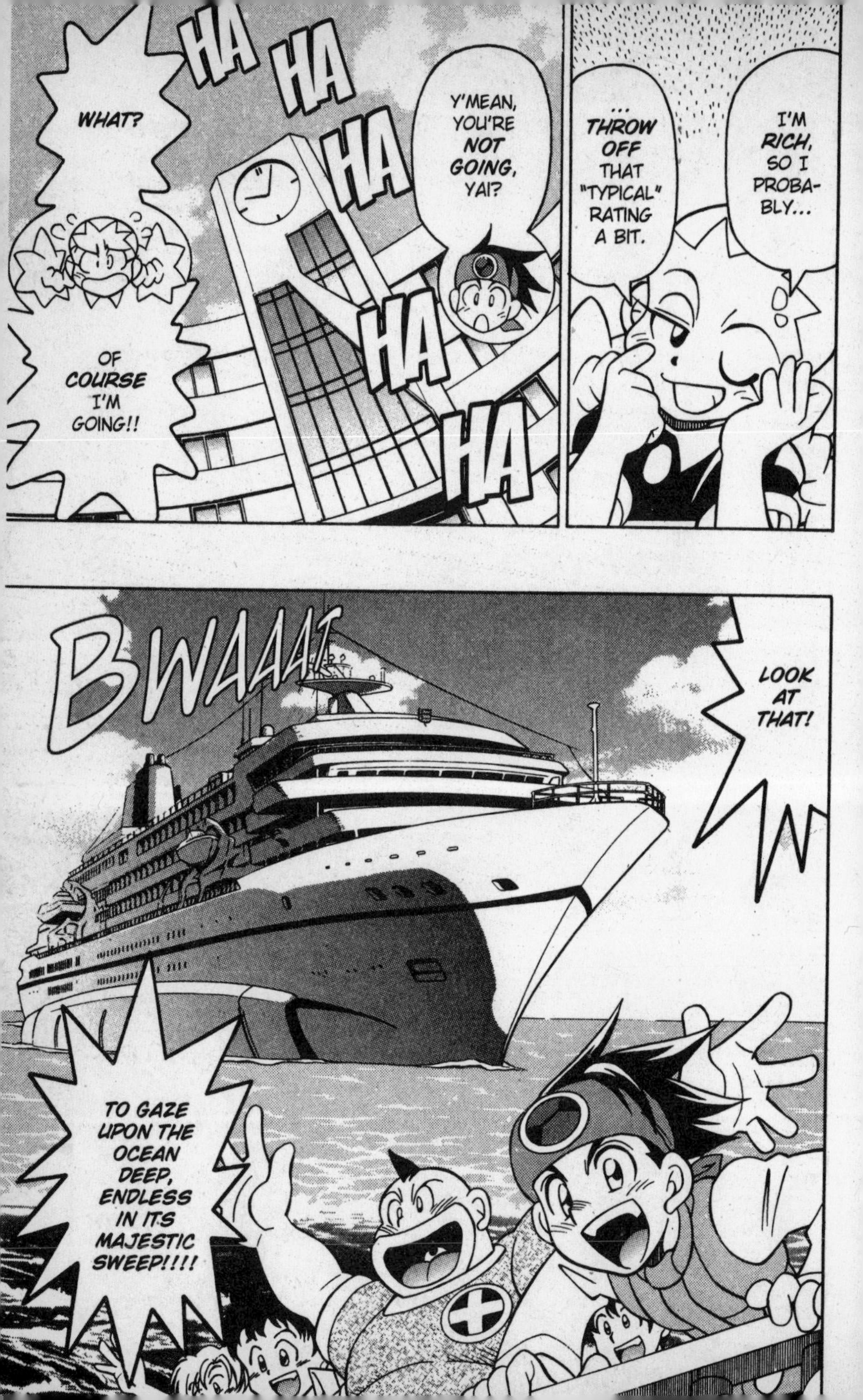
I'M RICH, SO I PROBABLY...
... THROW OFF THAT "TYPICAL" RATING A BIT.
Y'MEAN, YOU'RE NOT GOING, YAI?
HA HA HA HA HA
WHAT?
OF COURSE I'M GOING!!
LOOK AT THAT!
BWAAAT
TO GAZE UPON THE OCEAN DEEP, ENDLESS IN ITS MAJESTIC SWEEP!!!!

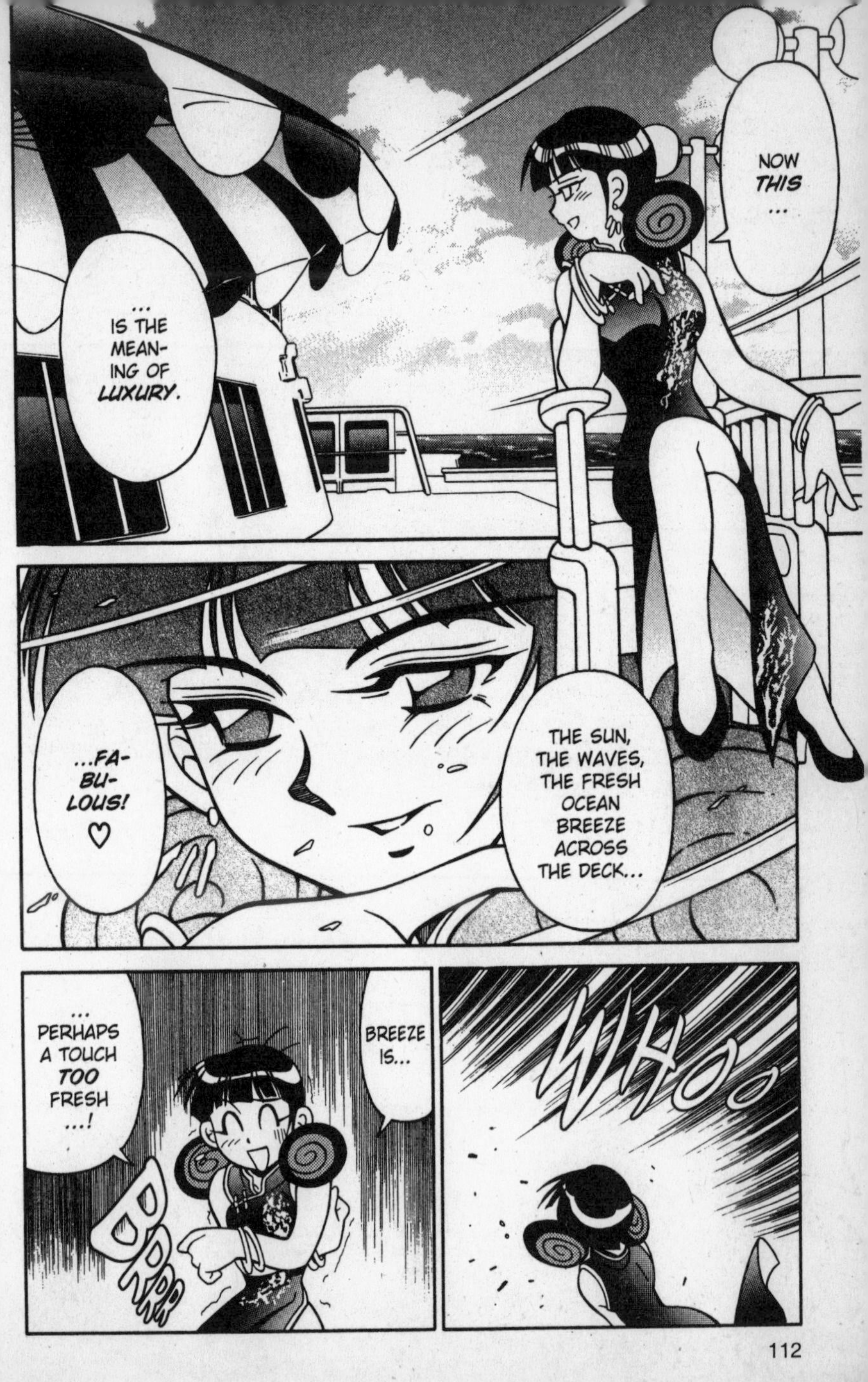
NOW THIS ...
... IS THE MEANING OF LUXURY.
THE SUN, THE WAVES, THE FRESH OCEAN BREEZE ACROSS THE DECK...
...FA-BU-LOUS! ♡
WHOO
BREEZE IS...
... PERHAPS A TOUCH TOO FRESH ...!
BRRRR

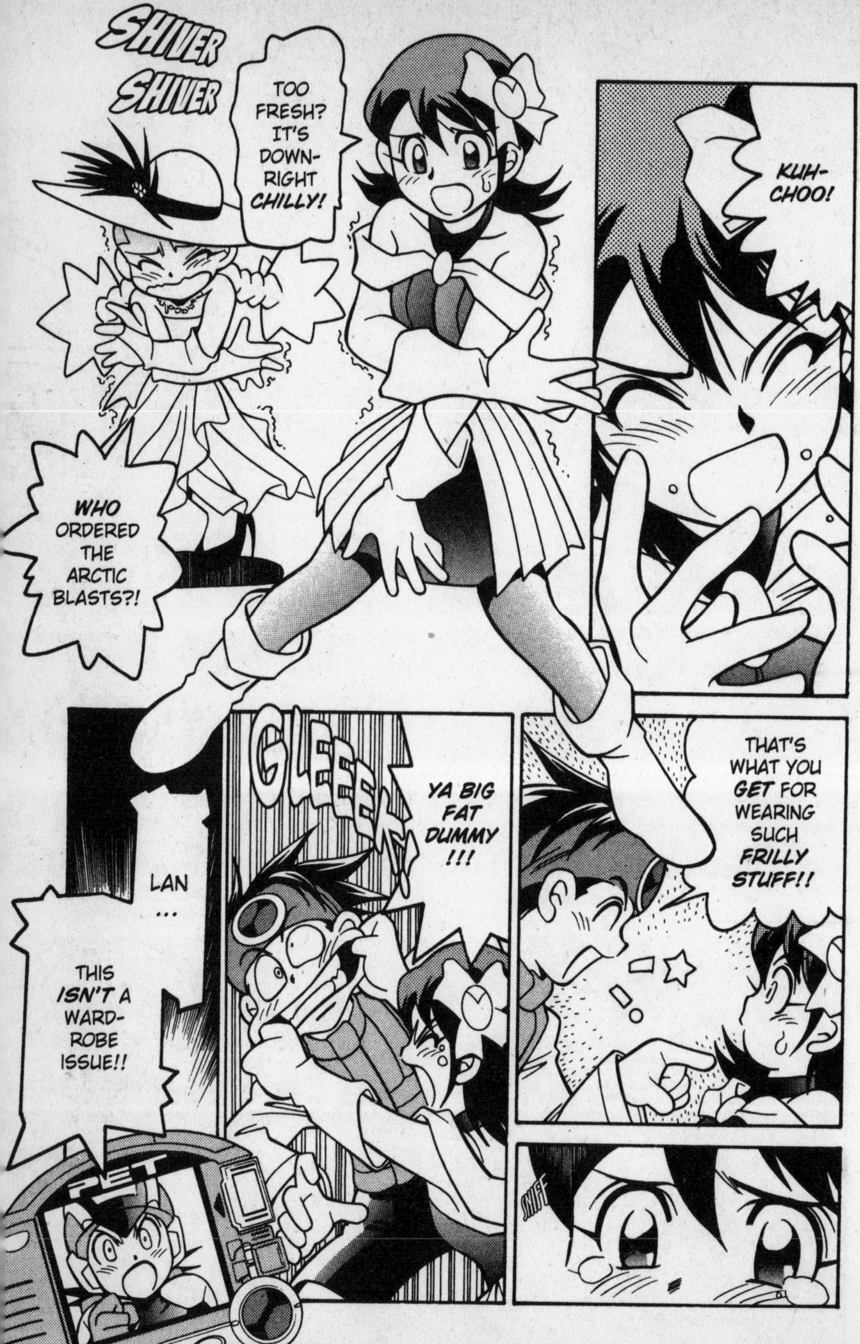
KUH-CHOO!
TOO FRESH? IT'S DOWN-RIGHT CHILLY!
SHIVER SHIVER
WHO ORDERED THE ARCTIC BLASTS?!
THAT'S WHAT YOU GET FOR WEARING SUCH FRILLY STUFF!!
SNIFF
GLEEEK
YA BIG FAT DUMMY!!!
LAN...
THIS ISN'T A WARD-ROBE ISSUE!!
PET

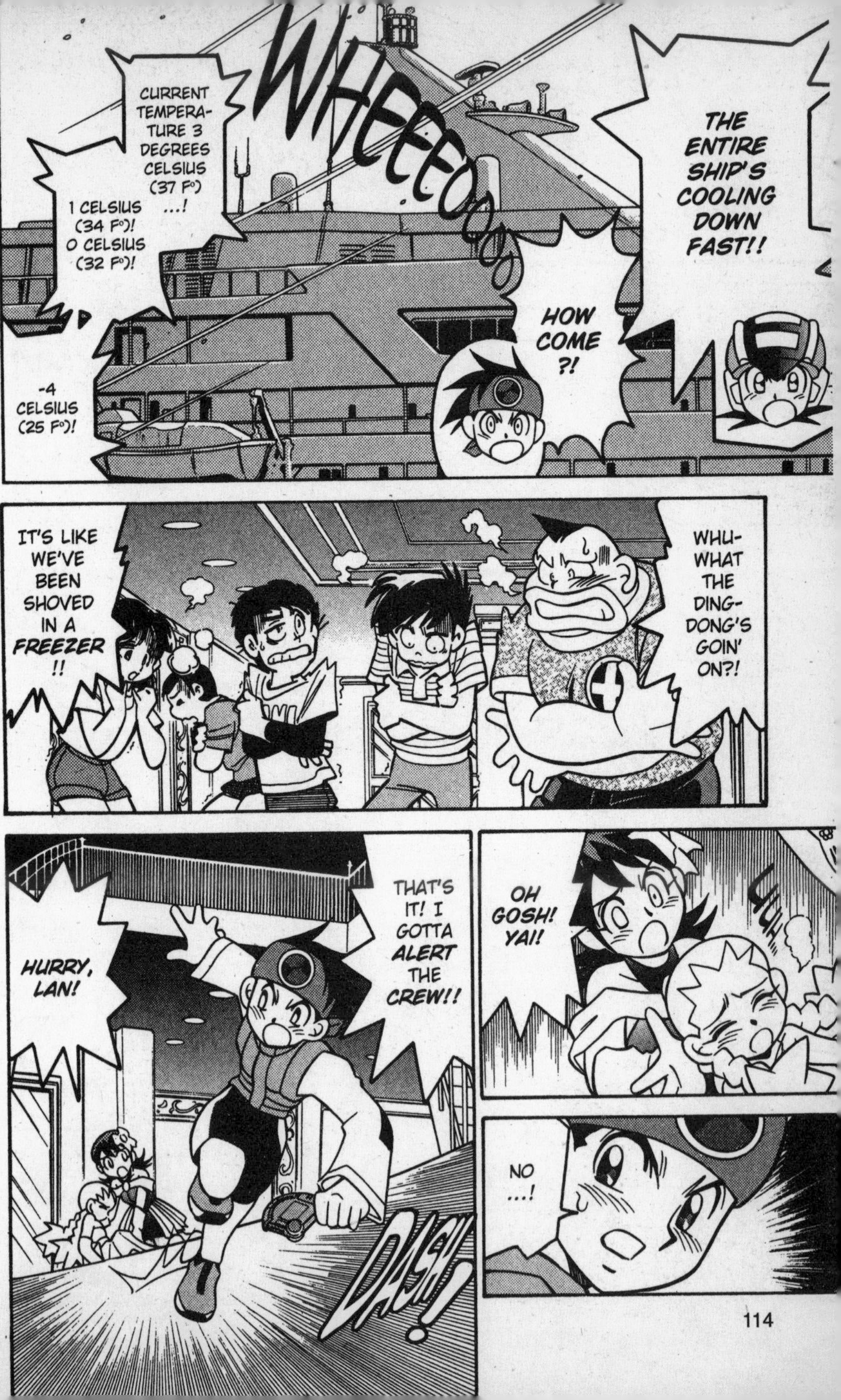
THE ENTIRE SHIP'S COOLING DOWN FAST!!
HOW COME?!
WHEEEOOOOO
CURRENT TEMPERATURE 3 DEGREES CELSIUS (37 F°) ...!
1 CELSIUS (34 F°)! 0 CELSIUS (32 F°)!
-4 CELSIUS (25 F°)!
WHU-WHAT THE DING-DONG'S GOIN' ON?!
IT'S LIKE WE'VE BEEN SHOVED IN A FREEZER!!
OH GOSH! YAI!
UGH
NO ...!
THAT'S IT! I GOTTA ALERT THE CREW!!
HURRY, LAN!
DASH!

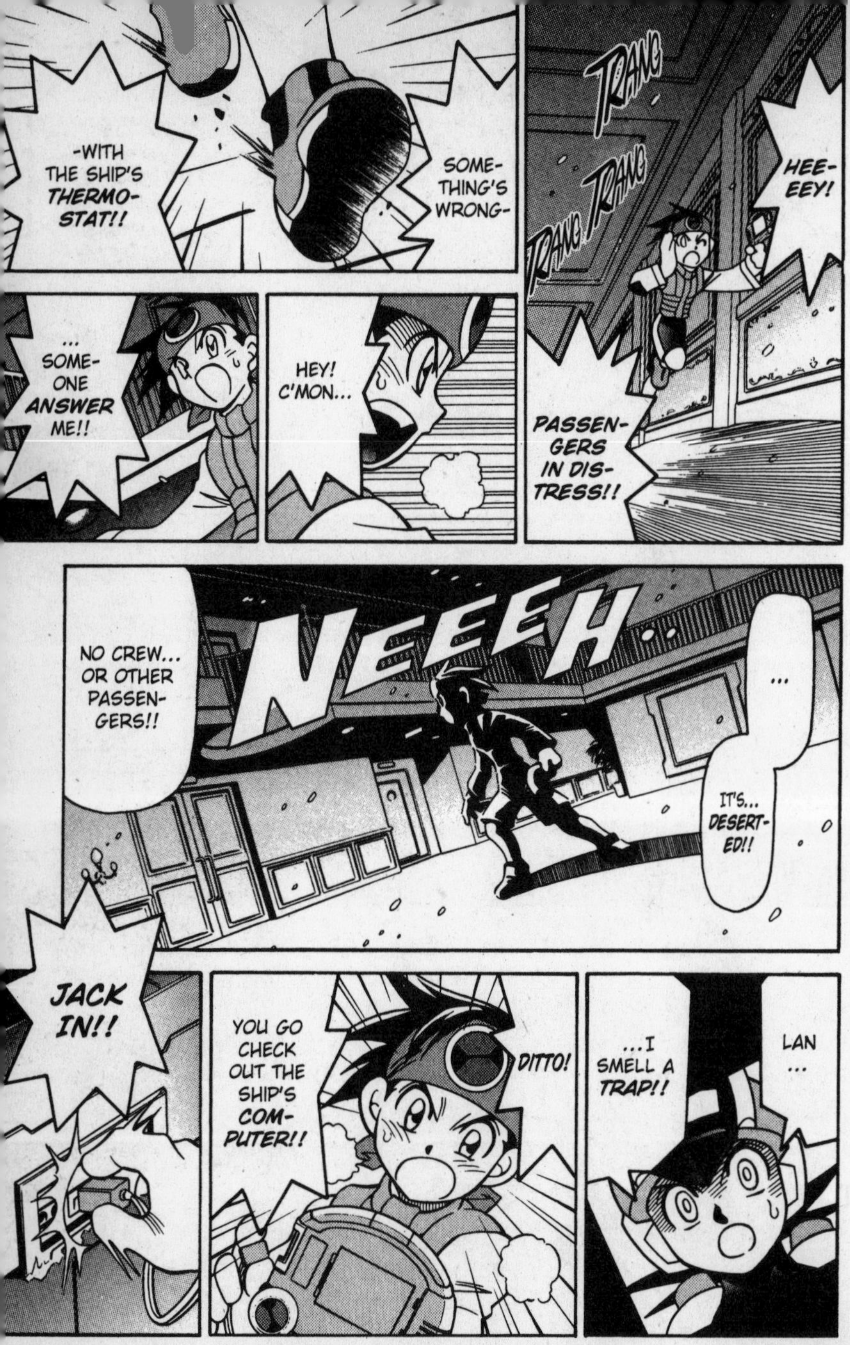
TRANG
TRANG TRANG
HEE-EEY!
PASSEN-GERS IN DIS-TRESS!!
SOME-THING'S WRONG-
-WITH THE SHIP'S THERMO-STAT!!
HEY! C'MON...
... SOME-ONE ANSWER ME!!
...
IT'S... DESERT-ED!!
NEEEH
NO CREW... OR OTHER PASSEN-GERS!!
LAN ...
...I SMELL A TRAP!!
DITTO!
YOU GO CHECK OUT THE SHIP'S COM-PUTER!!
JACK IN!!

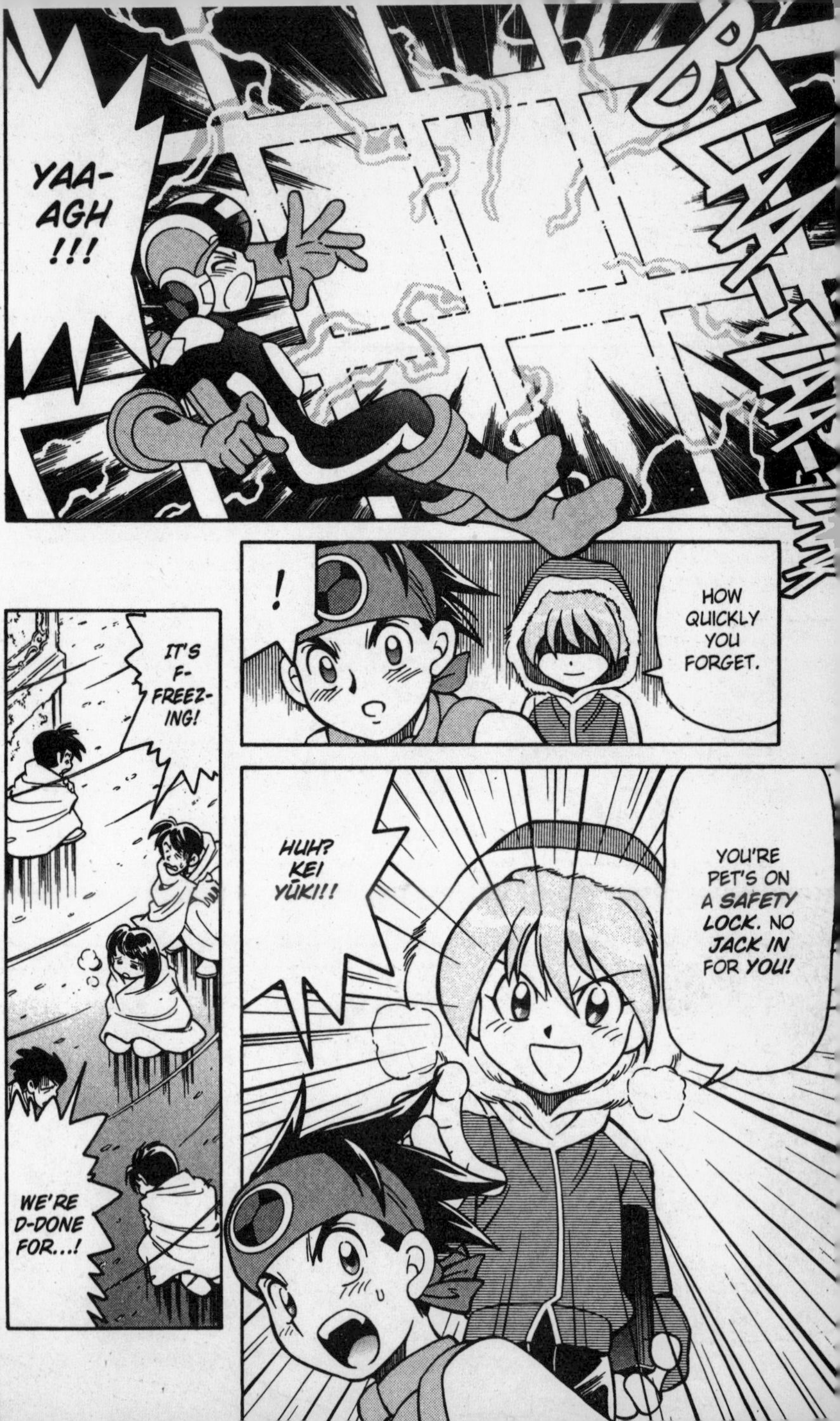
YAAA-AGH!!!
!
HOW QUICKLY YOU FORGET.
YOU'RE PET'S ON A SAFETY LOCK. NO JACK IN FOR YOU!
HUH? KEI YŪKI!!
IT'S F-FREEZ-ING!
WE'RE D-DONE FOR...!

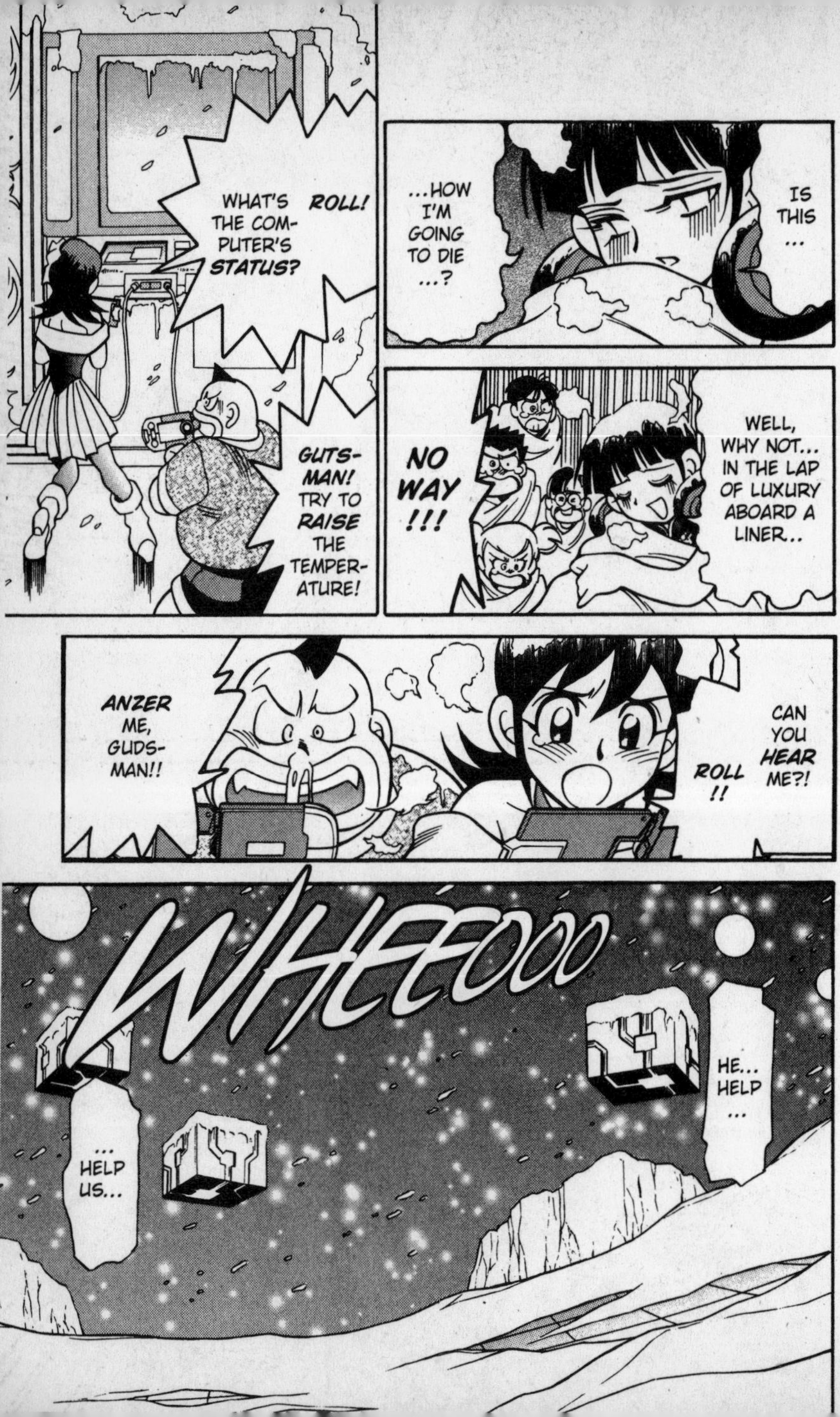
IS THIS ...
...HOW I'M GOING TO DIE ...?
WELL, WHY NOT... IN THE LAP OF LUXURY ABOARD A LINER...
NO WAY !!!
ROLL!
WHAT'S THE COM-PUTER'S STATUS?
GUTS-MAN! TRY TO RAISE THE TEMPER-ATURE!
CAN YOU HEAR ME?!
ROLL !!
ANZER ME, GUDS-MAN!!
WHEEOOO
HE... HELP ...
... HELP US...

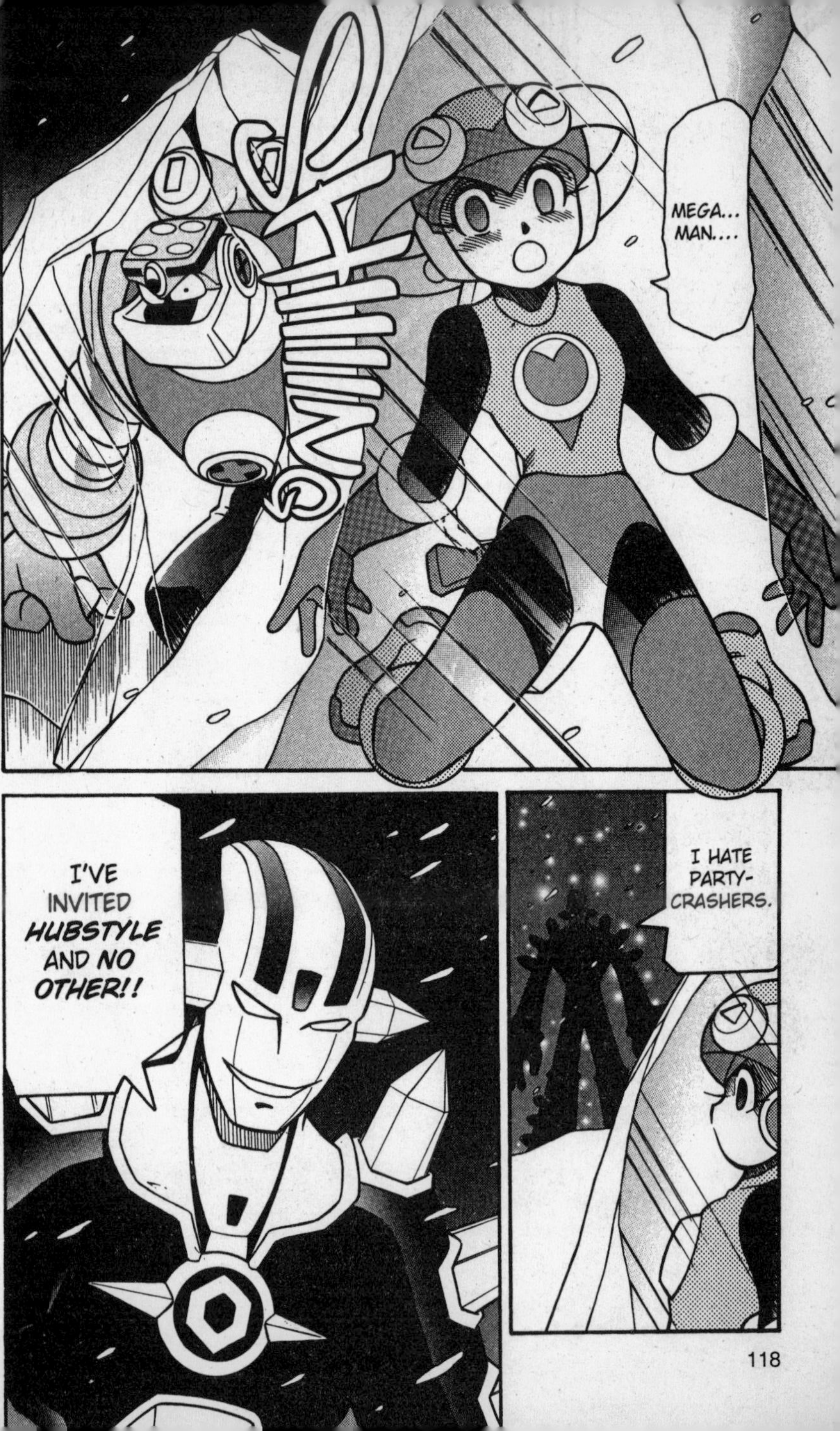
MEGA... MAN....
I HATE PARTY-CRASHERS.
I'VE INVITED ***HUBSTYLE*** AND ***NO OTHER!!***

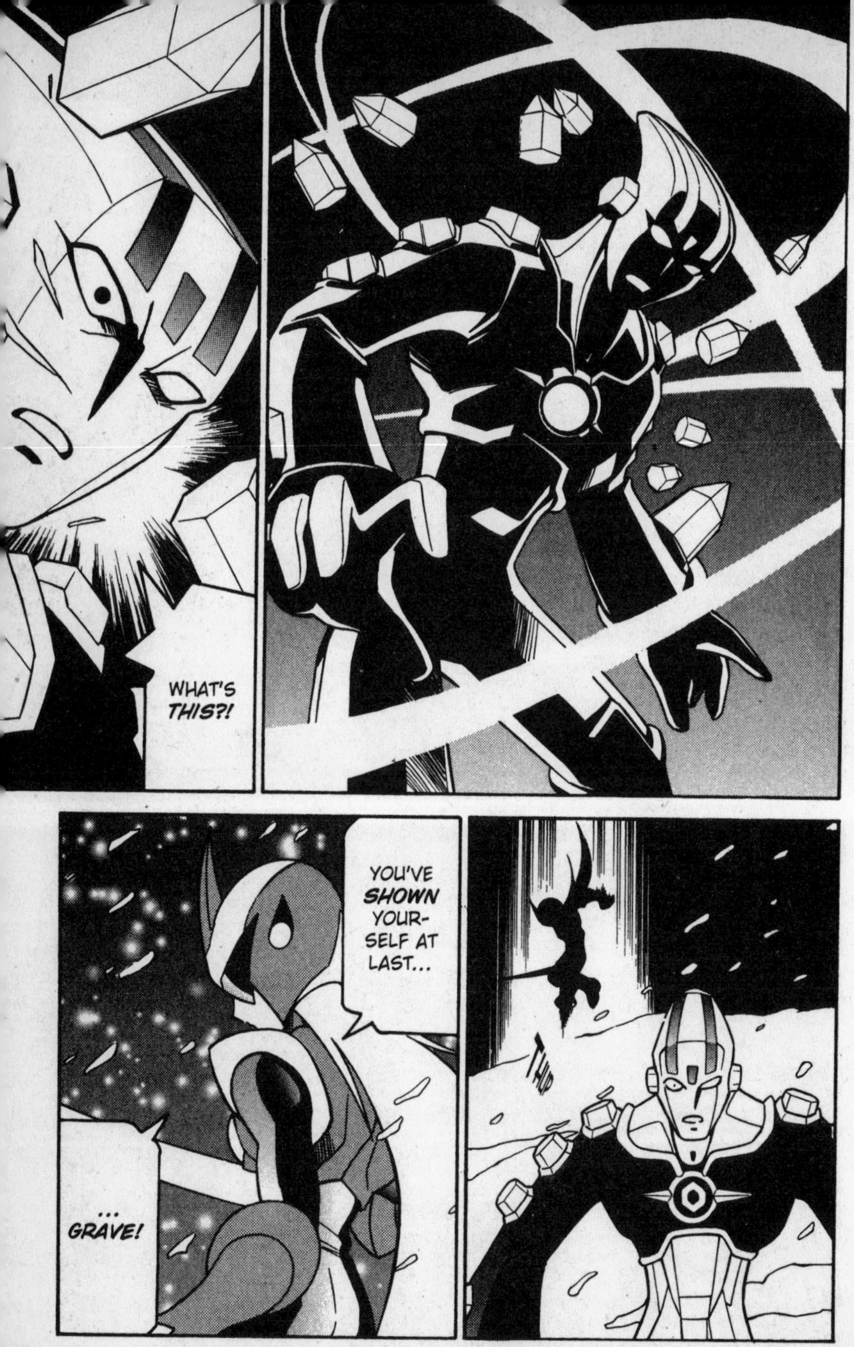
WHAT'S THIS?!
THUD
YOU'VE SHOWN YOUR-SELF AT LAST...
...GRAVE!

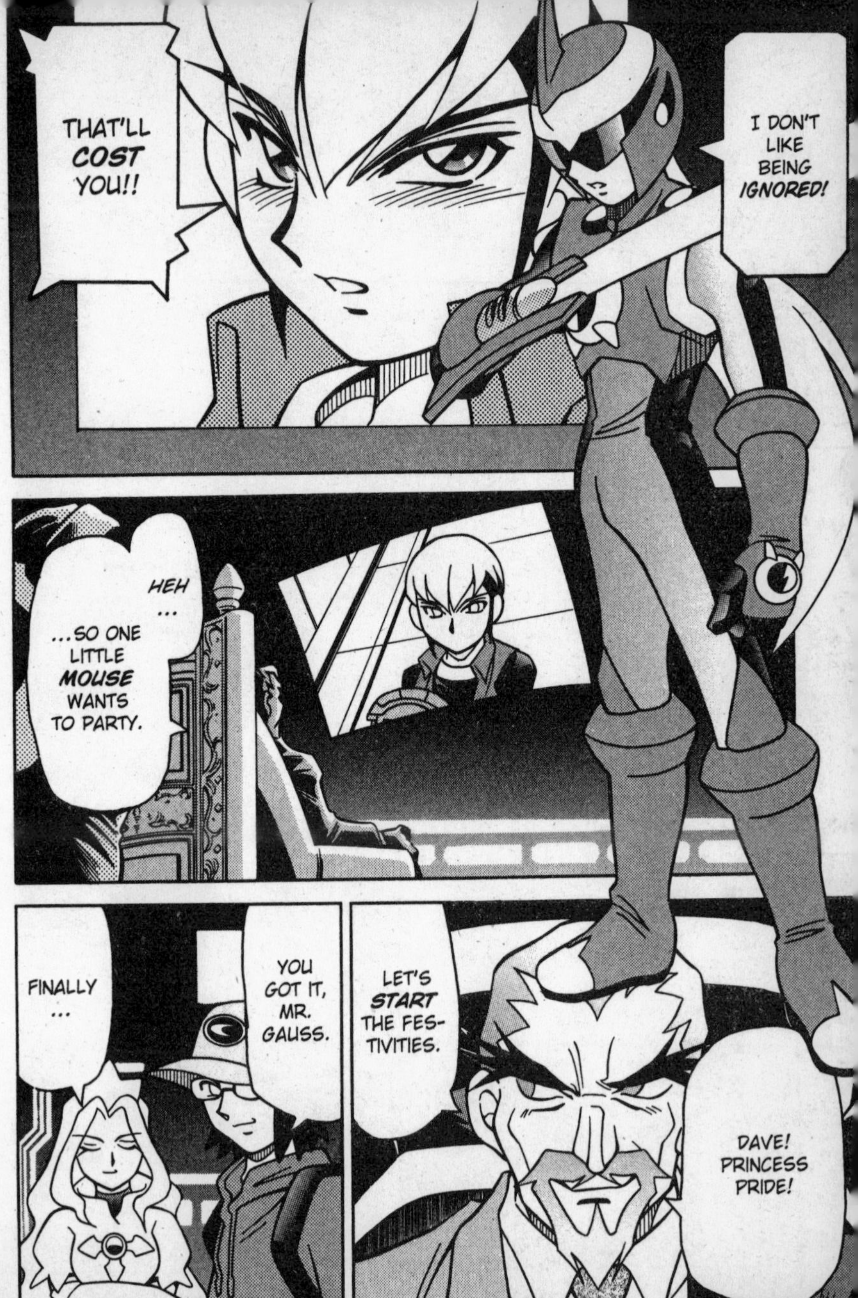
I DON'T LIKE BEING IGNORED!
THAT'LL COST YOU!!
HEH ...
...SO ONE LITTLE MOUSE WANTS TO PARTY.
LET'S START THE FES-TIVITIES.
DAVE! PRINCESS PRIDE!
YOU GOT IT, MR. GAUSS.
FINALLY ...

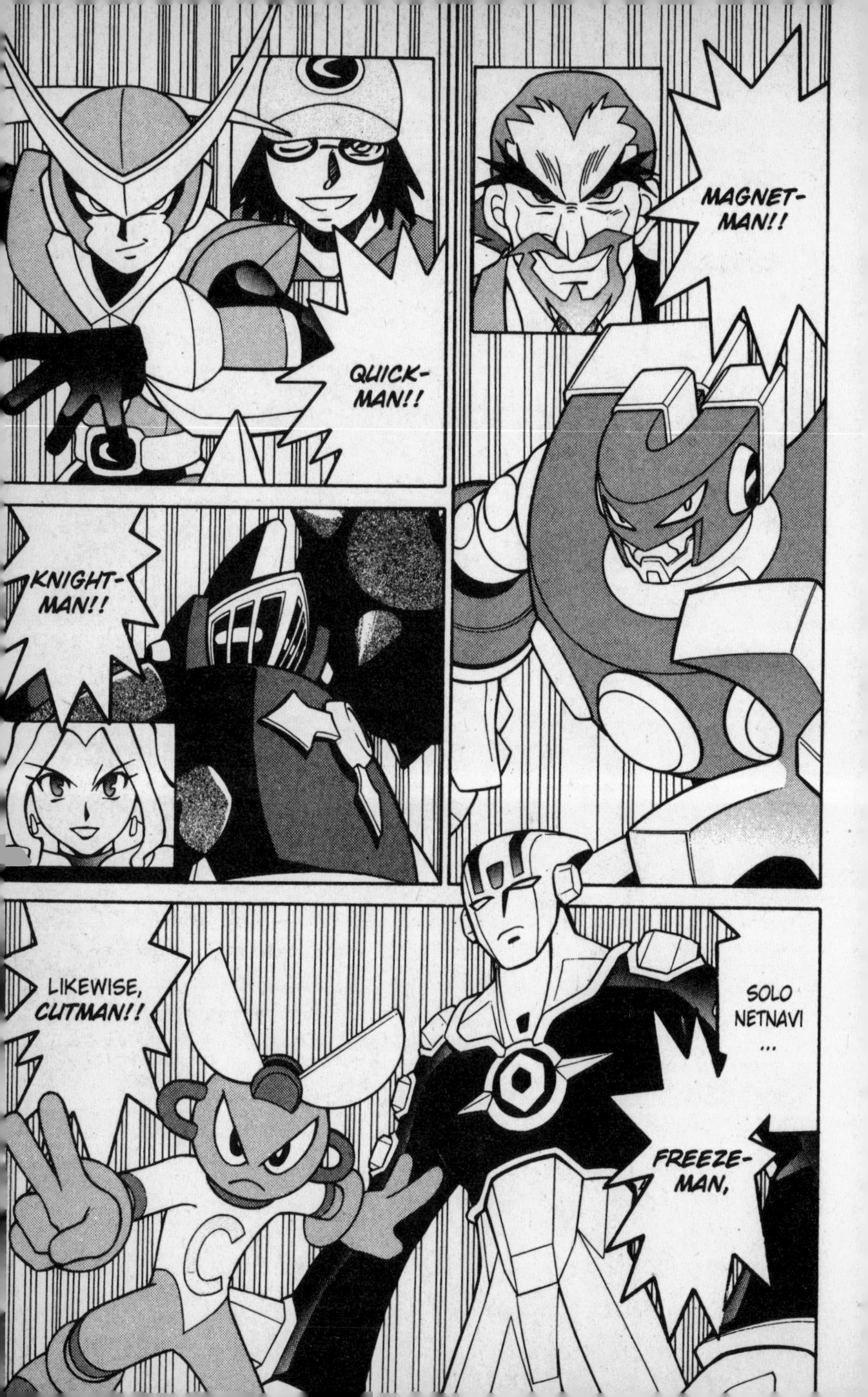
MAGNET-MAN!!
QUICK-MAN!!
KNIGHT-MAN!!
SOLO NETNAVI ...
FREEZE-MAN,
LIKEWISE, CUTMAN!!

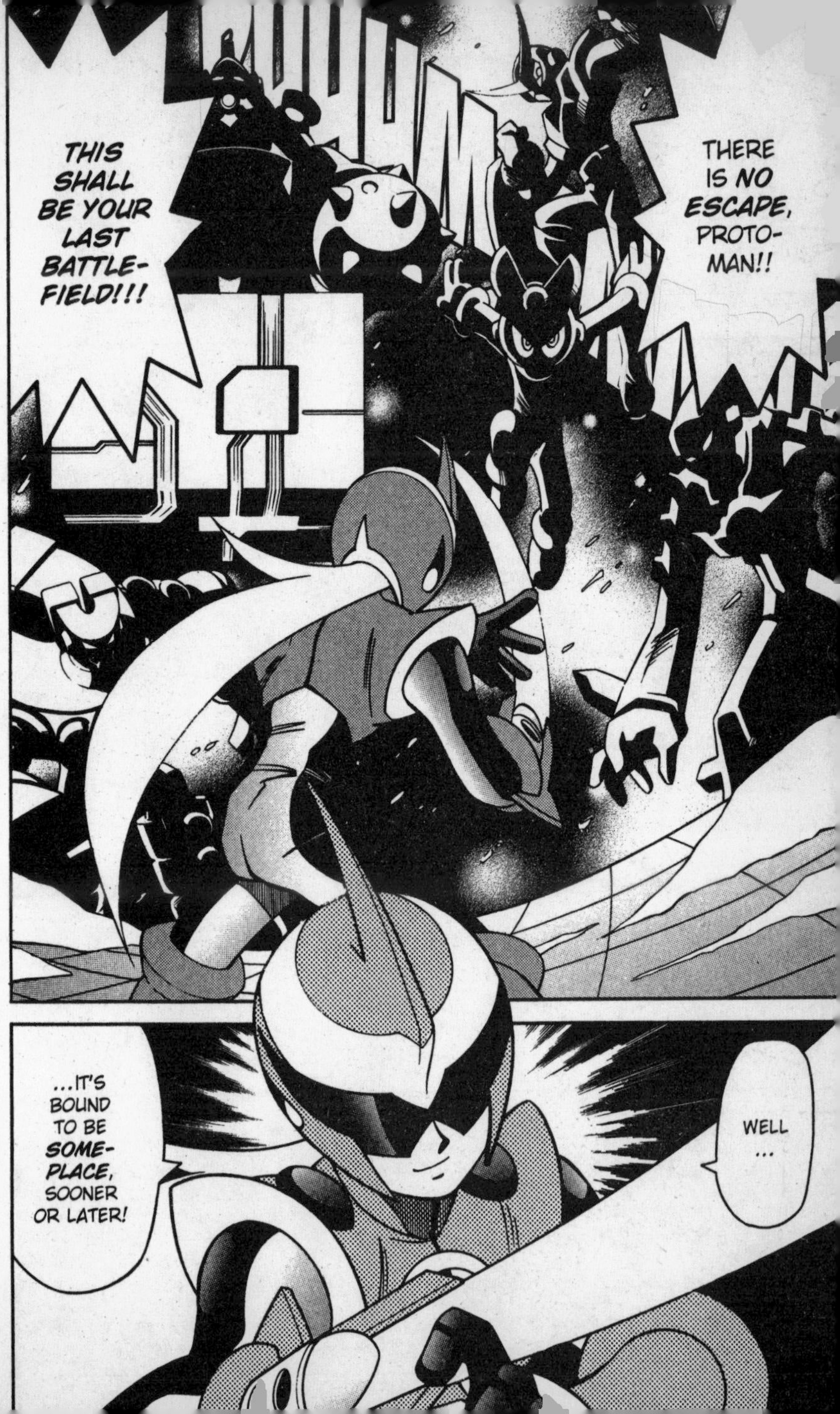
THERE IS NO ESCAPE, PROTO-MAN!!
THIS SHALL BE YOUR LAST BATTLE-FIELD!!!
WELL...
...IT'S BOUND TO BE SOME-PLACE, SOONER OR LATER!

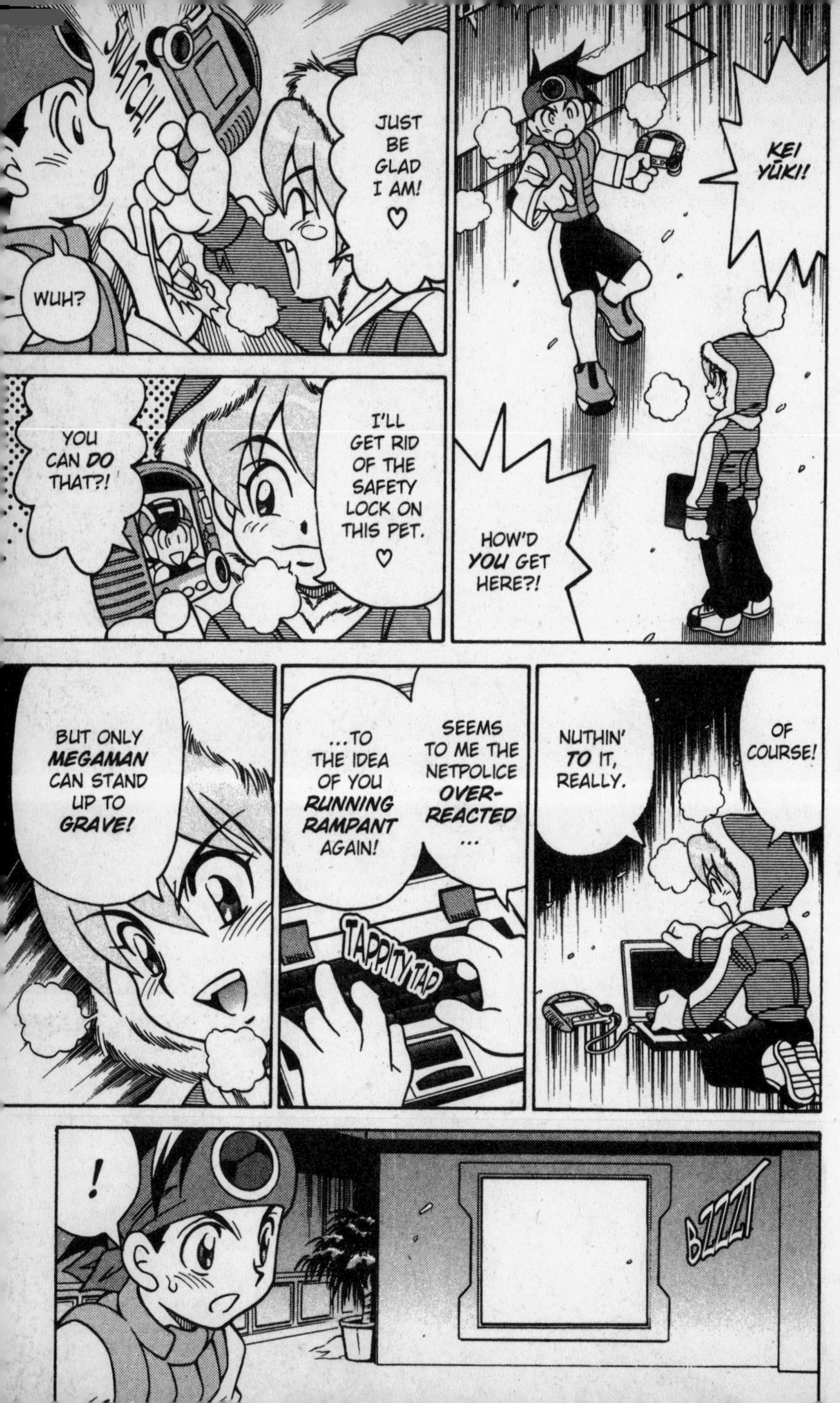
KEI YŪKI!
HOW'D YOU GET HERE?!
JUST BE GLAD I AM! ♡
SNATCH!!
WUH?
I'LL GET RID OF THE SAFETY LOCK ON THIS PET. ♡
YOU CAN DO THAT?!
OF COURSE!
NUTHIN' TO IT, REALLY.
SEEMS TO ME THE NETPOLICE OVER-REACTED...
...TO THE IDEA OF YOU RUNNING RAMPANT AGAIN!
TAPPITY TAP
BUT ONLY MEGAMAN CAN STAND UP TO GRAVE!
BZZZT
!

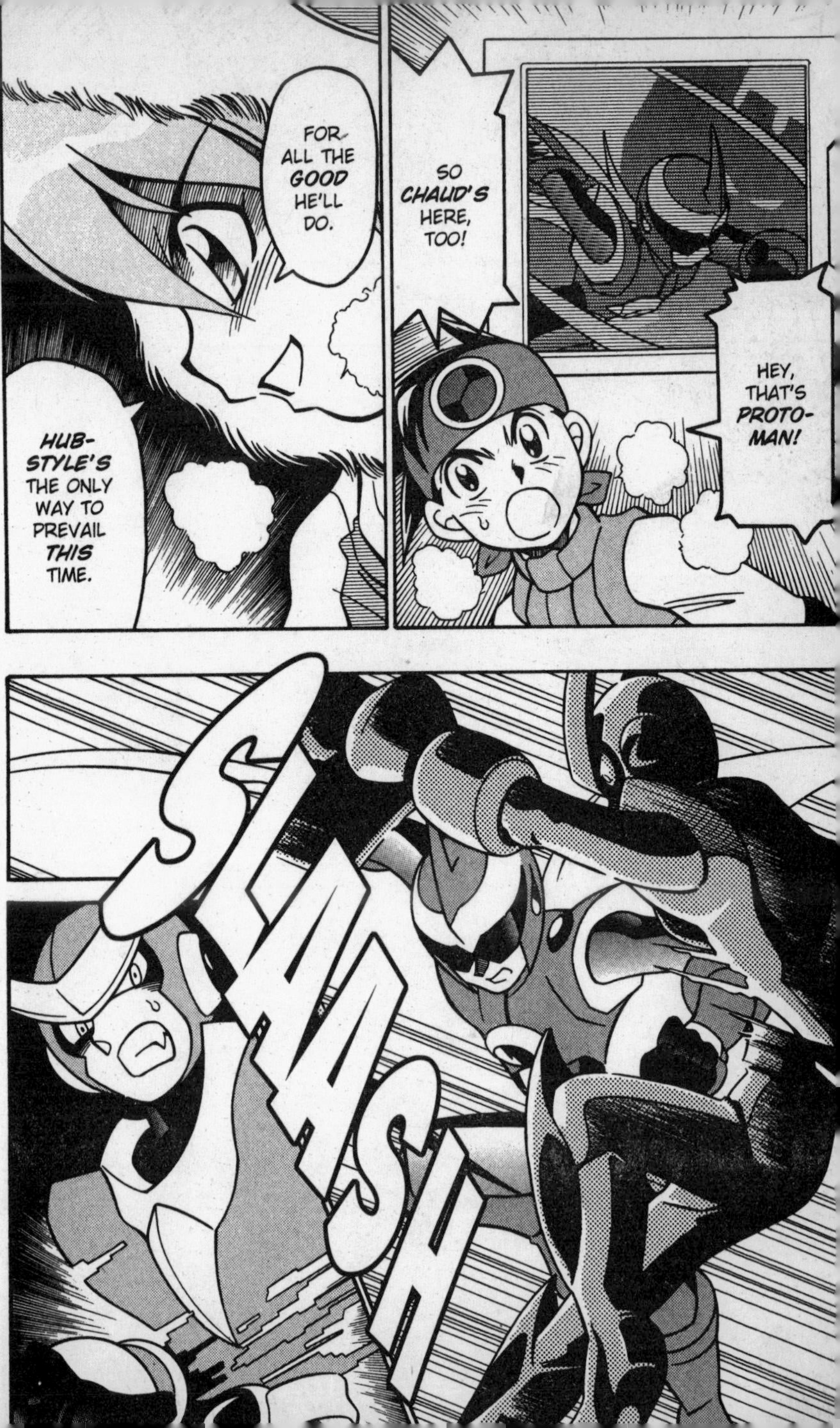
HEY, THAT'S PROTO-MAN!
SO CHAUD'S HERE, TOO!
FOR ALL THE GOOD HE'LL DO.
HUB-STYLE'S THE ONLY WAY TO PREVAIL THIS TIME.
SLASH

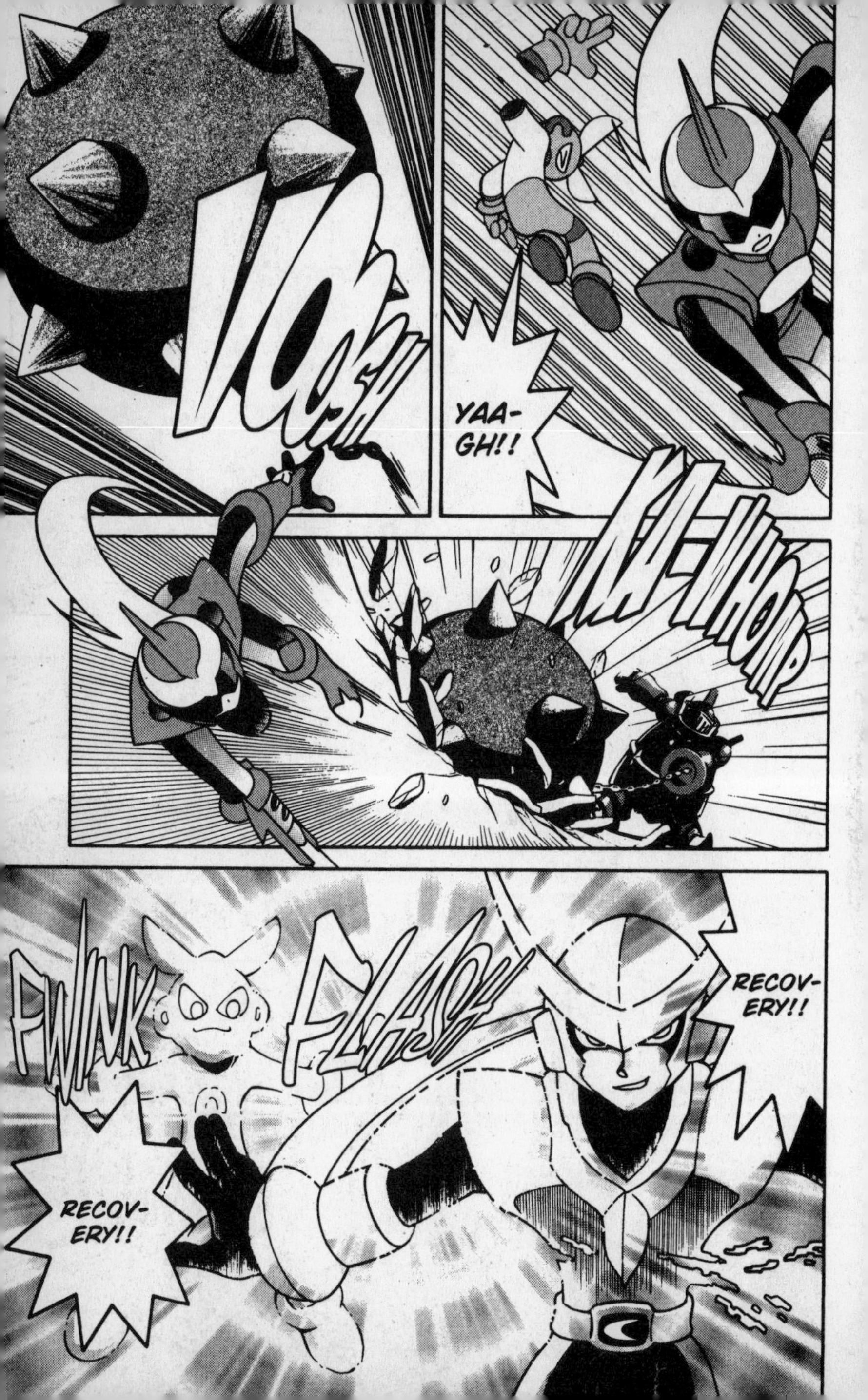
YAAG-
GH!!
KA-WHOMP
RECOV-
ERY!!
FLASH
FWINK
RECOV-
ERY!!

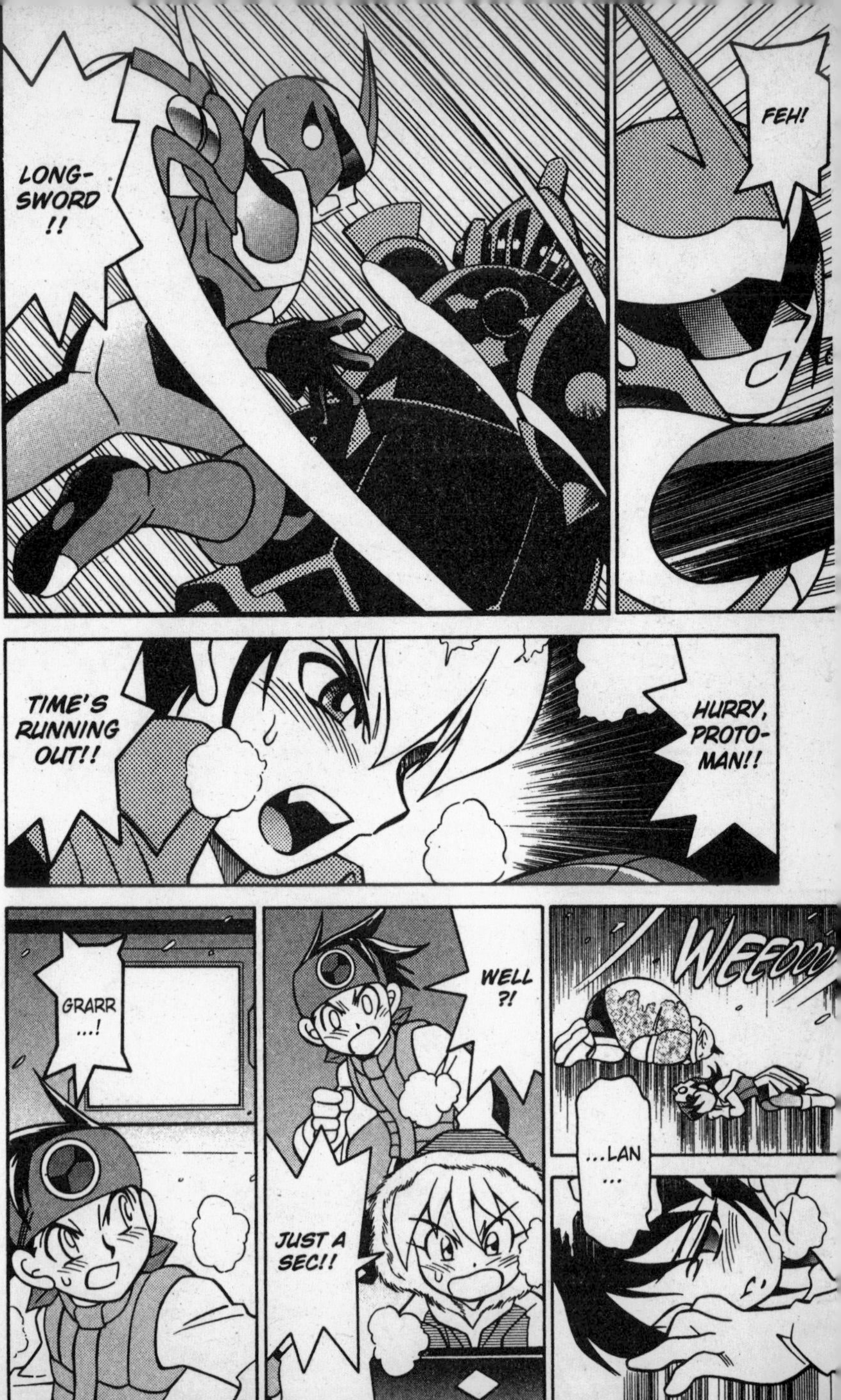
FEH!
LONG-SWORD!!
HURRY, PROTO-MAN!!
TIME'S RUNNING OUT!!
WEEOOO
...LAN...
WELL ?!
JUST A SEC!!
GRARR ...!

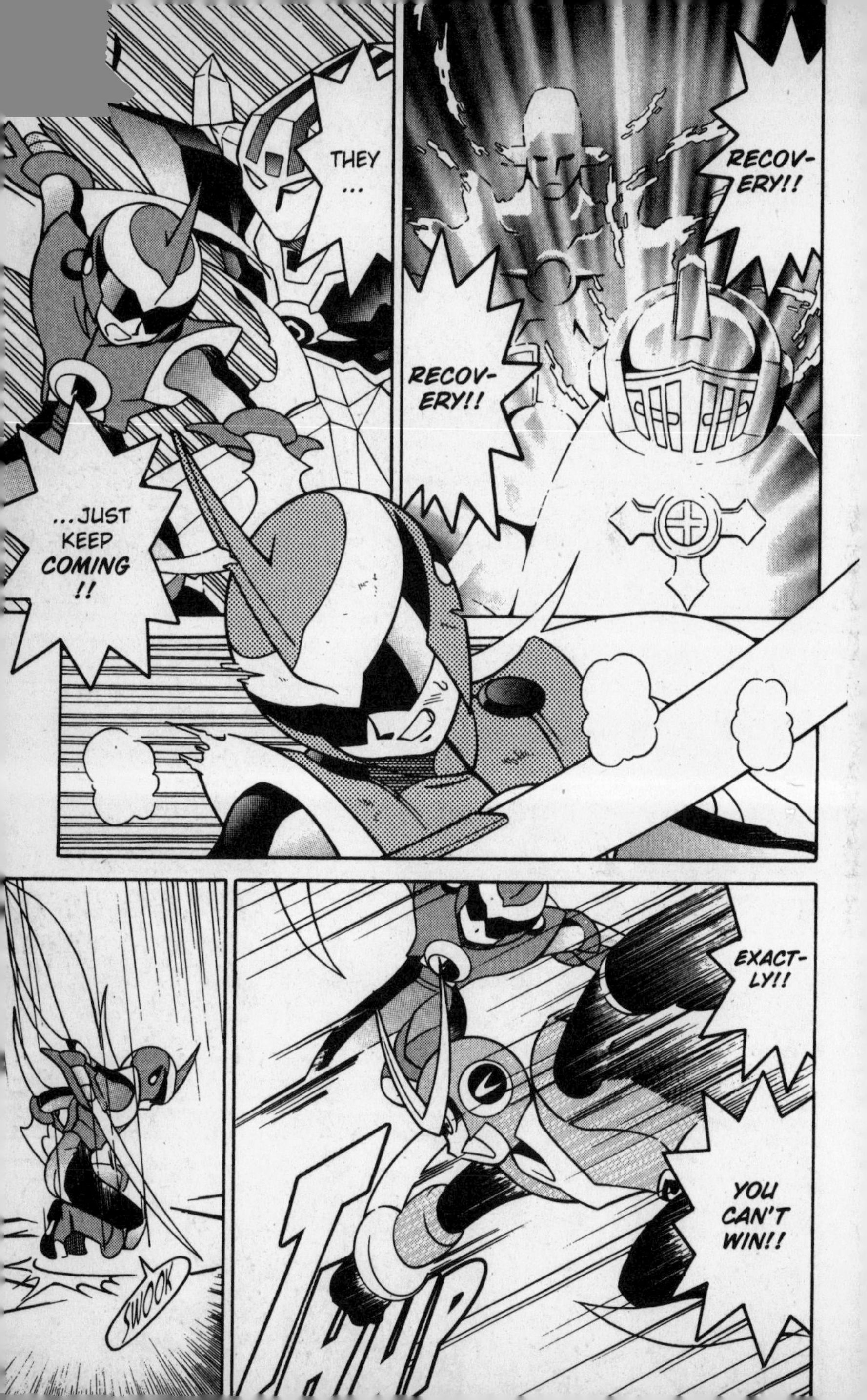
RECOV-ERY!!
RECOV-ERY!!
THEY ...
...JUST KEEP COMING !!
EXACT-LY!!
YOU CAN'T WIN!!
SWOOK

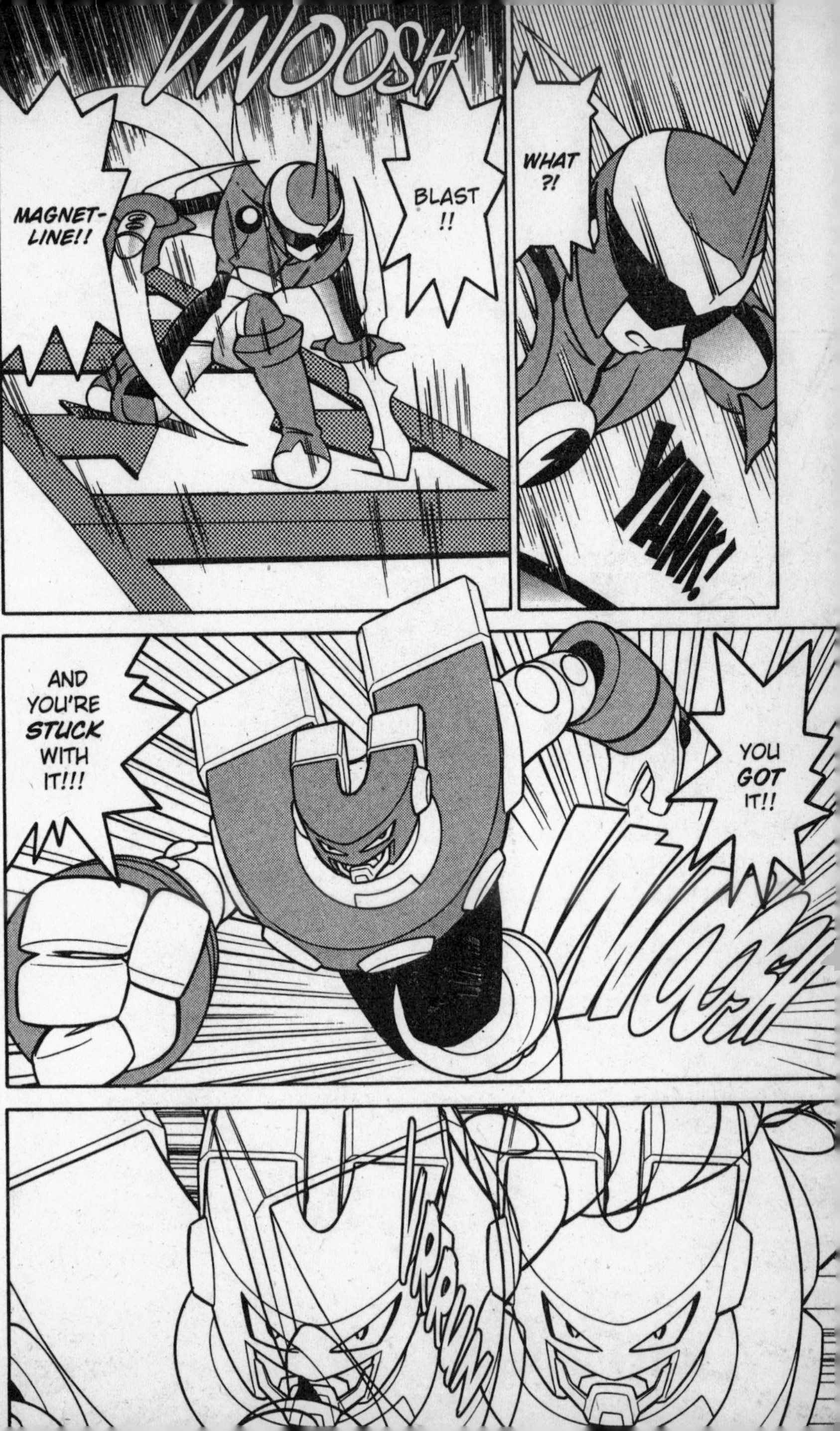
VWOOSH
MAGNET-LINE!!
BLAST !!
WHAT ?!
YANK!
AND YOU'RE STUCK WITH IT!!!
YOU GOT IT!!

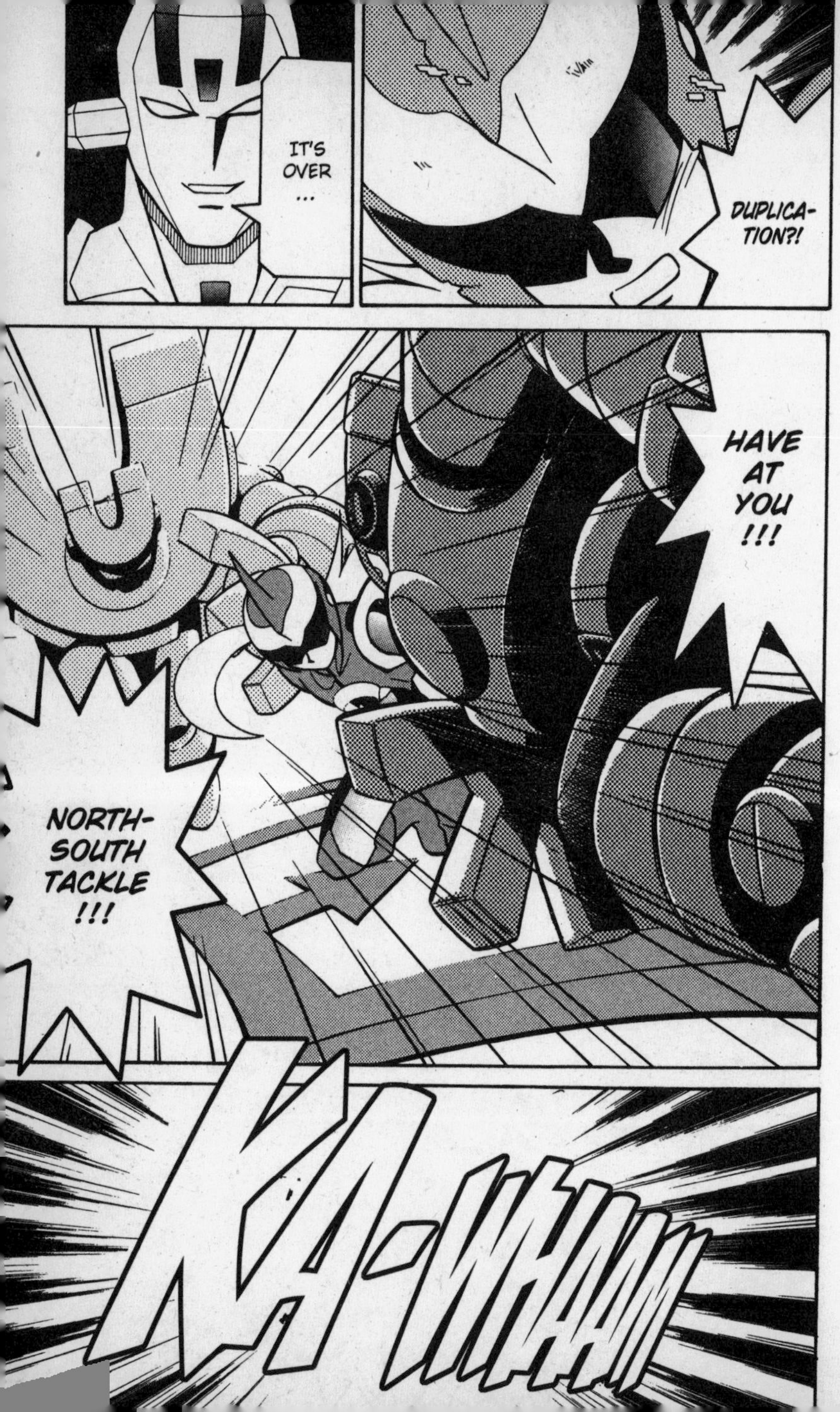
DUPLICA-TION?!
IT'S OVER ...
HAVE AT YOU !!!
NORTH-SOUTH TACKLE !!!
KA-WHAM

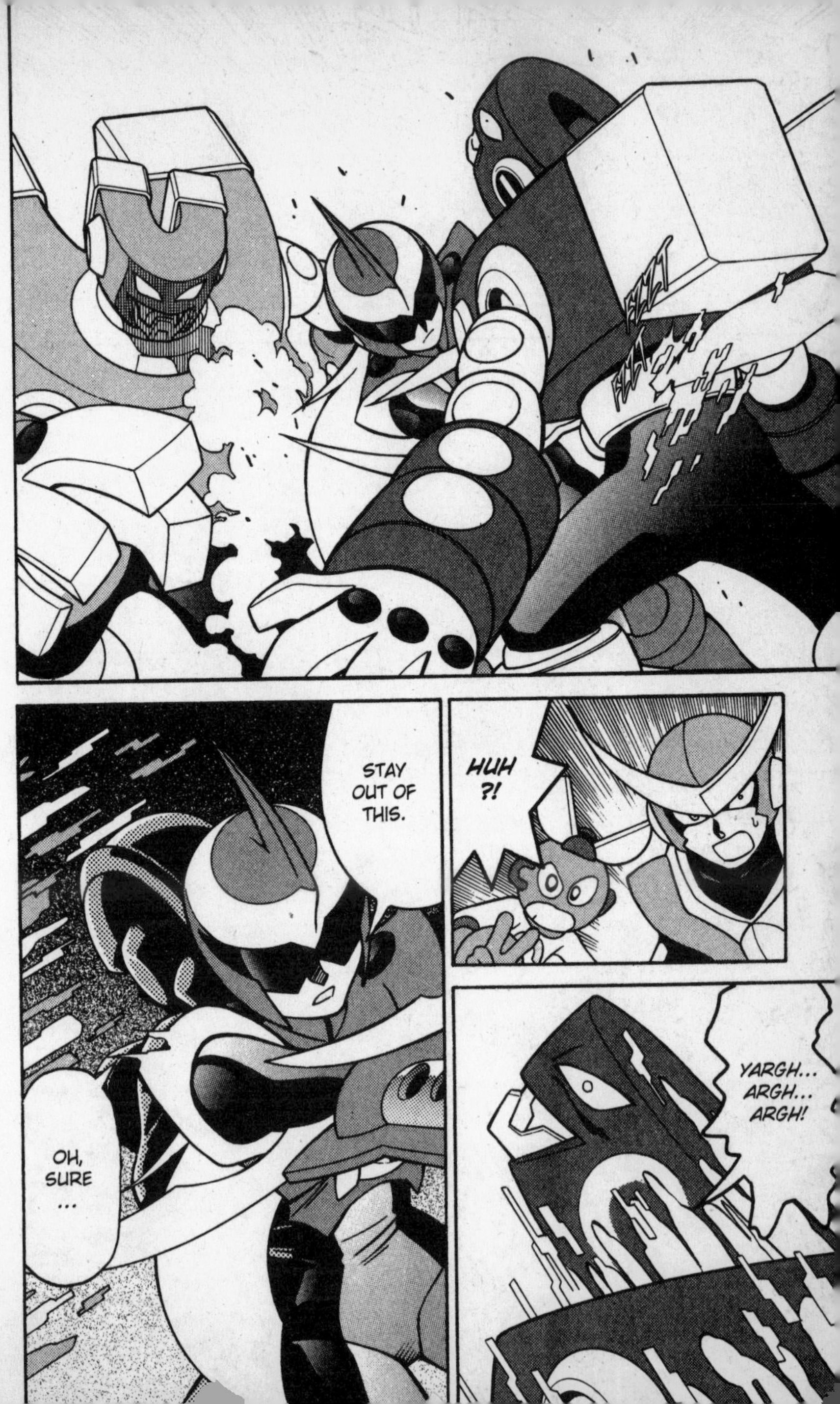
HUH ?!
YARGH... ARGH... ARGH!
STAY OUT OF THIS.
OH, SURE ...

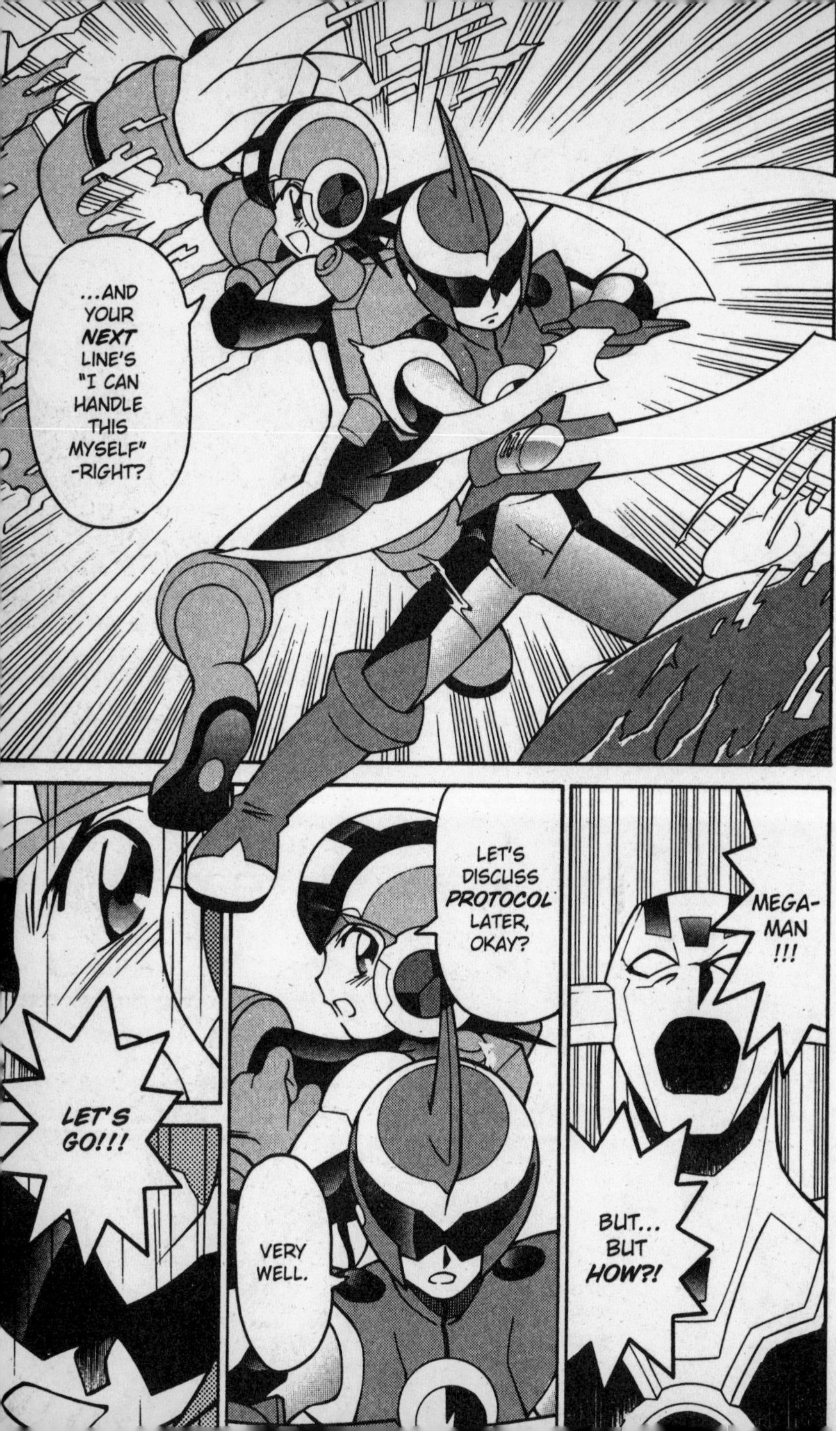
...AND YOUR ***NEXT*** LINE'S "I CAN HANDLE THIS MYSELF" -RIGHT?
MEGA-MAN!!!
BUT... BUT ***HOW?!***
LET'S DISCUSS ***PROTOCOL*** LATER, OKAY?
VERY WELL.
***LET'S GO!!!***

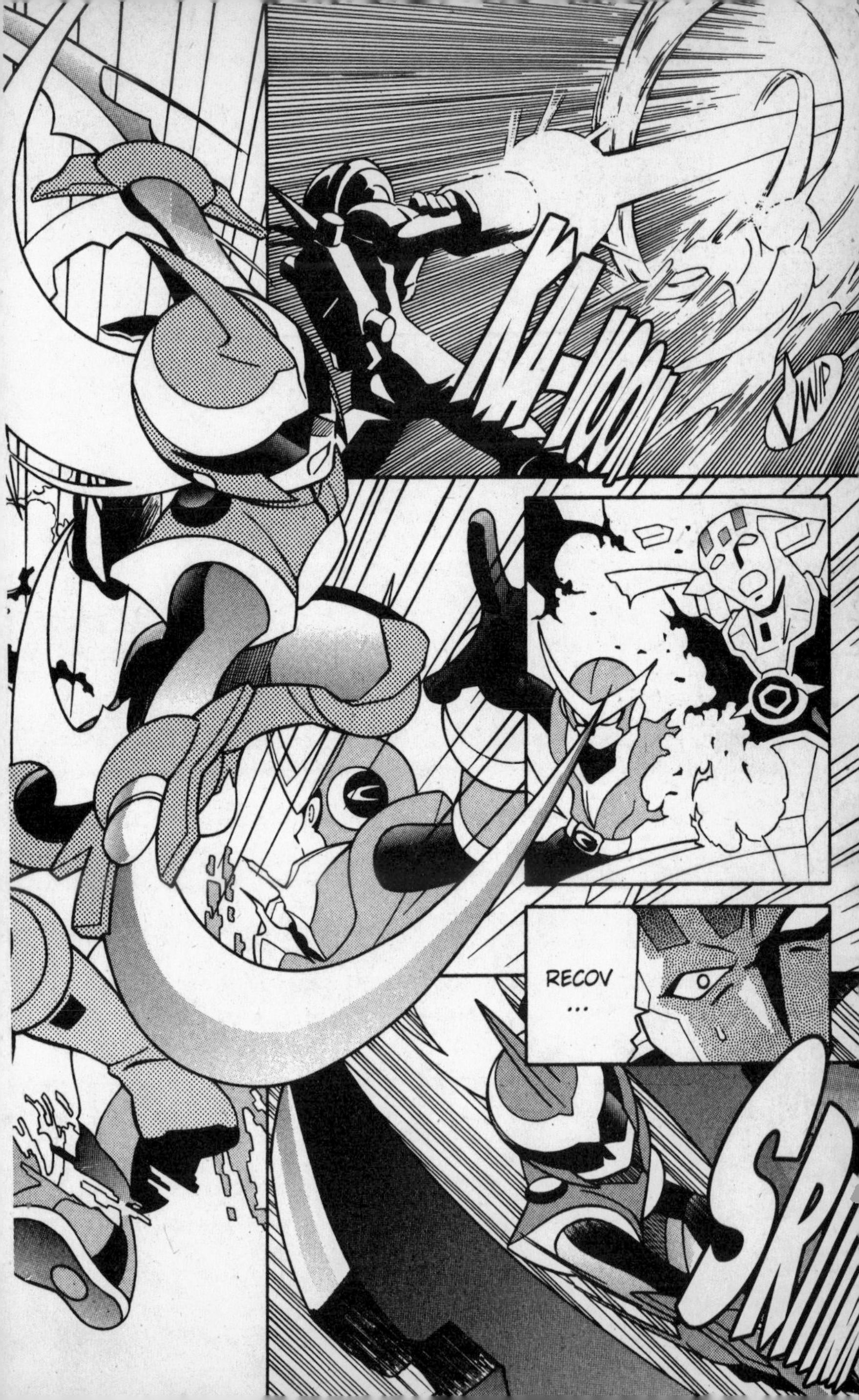
WHOOM
VWIP
RECOV ...

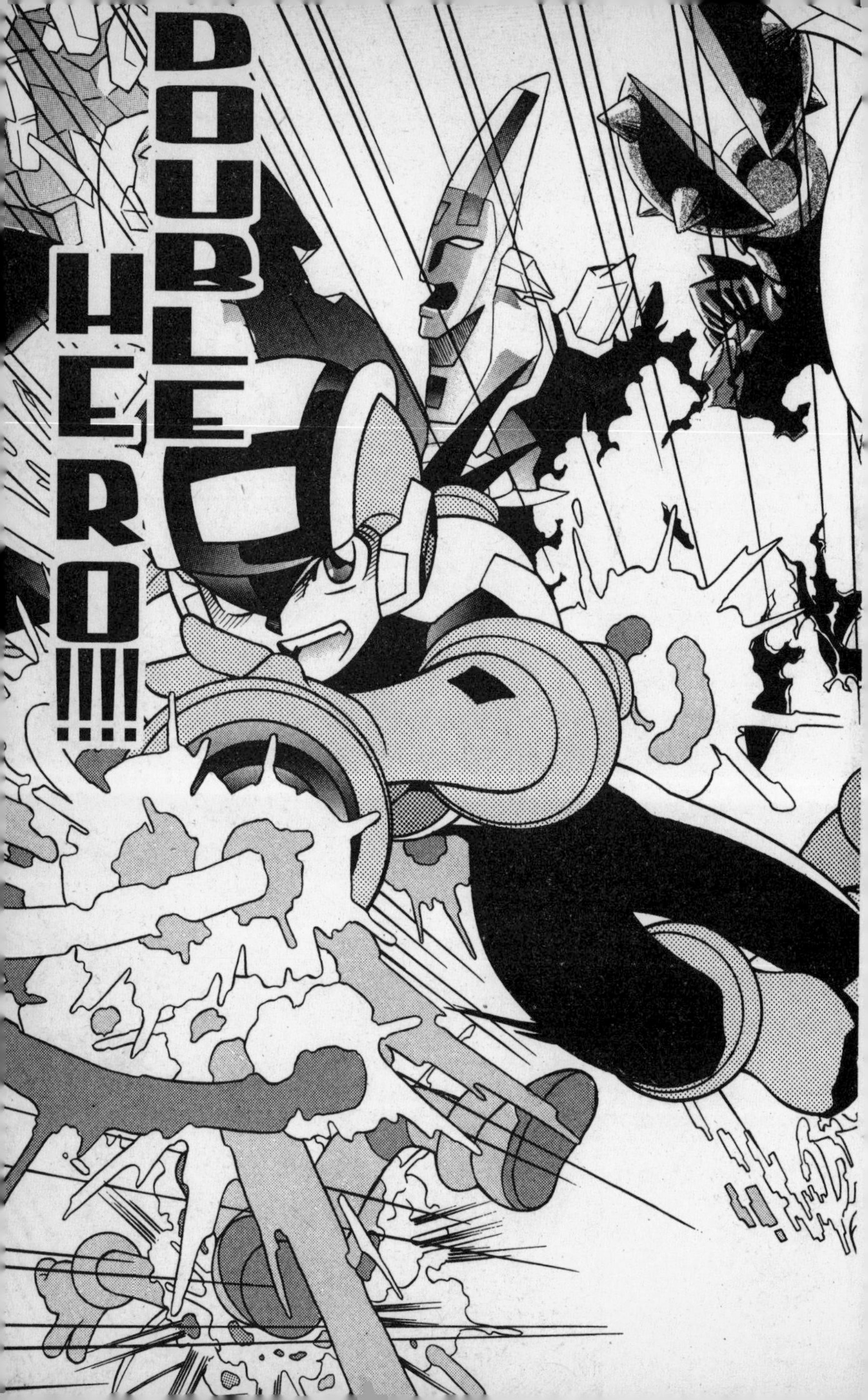
DOUBLE HERO!!!!

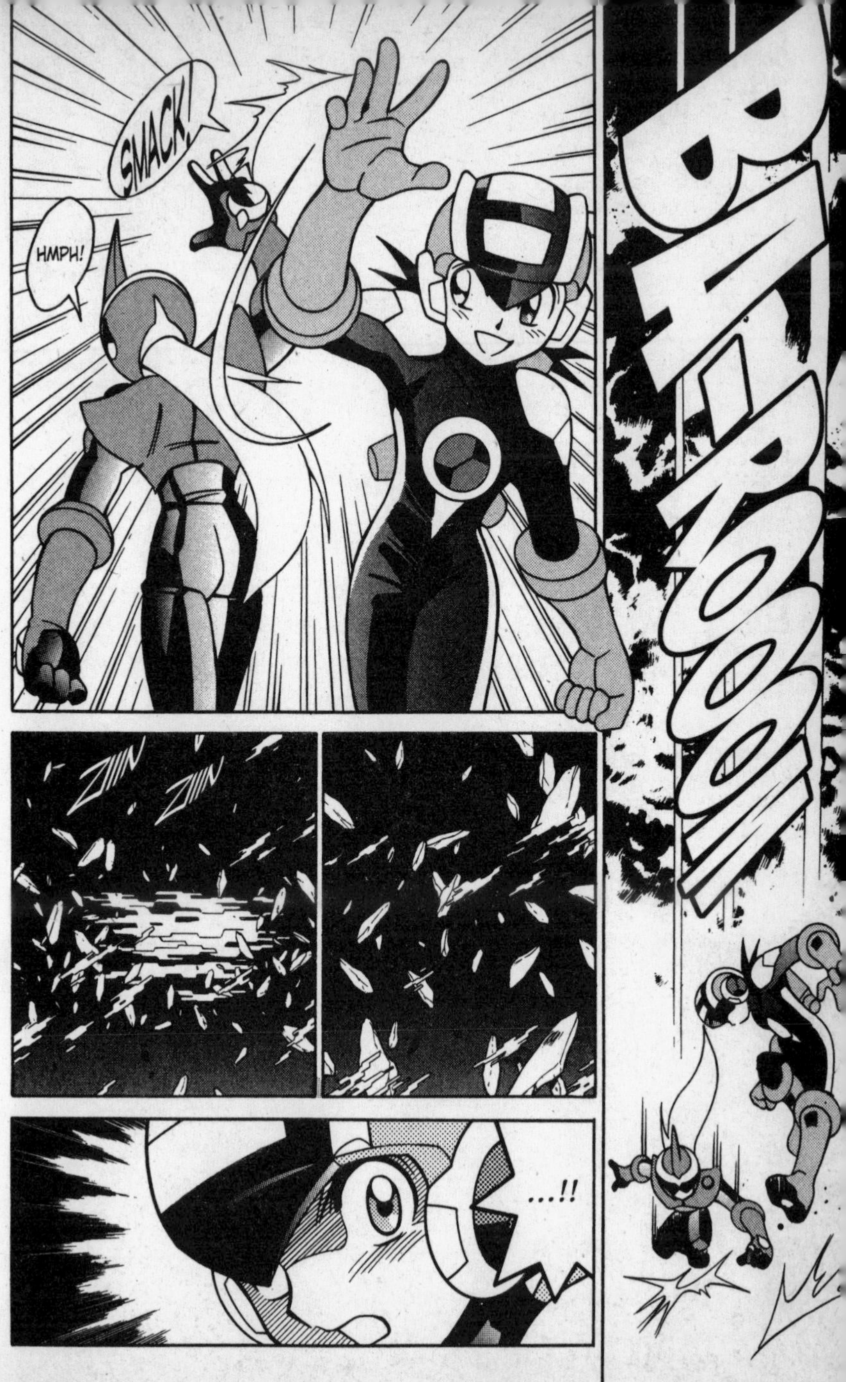
BA-ROOO!!
SMACK
HMPH!
ZIIIN
ZIIIN
...!!

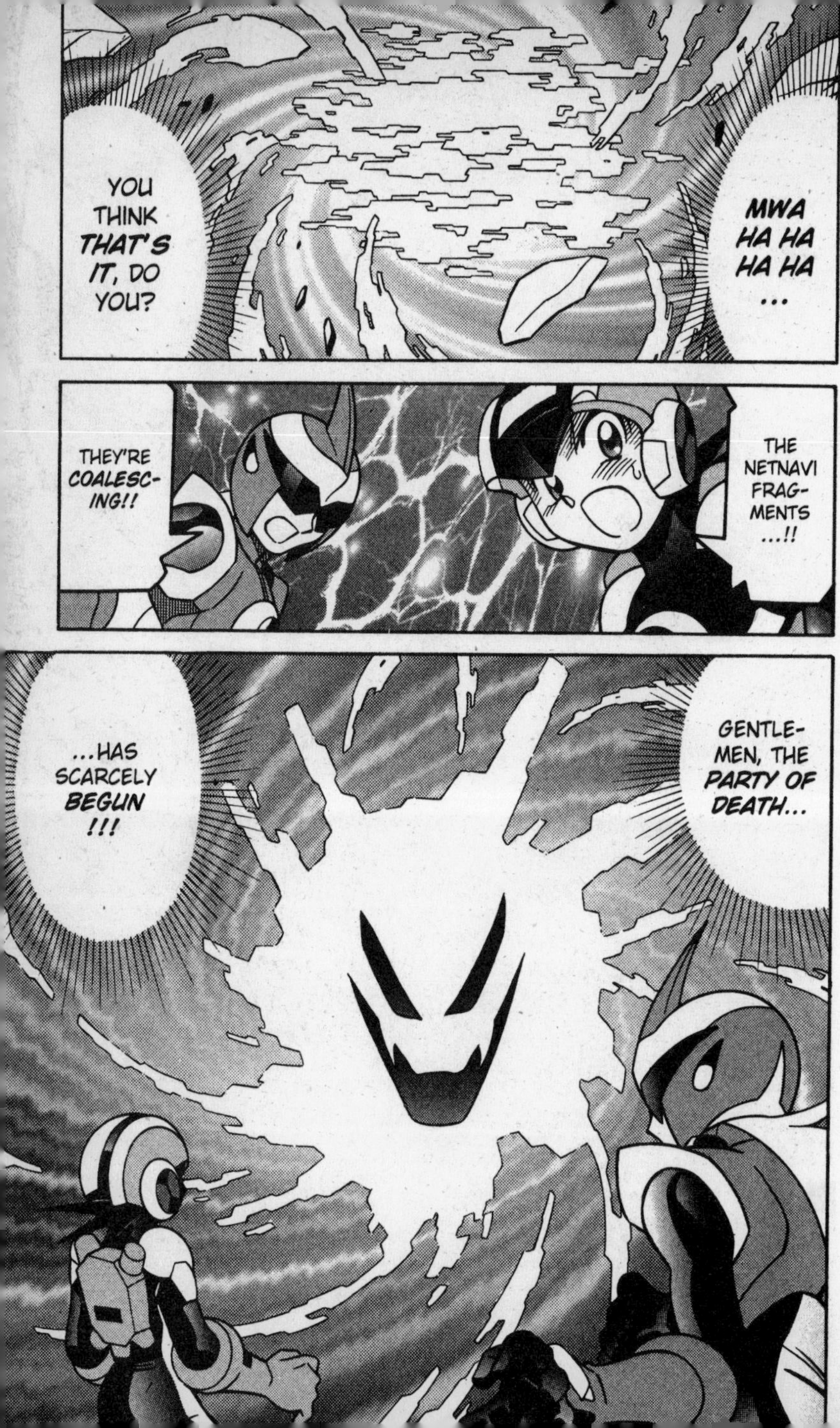
MWA HA HA HA HA ...
YOU THINK THAT'S IT, DO YOU?
THE NETNAVI FRAG- MENTS ...!!
THEY'RE COALESC- ING!!
GENTLE- MEN, THE PARTY OF DEATH...
...HAS SCARCELY BEGUN !!!

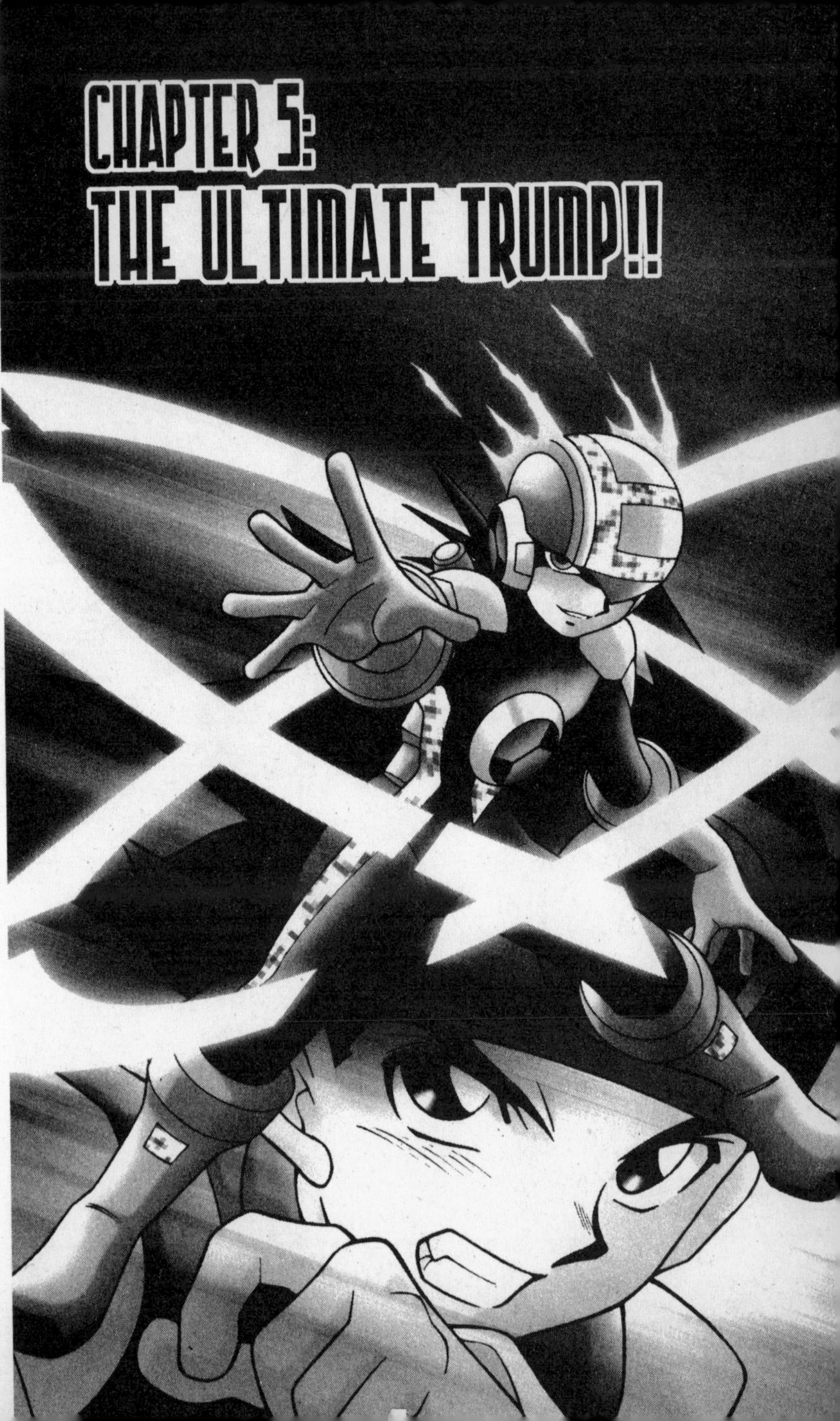
CHAPTER 5:
THE ULTIMATE TRUMP!!

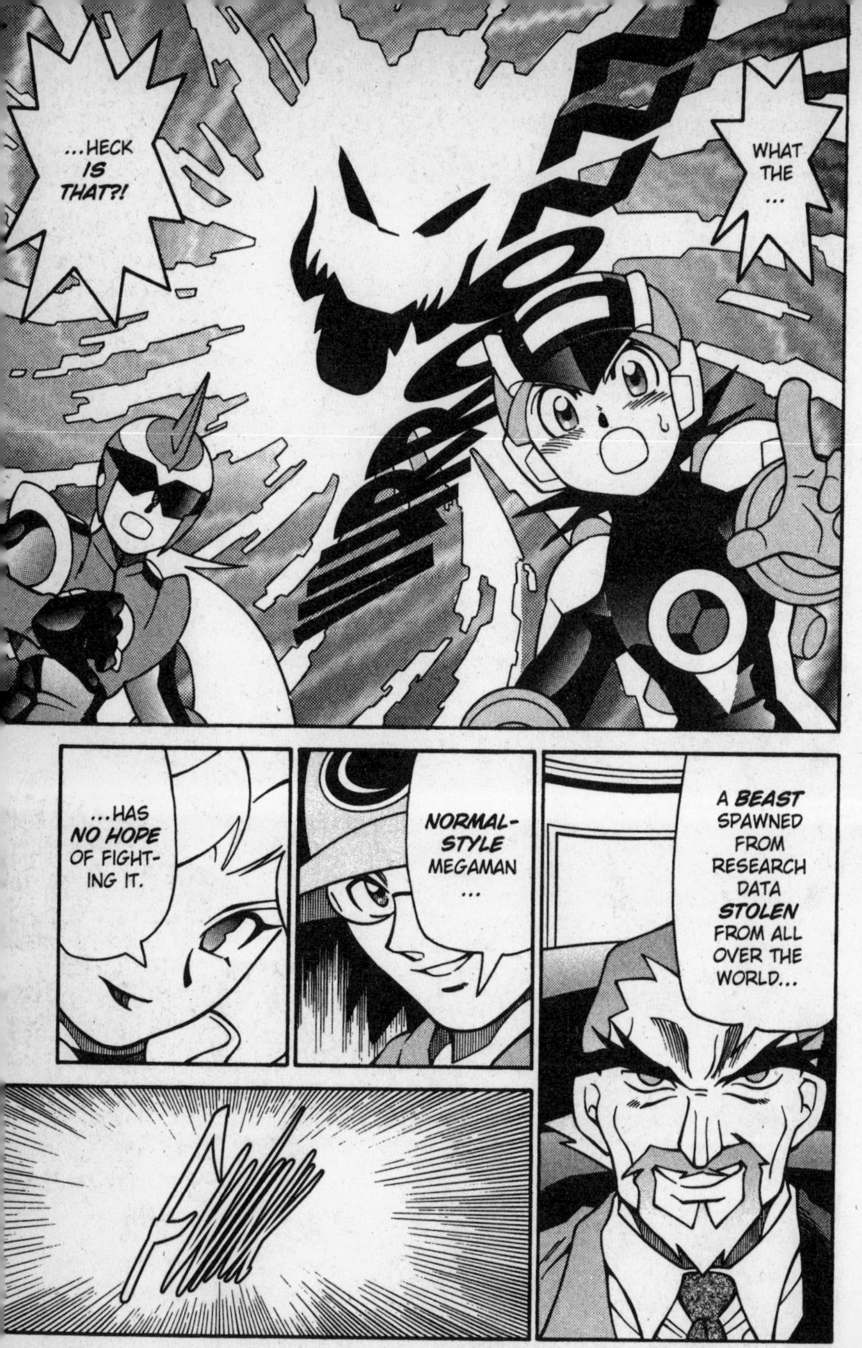
WHAT THE ...
...HECK IS THAT?!
A BEAST SPAWNED FROM RESEARCH DATA STOLEN FROM ALL OVER THE WORLD...
NORMAL-STYLE MEGAMAN ...
...HAS NO HOPE OF FIGHTING IT.

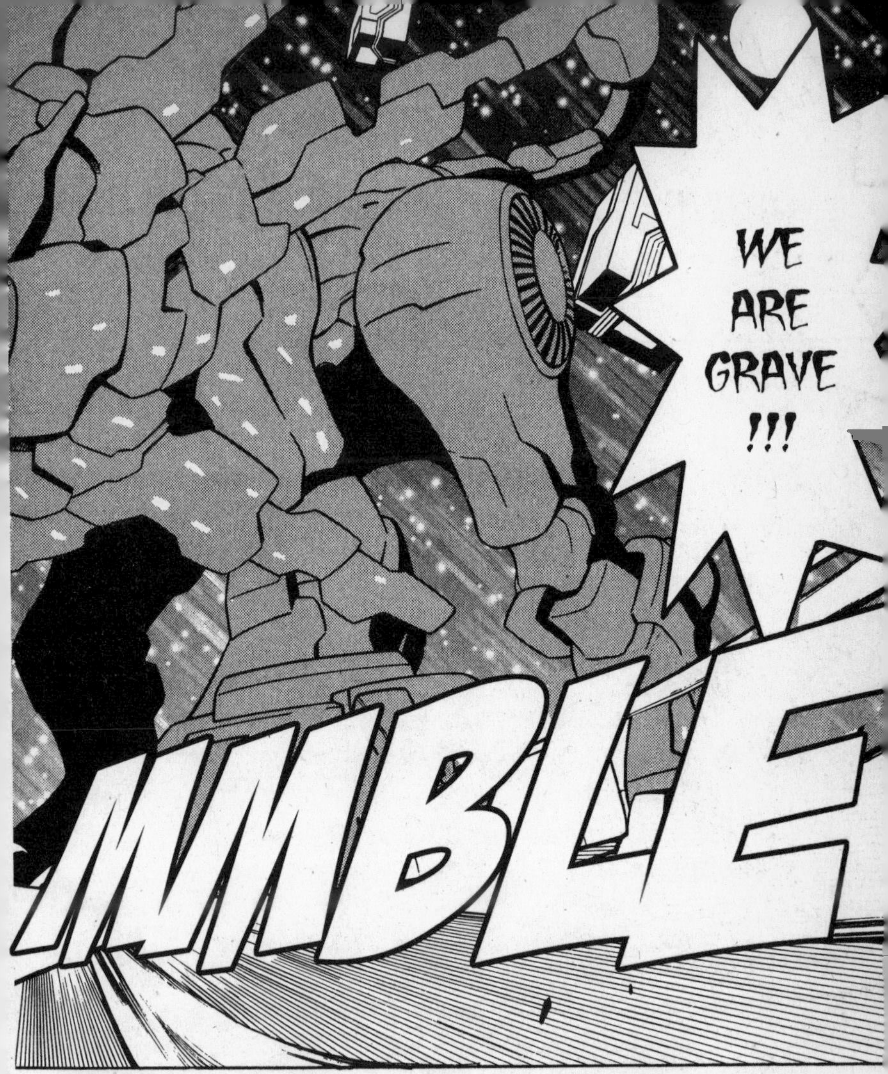
WE ARE GRAVE !!!
MMBLE

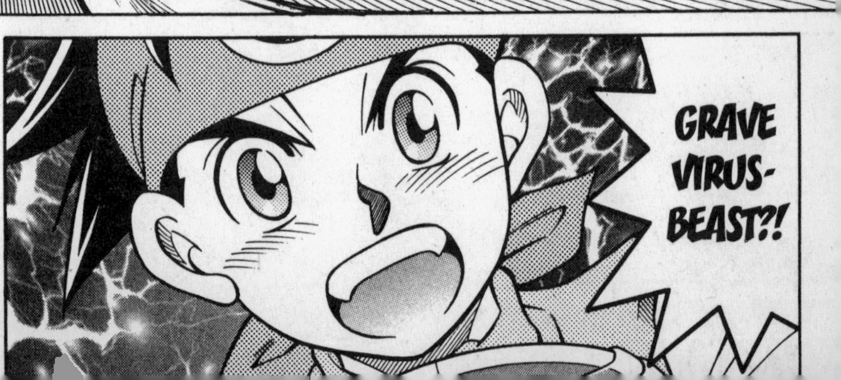
GRAVE VIRUS-BEAST?!

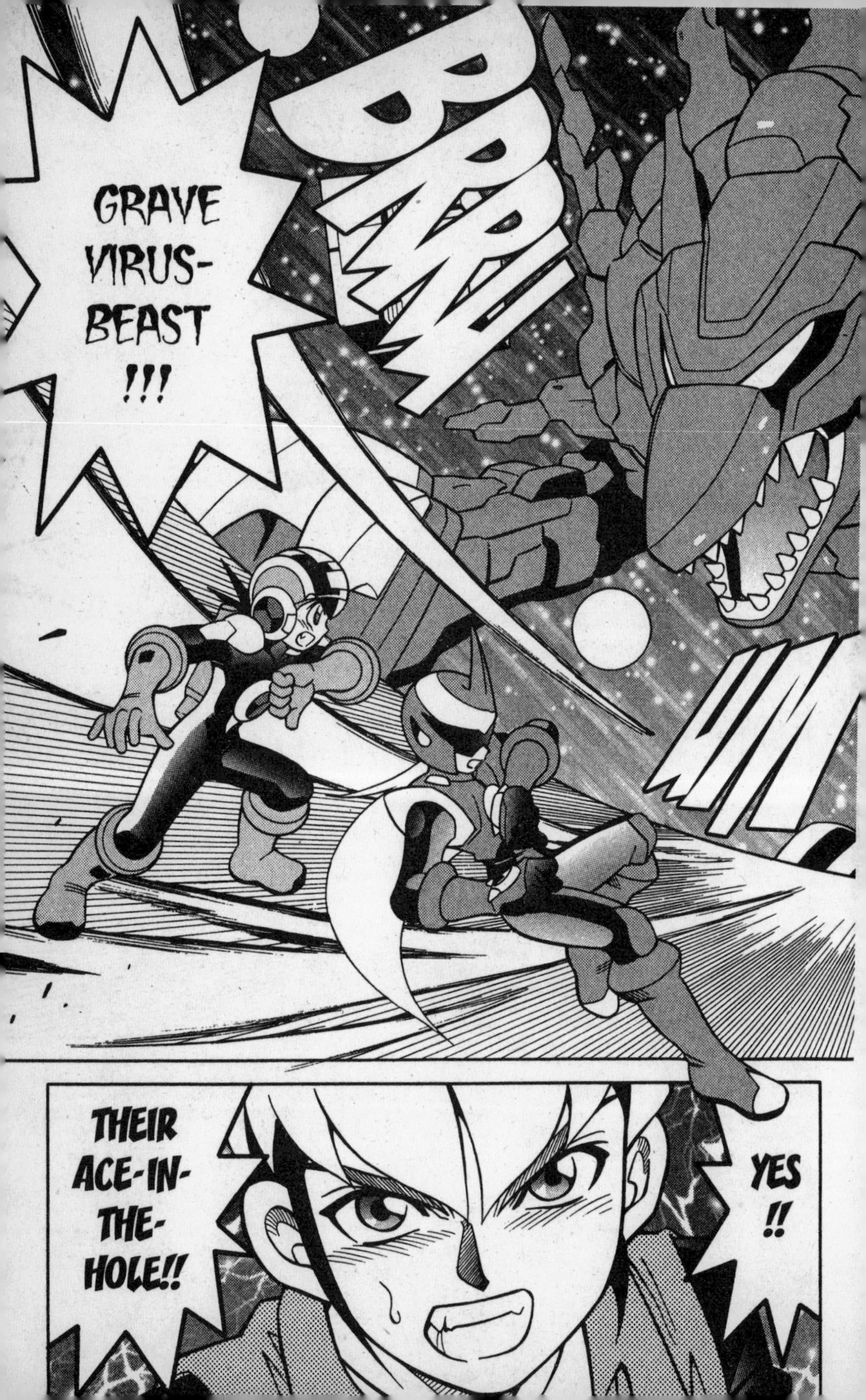
BRRM
GRAVE VIRUS-BEAST!!!
YES!!
THEIR ACE-IN-THE-HOLE!!

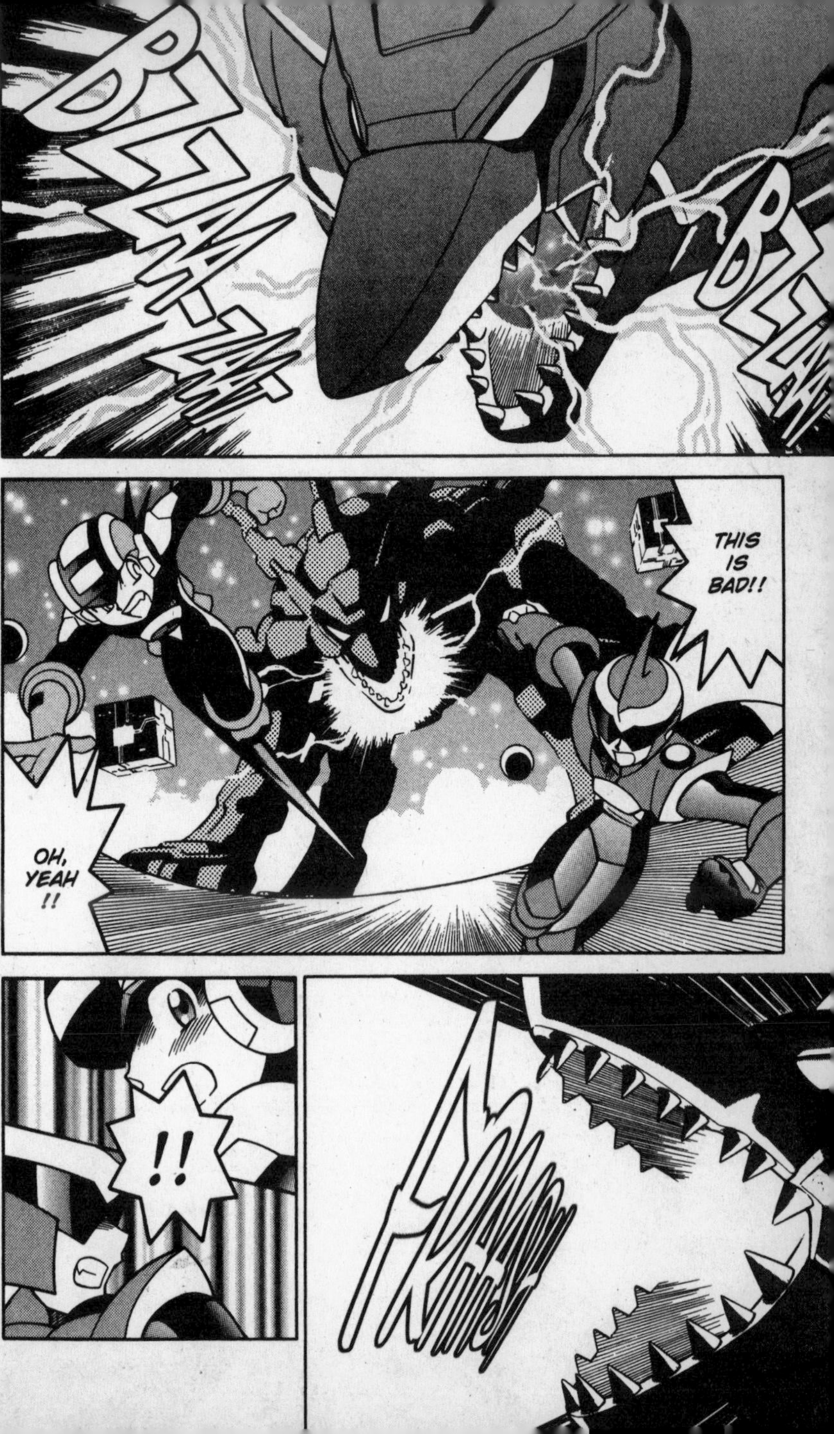
BZZAM-ZAM!!
THIS IS BAD!!
OH, YEAH !!
!!

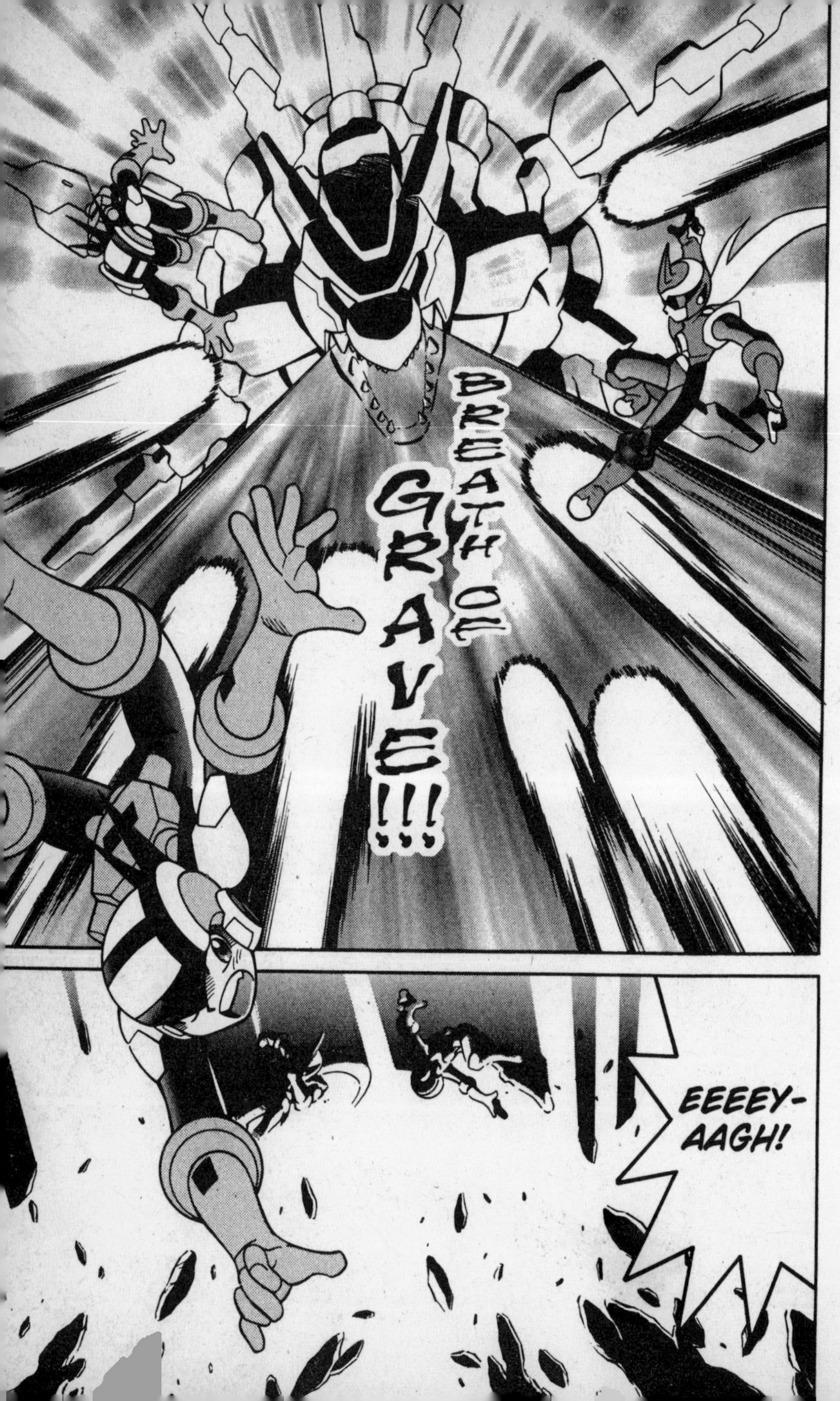
BREATH OF GRAVE!!!
EEEEY-AAGH!

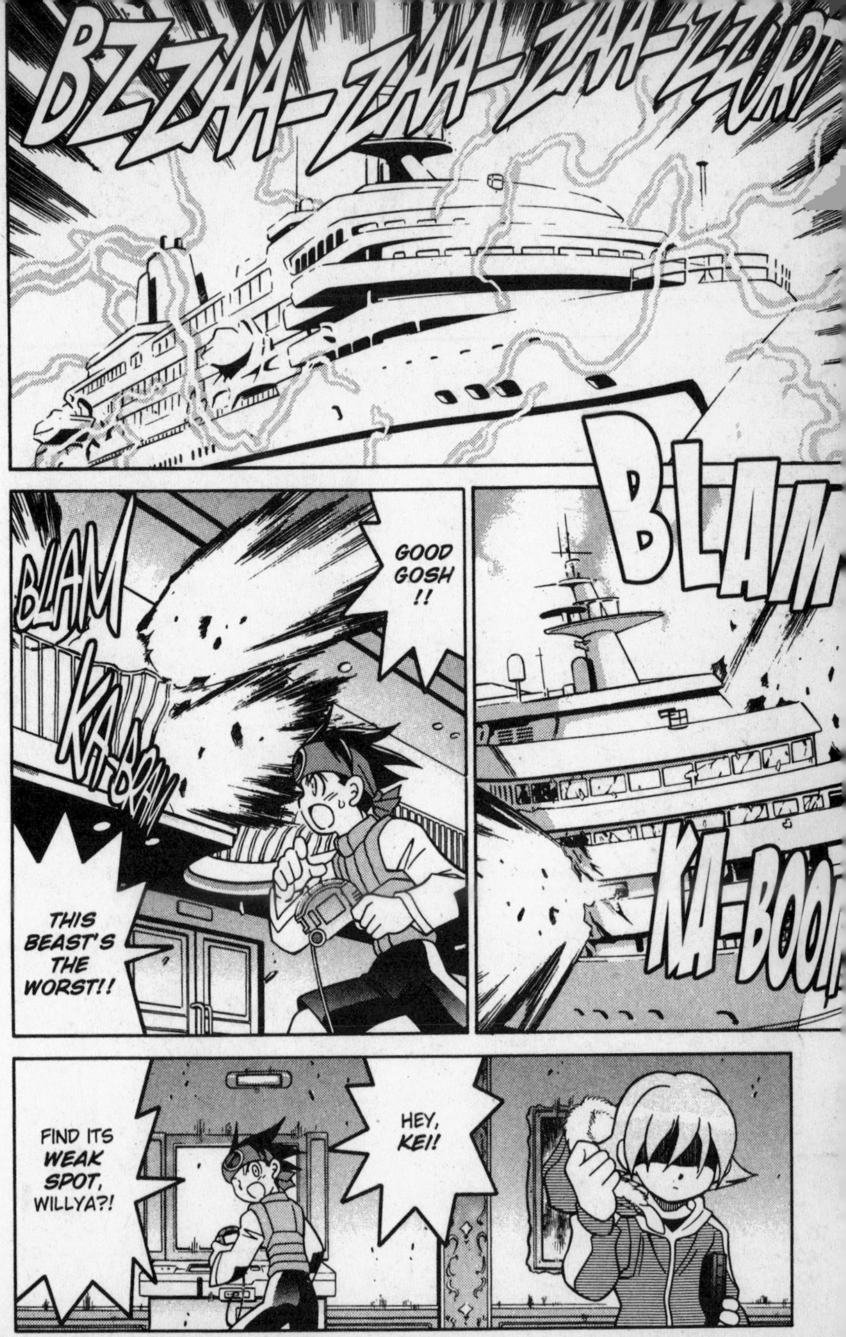
BZZAA-ZAA-ZAA-ZZOR
BLAM
KA-BOOM
BLAM
KA-BOOM
GOOD GOSH !!
THIS BEAST'S THE WORST!!
HEY, KEI!
FIND ITS WEAK SPOT, WILLYA?!

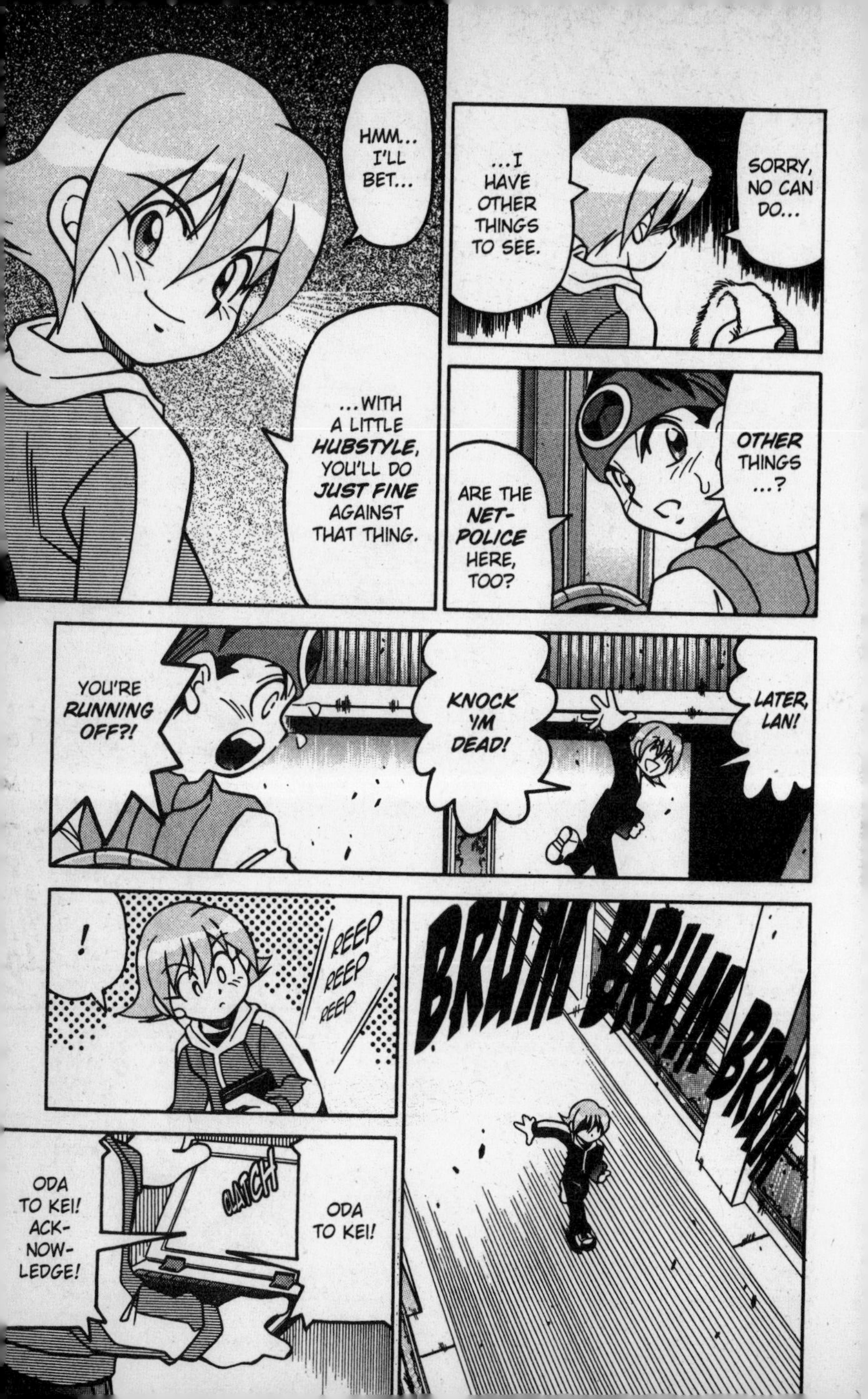
SORRY, NO CAN DO...
...I HAVE OTHER THINGS TO SEE.
OTHER THINGS ...?
ARE THE NET-POLICE HERE, TOO?
HMM... I'LL BET...
...WITH A LITTLE HUBSTYLE, YOU'LL DO JUST FINE AGAINST THAT THING.
LATER, LAN!
KNOCK 'YM DEAD!
YOU'RE RUNNING OFF?!
BRUM BRUM BRUM
!
REEP REEP REEP
ODA TO KEI!
CLATCH
ODA TO KEI! ACK-NOW-LEDGE!

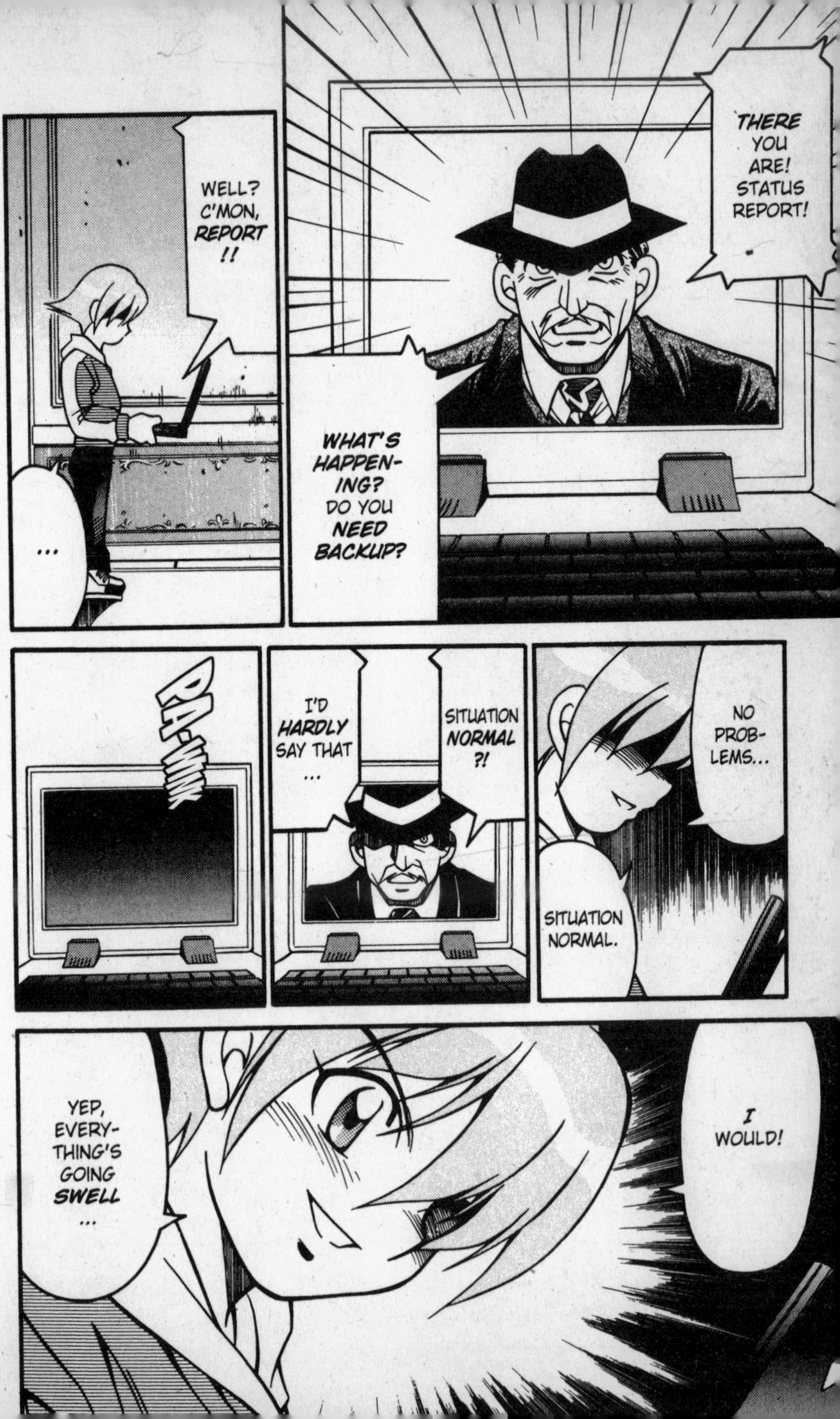
THERE YOU ARE! STATUS REPORT!
WHAT'S HAPPENING? DO YOU NEED BACKUP?
WELL? C'MON, REPORT !!
...
NO PROBLEMS...
SITUATION NORMAL.
SITUATION NORMAL ?!
I'D HARDLY SAY THAT ...
I WOULD!
YEP, EVERYTHING'S GOING SWELL ...

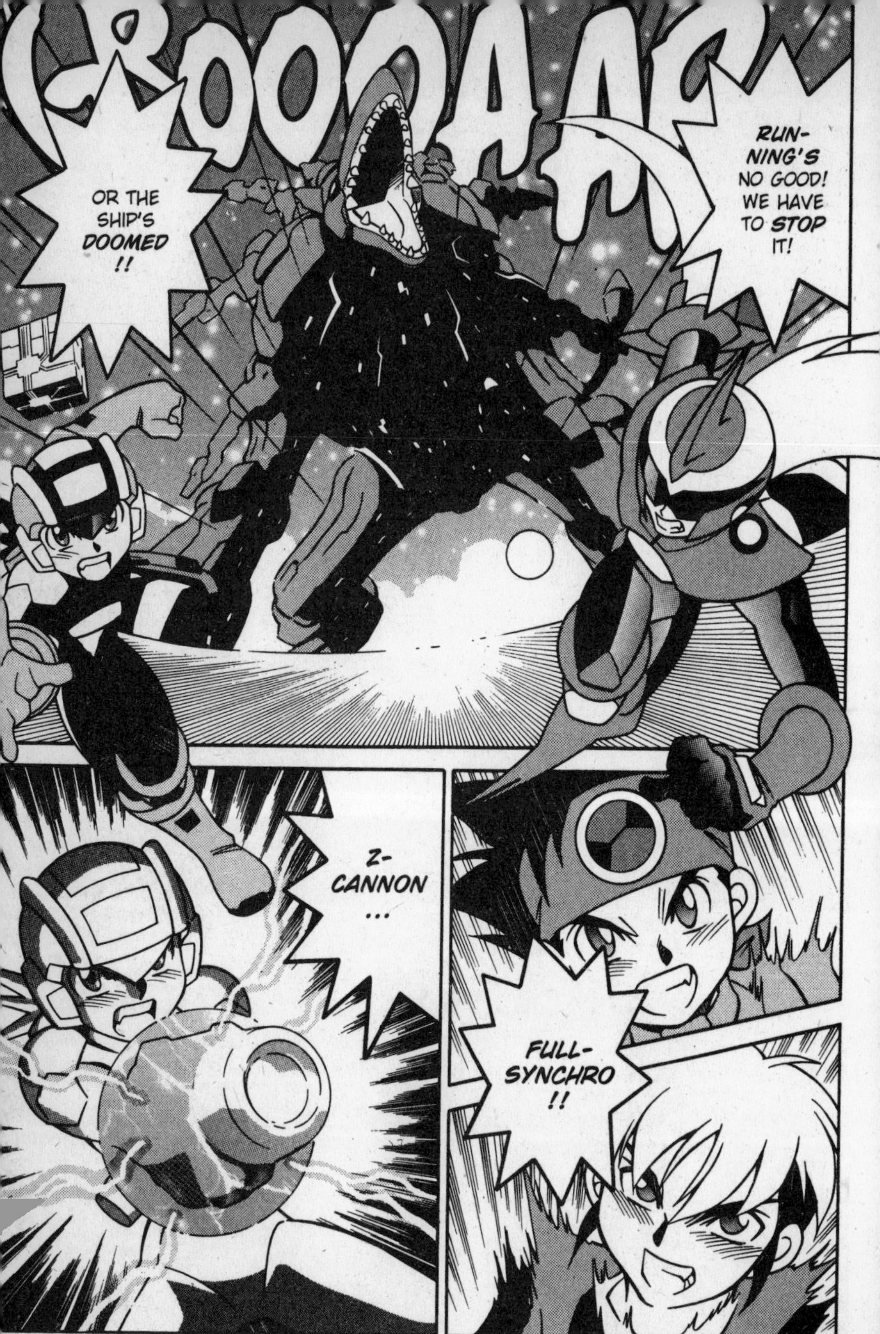
RUN-NING'S NO GOOD! WE HAVE TO STOP IT!
OR THE SHIP'S DOOMED!!
FULL-SYNCHRO!!
Z-CANNON...

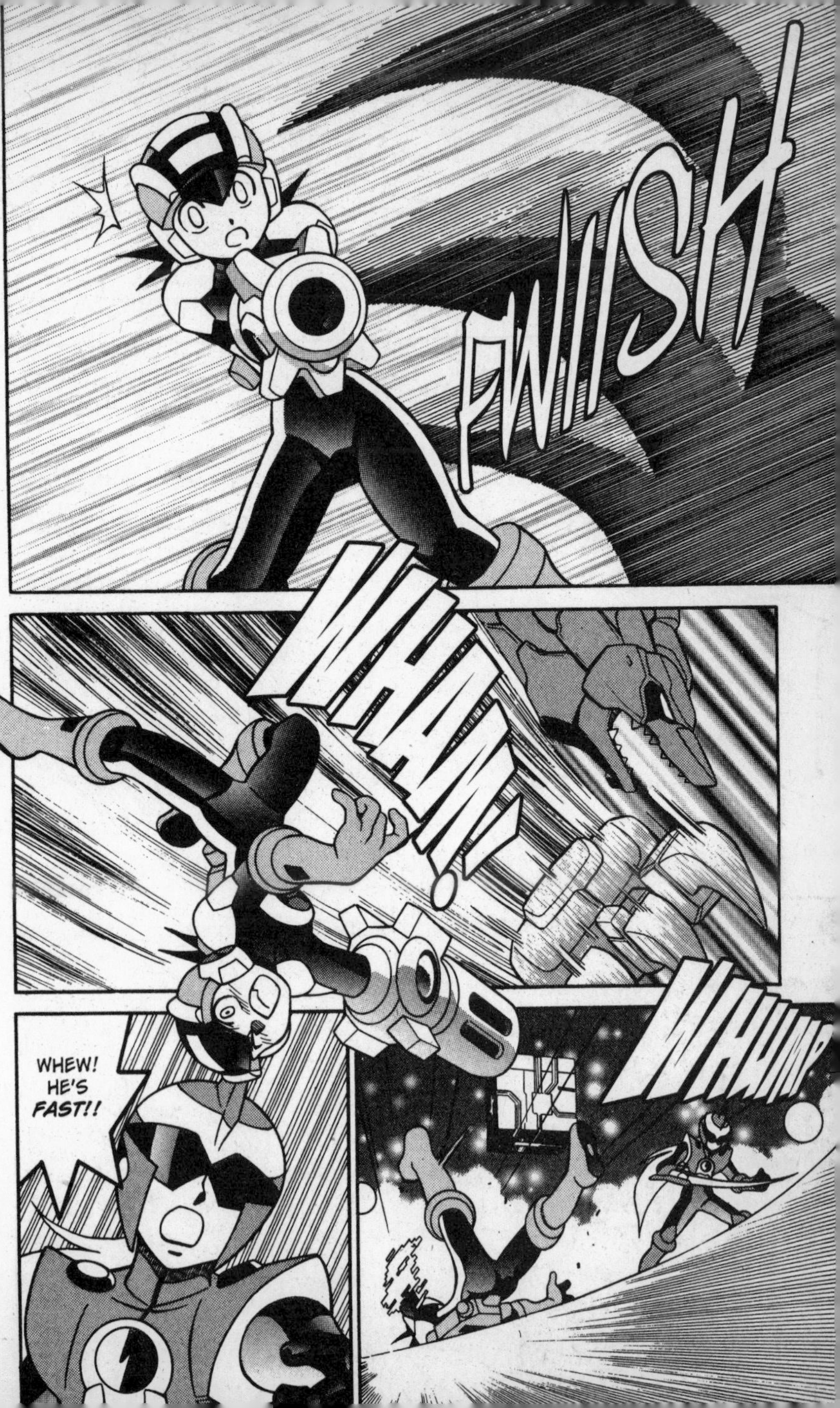
FWISH
WHAM!
WHUMP
WHEW! HE'S FAST!!

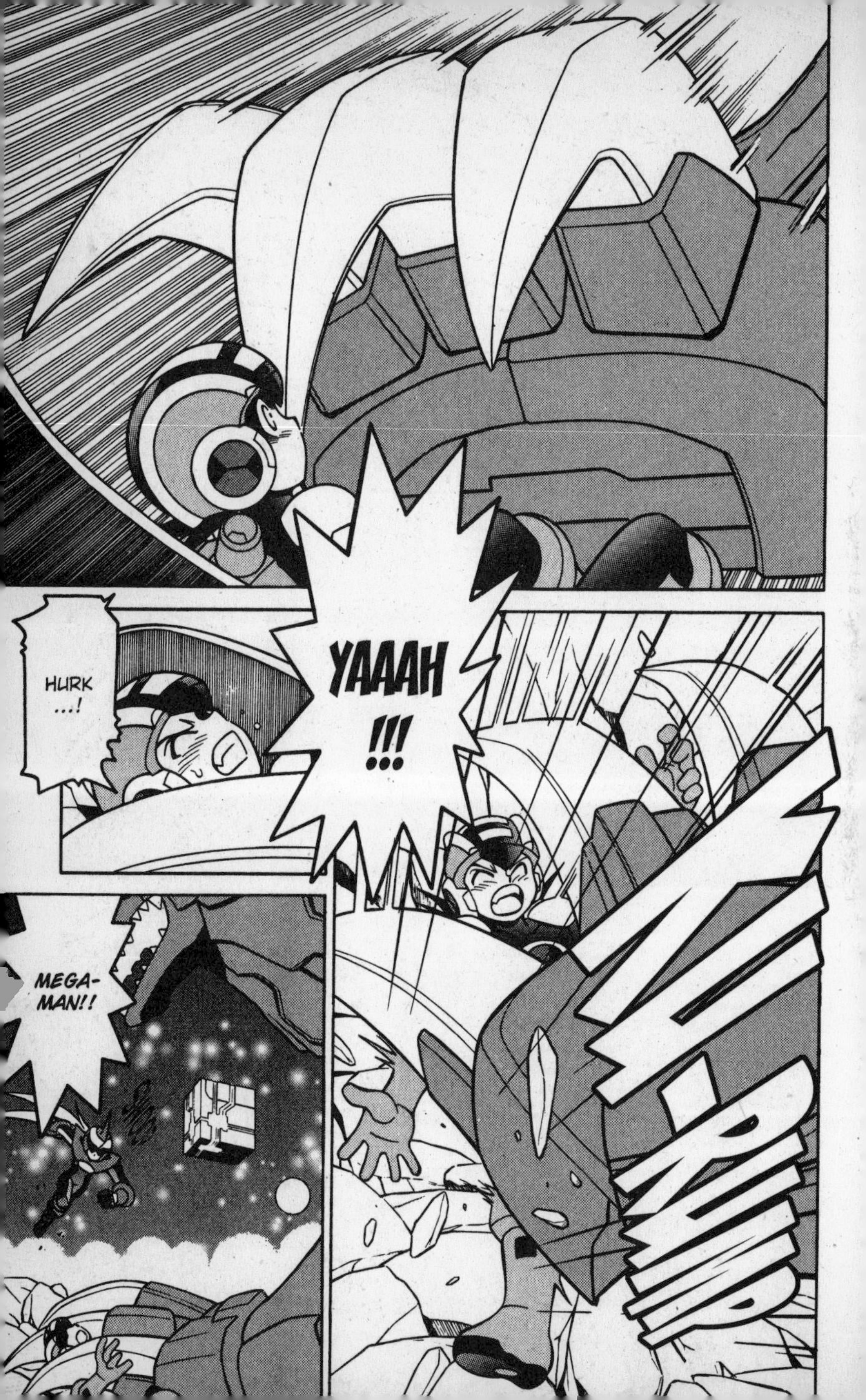
YAAAH !!!
HURK ...!
MEGA-MAN!!

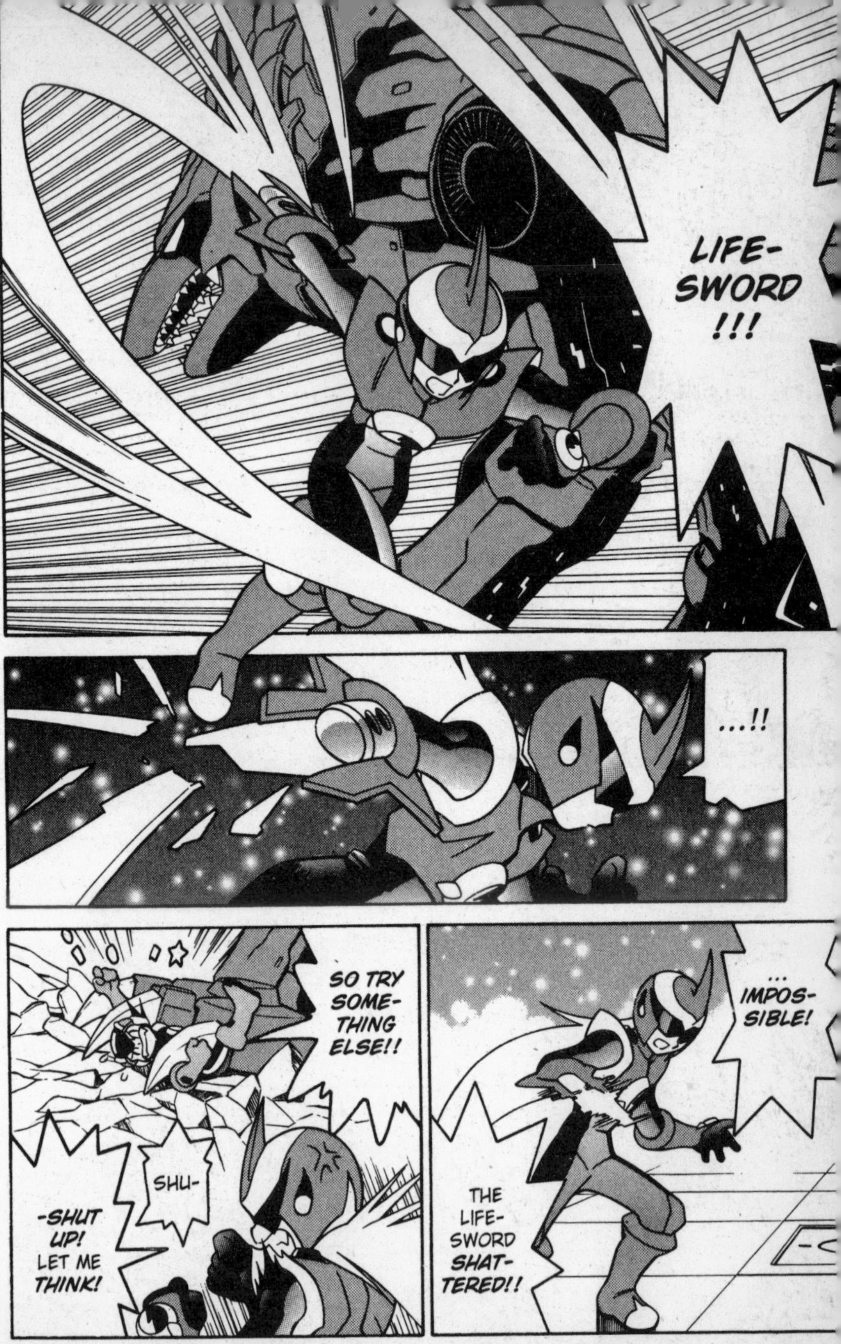
LIFE-SWORD!!!
...!!
...IMPOSSIBLE!
THE LIFE-SWORD SHATTERED!!
SO TRY SOMETHING ELSE!!
SHU-
-SHUT UP! LET ME THINK!

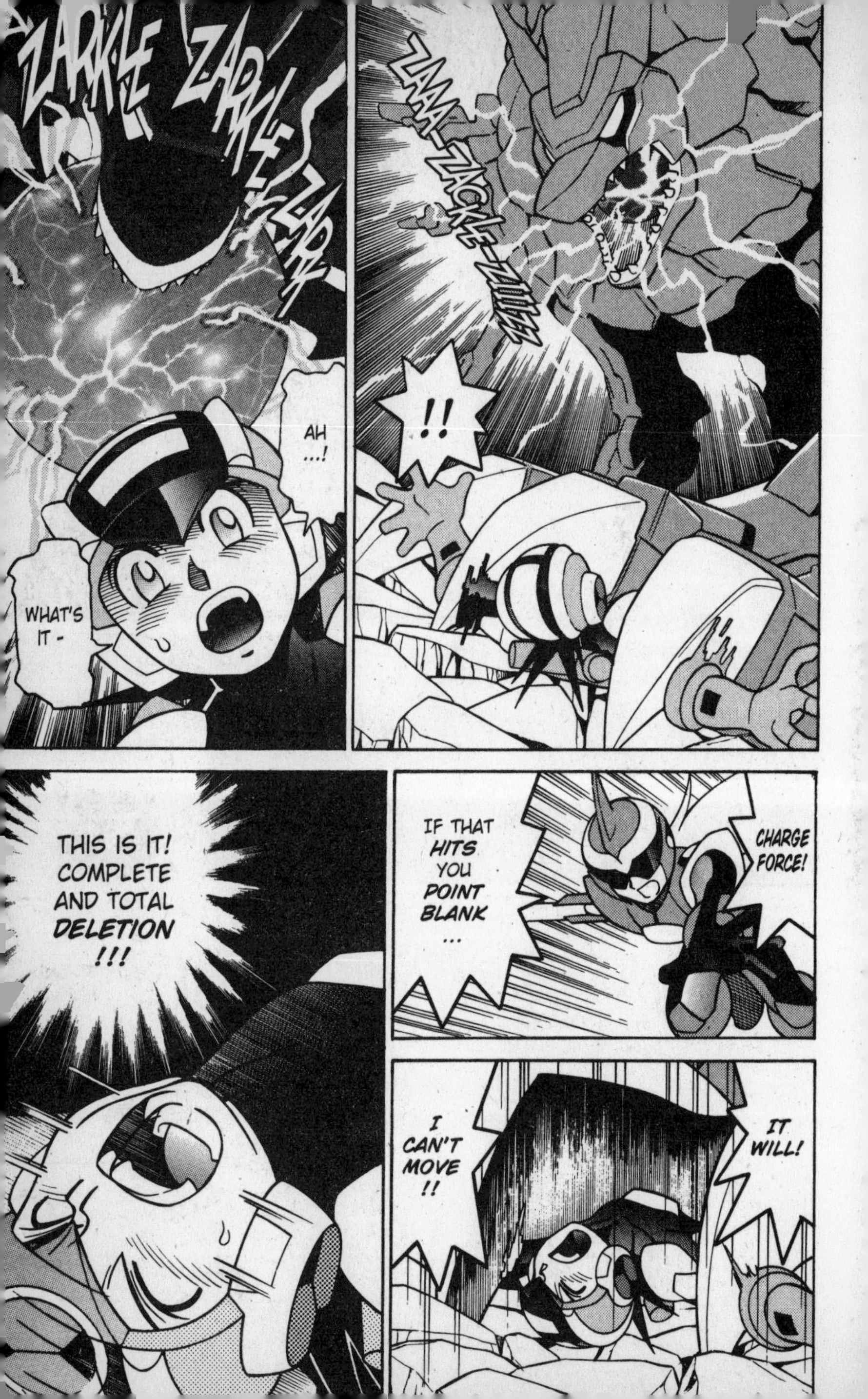

ZAAA-ZACKLE-ZIIIZZ
!!
ZARKLE ZARKLE ZARK
AH ...!
WHAT'S IT -
CHARGE FORCE!
IF THAT **HITS** YOU **POINT BLANK** ...
IT WILL!
I CAN'T MOVE !!
THIS IS IT! COMPLETE AND TOTAL **DELETION** !!!

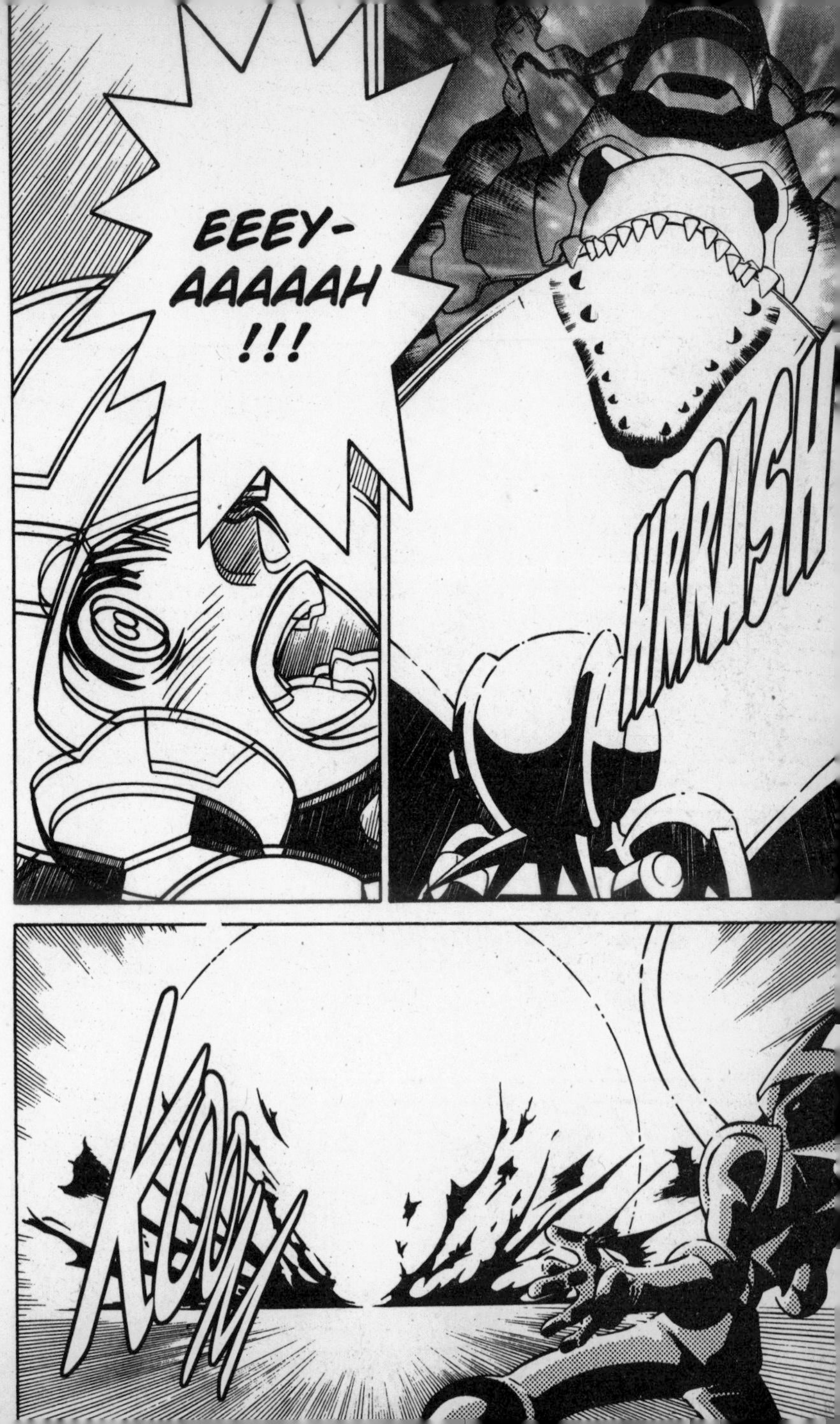
KRRASH
EEEY-AAAAAH!!!

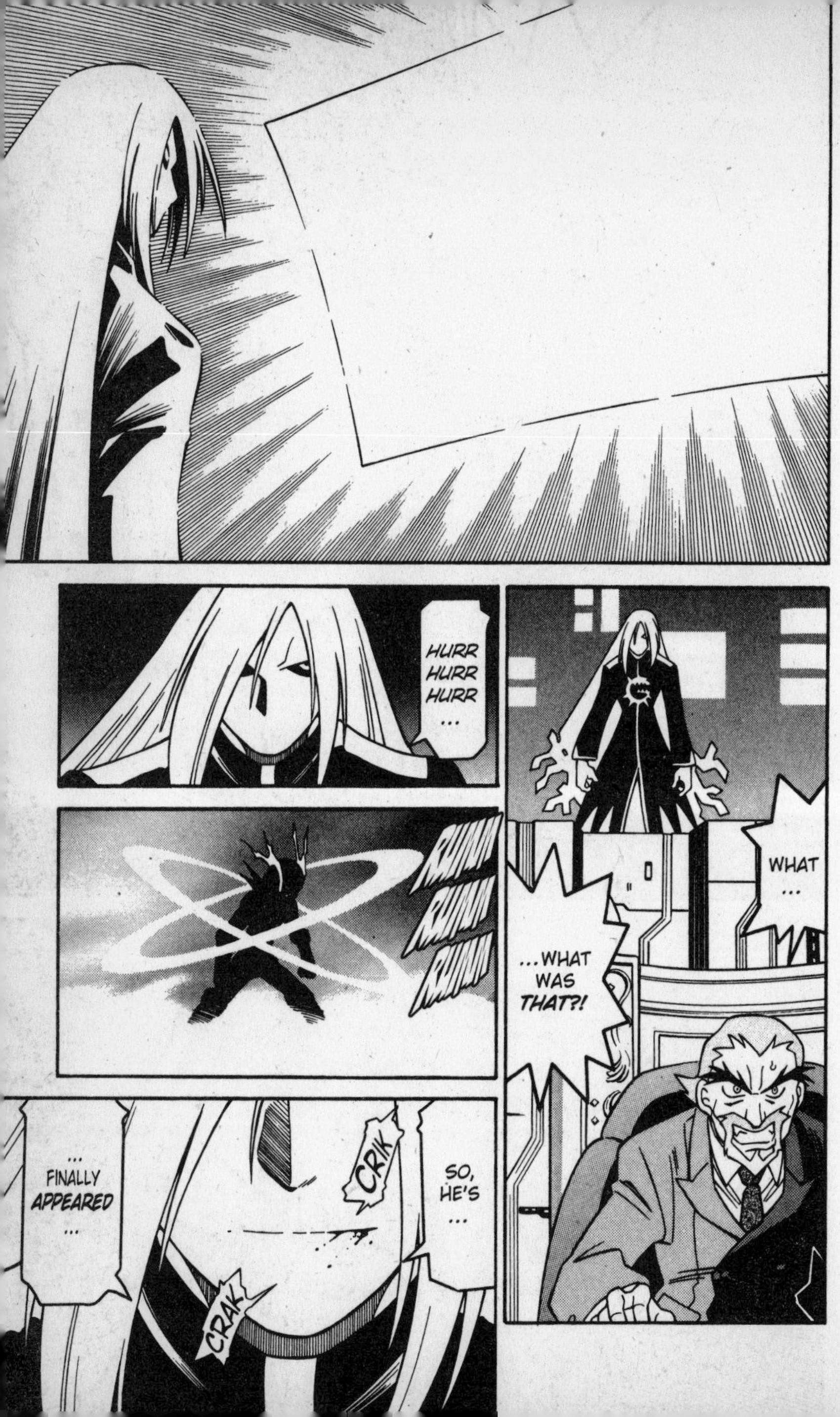
WHAT ...
...WHAT WAS THAT?!
HURR HURR HURR ...
CRIK
SO, HE'S ...
... FINALLY APPEARED ...
CRAK

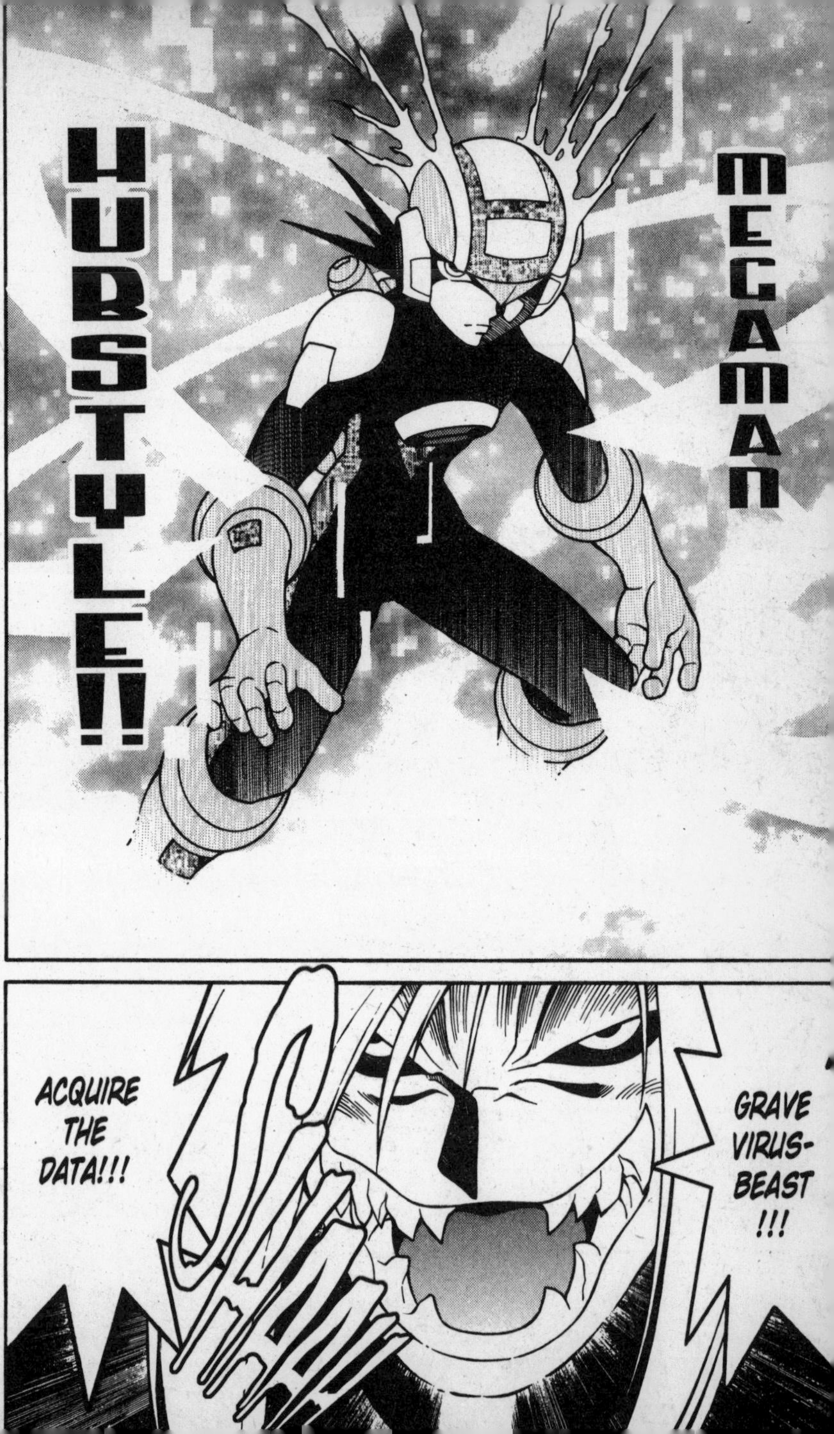
MEGAMAN
HUBSTYLE!!
GRAVE VIRUS-BEAST!!!
ACQUIRE THE DATA!!!

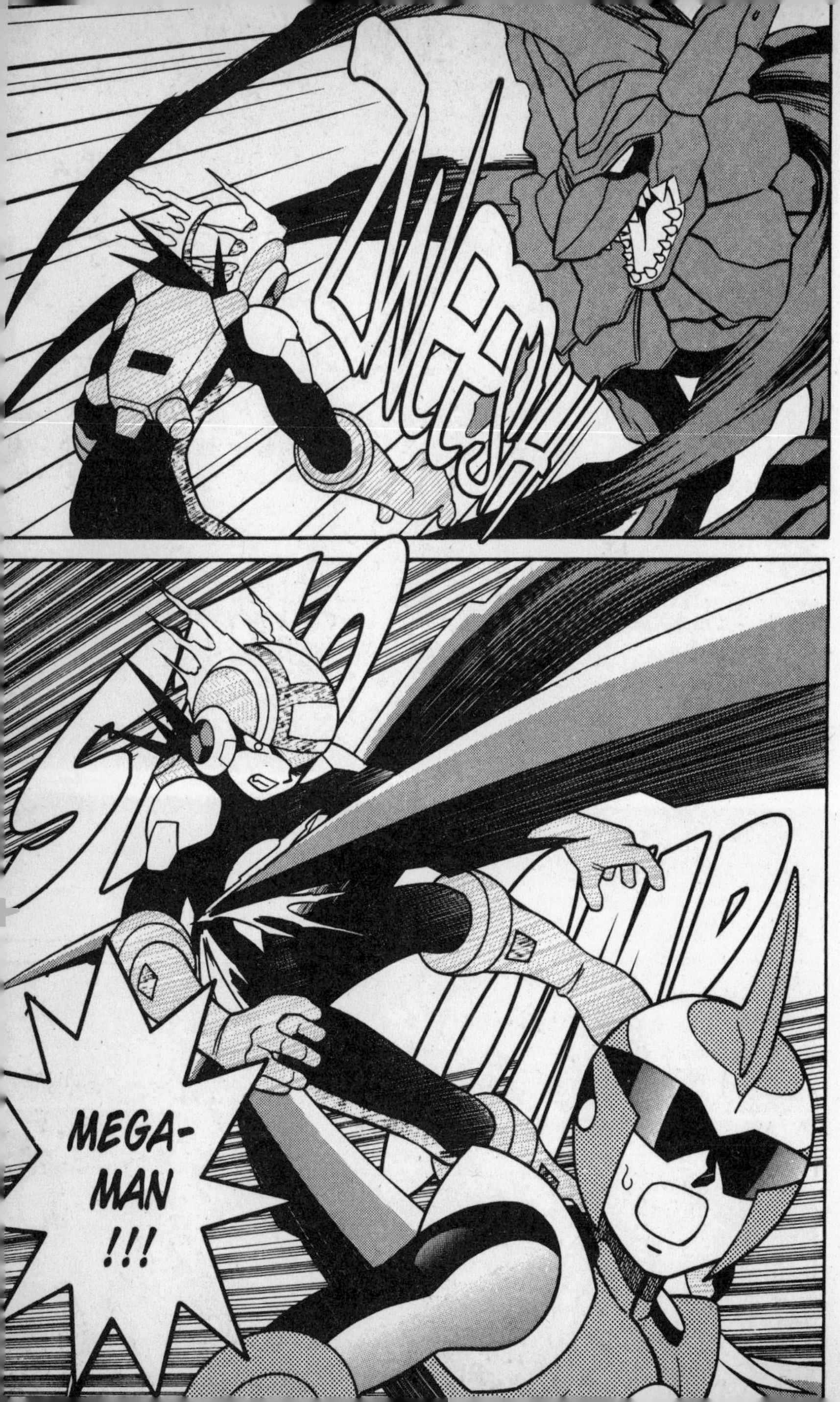
MEGA-
MAN
!!!

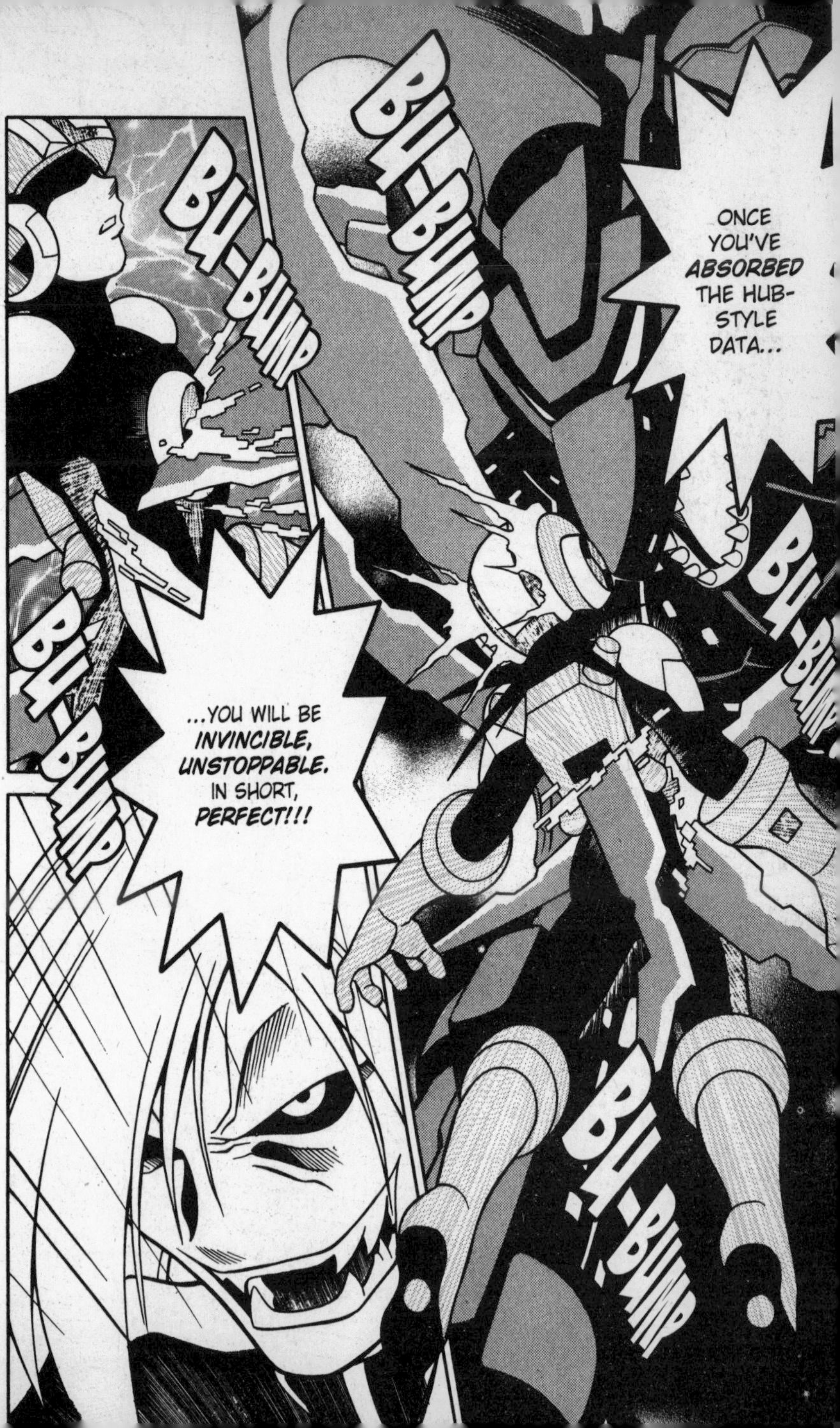
ONCE YOU'VE ABSORBED THE HUB-STYLE DATA...
BU-BUMP
BU-BUMP
BU-BUMP
BU-BUMP
BU-BUMP
BU-BUMP
...YOU WILL BE INVINCIBLE, UNSTOPPABLE. IN SHORT, PERFECT!!!

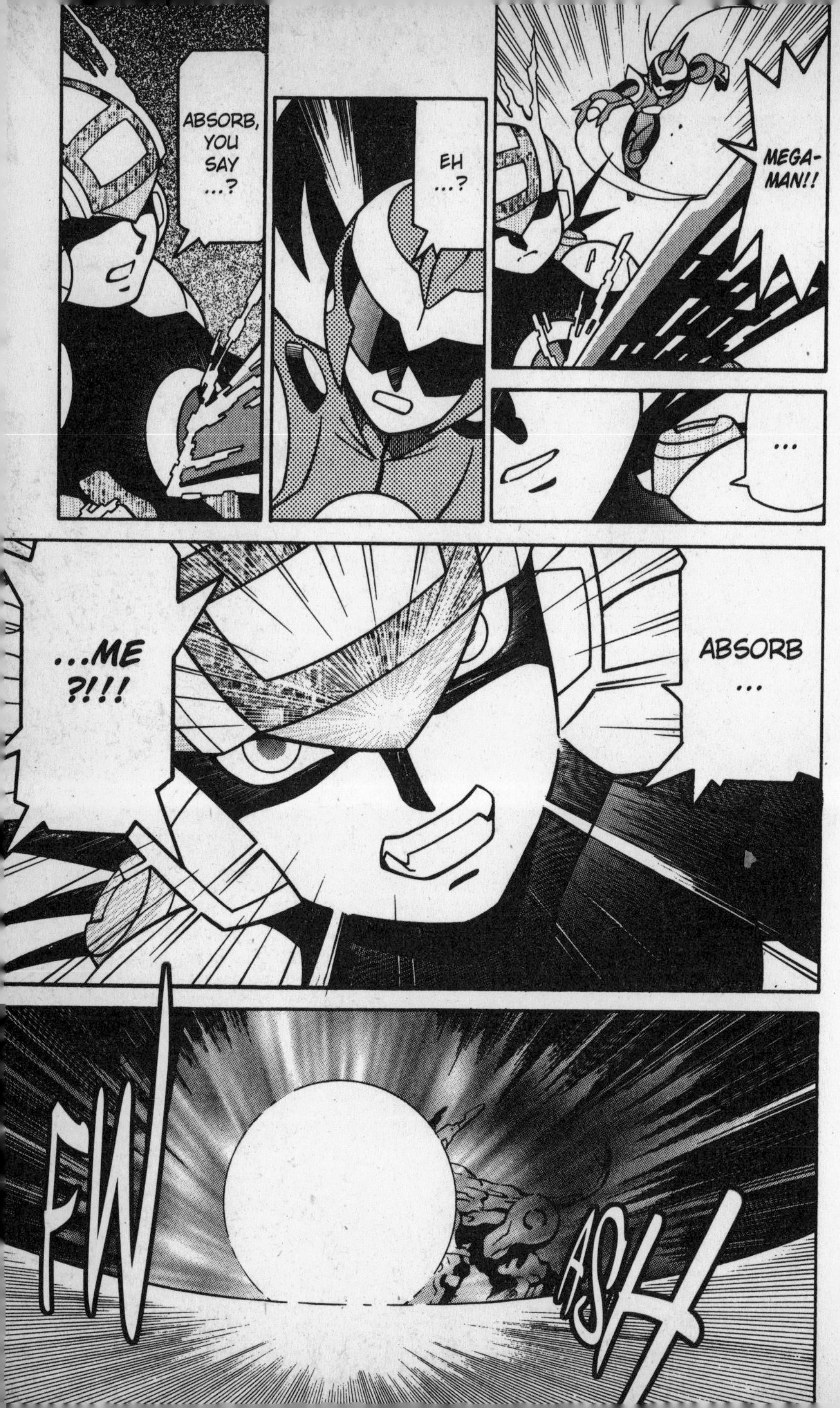
MEGA-MAN!!
...
EH ...?
ABSORB, YOU SAY ...?
ABSORB ...
...ME ?!!!
FWASH

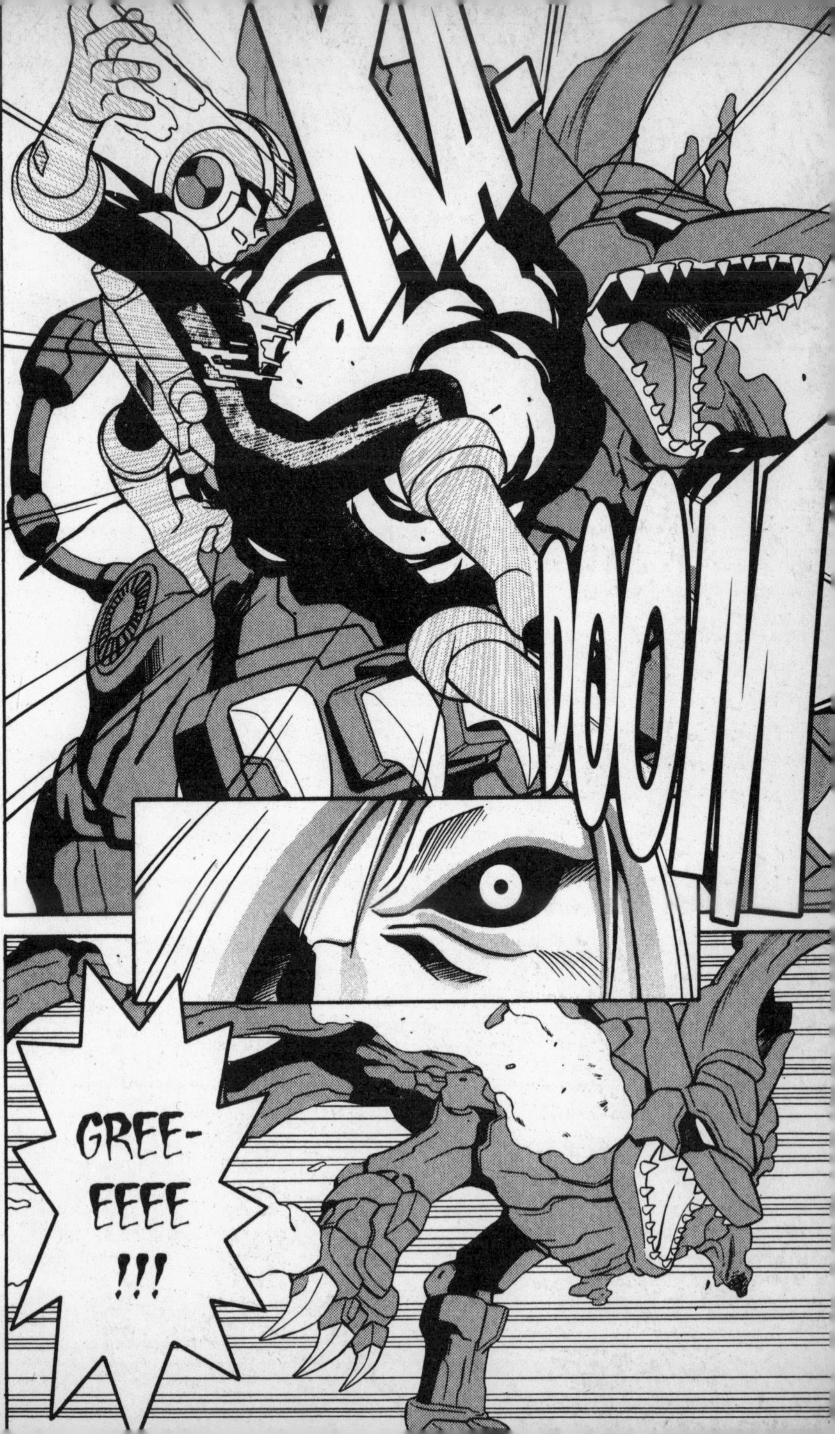
DOOM
GREE-
EEEE
!!!

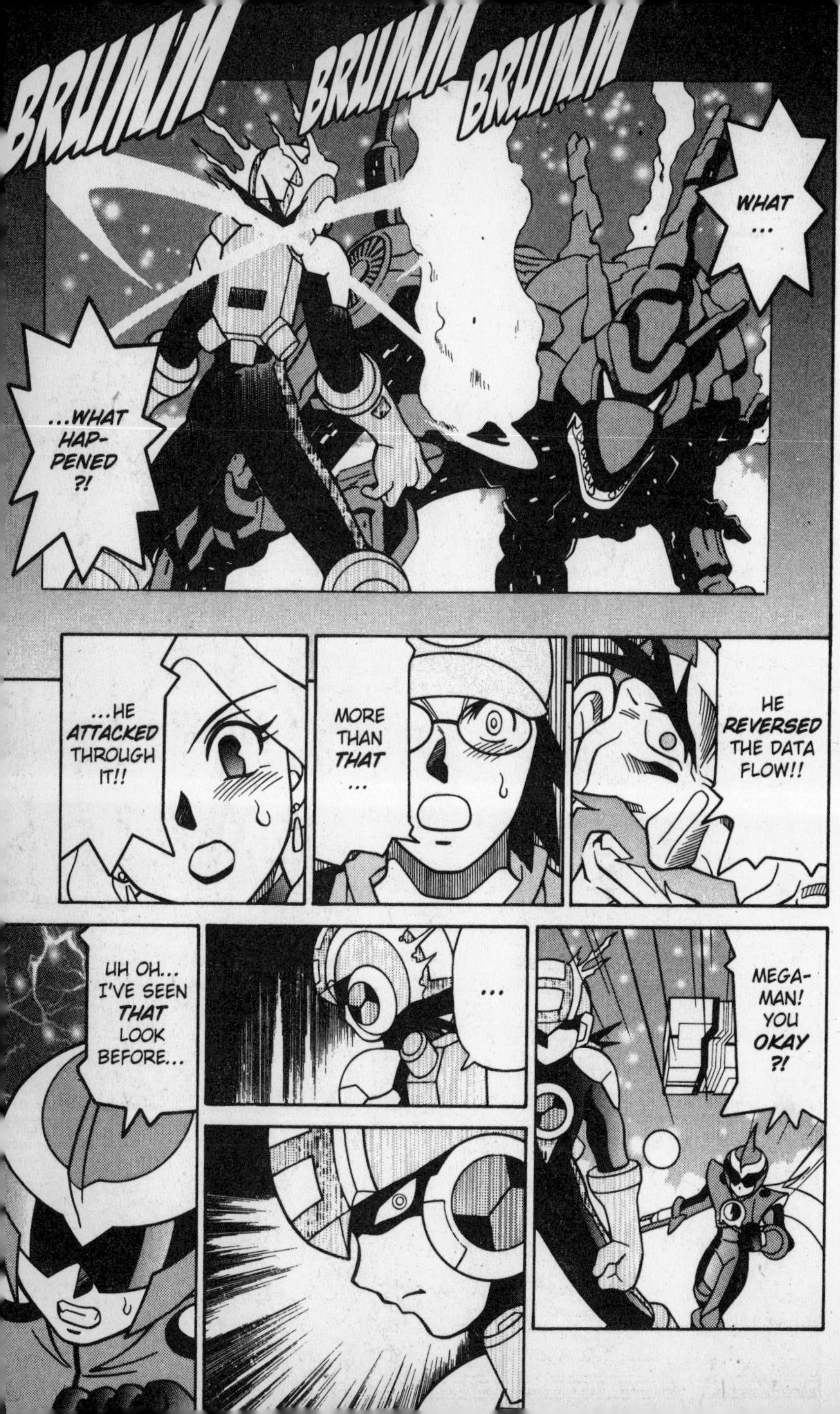
BRUMM BRUMM BRUMM
WHAT ...
...WHAT HAP-PENED ?!
HE REVERSED THE DATA FLOW!!
MORE THAN THAT ...
...HE ATTACKED THROUGH IT!!
MEGA-MAN! YOU OKAY ?!
...
UH OH... I'VE SEEN THAT LOOK BEFORE...

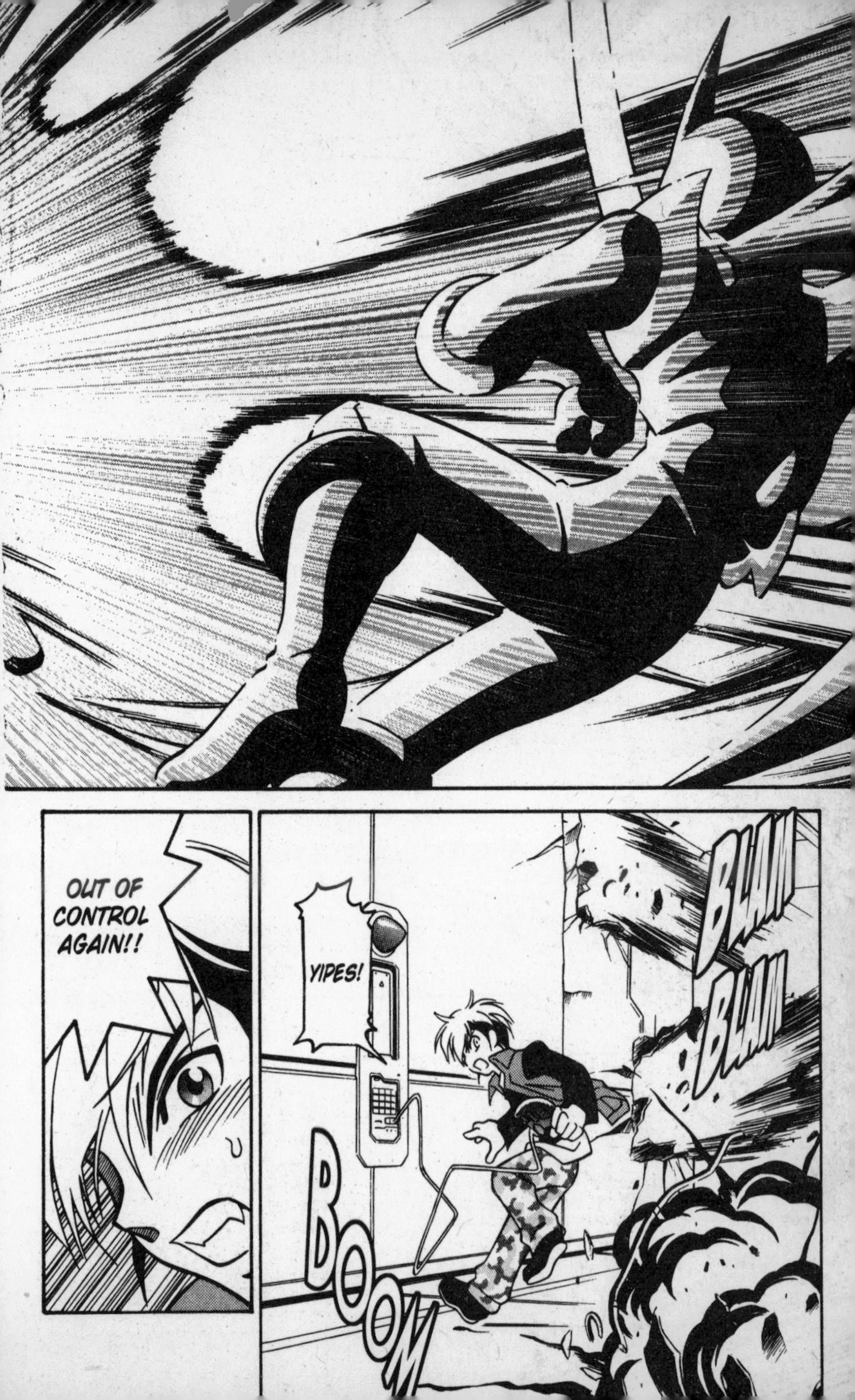
YIPES!
BLAM
BLAM
BOOM
OUT OF CONTROL AGAIN!!

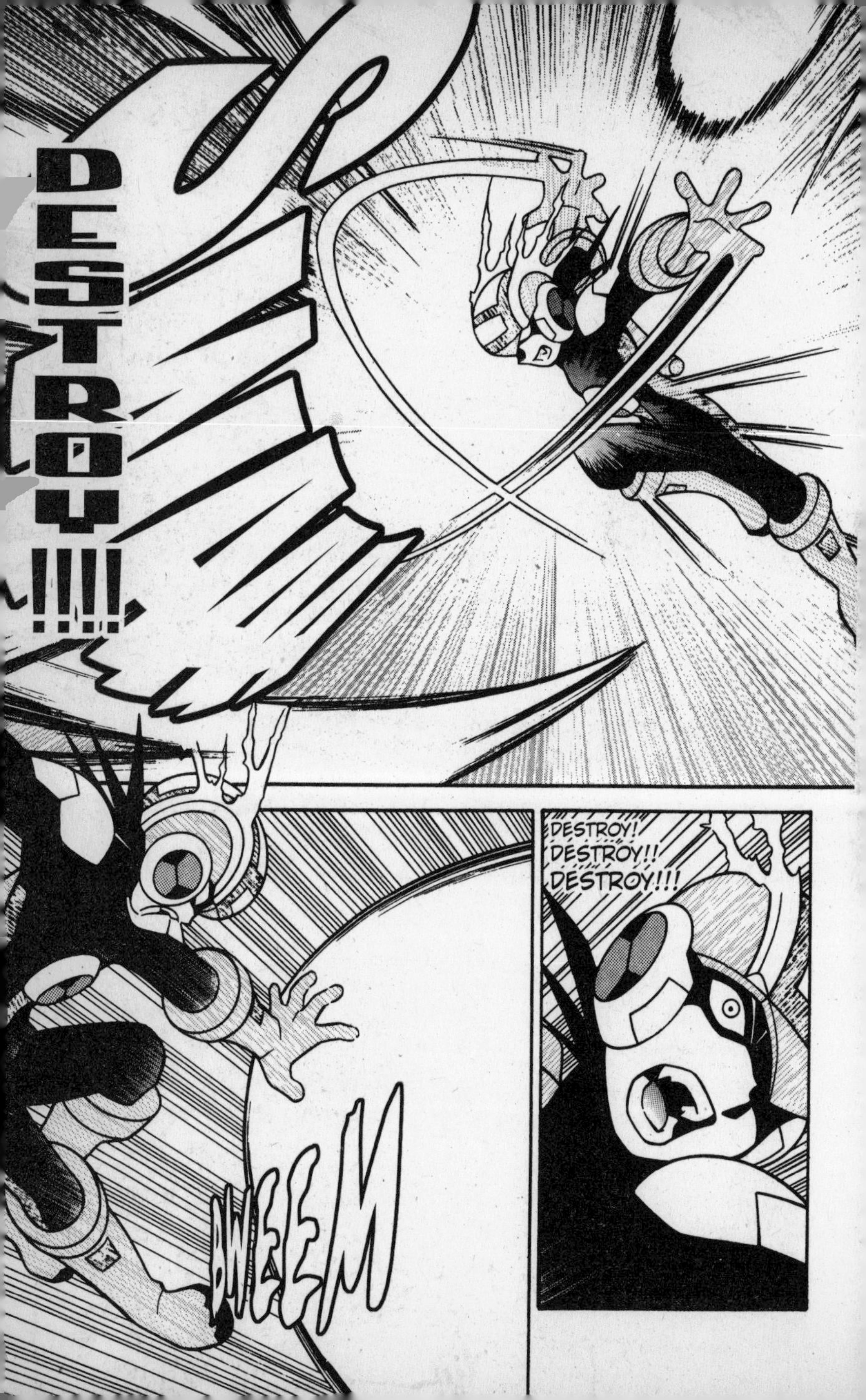
DESTROY!!!!
DESTROY! DESTROY!! DESTROY!!!
BWEEM

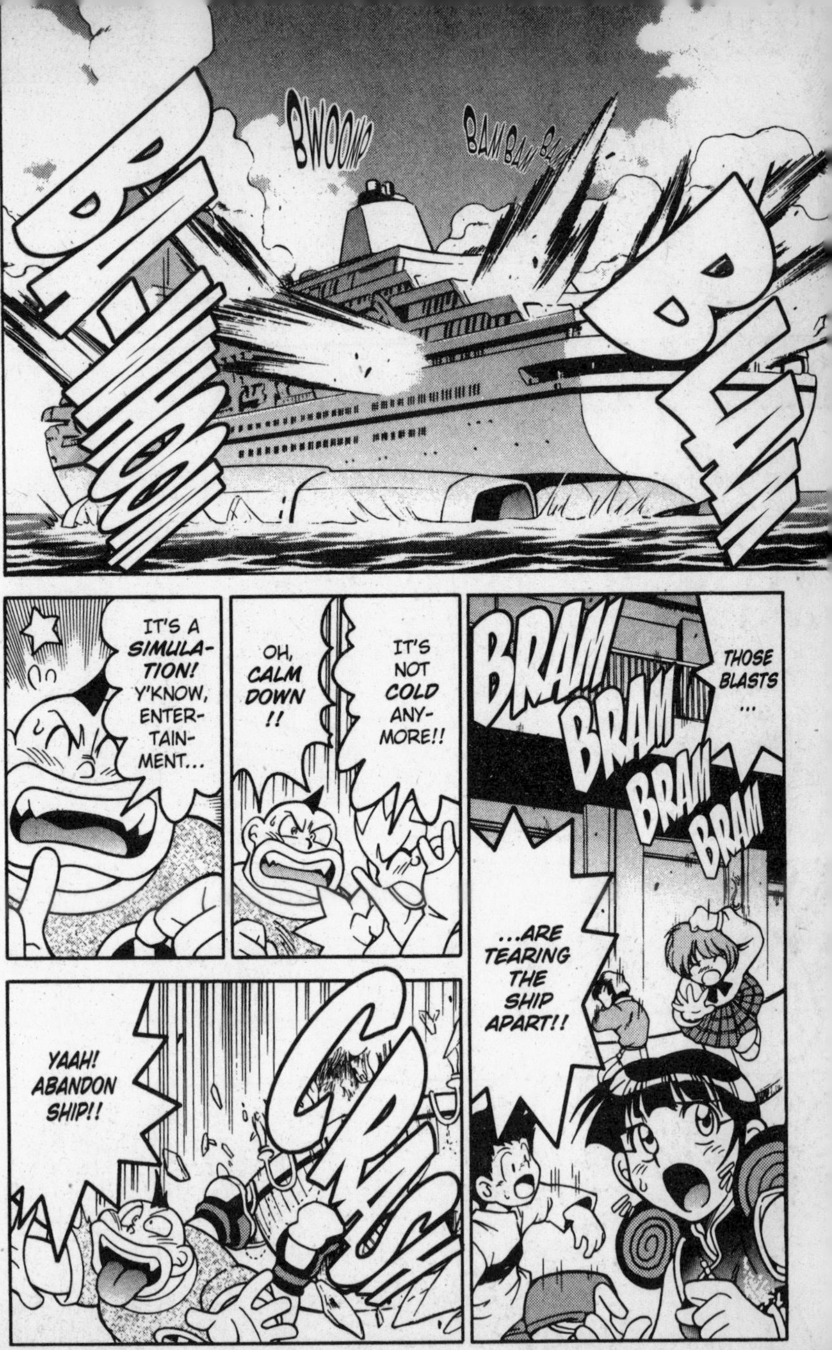
BLAM
BAM BAM BA
BWOOMP
THOSE BLASTS ...
BRAM BRAM BRAM BRAM
...ARE TEARING THE SHIP APART!!
IT'S NOT COLD ANYMORE!!
OH, CALM DOWN!!
IT'S A SIMULATION! Y'KNOW, ENTERTAINMENT...
YAAH! ABANDON SHIP!!

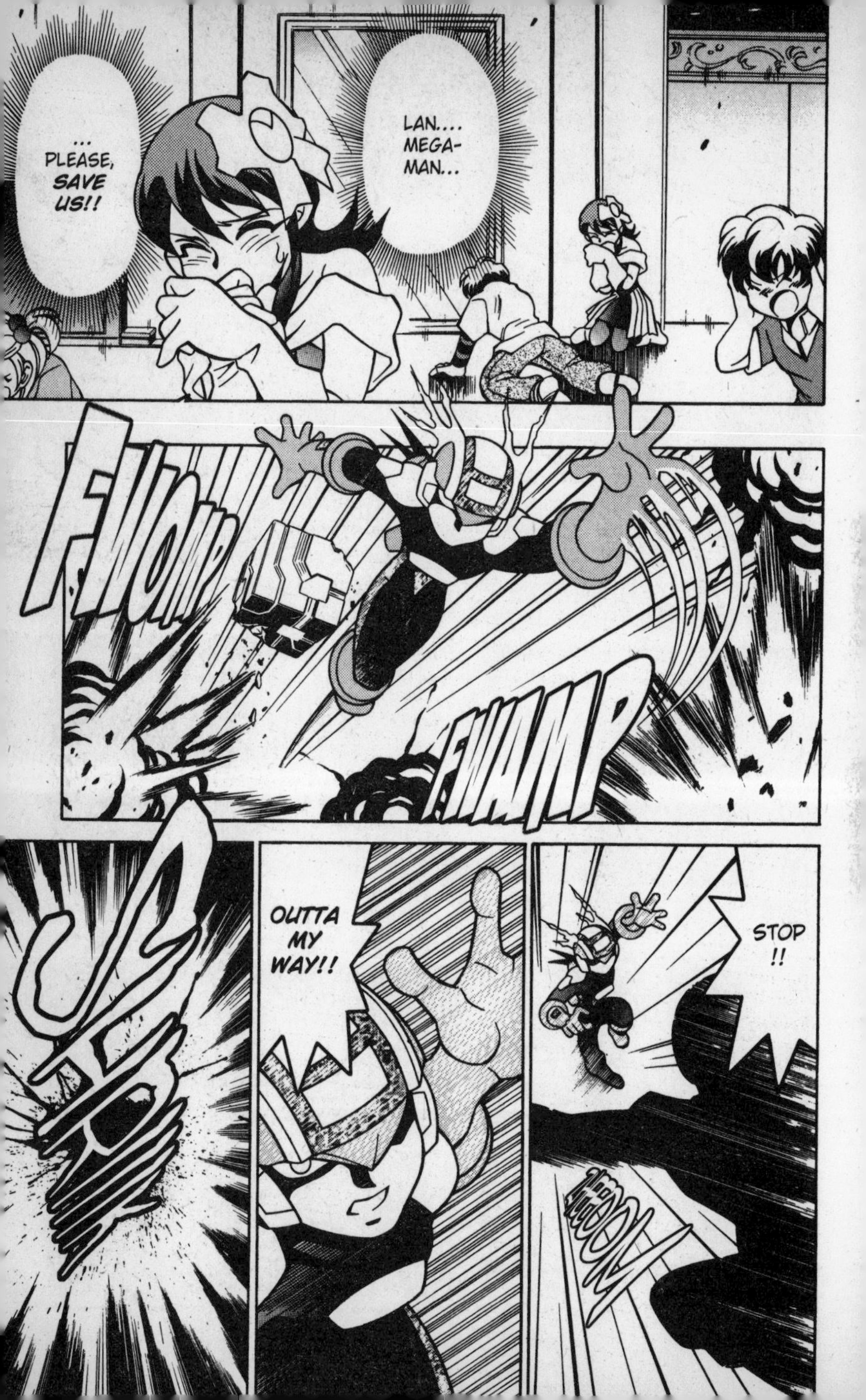
LAN.... MEGA-MAN...
... PLEASE, SAVE US!!
FWOMP
FWAMP
STOP !!
OUTTA MY WAY!!

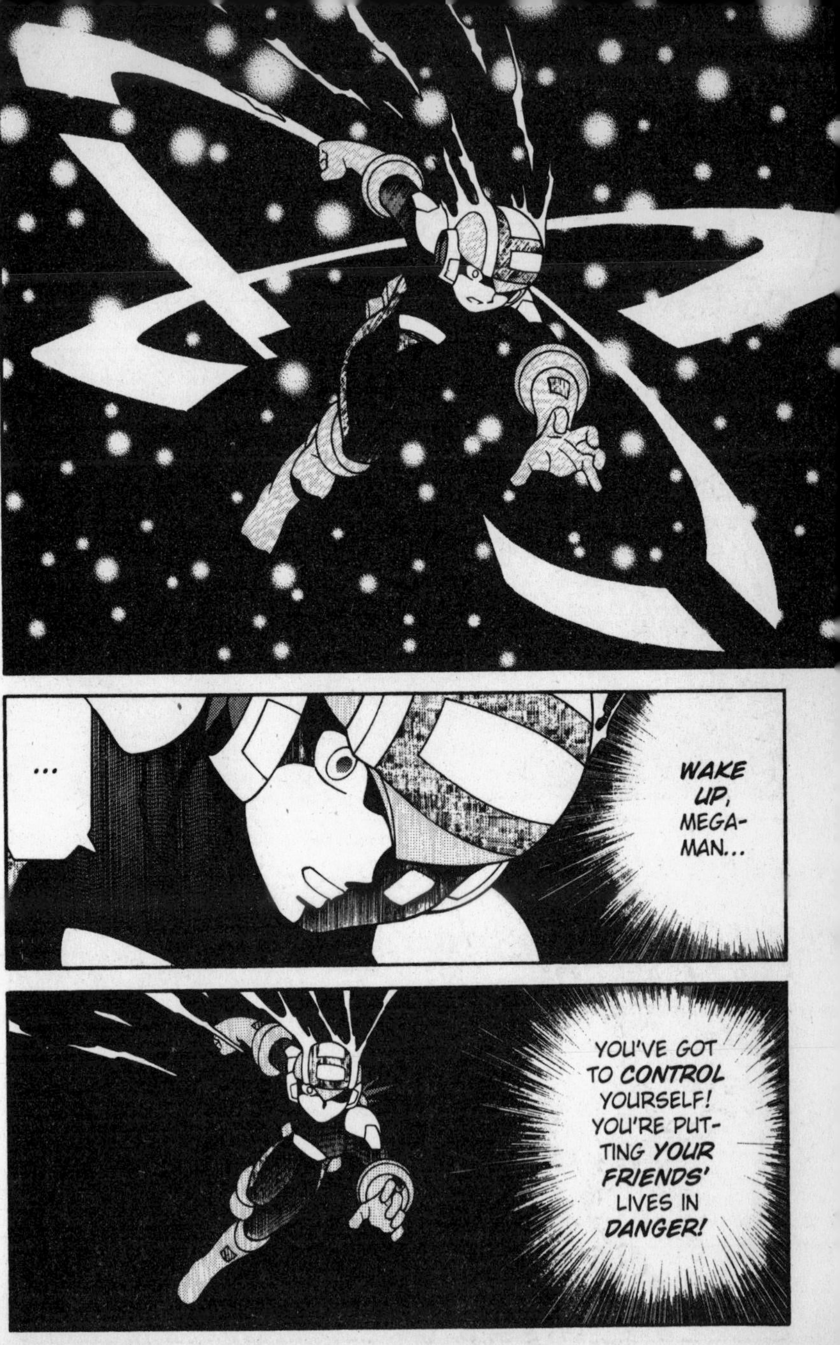
WAKE UP, MEGA-MAN...
...
YOU'VE GOT TO CONTROL YOURSELF! YOU'RE PUT-TING YOUR FRIENDS' LIVES IN DANGER!

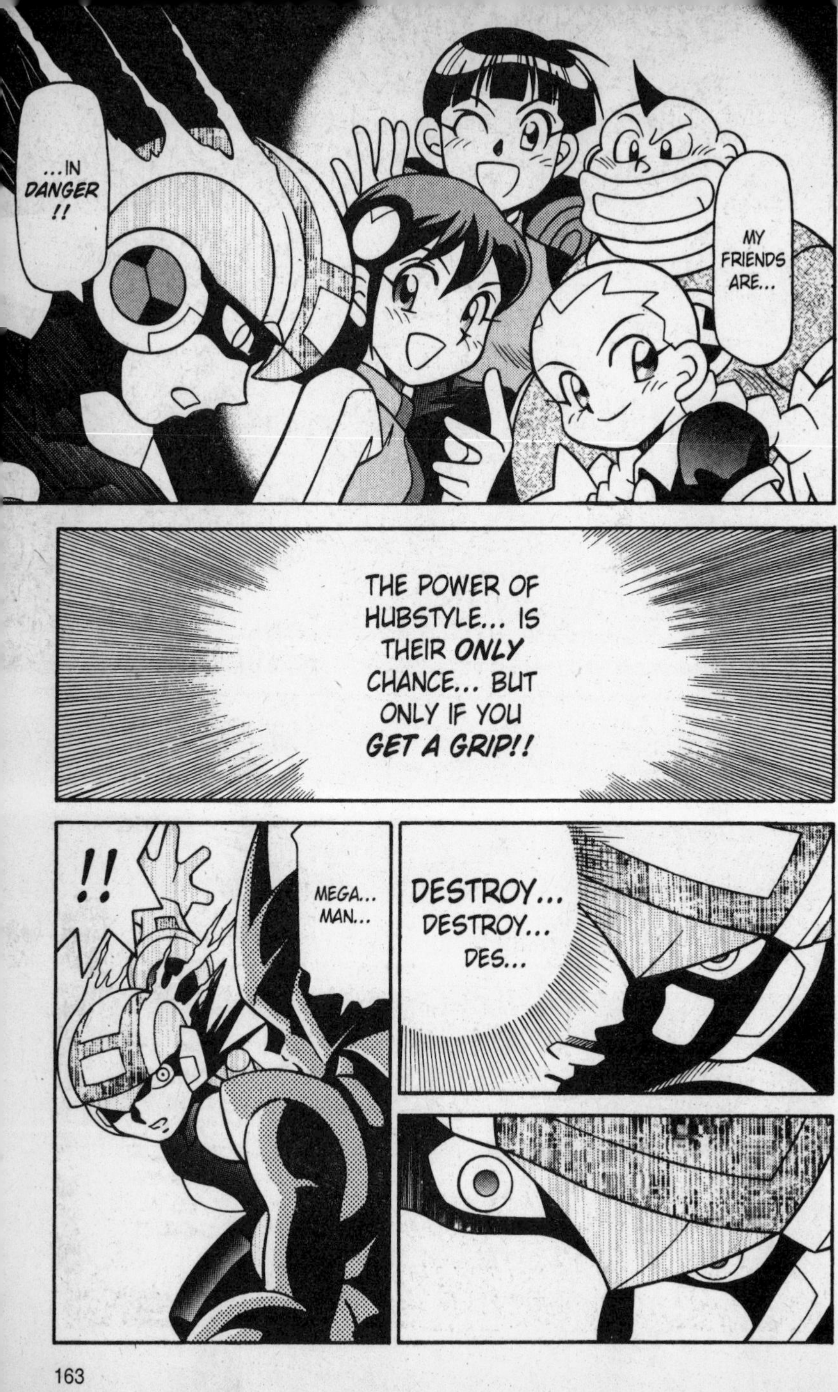
MY FRIENDS ARE...
...IN DANGER !!
THE POWER OF HUBSTYLE... IS THEIR *ONLY* CHANCE... BUT ONLY IF YOU *GET A GRIP!!*
DESTROY... DESTROY... DES...
MEGA... MAN...
!!

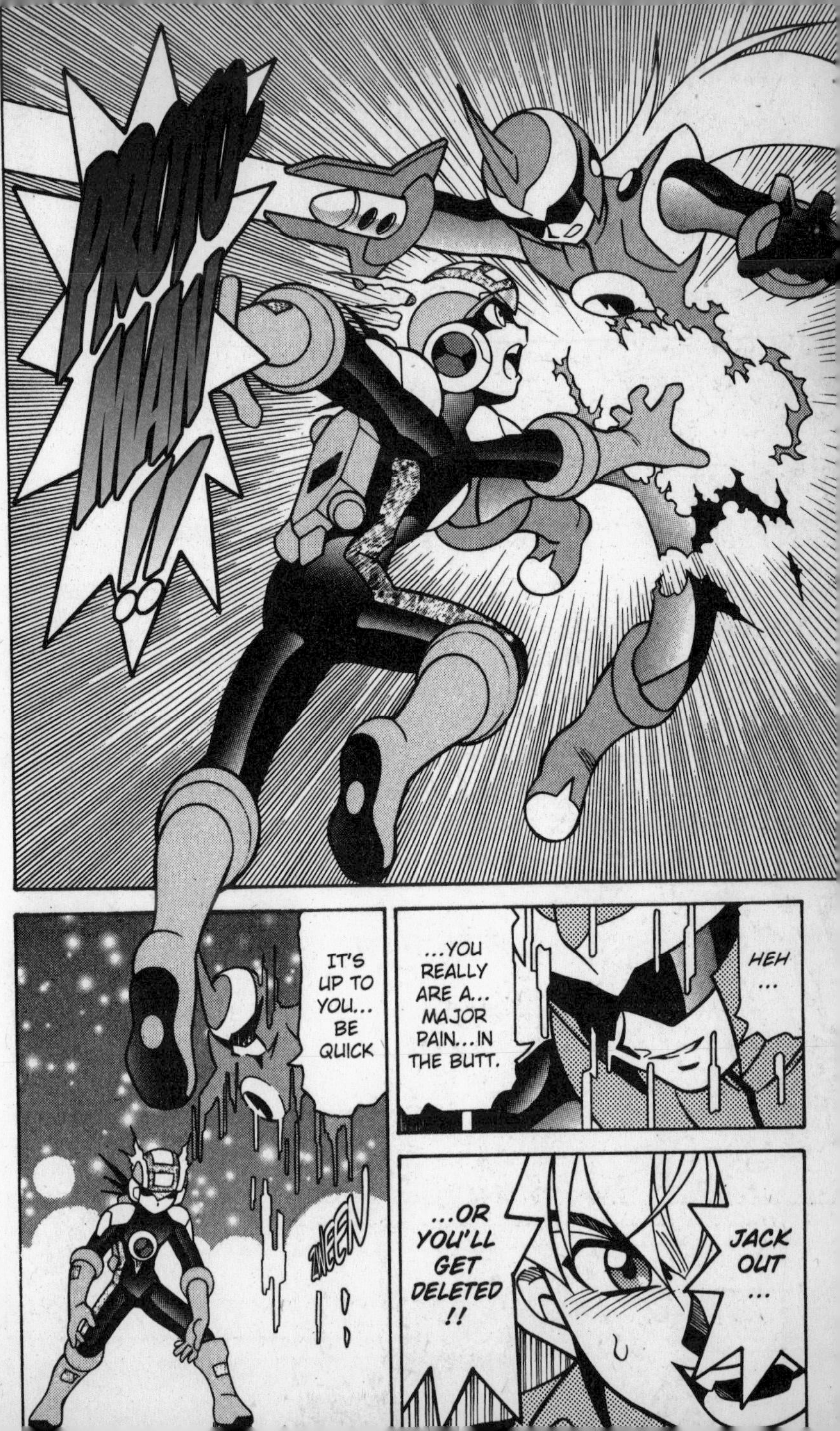
PROTO MAN!!
HEH...
...YOU REALLY ARE A... MAJOR PAIN...IN THE BUTT.
JACK OUT...
...OR YOU'LL GET DELETED!!
IT'S UP TO YOU... BE QUICK
ZWEEN

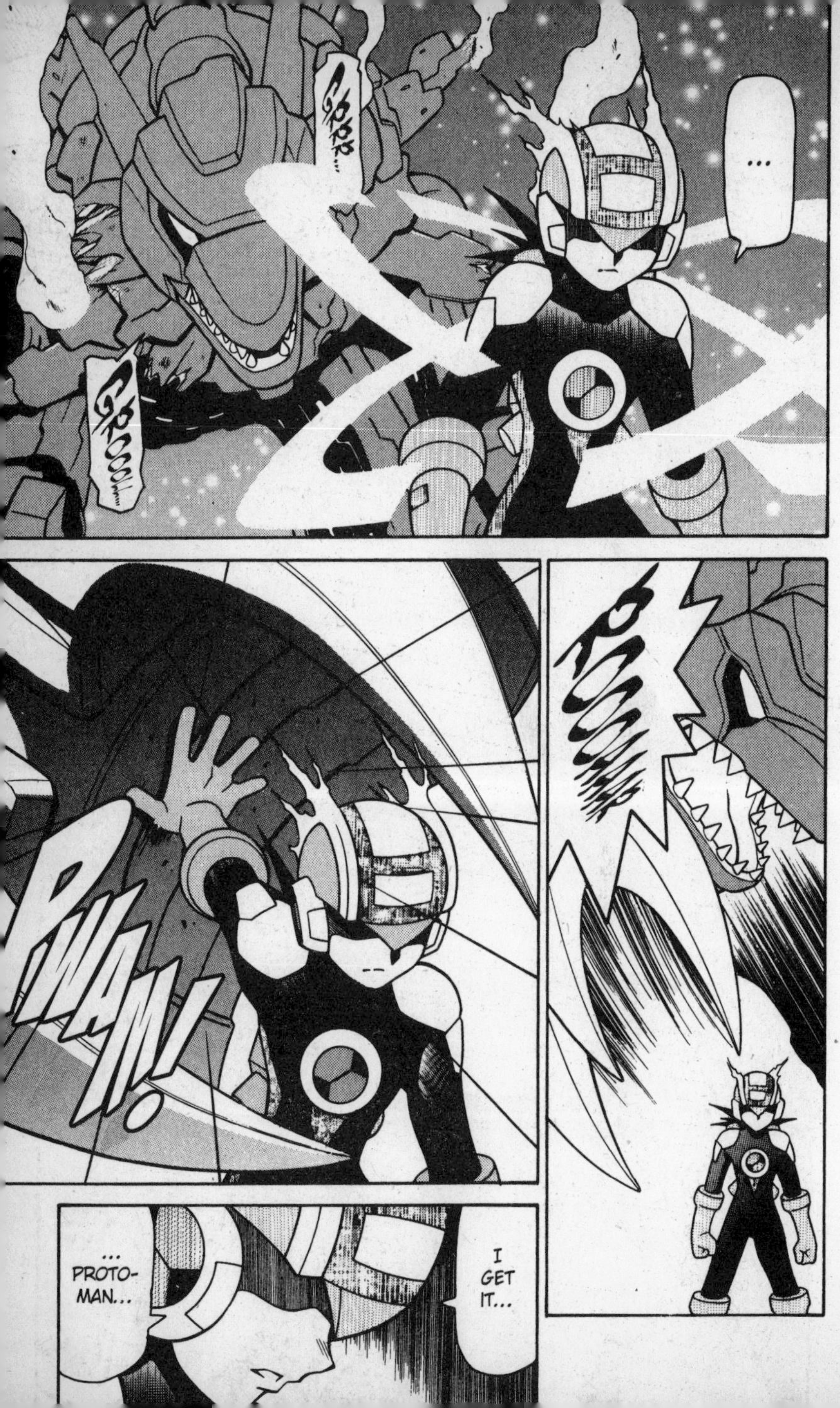
...
GRRRR...
GROOOOL...
BWAM!
I GET IT...
... PROTO-MAN...

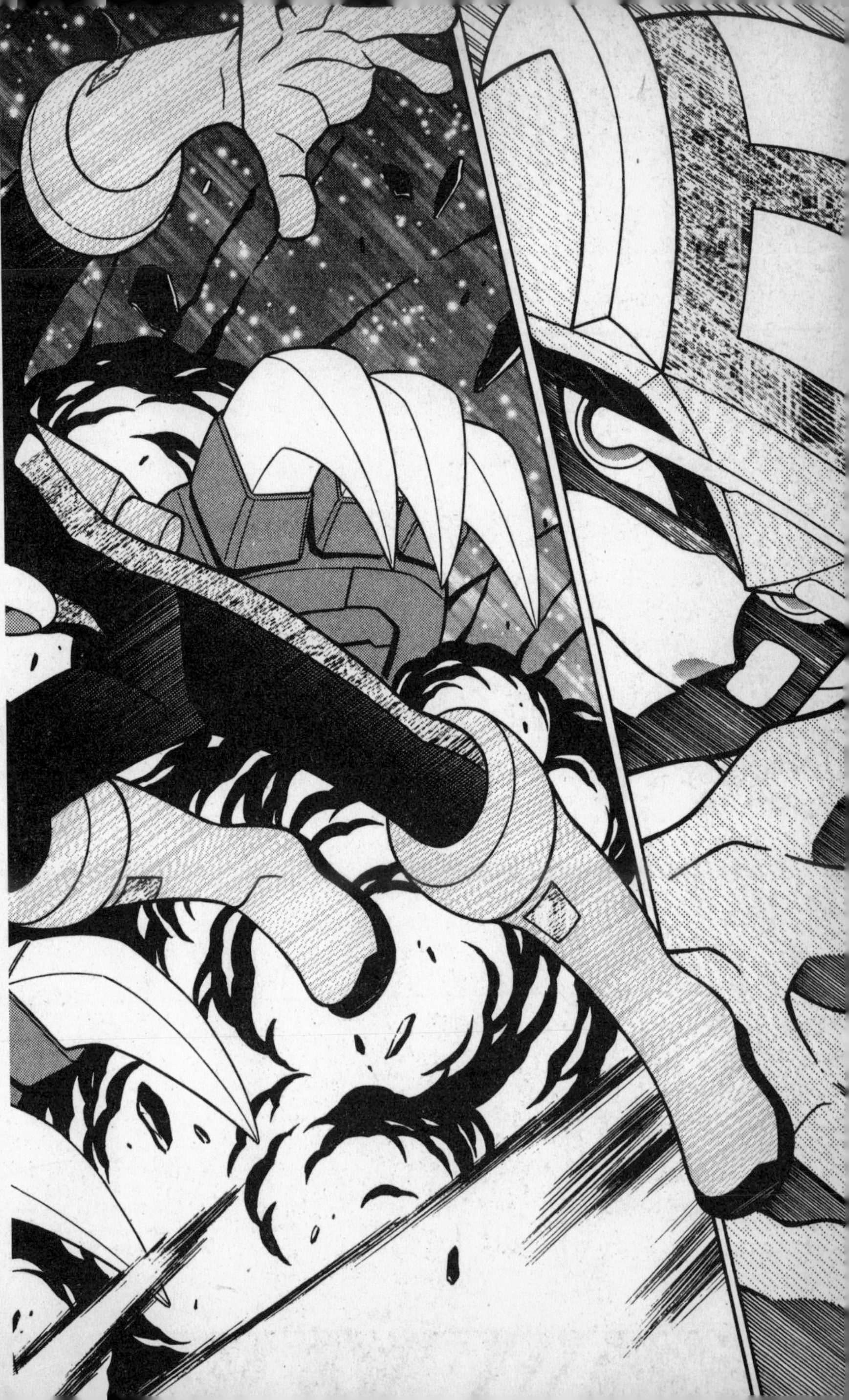

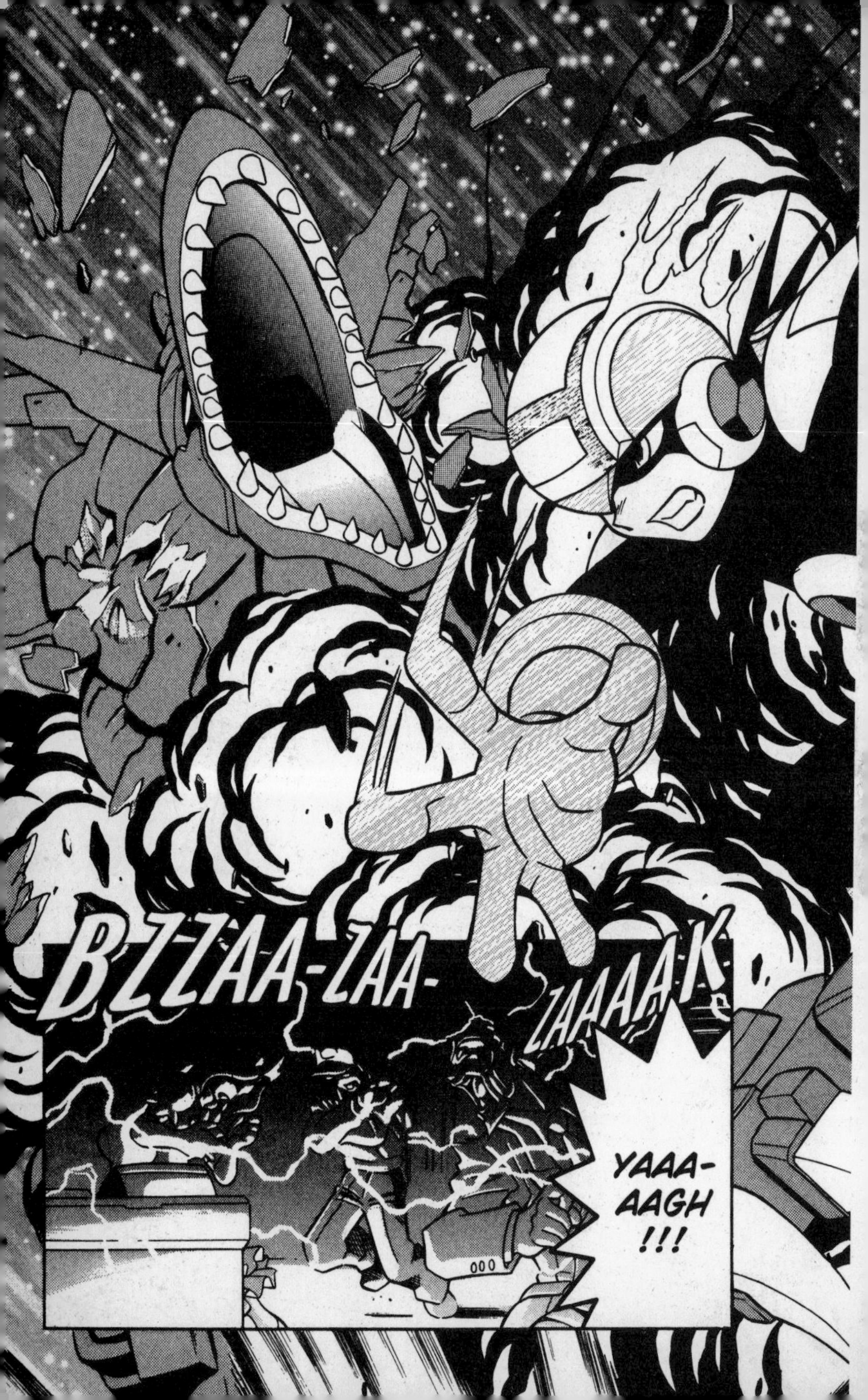
BZZAA-ZAA-
ZAAAAK
YAAA-AAGH!!!

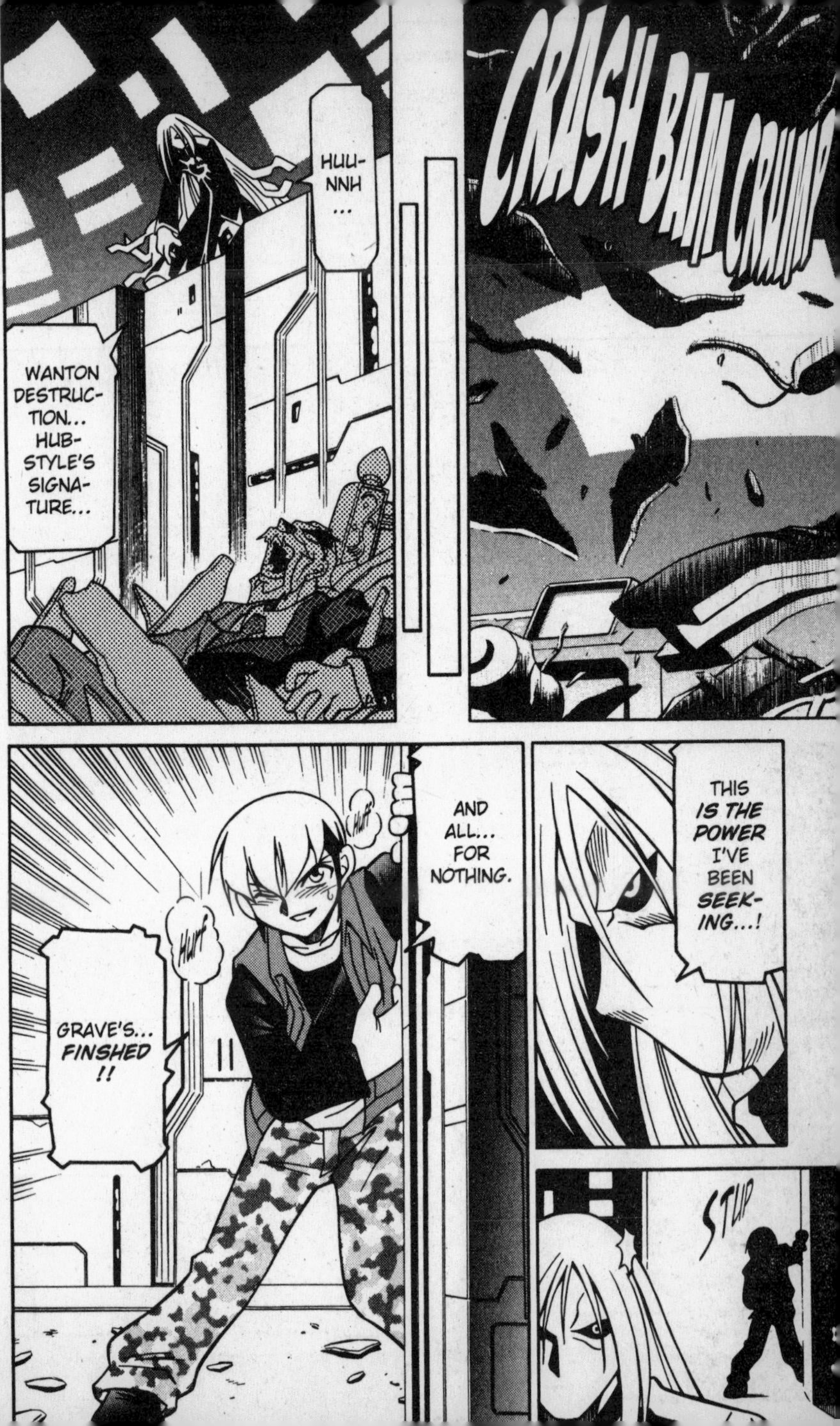
CRASH BAM CRUMP
HUU-NNH...
WANTON DESTRUCTION... HUBSTYLE'S SIGNATURE...
THIS IS THE POWER I'VE BEEN SEEKING...!
STUP
AND ALL... FOR NOTHING.
HUFF
HUFF
GRAVE'S... FINSHED!!

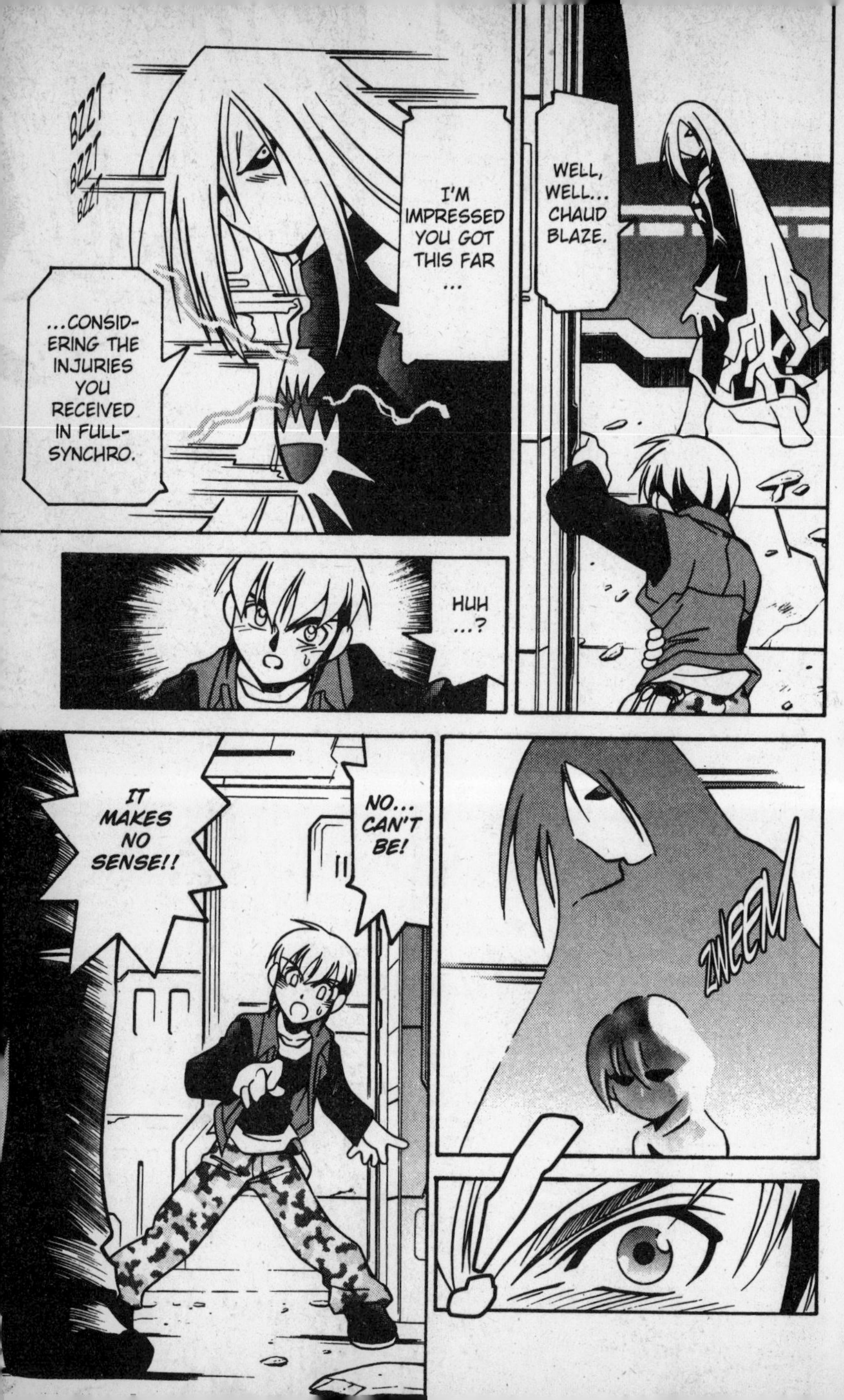
WELL, WELL... CHAUD BLAZE.
I'M IMPRESSED YOU GOT THIS FAR ...
BZZT BZZT BZZT
...CONSIDERING THE INJURIES YOU RECEIVED IN FULL-SYNCHRO.
HUH ...?
ZWEEM
NO... CAN'T BE!
IT MAKES NO SENSE!!

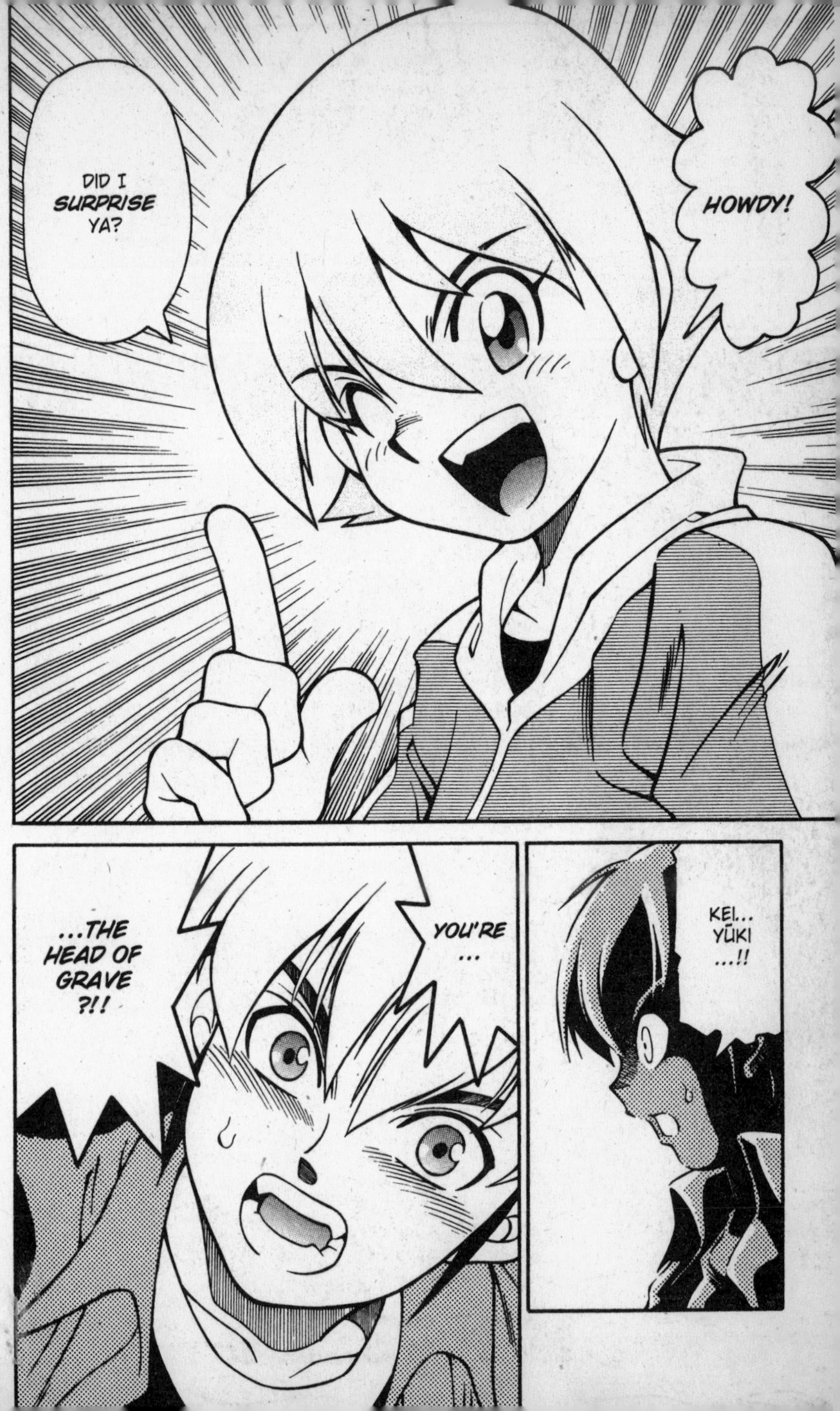
HOWDY!
DID I SURPRISE YA?
KEI... YŪKI ...!!
YOU'RE ...
...THE HEAD OF GRAVE ?!!

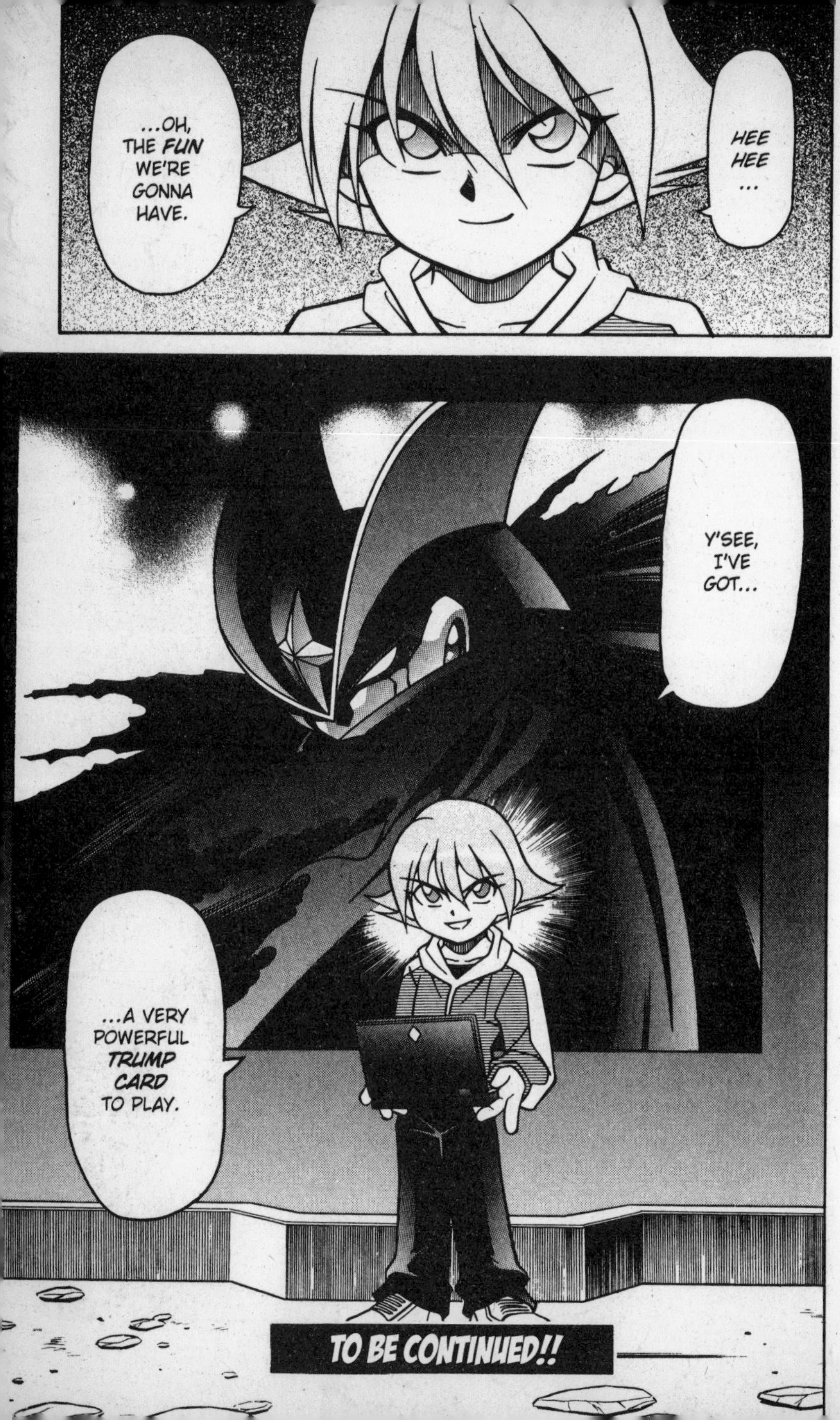
HEE HEE ...
...OH, THE FUN WE'RE GONNA HAVE.
Y'SEE, I'VE GOT...
...A VERY POWERFUL TRUMP CARD TO PLAY.
TO BE CONTINUED!!

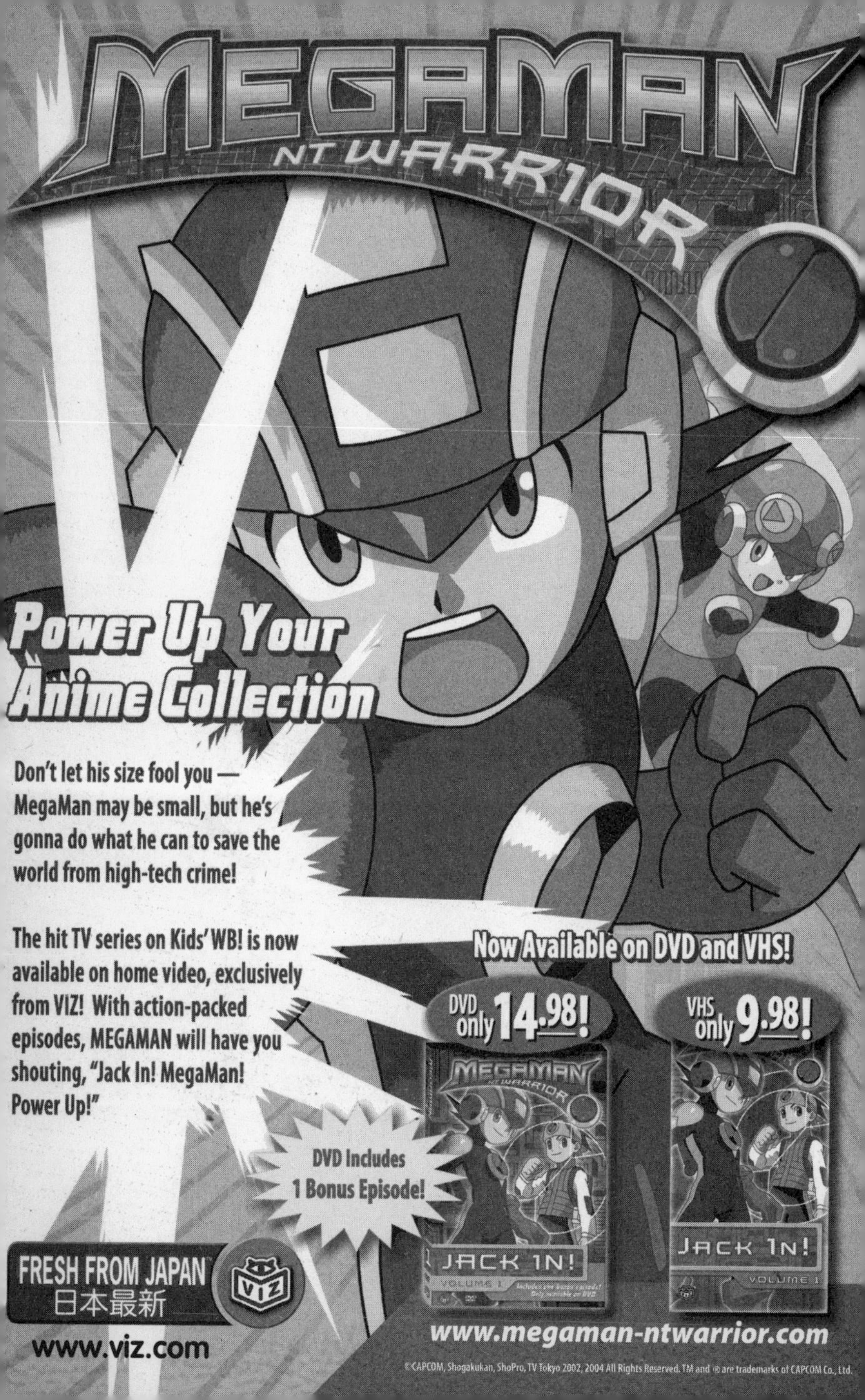
MEGAMAN
NT WARRIOR
Power Up Your Anime Collection
Don't let his size fool you — MegaMan may be small, but he's gonna do what he can to save the world from high-tech crime!
The hit TV series on Kids' WB! is now available on home video, exclusively from VIZ! With action-packed episodes, MEGAMAN will have you shouting, "Jack In! MegaMan! Power Up!"
Now Available on DVD and VHS!
DVD only 14.98!
VHS only 9.98!
MEGAMAN NT WARRIOR
JACK IN!
VOLUME 1
JACK IN!
VOLUME 1
DVD Includes 1 Bonus Episode!
FRESH FROM JAPAN
日本最新
VIZ
www.viz.com
www.megaman-ntwarrior.com
©CAPCOM, Shogakukan, ShoPro, TV Tokyo 2002, 2004 All Rights Reserved. TM and ® are trademarks of CAPCOM Co., Ltd.

# COMPLETE OUR SURVEY AND LET
# US KNOW WHAT YOU THINK!

☐ Please do NOT send me information about VIZ products, news and events, special offers, or other information.

☐ Please do NOT send me information from VIZ's trusted business partners.

**Name:** _____

**Address:** _____

**City:** _____ **State:** _____ **Zip:** _____

**E-mail:** _____

☐ **Male**  ☐ **Female**  **Date of Birth** (mm/dd/yyyy): ___/___/___  ( Under 13? Parental consent required )

## What race/ethnicity do you consider yourself? (please check one)

☐ Asian/Pacific Islander          ☐ Black/African American    ☐ Hispanic/Latino

☐ Native American/Alaskan Native  ☐ White/Caucasian           ☐ Other: _____

## What VIZ product did you purchase? (check all that apply and indicate title purchased)

☐ DVD/VHS _____

☐ Graphic Novel _____

☐ Magazines _____

☐ Merchandise _____

## Reason for purchase: (check all that apply)

☐ Special offer          ☐ Favorite title        ☐ Gift

☐ Recommendation         ☐ Other _____

## Where did you make your purchase? (please check one)

☐ Comic store            ☐ Bookstore             ☐ Mass/Grocery Store

☐ Newsstand              ☐ Video/Video Game Store ☐ Other: _____

☐ Online (site: _____ )

## What other VIZ properties have you purchased/own? _____

_____

**How many anime and/or manga titles have you purchased in the last year? How many were VIZ titles?** **(please check one from each column)**

| ANIME | MANGA | VIZ |
|---|---|---|
| ☐ None | ☐ None | ☐ None |
| ☐ 1-4 | ☐ 1-4 | ☐ 1-4 |
| ☐ 5-10 | ☐ 5-10 | ☐ 5-10 |
| ☐ 11+ | ☐ 11+ | ☐ 11+ |

**I find the pricing of VIZ products to be:** **(please check one)**

☐ Cheap ☐ Reasonable ☐ Expensive

**What genre of manga and anime would you like to see from VIZ?** **(please check two)**

☐ Adventure ☐ Comic Strip ☐ Science Fiction ☐ Fighting
☐ Horror ☐ Romance ☐ Fantasy ☐ Sports

**What do you think of VIZ's new look?**

☐ Love It ☐ It's OK ☐ Hate It ☐ Didn't Notice ☐ No Opinion



**Which do you prefer?** **(please check one)**

☐ Reading right-to-left
☐ Reading left-to-right

**Which do you prefer?** **(please check one)**

☐ Sound effects in English
☐ Sound effects in Japanese with English captions
☐ Sound effects in Japanese only with a glossary at the back

**THANK YOU! Please send the completed form to:**

VIZ Survey
42 Catharine St.
Poughkeepsie, NY 12601

**All information provided will be used for internal purposes only. We promise not to sell or otherwise divulge your information.**